Physical Activity and Health

Second edition

Physical Activity and Health explains clearly, systematically and in detail the relationships between physical activity, health and disease, and examines the benefits of exercise in the prevention and treatment of a wide range of important conditions.

Now in a fully updated and revised edition, and still the most complete and engaging textbook on this important subject, *Physical Activity and Health* offers a balanced examination of the very latest evidence linking levels of physical activity with disease and mortality. It offers a wide-ranging assessment of the importance of inactivity as a factor in major diseases and health conditions such as cardiovascular disease, diabetes, obesity, cancer and osteoporosis. The book is designed to help the reader evaluate the quality and significance of the scientific evidence, and includes an invaluable discussion of common study designs and the inherent difficulties of measuring physical activity. It also explores the full range of contemporary themes in the study of exercise and health, such as the hazards of exercise; exercise and the elderly; children's health and exercise; and physical activity and public health policy. It also includes a critical appraisal of current recommendations for physical activity.

Containing useful features throughout, such as chapter summaries, study tasks, guides to supplementary reading and definitions of key terms, and richly illustrated with supporting tables, figures and plates, *Physical Activity and Health* is an essential course text. Now supported by a companion website featuring self-test questions, PowerPoint slides for lecturers, additional learning activities and web links, this book is vital reading for degree-level students of sport and exercise science, public health, physical therapy, medicine and nursing.

Visit the companion website for *Physical Activity and Health* at www.routledge.com/textbooks/9780415421980.

Adrianne E. Hardman is Emeritus Professor of Human Exercise Metabolism at Loughborough University, the UK's leading centre for sport and exercise science. Adrianne has over 25 years experience in university teaching and research, has published widely, given invited lectures in many countries and has contributed to the development of guidelines on physical activity in the UK and in North America.

David J. Stensel is a Senior Lecturer in Exercise Physiology at Loughborough University and was formerly a lecturer at Nanyang Technological University, Singapore. An experienced teacher and researcher, David has also given invited lectures in the UK and overseas.

Physical Activity and Health
The evidence explained

Second edition

Adrianne E. Hardman and
David J. Stensel

Routledge
Taylor & Francis Group

LONDON AND NEW YORK

First edition published 2003
This edition published 2009
by Routledge
2 Park Square, Milton Park, Abingdon, Oxon OX14 4RN

Simultaneously published in the USA and Canada
by Routledge
711 Third Avenue, New York, NY 10017 (8th Floor)

Routledge is an imprint of the Taylor & Francis Group, an informa business

© 2009 Adrianne E. Hardman and David J. Stensel

Typeset in Adobe Garamond by Wearset Ltd, Boldon, Tyne and Wear

British Library Cataloguing in Publication Data
A catalogue record for this book is available from the British Library

Library of Congress Cataloging in Publication data
A catalog record for this book has been requested

ISBN10: 0-415-45585-5 (hbk)
ISBN10: 0-415-42198-5 (pbk)
ISBN10: 0-203-89071-X (ebk)

ISBN13: 978-0-415-45585-5 (hbk)
ISBN13: 978-0-415-42198-0 (pbk)
ISBN13: 978-0-203-89071-4 (ebk)

Contents

Figures

Tables

Plates

Boxes

Foreword to the second edition

I am delighted to welcome this second updated edition that seeks to report and interpret the international study effort. This could not be more timely. It appears that at long last our government is serious about its responsibility to promote physical activity as essential for the health of the nation. Mounting concern over children's obesity, treated here in model new theoretical and practical chapters, may have triggered the shift in policy. Newcomers to physical activity and health can be expected, including many newly involved in public approaches. They will be seeking instruction, understanding and guidance – and will find a splendid resource in this distinguished text.

Jerry N. Morris, January 2009

Foreword to the first edition

It is a privilege and pleasure to welcome this fine work by a leading investigator and her colleague, both of them experienced teachers in the famous school at Loughborough. The text meets the needs of countless students of physical activity and health now to be found in university sports sciences, clinical medicine, epidemiology, and in the social domain, from transport planning to the fitness industry. Many of these students, like myself, have not had systematic teaching in the physiology of exercise. Yet, we are constantly meeting its concepts and observations that are plainly fundamental to understanding and to application. Until now, there hasn't been a book to meet our needs. Two features, moreover, characterize their contribution: throughout, the nature and quality of the evidence are clearly described, and the collective – the population – aspects as well as the individual and personal are emphasized.

Our field today presents some remarkable features. In the half-century since the Second World War, there has been an explosion of research and thinking on the needs for, and benefits of, physical activity/exercise across the lifespan and bodily systems. This knowledge is widely not being applied in practice. In consequence there is an epochal waste of human potential for health, functional capacities, well-being. This the authors document and illuminate.

Three of today's major associated issues may be cited. First, the pandemic of obesity in the developed and, increasingly, the developing world. The scientific consensus now is that physical inactivity bears much and possibly most of the responsibility. The authors devote two chapters to the issue, giving us a lucid straightforward description plus a highly instructive account of the metabolic, insulin resistance, syndrome, a seminal concept that Public Health has not yet begun to take on board. The characteristic 'modern epidemic' of coronary heart disease is dealt with again in two chapters. These are typically helpful in elucidating the roles of physical activity and physical fitness and in distinguishing disease and risk factors for disease. A third instance is the welfare of old people. When history comes to be written, society's failure to apply modern knowledge of normal ageing processes, in particular the loss of muscle, and the remedial possibilities, is likely to shame us. Scientific evidence in randomized controlled trials is impeccable. And yet, one of the great gifts of physiology to public health is massively ignored. There cannot be any excuse for any in health care with such a convincing demonstration now so readily available in this book.

We are, the generality of us, the first generation in history to require little, often scarcely any, physical activity in our everyday lives. We have therefore deliberately to introduce this ourselves, and commonly in an unhelpful environment. Many readers will be seeking one way and another to serve in this field. They will find much support in this splendid book. It is surely a tract for the times. Bon voyage!

Jerry N. Morris
Public and Environmental Health Research Unit
London School of Hygiene and Tropical Medicine

Author's preface

In writing the first edition of this book we hoped to help students to understand and evaluate the evidence linking physical activity to personal and public health. Based on feedback from a variety of sources, we have had success in achieving this aim. Why then is a second edition necessary?

Since 2002 when we submitted the text of our first edition to the publishers there has been much progress across the whole of our field. In already well-developed areas, research has sought out more detail of relationships between the amount, pattern and intensity of activity and disease risk as well as pursuing plausible biological mechanisms that might explain the observed associations. In other, less well-developed areas progress has been to confirm or deny reported associations and explore these within a wider range of populations. So, whilst this second edition (like the first) relies on classic, 'landmark' studies to illustrate existing knowledge, it also draws on recent research where this extends our knowledge, including understanding of mechanisms.

In our first edition, we identified three modern trends associated with the increased prevalence of chronic diseases. These were the epidemic of obesity, inactivity in children and the ageing of populations. All three trends have continued in recent years, generating even more research interest into their links with physical activity and inactivity. Thus our chapters on obesity and its seemingly inevitable metabolic consequence, type 2 diabetes, have been extensively revised. Serious weight-related problems that may be expected to lead to life-threatening disease in adulthood are being diagnosed in obese adolescents, increasing concern for the health of future generations. The influence of activity/inactivity on the health of children is therefore a topic of increasing research interest and this has been addressed in a comprehensive new chapter. Research on physical activity in older people has also burgeoned and this is reflected in our expanded chapter on ageing and physical activity that includes, for instance, recent findings related to cognitive function.

As well as updating each chapter, we have taken the opportunity presented by this new edition to restructure our book in several ways. The first has already been referred to, that is the addition of a new chapter dealing specifically with physical activity and children's health. The second was to integrate all information relating to cardiovascular disease and its risk factors (previously in separate chapters) into a single chapter in order to make coverage of this topic more coherent. Finally because the focus of our book is disease prevention rather than management of existing disease, discussion of the therapeutic role of exercise is presented in each relevant chapter rather than in one discrete chapter as in the first edition.

In writing the first edition of 'Physical activity and health' we drew heavily on advice and comment from colleagues, many of whom are friends. Thus, we remain indebted to Leslie Boobis, FRCS and to Drs Lettie Bishop, Michael Morgan, Greg Atkinson, Katherine Brooke-Wavell and Jason Gill for their valued input. Professor Jerry Morris has been a constant source of constructive comment for this edition, as he was for the first. He has shared his unique insight and experience in the field unstintingly and Adrianne has looked forward to his telephone 'tutorials'!

Adrianne thanks her husband, Professor Peter Jones, for his valued comments on the text and for his patience during the long hours she has spent at the keyboard. David thanks Para, his wife and soul-mate, and his daughters Chandini and Rohini for their unceasing patience, support and understanding. Finally, both authors extend warm and wholehearted thanks to Simon Whitmore and Brian Guerin of Routledge for their understanding when writing was slow and for their recognition of the value of our book.

Illustrations acknowledgements

The authors and publishers would like to thank the institutions below for permission to use tables and figures that originated from other original works. Every effort has been made to trace copyright holders, but in a few cases this has not been possible. Any omission brought to our attention will be remedied in future editions.

Figure 2.1: Copyright Harvard University Press (adapted from Keys, A. (1980) 'Seven countries: a multivariate analysis of death and coronary heart disease', Figure 8.2).

Figure 3.4: This is a slight modification of Figure 2 on page 798 of Myers, J., Prakash, M., Froelicher, V., Do, D., Partington, S. and Atwood, J.E. (2002) 'Exercise capacity and mortality among men referred for exercise testing', *New England Journal of Medicine* 346: 793–801.

Figure 3.5: This is a slight modification of Figure 1 on page 797 of Myers, J., Prakash, M., Froelicher, V., Do, D., Partington, S. and Atwood, J.E. (2002) 'Exercise capacity and mortality among men referred for exercise testing', *New England Journal of Medicine* 346: 793–801.

Figure 4.3: This is a reproduction of Figure 2 on page 462 of Hajjar, D.P. and Nicholson, A.C. (1995) 'Atherosclerosis. An understanding of the cellular and molecular basis of the disease promises new approaches for its treatment in the near future', *American Scientist* 83: 460–7.

Figure 4.4: This is a reproduction of Figure 7.4 from Wheater, P.R., Burkitt, H.G., Stevens, A. and Lowe, J.S. (1985) *Basic Histopathology. A Colour Atlas and Text,* Edinburgh: Churchill Livingstone.

Figure 4.5: This is a reproduction of Figure 1 on page 42 of McGill, H.C. Jr., Geer, J.C. and Strong, J.P. (1963) 'Natural history of human atherosclerotic lesions', in Sandler, M. and Bourne, G.H. (eds) Atherosclerosis and its Origin. New York: Academic Press, pp. 39–65.

Figure 4.6: This is a slight modification of Figure 1 on page 546 of Paffenbarger, R.S. and Hale, W.E. (1975) 'Work activity and coronary heart mortality', *New England Journal of Medicine* 292: 545–50.

Figure 5.2: This is a reproduction of the Figure on page 78 of Mokdad, A.H., Ford, E.S., Bowman, B.A., Dietz, W.H., Vinicor, F., Bales, V.S. and Marks, J.S. (2003) 'Prevalence of obesity, diabetes, and obesity-related health risk factors, 2001', *Journal of the American Medical Association* 289: 76–9.

Figure 6.4: This is a reproduction of Figure 1, page 195 from Stunkard, A.J., Sorensen, T.I.A., Hanis, C., Teasdale, T.W., Chakraborty, R., Schull, W.J. and Schulsinger, F. (1986) 'An adoption study of human obesity', *New England Journal of Medicine* 314: 193–8.

Figure 6.5: This is a reproduction of Figure 1, page 1479 and Figure 2, page 1481 from Bouchard, C., Tremblay, A., Despres, J.P., Nadeau, A., Lupien, P.J., Theriault, G., Dussault, J., Moorjania, S., Pineault, S. and Fournier, G. (1990) 'The response to long-term overfeeding in identical twins', *New England Journal of Medicine* 322: 1477–82.

Figure 6.13: This is a reproduction of Figure 5, page 439 from Prentice, A.M. and Jebb, S.A. (1995) 'Obesity in Britain: gluttony or sloth?', *British Medical Journal* 311: 437–9.

Figure 6.14: This is a reproduction of Figure 4, page 1560 from Jakicic, J.M., Winters, C., Lang, W. and Wing, R.R. (1999) 'Effects of intermittent exercise and use of home exercise equipment on adherence, weight loss, and fitness in overweight women. A randomized trial', *Journal of the American Medical Association* 282: 1554–60.

Figure 6.15: This is a reproduction of part of Figure 1, page 404 and part of Figure 2, page 406 from Bouchard, C., Tremblay, A., Després, J.P., Thériault, G., Nadeau, A., Lupien, P.J., Moorjani, S., Prudhomme, D. and Fournier, G. (1994) 'The response to exercise with constant energy intake in identical twins', *Obesity Research* 2: 400–10.

Figure 7.5: *Medicine and Science in Sports and Exercise.* Copyright Lippincott, Williams and Wilkins. (Jurca, R., Lamonte, M.J., Church, T.S., Earnest, C.P., Fitzgerald, S.J., Barlow, C.E., Jordan, A.N., Kampert, J.B. and Blair, S.N. (2004) 'Associations of muscle strength and fitness with metabolic syndrome in men', *Medicine and Science in Sports and Exercise* 36: 1301–7. Figure 1, p. 1306.)

Figure 7.6: *Circulation.* Copyright Lippincott, Williams and Wilkins. (LaMonte, M.J., Barlow, C.E., Jurca, R., Kampert, J.B., Church, T.S. and Blair, S.N. (2005) 'Cardiorespiratory fitness is inversely associated with the incidence of metabolic syndrome: a prospective study of men and women', *Circulation.* 112: 505–12. Epub 2005 July 11. Figure (no number) on p. 508.)

Figure 7.9: *Medicine and Science in Sports and Exercise.* Copyright Lippincott, Williams & Wilkins. (Tsetsonis, N.V. and Hardman, A.E. (1996) 'Reduction in postprandial lipemia after walking: influence of exercise intensity', *Medicine and Science in Sports and Exercise* 28: 1235–42. Figure 2, p. 1237.)

Figure 9.2: Copyright Human Kinetics (Khan, K.M. *et al.* (2001) 'Physical activity and bone health', Figure 1.6, p. 7. Champaign, Illinois: Human Kinetics.)

Figure 9.4: By kind permission of L Mosekilde, MD, DMSci, University Hospital of Aarhus.

Figure 9.6: The *Lancet*, Elsevier. (Heinonen, A., Kannus, P., Sievänen, H., Oja, P., Pasanen, M., Rinne, M., Uusi-Rasi, K. and Vuori, I. (1996) 'Randomised controlled trial of the effect of high-impact exercise on selected risk factors for osteoporotic fractures', *Lancet* 348: 1343–7, Figure 2, p. 1344.)

Figure 10.2: This is a reproduction of Figure 2 from page 713 of Kimm, S.Y.S., Glynn, N.W., Kriska, A.M., Barton, B.A., Kronsberg, S.S., Daniels, S.R., Crawford, P.B., Sabry, Z.I. and Liu, K. (2002) 'Decline in physical activity in black girls and white girls during adolescence', *New England Journal of Medicine* 347: 709–15.

Figure 10.3: This is a reproduction of the figure on page 592 from Mallam, K.M., Metcalf, B.S., Kirkby, J., Voss, L.D. and Wilkin, T.J. (2003) 'Contribution of time-tabled physical education to total physical activity in primary school children: cross sectional study', *British Medical Journal* 327: 592–3.

Figure 10.11: This is a reproduction of Figure 1 from Kannus, P., Haapasalo, H., Sankelo, M., Sievanen, H., Pasanen, M., Heinonen, A., Oja, P. and Vuori, I. (1995) 'Effect of starting age of physical activity on bone mass in the dominant arm of tennis and squash players', *Annals of Internal Medicine* 123: 27–31.

Figure 10.12: This is a reproduction of Figure 1 on page 470 from Karlsson, M.K., Linden, C., Karlsson, C., Johnell, O., Obrant, K. and Seeman, E. (2000) 'Exercise during growth and bone mineral density and fractures in old age', *Lancet* 355: 469–70.

Figure 11.2: This is a reproduction of Figure 1 on page 1511 of Pollock, M.L., Mengelkoch, L.J., Graves, J.E., Lowenthal, D.T., Limacher, M.C., Foster, C. and Wilmore, J.H. (1997) 'Twenty-year follow-up of aerobic power and body composition of older track athletes', *Journal of Applied Physiology* 82: 1508–16.

Figure 11.7: This is a reproduction of Figure 2 on page 1041 of Frontera, W.R., Meredith, C.N., O'Reilly, K.P., Knuttgen, H.G. and Evans, W.J. (1988) 'Strength conditioning in older men: skeletal muscle hypertrophy and improved function', *Journal of Applied Physiology* 64: 1038–44.

Figure 11.8: This is a reproduction of Figure 5 on page 1042 of Frontera, W.R., Meredith, C.N., O'Reilly, K.P., Knuttgen, H.G. and Evans, W.J. (1988) 'Strength conditioning in older men: skeletal muscle hypertrophy and improved function', *Journal of Applied Physiology* 64: 1038–44.

Figure 11.13: This is a reproduction of Figure 1 on page 156 of Cherkas, L.F., Hankin, J.L., Kato, B.S., Richards, B., Gardner, J.P., Surdulescu, G.L., Kimura, M., Lu, X., Spector, T.D. and Aviv, A. (2008) 'The association between physical activity in leisure time and leukocyte telomere length', *Archives of Internal Medicine* 168: 154–8.

Figure 12.1: *Medicine and Science in Sports and Exercise*, Lippincott, Williams and Wilkins. (Hootman, J.M., Macera, C.A., Ainsworth, B.E., Addy, C.L., Martin, M. and Blair, S.N. (2002) 'Epidemiology of musculoskeletal injuries among sedentary and physically active adults', *Medicine and Science in Sports and Exercise* 34: 838–44. Figure 1, p. 841.)

Figure 12.2: *New England Journal of Medicine*. Massachusetts Medical Society (Mittleman, M.A., Maclure, M., Tofler, G.H., Sherwood, J.B., Goldberg, R.J. and Muller, J.E. (1993) 'Triggering of acute myocardial infarction by heavy physical exertion. Protection against triggering by regular exertion', *New England Journal Medicine* 329: 1677–83. Figure 2, p. 1680.)

Figure 12.3: *Medicine and Science in Sports and Exercise*. Lippincott, Williams and Wilkins. (Torstveit, M.S. and Sundgot-Borgen, J. (2005) 'The female athlete triad: are elite athletes at increased risk?', *Medicine and Science in Sports and Exercise* 37: 184–93. Figure 2, p. 1453 and Figure 3, p. 1455.)

Figure 12.5: *Journal of the American Medical Association*, Drinkwater, B.L., Bruemner, B. and Chesnut, C.H. (1990) 'Menstrual history as a determinant of current bone density in young athletes', *Journal of the American Medical Association* 263: 545–8. Figure on p. 546.

Figure 13.1(a): *Journal of Applied Physiology*. Lippincott, Williams and Wilkins. Hardman, A.E., Lawrence, J.E.M. and Herd, S.L. (1998) 'Postprandial lipemia in endurance-trained people during a short interruption to training', *Journal of Applied Physiology* 84: 1895–901. Figure 1, p. 1897.

Plates acknowledgements

Plate 2: This is the front page of the paper by Paffenbarger, R.S., Hyde, R.T., Wing, A.L. and Hsieh, C.C. (1986) 'Physical activity, all-cause mortality, and longevity of college alumni', *New England Journal of Medicine* 314: 605–13.

Plate 3: This is a reproduction of Figure 7 (page 992) and Figure 8 (page 993) of the article by Currens, J.H. and White, P.D. (1961) 'Half a century of running. Clinical, physiologic and autopsy findings in the case of Clarence DeMar ("Mr. Marathon")', *New England Journal of Medicine* 265: 988–93.

Plate 4: This is the reproduction of a photograph from Bliss, M. (2007) 'The discovery of insulin', Chicago, The University of Chicago Press.

Plate 5: This is a reproduction of part of Figure 4, page 62 from Ross, R. (1997) 'Effects of diet and exercise induced weight loss on visceral adipose tissue in men and women', *Sports Medicine* 24: 55–64.

Plate 8: Copyright McGraw-Hill Education (Carola, R. *et al.*, (1992) Human anatomy and physiology, 2nd edn, figure 6.2, p. 131.)

Plate 10: This is a direct reproduction of Figure 17.6 on page 544 of Wilmore, J.H. and Costill, D.L. (2004) 'Physiology of Exercise and Sport' (3rd ed.), Champaign, IL: Human Kinetics.

Conversion factors for commonly used units

Length: 1 kilometre = 0.62137 mile
Mass: 1 kilogram = 2.2046 pounds
Energy: 1 kJ = 0.23889 kcal
Concentration cholesterol: 1 mmol l^{-1} = 38.67 mg dl^{-1}
Concentration triglycerides: 1 mmol l^{-1} = 88. mg dl^{-1}
Concentration glucose: 1 mmol l^{-1} = 18 mg dl^{-1}
Concentration insulin: 1 pmol l^{-1} = 0.1389 μU ml^{-1}

Part I
Assessing the Evidence

1 Introduction

Knowledge assumed
Principle of energy balance
Procedures for testing aerobic
fitness, including prediction of
maximal oxygen uptake

EARLY OBSERVATIONS

Physical activity and physical fitness have been linked with health and longevity since ancient times. The earliest records of organized exercise used for health promotion are found in China, around 2500 BC. However, it was the Greek physicians of the fifth and early fourth centuries BC who established a tradition of maintaining positive health through 'regimen' – the combination of correct eating and exercise. Hippocrates (c.460–370 BC), often called the Father of Modern Medicine, wrote

all parts of the body which have a function, if used in moderation and exercised in labours in which each is accustomed, become thereby healthy, well-developed and age more slowly, but if unused and left idle they become liable to disease, defective in growth and age quickly.

(Jones 1967)

Plate 1   A London double-decker bus in the 1950s. Jeremy Morris *et al.* compared the incidence of heart attack in sedentary drivers with that in physically active conductors.

Source: Getty.

Modern-day exercise research began after the Second World War in the context of post-war aspirations to build a better world. Public health was changing to focus on chronic, non-communicable diseases and the modification of individual behaviour. Whilst Doll and Hill worked on the links between smoking and lung cancer, Professor Jeremy Morris and his colleagues set out to test the hypothesis that deaths from coronary heart disease (CHD) were less common among men engaged in physically active work than among those in sedentary jobs. In seminal papers published in 1953, they reported that conductors working on London's double-decker buses who climbed around 600 stairs per working day experienced less than half the incidence of heart attacks as the sedentary drivers who sat for 90% of their shift.

Subsequent studies by Morris and others, in particular Morris' close friend Ralph Paffenbarger in the US, confirmed that the postponement of cardiovascular disease through exercise represents a cause-and-effect relationship. For their contribution, Morris and Paffenbarger were, in 1996, jointly awarded the first International Olympic Medal and Prize for research in exercise sciences.

In the 50 years since Morris' early papers, research into the influence of physical activity on health has burgeoned. This book is not a comprehensive account of this literature; rather it is an attempt to illustrate its extent, strengths and weaknesses and to help students understand the process of evaluation of evidence. Our emphasis will be on topics that comprise major public health issues. But first, it is necessary to 'paint a picture' of some relevant features of today's societies.

MODERN TRENDS

Just three behaviours – smoking, poor diet and physical inactivity – are the root cause of around one-third of deaths in developed countries. These risk factors often underlie today's leading chronic disease killers: heart disease, cancer, stroke and diabetes. Sadly, three modern trends will increase the prevalence of these diseases in the twenty-first century. These are the epidemic of obesity, inactivity in children and the increasing age of the population.

Epidemic of obesity

In parts of the world such as North America, the United Kingdom, Eastern Europe and Australasia, obesity prevalence has risen three-fold or more in the last 25 years. Nearly one-third of American adults are obese, and rates in England are the worst in Europe, with 24% of adults obese and a further 38% overweight in 2006, with no real slowing of the upward trend (Figure 1.1). Moreover, all the signs are that the increase in obesity is often faster in developing countries than in the developed world. For example, in South Africa, nearly 60% of black women have been reported to be either obese or overweight. Even in China, where the overall prevalence is below 5%, rates of obesity are almost 20% in some cities.

While the figures for adult obesity give rise to concern, those for children presage an even more major public health problem – perhaps one of the most consequential of the twenty-first century. Serious weight-related problems that may be expected to lead to life-threatening disease in adulthood are already being diagnosed in obese adolescents. In England, 16% of children aged between 2 and 15 were classed as obese in 2006, an increase from 11% in 1995 (Figure 1.1); and in the US almost one in three children and adolescents is either overweight or obese. The problem is global, and increasingly extends into the developing world. For example, in Thailand the prevalence of obesity in 5–12-year-olds rose from 12% to 15% in just two years.

The health hazards of obesity and the ways in which physical activity influences weight regulation are discussed fully in Chapter 6, but one general point will be made here. For many people today, everyday life demands only low levels of physical activity and hence energy expenditure. The average decline in daily energy expenditure in the United Kingdom from the end of the Second World War to 1995 has been estimated

Figure 1.1 Prevalence of obesity among men and women (1993 to 2006) and among boys and girls aged 2–15 (1995–2006) in England.

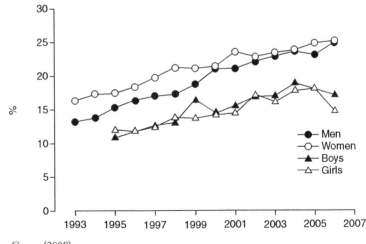

Source: Information Centre (2008).

as 3,360 kJ (800 kcal) (James 1995), the equivalent of walking about 16 km (10 miles) less. A large population-based study in which Swedish women recalled retrospectively their daily physical activity at ages 15, 30 and 50 years found a decrease over the last 60 years of the twentieth century equivalent to 45 minutes of brisk walking (approximately 3 miles) (Orsini *et al.* 2006). The modern phase of the obesity epidemic (from 1980 onwards) is therefore probably mediated more by inactivity than by overeating (Prentice and Jebb 1995).

Inactivity in children

The high prevalence of sedentary behaviours in children and youths partly explains their low total levels of physical activity. In industrialized countries young people typically watch 2–2.5 hours of television each day (Marshall *et al.* 2006), but in America around 40% of children in some ethnic groups watch at least four hours daily (Andersen *et al.* 1998). Total 'screen time' is even higher among those with access to computers and video/DVD games. For example, Canadian children aged 10–16 are spending, on average, six hours per day in front of a computer or television screen (Health Canada 2007).

Another factor contributing to low levels of physical activity is the general decline in children's walking and cycling, and the dramatic decline in physically active transport to school. For example, the percentage of Australian children (aged 5–14) that walked to school halved between 1971 and 1999/2003 (van der Ploeg *et al.* 2008). The corollary is, of course, that more children are being driven to school (Figure 1.2). In the United Kingdom the number of primary school children travelling to school by

Figure 1.2 Prevalence of walking and being driven to school 1971 to 2003.

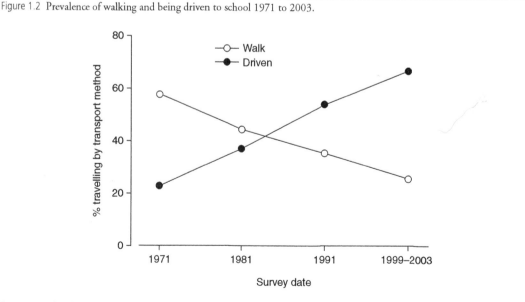

Source: van der Ploeg *et al.* (2008).

car has doubled in the past 20 years, despite the fact that a majority of these trips are under 1 mile (Black *et al.* 2001).

Estimates of overall physical activity levels in children world-wide show a marked decline as age increases, with a particularly steep fall in girls. For example, by the age of 15, only 41% of English girls reach the recommended 60 minutes of moderate-intensity activity daily. In Canada – a country long committed to monitoring and increasing physical activity levels – objective pedometer evidence indicates that 91% of children and young people do not meet the guideline of 16,500 steps per day (Health Canada 2007), raising the prospect that self-report (the basis of most descriptive data) may underestimate the extent of inactivity.

Thus the summary by the World Health Organization (WHO) that 'in many countries, developed and developing, less than one-third of young people are sufficiently active to benefit their present and future health' may well understate the problem (WHO 2008a).

Ageing population

The world is experiencing a demographic transition characterized by an improvement in life expectancy for both men and women, leading to an increase in the total number of older people world-wide. To illustrate the effect on the age structure of populations, using New Zealand as an example, Figure 1.3 shows population 'pyramids' for 2006

Figure 1.3 Age structure of the population of New Zealand in 2006 and projection for 2061.

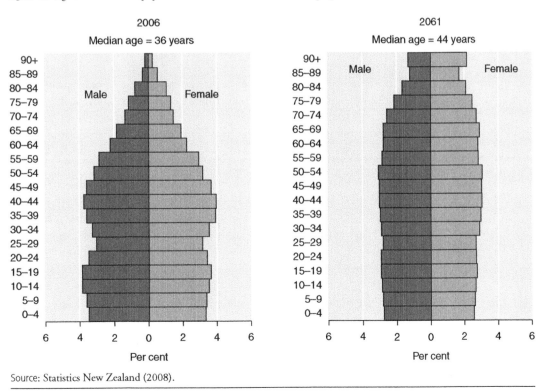

Source: Statistics New Zealand (2008).

Figure 1.4 Proportion of population aged 60 or over: world and development regions, 1950–2050.

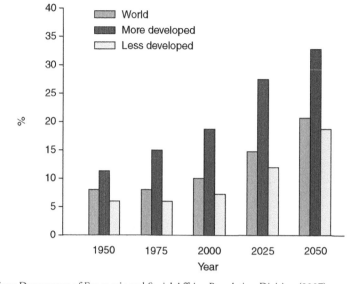

Source: United Nations Department of Economic and Social Affairs: Population Division (2007).

(real data) and 2061 (projections). The 2061 pyramid has a narrower base and a broader top, indicating a smaller number of children, a larger number of old people and a median age of the population that is older by eight years.

The impact, world-wide, of the ageing of populations is shown in Figure 1.4. This histogram shows the percentage of individuals aged 60 in 1950, and at 25 year intervals up to 2050. Developed countries have the highest proportion of older people, the population of Europe being the oldest. A notable aspect of population ageing is the progressive ageing of the older population itself. In most countries, the population aged 80 or over (the oldest old) is growing faster than any other segment of the population. Globally, this sector will likely increase more than four-fold by 2050 (United Nations Department of Economic and Social Affairs 2007).

The ageing of a population has enormous social and economic implications, including an increase in age-related diseases and an increased number of frail elderly people. Physical activity has much to offer the elderly in terms of personal and public health: it helps to prevent some important age-related diseases (e.g. type 2 diabetes, osteoporosis[1] and cardiovascular disease); and it enhances functional capacities, leading to a better quality of life and increased capability for independent living (see Chapter 11). Public health policies to attenuate the marked age-related decline in physical activity levels (see following section) are therefore sorely needed.

PREVALENCE OF ACTIVITY/INACTIVITY WORLD-WIDE

Governments and other agencies monitor health behaviours, including physical activity, to inform public health policy and to review the progress of interventions that aim to change behaviours. Many countries survey only leisure-time physical activity, because this type of activity is assumed to be the most amenable to interventions and because occupational work is now uncommon in westernized countries – the source of most national data. The assessment methods used to monitor physical activity unfortunately are varied, but it is clear that physical activity levels are low in many, probably most, countries.

There are two frequently used approaches to presenting data on population physical activity levels: one is to report the proportion of individuals in a specified age/sex-group who are judged to be inactive; the other is to report the proportion of individuals meeting the criteria that identify the minimal 'dose' of activity needed for health benefits. Figure 1.5 shows the percentage of adults in selected European countries that are classified as 'inactive' because they report doing no moderate-intensity

Figure 1.5 Percentage of adults who do no moderate-intensity physical activity in a typical week, 2005, selected European Countries.

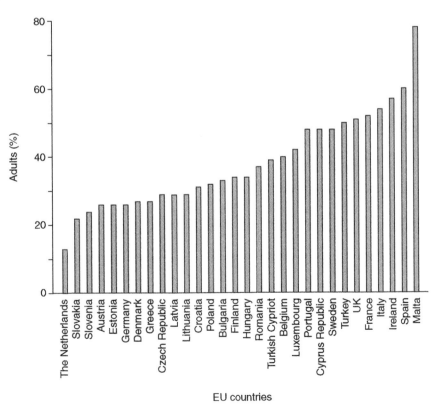

Source: European Commission (2006).

Figure 1.6 Proportion of adults in England achieving the physical activity guidelines in 2006, by age and gender.

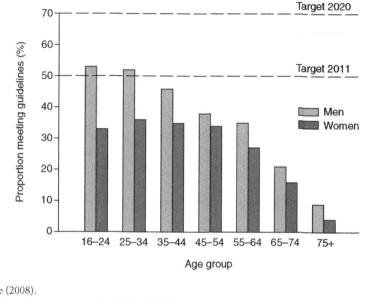

Source: Information Centre (2008).
Note: Horizontal lines depict government targets for 2011 and 2020.

physical activity. The United Kingdom scores worse than average, with around half the adult population classed as inactive. In the US around 38% of adults are reported to engage in no leisure-time physical activity.

Reporting the proportion of individuals who meet national guidelines has the advantage of allowing governments to set targets for increasing activity levels and then monitor progress towards that target. In England in 2006, only 40% of men and 30% of women achieved the recommended amount of activity – far short of the target of 50% that has been established for 2011 (Figure 1.6). Only one-third of American adults are deemed to be sufficiently active and, although Australians and Canadians appear to do better (46% and 49%, respectively, are classified as sufficiently active), active individuals still comprise a minority of the population.

Two features of the data on physical activity are common to most developed countries: the rapid decline with increasing age; and higher levels of activity in men than in women. For example, the data from the United Kingdom in Figure 1.6 show that, whereas 54% of men and 33% of women aged 16–24 fulfil the guideline for health benefits, these figures decline to 17% and 12%, respectively, in the age group 65–74 years.

Activity levels within countries also vary considerably with racial/ethnic group. In the United Kingdom, adults of Bangladeshi or Pakistani origin are the least active, and in the US there is particular concern at the low levels of activity among Hispanics. In developing countries, a decline in physical activity appears to follow in the wake of economic growth, so the prevalence of inactivity world-wide may be expected to rise as the economies of these countries progress.

TRENDS OVER TIME IN PHYSICAL ACTIVITY LEVELS

Few countries have collected comprehensive data in a standardized manner over enough decades to identify long-term trends in physical activity levels. Exceptions are Canada and Finland.

Canada has a long history of commitment to the study of physical activity levels. National surveys of leisure-time physical activity were carried out in 1981 (fitness as well as activity), 1988, 1995, 1998, 1999, 2000, 2001 and 2005. From 1995 onwards the same instrument, the Physical Activity Monitor, has been used. Comparison over time reveals that substantial inroads were made in reducing sedentary living during the 1980s and early 1990s. In 1981, over three-quarters of adults aged 18 and older were considered insufficiently active for health benefits, but levels of inactivity decreased to 71% in 1988 and to 63% by the mid-1990s. Subsequent progress has been slow, although the percentage of the population that was at least moderately active increased significantly between 1994/5 and 2004/5 (Figure 1.7). However, a majority of adult Canadians are still not sufficiently active, despite considerable efforts by government agencies to promote physical activity.

Health behaviours have been monitored in Eastern Finland at five-year intervals since 1972, when the community-wide North Karelia Project was initiated with the aim of reducing high rates of cardiovascular diseases. Twenty-five years of change in leisure-time, occupational and commuting physical activity have been described

Figure 1.7 Trends in the proportion of inactive and moderately active adults in Canada 1994/5–2004/5.

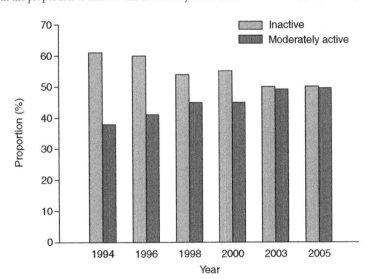

Source: Canadian Fitness and Lifestyle Research Institute (2005).
Note: Activity levels based on estimated average daily energy expenditure. Inactive: less than 1.5 kcal per kilogram of body mass per day (equivalent to walking no more than 15 minutes per day). Moderately active: more than 1.5 kcal per kilogram of body mass per day (walking for 0.5 hours per day is equivalent to 1.5–2.9 kcal per kilogram per day, walking for one hour per day is equivalent to just over 3 kcal per kilogram per day).

(Barengo *et al.* 2002). The proportion of both men and women engaging in high levels of leisure-time physical activity has increased since 1972, as has the proportion of women participating at a moderate level (defined as at least four hours per week of activities such as walking or cycling). Repeated surveys of representative samples of the Finnish population overall confirm that participation in recreational physical activity has increased over the past two decades in young, working-age and elderly people – although walking and cycling in commuting have decreased (Vuori *et al.* 2004).

More recently, other countries have begun to monitor activity levels in a consistent manner. Since 1996 the UK government recommendation on physical activity has been that adults should participate in a minimum of 30 minutes of activity of at least moderate intensity on five or more days of the week. The proportion achieving this level has increased over recent years to 40% of men and 28% of women in 2006, but nevertheless a majority of adults are still insufficiently active (Information Centre 2008). Progress has also been slow in the US, with only 33% of adults sufficiently active in 2003, compared with 32% in 1997: a small positive is that the prevalence of walking has improved somewhat over these years. In Australia, the proportion of those aged 15 and over reporting sedentary or low exercise levels has not changed significantly over the last ten years (69% in 1995, 69% in 2001 and 70% in 2004–5) (Australian Bureau of Statistics 2006).

In summary, it is clear that the prevalence of physical inactivity remains high in developed countries. In rapidly growing cities of the developing world, inactivity is an even greater problem. The WHO Global Strategy on Diet, Physical Activity and Health summarizes the available data thus: 'More than 60% of the world population is inactive or insufficiently active to gain health benefits' (WHO 2008b).

NATIONAL SURVEYS OF FITNESS

Three countries, Canada (1981 and 1988), England (1992) and the US (1999–2000 and 2001–2002) have published representative national surveys of fitness. In the Canadian survey, more than 20,000 participants completed a battery of tests. Cardiorespiratory fitness was assessed on the basis of the heart rate response to a standard step test, and participants were allocated to one of three fitness levels: 'an undesirable personal fitness level'; 'the minimum personal fitness level'; or 'a satisfactory personal fitness level'. This approach reflected the original purpose of the step test (to give individuals a means to monitor changes in their own fitness), but it made it difficult to relate the data to epidemiological findings. Average values for maximal oxygen uptake were predicted, without direct measurement of respiratory gases, and found to correspond quite closely with 'world averages' (Shephard 1986). The latter were not drawn from representative samples, however, and the prediction of VO_2max from the step test data was fraught with problems. Repeat measurements were made in 1988 on most of a 20% subset of the original sample, but results have not been widely disseminated.

The English National Fitness Survey used a graded treadmill test to estimate VO_2max from measurements of oxygen uptake and heart rate in a much smaller, but still representative, sample (858 men, 883 women). These values were reported by age and sex, but researchers used functional criteria as the main outcome measures (did people have sufficient aerobic capacity or muscle strength to carry out everyday tasks without fatigue?). For example, it was determined that nearly one-third of men and two-thirds of women would find it difficult to sustain a walking pace of about $4.8\,km\,h^{-1}$ ($3\,mile\,h^{-1}$) up a 1-in-20 (5%) slope for more than a few minutes (Sports Council and Health Education Authority 1992). The proportion of men who could not do this rose sharply with age, that is, from 4% of 16–24-year-olds to 81% of 65–74-year-olds. Equivalent figures for women rose from 34% to 92%. These findings strongly suggest that the prevalence of low fitness was widespread in England. To the authors' knowledge, there are no plans to update these data.

The American data derives from the National Health and Nutrition Examination Survey (NHANES) and also comprises predicted values for maximal oxygen uptake, based on heart rate responses to a submaximal treadmill test. Analysis revealed low fitness in adults of non-Hispanic black race, particularly among women (Duncan *et al.* 2005). Uniquely, NHANES also obtained data for young people aged 12 to 19 years. Fitness was lower among overweight individuals but unrelated to race/ethnicity (Pate *et al.* 2006).

DEFINITIONS OF KEY TERMS

Disease is relatively easy to define, either according to aetiology (e.g. tuberculosis is caused by a bacterium, *Mycobacterium tuberculosis*) or in terms of symptoms (e.g. the term asthma describes a disease characterized by fits of laboured breathing). Defining health is more problematic. Is health merely the 'other side of the coin', that is, the absence of disease? Somehow this fails to capture the essence of our everyday use of the term health as encapsulated in phrases such as 'picture of health' and 'rude health'. Something wider is needed. The most ambitious definition is probably that proposed by the WHO (1946): 'Health is a state of complete physical, mental and social well-being and not merely the absence of disease or infirmity.' This definition, although criticized because of the difficulty of defining and measuring well-being, remains an ideal. It is helpful in the context of this book because physical activity contributes more to health than just helping to prevent disease.

Finally – a note on our use of the terms 'physical activity' and 'exercise'. We have adopted the definitions that have acquired currency over recent years (Howley 2001). Thus physical activity is 'any bodily movement produced by contraction of skeletal muscle that substantially increases energy expenditure'. Hence the title of this book is broad – *physical activity* and health. Exercise (or exercise training) is defined as 'a subcategory of leisure-time physical activity in which planned, structured and repetitive bodily movements are performed to improve or maintain one or more components of physical fitness'. However, the distinction between physical activity and exercise is sometimes neither helpful nor necessary, so there are occasions in the text where these terms are used more loosely.

SUMMARY

- The modern history of exercise science began after the Second World War, when epidemiologists began the scientific study of the role of exercise in protection against heart disease.

- An epidemic of obesity in adults and children is leading to an increase in obesity-related diseases.
- In many countries, developed and developing, less than one-third of young people are sufficiently active to benefit their present and future health.
- Improvements in life expectancy for both men and women mean that the total number of older people world-wide is increasing, changing the age structure of populations. This means more age-related disease and an increased number of frail elderly people.
- The findings of representative surveys of physical activity levels generally have two features in common: a rapid decline in activity levels with increasing age; and higher levels of activity in men than in women.
- A decline in physical activity appears to follow in the wake of economic growth, so that the prevalence of inactivity world-wide may be expected to rise as the economies of developing countries progress.
- The National Fitness Survey for England determined that nearly one-third of men and two-thirds of women would find it difficult to sustain a walking pace of about $4.8\,km\,h^{-1}$ ($3\,mile\,h^{-1}$) up a 1-in-20 (5%) slope for more than a few minutes.

STUDY TASKS

1 Typical daily energy expenditure in western countries is estimated to have fallen by as much as 3,360 kJ (800 kcal) in the last 50 years. Is this a lot or a little? Explain your answer as fully as possible.
2 Why do the figures describing the prevalence of overweight and obese children give rise to so much concern?
3 In your opinion, what factors can be invoked to explain the low levels of physical activity in children and adolescents?
4 Why is the age structure of the population of a country such as New Zealand expected to change so much in the decades to come? What are the implications of this change for public health policy?
5 Basing your answer on Figure 1.6, describe and evaluate the public health importance of the data describing physical activity levels in England.
6 Which two countries have the best data on long-term changes in physical activity? What, in your opinion, is the value of making objective comparisons over time of physical activity in population levels?

NOTE

1 There are more women than men in the older age groups, and this proportion is expected to rise still further as the population ages. Thus the prevalence of osteoporosis will increase.

FURTHER READING

Allender, S., Peto, V., Scarborough, P., Boxer, A. and Rayner, M. (2007) 'British Heart Foundation CHD statistics'. Online, available at: www.heartstats.org/datapage.asp?id=6799, page updated 25 February 2008 (accessed 28 February 2008).

Aylin, P., Williams, S. and Bottle, A. (2007) 'Dr Foster's case notes: obesity and type 2 diabetes in children, 1996–7 to 2003–4', *British Medical Journal* 331: 1167.

Council on Sports Medicine and Fitness and Council on School Health (2006) 'Active healthy living: prevention of childhood obesity through increased physical activity', *Pediatrics* 117: 1834–42.

Ludwig, D.S. (2007) 'Childhood obesity: the shape of things to come', *New England Journal of Medicine* 357: 2325–7.

Paffenbarger, R.S., Blair, S.N. and Lee, I.-M. (2001) 'A history of physical activity, cardiovascular health and longevity: the scientific contributions of Jeremy N Morris, DSc, DPH, FRCP', *International Journal of Epidemiology* 30: 1184–92. Online, available at: http://ije.oxfordjournals.org/cgi/content/full/30/5/1184.

United Nations Department of Economic and Social Affairs: Population Division (2007) 'World population ageing 2007', Online, available at: www.un.org/esa/population/publications/WPA2007/wpp.2007.htm (accessed 10 October 2008).

2 Nature of the evidence

Knowledge assumed
Principles of measurement and categories of measurement scales
Basic statistics (including inference, estimation and statistical power)

INTRODUCTION

Evidence concerning physical activity and health takes a variety of forms. Like evidence on other topics, it is constrained by the nature of investigations and the methods employed. The reader needs to understand these constraints and to be able to identify research that has been well-conducted. Good research requires a plausible hypothesis, a robust design and that data are collected and interpreted with adequate allowance for potential sources of error. It also has to be concerned with the complexity caused by the interrelation of physical activity levels with social and environmental factors.

Research in physical activity and health can be divided into epidemiological and laboratory-based studies. Within each category, studies may be either observational or experimental. However, in this field, most epidemiological studies are observational and most laboratory-based studies are experimental. In observational studies researchers allow nature to take its course and merely collect information about one or more groups of subjects. The simplest observational studies are purely descriptive, but most go further by analysing relationships between health status and other variables. In experimental studies the researchers intervene to affect what happens to some or all of the individuals.

WHAT IS EPIDEMIOLOGY?

Epidemiology has been defined by the World Health Organization (WHO) as 'the study of the distribution and determinants of health-related states or events in specified populations,[1] and the application of this study to control of health problems' (Porta 2008). The use of the phrase 'health-related states or events' (rather than the older term 'disease frequency') reflects the fact that our concept of health now includes aspects of positive health – for example, a good quality of life – and not only the absence of disease. For simplicity, the term 'health-related outcome' will be used in this text to include both disease and other health-related states or events. Health-related outcomes may be defined simply, for example, as 'disease present' or 'disease absent', or graded, for example 'normal weight', 'overweight' or 'obese'.

Types of study

The main types of epidemiological study are summarized in Table 2.1.

Case reports or case series describe the experience of a single patient or group of patients with a similar diagnosis. Such studies usually report an unusual feature and may lead to the formulation of a new hypothesis. Few studies on physical activity or fitness are of this form, but one example is the autopsy study of Clarence DeMar, a runner who had participated in over 1,000 distance races, including 100 marathons; the diameter of his coronary arteries was estimated to be two or three times the normal diameter, leading to conjecture that years of running training might lead the arteries to adapt to the larger demand for blood flow (Currens and White 1961).

In correlational studies (sometimes called ecological studies), the characteristics of entire populations are used to describe the frequency of a health-related outcome in

Table 2.1 Types of epidemiological study

CATEGORY	TYPE OF STUDY	UNIT OF STUDY
Observational		
Descriptive studies	Case reports or case series	Individuals
Analytical studies	Correlational	Populations
	Cross-sectional surveys	Individuals
	Case-control studies	Individuals
	Cohort studies	Individuals
Experimental	Randomized, controlled trials	Individuals

Source: Adapted from Beaglehole *et al.* (1993).

Figure 2.1 Relationship between the median serum cholesterol concentration and ten-year mortality from CHD in 16 cohorts of men in the Seven Countries Study.

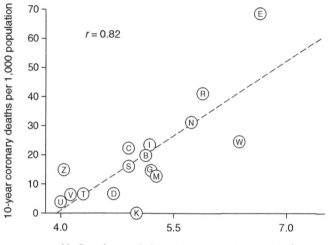

Source: Keys (1980).

Notes: B = Belgrade (Yugoslavia, formerly Serbia); C = Crevalcore (Italy); D = Dalmatia (Yugoslavia, formerly Croatia); E = East Finland; G = Corfu; I = Italian railroad; K = Crete; M = Montegiorgio (Italy); N = Zutphen (the Netherlands); R = American railroad; S = Slavonia (Yugoslavia, formerly Croatia); T = Tanushimaru (Japan); U = Ushibuka (Japan); V = Velike Krsna (Yugoslavia, formerly Serbia); W = West Finland; Z = Zrenjanin (Yugoslavia).

relation to some factor/s relevant to the research question or hypothesis. An example would be the Seven Countries Study where patterns of mortality from coronary heart disease (CHD) were highly correlated with the median plasma cholesterol concentration in the different populations (Figure 2.1). One interpretation of this finding is that CHD mortality in a community depends strongly on the typical plasma cholesterol concentration of its people.

Cross-sectional surveys describe the prevalence of a health-related outcome in representative samples and relate this to personal or demographic characteristics. For example, the 1981 Canada Fitness Survey found distinct differences between active and sedentary Canadians in measures of their health. If such surveys are repeated, they offer a means to evaluate population-based interventions.

In a case-control study (also called a retrospective study), the occurrence of a possible cause is compared between people known to have a disease (the cases) and a reference group who do not have the disease (the controls). The investigators look back from the disease to a possible cause, seeking associations with exposure to the factors of interest. The most difficult aspect of this design is the selection of controls because this can introduce bias (systematic error). However, case-control studies offer a way to identify adequate numbers of patients even when the outcome under study is relatively rare. Many studies of physical activity and the risk of cancer are therefore of this type.

Cohort studies, sometimes called follow-up studies, are conceptually simple. They begin with a group of people who are free of disease (or other health-related outcome) and determine their exposure to a suspected risk factor. Subgroups are defined on the basis of exposure to the risk factor. For a study of physical (in)activity, subgroups might comprise: sedentary individuals; those engaging in moderate activity; and those engaging in vigorous activity. Participants are then followed for a period of time, usually some years, so that the occurrence of the specified outcome can be compared between subgroups. In contrast to case-control studies, a range of outcomes can be studied. For example, the Harvard Alumni (graduates) Health Study, a cohort study which began in 1962, has investigated physical inactivity as a risk factor for cardiovascular diseases, longevity, diabetes, several site-specific cancers, gallbladder disease, Parkinson's disease and even depression and suicide. Such studies are expensive, but offer the best potential for establishing causality.

Experimental studies are sometimes called intervention studies because the researchers attempt to 'intervene', that is, change a variable in one or more groups of people and measure the effect on the outcome of interest. In a randomized controlled trial, considered to be the strongest design, subjects are assigned to one or more intervention groups and a control group in a random manner. This ensures that any differences between groups are due to chance rather than to bias introduced by the investigators. One framework for summarizing research on health-related issues assigns the highest level of evidence (Category A) only when a 'rich body of data' from randomized controlled trials is available (National Institutes of Health 1998). However, obvious ethical and practical constraints mean that this type of epidemiological study will probably never be conducted with a physical activity intervention because researchers cannot ask people to remain physically inactive for 20 years to see if this increases their risk of developing, say, CHD.

Measures of health-related outcomes

Measures of the occurrence of health-related outcomes are basic tools of epidemiology. They permit comparison of the frequency of the outcome(s) of interest between populations, as well as among individuals, with and without exposure to a particular risk factor. A number of measures are in common usage, giving different types of information. All require correct definition of the population at risk. For instance, sports injuries only occur among people who play sport, so the population at risk are sports players.

Prevalence and incidence are the measures most commonly used. Prevalence quantifies the proportion of individuals in a population that exhibits the outcome of interest at a specified time. For example, in the Health Survey for England 2004, the prevalence of raised waist:hip ratio among women of Pakistani origin was 39%. Prevalence is helpful in assessing the need for health care or preventive strategies. The formula for calculating prevalence (P) is:

$$P = \frac{\text{number of people with the health-related outcome at a specified time}}{\text{number of people in the population at risk at the specified time}}$$

Incidence quantifies the number of new occurrences of an outcome that develop during a specified time interval in the population at risk of experiencing the event during this period. The most accurate is the person–time incidence rate (I), calculated as:

$$I = \frac{\text{number of people who develop the health-related outcome in a specified period}}{\text{sum of the periods of time for which each person in the population is at risk}}$$

The denominator is the best available measure of the total time for which individuals are free of the outcome in question. Each person in the study population contributes one person-year for each year of observation before the outcome develops or that person is lost to follow-up. Figure 2.2 illustrates this schematically, based on a study of five subjects over a five-year observation period.

The commonest outcome measures are rates of morbidity (illness) and mortality (death). Because the age structure of a population affects both rates, these are often reported as age-specific or age-adjusted rates. This is essential when older people are more likely to become ill, as is the case, for instance, for CHD or stroke. Measures of health status may also encompass some measure of the quality of life – for example, life expectancy free from disability, quality-adjusted life years or disability-adjusted life years lost.

Comparisons of disease occurrence between exposed and unexposed groups, for example smokers versus non-smokers, or sedentary people versus physically active people, are essential tools in epidemiology. These include risk difference, relative risk and population-attributable risk. (The odds ratio is used to measure the association between an exposure and a disease (or other outcome) in case-control studies. It is very similar to the relative risk, particularly if the outcome is a rare disease.) The risk difference (also called the excess risk) is the absolute difference in rates of occurrence between groups of individuals who have and have not been exposed to the factor of interest. The relative risk (also called the risk ratio) is the ratio of the risk of occurrence among exposed people to that among the unexposed; it measures the strength of an association. For example, let us assume that the incidence of stroke is 17.7 per 100,000 person-years among non-smokers and 49.6 per 100,000 person-years among smokers. The relative risk of stroke in smokers compared with non-smokers is therefore 2.8 (49.6/17.7). Put another way, smokers are 2.8 times more likely to have a stroke than

Figure 2.2 Calculation of person-time incidence rate.

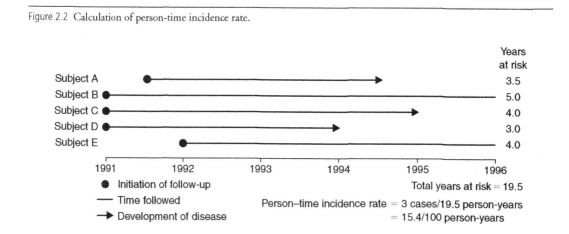

Source: Adapted from Hennekens and Buring (1987).

non-smokers. When dealing with exposures that are associated with a *decreased* risk of disease – as is often the case for physical activity – researchers sometimes take the *unexposed* group (the *inactive* group) as the reference category. The relative risk in the group exposed to physical activity is thus less than 1. Box 2.1 illustrates both approaches.

For public health policy, it is informative to estimate the incidence of a disease (or other health outcome) in a population that can be attributed to exposure to a particular risk factor. This measure is the population-attributable risk. It reflects not only the strength of the risk associated with an exposure (information vital for assessment of the risk to an individual) but also its prevalence. Population-attributable risk estimates can therefore help to determine which exposures have the most relevance to the health of a community. For example, the relative risk of developing lung cancer in smokers is high (14 in a classic study of British doctors). Nevertheless, if only 1% of the population

---

BOX 2.1 COMPARISONS OF DISEASE OCCURRENCE

Table 2.2 Vigorous sports and attack rate of CHD in male civil servants

EPISODES OF VIGOROUS SPORT IN PREVIOUS FOUR WEEKS, REPORTED IN 1976	CHD CASES	MAN-YEARS	AGE STANDARDIZED RATE* (CASES PER 1000 MAN-YEARS)
None (reference group)	413	72,282	5.8
1–3	37	7,786	4.5
8–12+	7	3,349	2.1

Source: Adapted from Morris *et al.* (1990).

Note: *rates are slightly different from values obtained from calculations based on data in columns 2 and 3 because of adjustment for age.

In Table 2.2, the absolute difference in risk of CHD between men reporting no vigorous sports and those reporting between eight and ≥12 episodes is (5.8–2.1), that is, 3.7 cases per 1,000 man-years. This gives no indication of the *strength* of the association, however, which is estimated by calculating the relative risk. Relative risk can be expressed in two ways.

1 Taking men reporting no vigorous sport as the reference group, the relative risk in men reporting between 8 and ≥12 episodes is (2.1/5.8), or 0.36. Thus, the men who were most active in vigorous sport had a risk of developing CHD that was around one-third of that experienced by the men least active in such sports.
2 Taking men with the highest level of participation in vigorous sports as the reference group, the relative risk of not engaging in these is (5.8/2.1), or 2.76. Thus, men who did not engage in vigorous sport were more than two-and-a-half times as likely to develop CHD as those with the highest level of participation in such sport.

CHARACTERISTIC	PREVALENCE (% OF MAN-YEARS)	RELATIVE RISK	POPULATION-ATTRIBUTABLE RISK (%)
Sedentary lifestyle	62.0	1.31	16.1
Hypertension	9.4	1.73	6.4
Cigarette smoking	38.2	11.76	22.5

Table 2.3 Relative and population-attributable risks of death from all causes among 16,936 male Harvard Alumni, 1962–78

Source: Adapted from Paffenbarger *et al.* (1986).

smoke, the population-attributable risk is low; on the other hand, if 30% of people smoke, then the population-attributable risk is high and this behaviour represents a considerable public health burden that justifies investment in strategies to reduce its prevalence. A second example, based on data from the Harvard Alumni Study, is shown in Table 2.3. Although the relative risk of death among alumni was nearly nine-fold greater for cigarette smoking than for a sedentary lifestyle, the estimates of population-attributable risk for these two exposures were similar because the prevalence of a sedentary lifestyle was much higher than the prevalence of smoking.

MEASURING PHYSICAL ACTIVITY AND FITNESS IN POPULATION STUDIES

In epidemiology, health-related outcomes are often compared between groups differing in their level of physical activity and/or fitness. The measurement tools employed are varied and have different strengths and weaknesses. While the number of studies relying on measurements of fitness is now substantial, large epidemiological studies most commonly measure physical activity and/or inactivity.

Physical activity/inactivity

In the early years of research into physical activity and health, job classification was a useful tool. For example, the classic study by Morris and co-workers compared the incidence of CHD in London postmen who delivered mail on foot or by bicycle (a physically active group) with that in colleagues who sorted the mail (designated as less active) (Morris *et al.* 1953). Occupational tasks have sometimes been classified based on 'on-the-job' measurements of oxygen uptake as in Paffenbarger's study of San Francisco longshore men (dockworkers) in the 1970s (Paffenbarger and Hale 1975). However, as the physical demands of so many occupations decreased, leisure-time physical activity became the dominant component of total activity. This has most commonly been measured using a questionnaire or diary (in 'real-time' or retrospectively). For some purposes, self-reported indices of *in*activity, such as number of cars per family or hours spent watching television, provide useful information. Approaches that are increasingly adopted as technology progresses include monitoring physical activity using a pedometer or accelerometer and measurement of total energy expenditure using the doubly labelled water technique.

Questionnaires

The simplest of these classify people as active or inactive, based on two or three questions. However, physical activity is a complex behaviour, with components of type, intensity, frequency and duration. Consequently, if a more comprehensive measure is desired, researchers have to ask those questions that elicit the information relevant to their study hypothesis. If this is that improvements in fitness arising from physical activity determine the health outcome, then the questionnaire needs to obtain information on the intensity of activity (because fitness improvements are positively related to exercise intensity). A direct approach is to ask about participation in specific activities known to demand a high rate of energy expenditure. Alternatively, the questionnaire may ask how often the individual participates in exercise that he or she would describe as 'vigorous' or which elicits physiological responses associated with vigorous exercise. An example of the latter approach is: 'How many times per week do you engage in exercise which makes you sweat?' These indirect questions are probably a good way to tease out the level of 'physiological stress' on the individual that is determined by the relative,[2] rather than the absolute, intensity of physical activity. Yet another way to characterize the intensity of activity is to use metabolic equivalents (METs). This unit measures intensity in multiples of the resting metabolic rate (assumed to be $3.5\,ml\,kg^{-1}\,min^{-1}$). For example, light housework demands about 2.5 METs, very brisk walking at $6.4\,km\,h^{-1}$ ($4\,mile\,h^{-1}$) demands about 4 METs and doubles tennis about 6 METs (Ainsworth *et al.* 2000).

If the research hypothesis is that the total energy expended in physical activity, rather than its intensity per se, determines its effects on the outcome under study, data must be collected to describe the absolute intensity, the duration and the frequency of physical activity, so that a collective measure of its 'volume' may be obtained (Howley 2001). This information can be converted into energy units by referring to data that describe typical rates of energy expenditure during a whole range of physical activities (McArdle *et al.* 2006). Energy expenditure in activity is then reported as kJ or kcal over a specified time, often per week. An alternative is to report activity in MET-h or MET-min per week. For example, if a woman did two hours of high-impact aerobic dance (intensity 7 METs) each week, as well as three hours of brisk walking at 4 METs, her total physical activity could be described as $[(2 \times 7) + (3 \times 4)] = 26\,MET\text{-}h\,week^{-1}$. The woman's energy expenditure in these two activities can then be estimated, provided that body mass is known, because the resting metabolic rate is fairly constant at $4.2\,kJ\,kg\,body\,mass^{-1}\,h^{-1}$ ($1\,kcal\,kg\,body\,mass^{-1}\,h^{-1}$). For a 65 kg woman, $26\,MET\text{-}h\,week^{-1}$ is equivalent to an energy expenditure of approximately $(4.2 \times 26 \times 65)\,kJ$, that is 7,098 kJ or 7.1 MJ.

Historically, physical activity questionnaires were developed to be relevant to cardiovascular disease. Research into skeletal health requires different or additional information because the pattern of skeletal loading – rather than its energy expenditure – determines the adaptation of bone. Attempts are in progress to devise and validate a questionnaire that elicits the information on physical activity that is relevant to skeletal health (Dolan *et al.* 2006). Such targeted questionnaires, particularly if used in combination with motion sensors, may improve measurement of bone loading.

In order to assess exposure, researchers ask participants about 'usual' or 'habitual' physical activity. Alternatively, participants may be asked to recall their physical activity levels in earlier years. This may be necessary if the hypothesis is that physical activity exerts its influence on the outcome mainly at particular stages of life. For example, in a case-control study of breast cancer, women aged between 36 and 40 years were asked to estimate their participation in various sports and leisure activities when they were 10, 16 and 25 years old (see Figure 2.3). This approach requires recall over long periods, with obvious potential for error. An alternative is to ask questions about activity during a specified period – for example, the last four weeks. This improves recall, but the validity of the data is limited by the extent to which the period sampled reflects each individual's usual behaviour. Researchers have to prioritize the need for data on long term and/or current exposure according to the outcome under study. If, as for CHD, there is reason to suppose that physical activity may influence both the long-term development of the disease and the acute events that precipitate a heart attack, both sorts of information are relevant.

The precision (repeatability) of questionnaires, assessed by test–retest correlation coefficients, is high (at an interval of one month this mostly exceeds 0.75). It is, however, best for high-intensity leisure-time activities and much poorer for those of moderate and light intensity. It tends to be poorer in women than in men, mainly because women report very little vigorous exercise and because questionnaires do not record household activities comprehensively. Walking, in particular, is unreliably recalled and this is the most popular leisure-time physical activity for many people.

Figure 2.3 Recall of lifetime participation in physical activity.

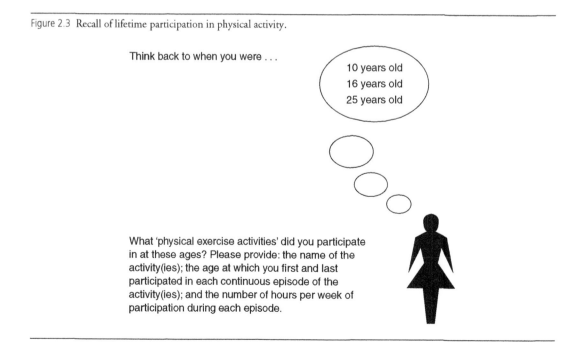

Questionnaires have been validated using a variety of approaches, including: detailed interview by a trained interviewer; use of a motion detector, usually an accelerometer; and assessment of cardiorespiratory fitness. Questionnaire measures do not correlate well with accelerometer recordings or with measurements of total energy expenditure obtained by the doubly labelled water method. The relationships between questionnaire scores of physical activity and fitness tend to be modest (typical correlation coefficients 0.3–0.5); this may reflect the genetic influence on fitness and/or the imprecision involved in measuring physical activity by questionnaire. Misclassification in self-reports of physical activity is important because it may lead to type I error (discussed later in this chapter).

There has long been a need for a standardized approach to obtaining data on self-reported physical activity levels to facilitate international comparisons and global surveillance. To this end the International Physical Activity Questionnaire has now been developed in both long and short forms. Details are available at www.ipaq.ki.se. Its reliability and validity are 'at least as good as other established self-reports', even in diverse settings (Craig *et al.* 2003).

Doubly labelled water

This non-intrusive method for measuring total energy expenditure in free-living situations will increasingly be used. It is more objective and accurate than questionnaire-based methods. On the other hand, it is expensive and cannot distinguish different *rates* of energy expenditure. A brief description of the principle and procedures involved are given in Box 2.2.

Motion sensors

Both types of motion sensors (pedometers and accelerometers) are objective alternatives or adjuncts to self-reports of behaviours. Subjects wear the devices during waking hours, except during bathing, showering or swimming. Motion sensors can

---

BOX 2.2 MEASUREMENT OF ENERGY EXPENDITURE USING DOUBLY LABELLED WATER

The principle is as follows:

- subjects drink water containing stable (non-radioactive) isotopes of hydrogen (^2H, or deuterium) and oxygen (^{18}O or oxygen-18);
- the isotopes distribute throughout all body fluids;
- ^2H leaves the body as water (^2H_2O) in urine, sweat and vapour from breathing;
- ^{18}O leaves the body as both water ($H_2{}^{18}O$) and carbon dioxide ($C^{18}O_2$);
- the difference between the rates of loss of ^{18}O and ^2H enables carbon dioxide production to be estimated;
- oxygen consumption is calculated from carbon dioxide production;
- energy expenditure is calculated using stoichiometry.

quantify physical activity as a continuous variable, whereas data from questionnaires are best reduced to categorical variables. Both measure walking with greater sensitivity than questionnaires.

Pedometers typically operate using a horizontal, spring-suspended lever arm that bounces with vertical motion during walking or running. Each movement detected above a pre-determined critical threshold is counted as a step taken. Data are typically reported as steps per day. Pedometers do not capture intensity of activity, but detect steps taken with acceptable accuracy.

As their name implies, accelerometers measure body movement in terms of acceleration. Most are piezoelectric sensors that detect acceleration in one plane. Processed data is recorded in internal memory and subsequently downloaded to a computer. Dedicated hardware and software are then employed to reduce what can be an overwhelming amount of data and analyse it. Most instruments in common use are uniaxial and sensitive only in a vertical plane. They are small in size, attached to the hip or lower back and thus minimally intrusive to the wearer. Tri-axial accelerometers provide a theoretically more comprehensive assessment of body movements, but techniques are still being developed to take full advantage of the three-dimensional data they output (Plasqui *et al.* 2005).

Raw outputs from an accelerometer are known as 'counts'. Counts are averaged over a specified time period and researchers have to translate these counts into meaningful indicators such as energy expenditure or time spent in moderate to vigorous activity. Calibration – mostly built into the instrument – typically involves relating counts to measures of energy expenditure, usually oxygen uptake during treadmill walking/running through a range of speeds or during a variety of physical tasks. Accuracy of accelerometer data depends on this calibration process as it does on the methods of data reduction and analysis employed. Further checks are necessary to ensure that output from individual accelerometers is standardized and internally reproducible. An exciting development is the coupling of accelerometers with other technologies. For example, the addition of heart rate monitoring to accelerometry may provide a more accurate assessment of energy expenditure. The two techniques are complementary because heart rate monitoring alone is problematic as heart rate is subject to so many influences beyond activity level.

The use of accelerometry in research is increasing exponentially, but it is now beginning to be used also in population surveillance of activity levels (e.g. US National Health and Nutrition Examination Survey 2003–4). However, more than with many other techniques, investigators need to make sure that they adopt best practice and balance completeness of data with the burden on their subjects. Readers wishing to consider methodological issues further will find the series of papers 'Objective monitoring of physical activity: closing the gaps in the science of accelerometry' a valuable resource (*Medicine and Science in Sports and Exercise* 2005 37 (11) (Supplement)).

Fitness

Some epidemiological studies classify individuals according to a measure of fitness. Direct measurements of VO_2max have been made during cycle ergometry or, less commonly, treadmill walking/running. Usually, however, because of practical and ethical constraints, a sub-maximal test has been employed. Maximal oxygen uptake may be predicted from sub-maximal heart rates (and sometimes oxygen uptake) measured during cycling. Alternatively, the heart rate at a given work rate may be adopted as a marker. In one large cohort study of men and women, time to 'volitional fatigue' during an incremental treadmill test has been used as a surrogate measure of $\dot{V}O_2$max (Blair *et al.* 1989). The validity of this method derives from the strong, essentially linear, relationship between $\dot{V}O_2$max and treadmill test performance. As with measures of physical activity, each approach has its strengths and limitations. Indirect measures are less accurate but can permit larger numbers to be studied. Maximal testing improves accuracy but has to be restricted to apparently healthy people. Treadmill walking/running may reflect performance in weight-bearing activities better than cycle ergometry, but will be more time-consuming if subjects require lengthy familiarization. In clinical research, simple walking tests such as the shuttle walking test (Singh *et al.* 1992) are commonly employed. These can be conducted in a physiotherapy department or even in a hospital corridor, and are appropriate and safe for various patient groups. A limitation to all tests of fitness as measures of exposure to physical activity is that they are influenced to some degree by genetic factors.

LABORATORY-BASED RESEARCH

Laboratory-based studies of physical activity/fitness and health complement epidemiology and help to establish causality, often by examining potential mechanisms. They may be either observational (descriptive or analytical) or experimental. Observational studies have limited potential to identify causal factors, but often lead to the generation of a hypothesis that is subsequently tested experimentally. For example, early descriptive studies reported that people with exercise-induced asthma could undertake repeated short bouts of exercise without undue distress. This led to experimental studies that tested the hypothesis that intermittent exercise was better tolerated by asthmatics than continuous exercise. Cross-sectional comparisons of athletes with inactive controls have often indicated potentially fruitful lines of enquiry. For example, studies in the 1960s found that endurance athletes have low plasma insulin responses to a glucose tolerance test, something later found to derive from their enhanced sensitivity to this hormone. Such cross-sectional studies are always dogged by the problem of self-selection, however, and some genetic factor common in athletic individuals may influence the health outcome under study.

Experimental studies, by manipulating single factors independently, can remove this problem and provide good control of extraneous influences. A range of designs can be used. Randomly controlled studies generate the highest degree of confidence and have strong internal validity. In other words, the findings are unlikely to be influenced by chance, bias or confounding. (These sources of error are discussed later.) Such studies are commonly employed to test hypotheses related to the effects on health outcomes of increasing (or decreasing) levels of physical activity or fitness over weeks, months or sometimes years. The steps in setting up a randomly controlled study are shown in Figure 2.4.

Figure 2.4 Steps in setting up a randomized, controlled, laboratory-based intervention study.

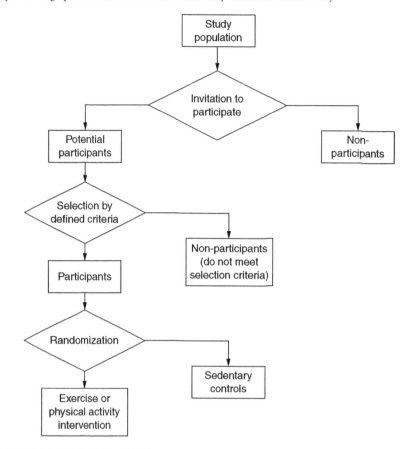

Without control groups, studies risk being confounded by systematic effects unrelated to the intervention. For example, participants in an uncontrolled exercise intervention study may respond to advice to the population at large to decrease their consumption of saturated fat. Investigators might conclude that exercise decreases plasma total cholesterol when this was, in reality, due to the change in diet (decreasing the intake of saturated fat lowers plasma total cholesterol). Figure 2.5 shows another example. Heart rates were measured during an incremental treadmill running test in an intervention group and a control group, before and after the intervention group did 13 weeks of running training. The decrease in heart rate in the control group may be explained by lower levels of anxiety on the second test occasion and/or by improved running economy through getting used to running on a treadmill. The true effect of training in reducing heart rate is the difference between the decrease in the intervention group and that in controls. The absence of a control group often leads to overestimation of the effect of an exercise intervention.

Moreover, without randomization, even a controlled laboratory study can be biased. For example, given the choice, 'couch potatoes' will typically choose to be controls, while those who are already active and fit will happily volunteer to be exercisers. This

Figure 2.5 Heart rate during treadmill running in intervention group (upper panel) and controls (lower panel) before and after the intervention group completed a 13-week programme of running training.

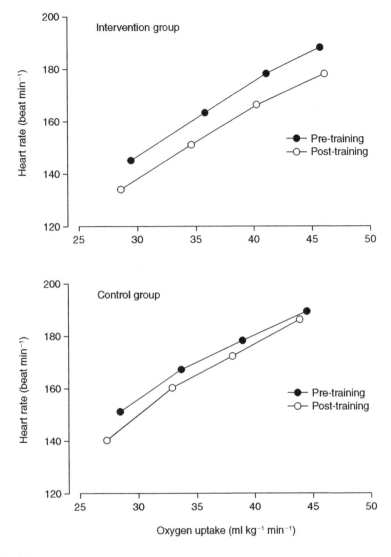

Source: Unpublished data.

will lead to differences in variables of interest between the two groups that confound findings.

Laboratory studies of exercise often use a repeated measures design where subjects act as their own control. Where the research question permits, a counterbalanced design will be used, with subjects allocated randomly to different orders of presentation. For example, if researchers wish to investigate the effects of a single session of exercise on markers of bone metabolism, each subject will be studied in two conditions, that is, with and without prior exercise. If all subjects were to do the exercise trial first, findings could be confounded by order-of-testing effects. These effects might derive from, for example, the environment (hot weather during the first trials, followed by a cold snap), but more often relate to changes in the subjects themselves. Subjects' anxiety levels decrease with repeated trials, resulting in changes to physiological and metabolic responses. One approach to the analysis of data from a typical laboratory exercise study is shown in Figure 2.6.

Laboratory studies of human volunteers can encounter problems with both statistical power and generalizability (external validity). A hypothesis is never proven to be true or false, it is accepted or rejected on the basis of statistical tests. Two types of error are associated with this decision: to reject the null hypothesis when it is true (type I or alpha error), and to accept the null hypothesis when it is false (type II or beta error). The probability of making a type I error is the level of significance of a statistical test. The probability of rejecting the null hypothesis when it is in fact false and should be rejected is known as its power. This reflects the potential of a study to detect an important effect. ('Important' has to be defined by the investigators, often on the basis

---

Figure 2.6 Experiment to test the hypothesis that prior exercise influences fat oxidation during exercise and recovery: data analysis using ANOVA with repeated measures.

Design: six subjects each undertook two exercise trials, one low intensity (40%) and one high intensity (70%), in a counterbalanced design, i.e. three subjects did the low intensity trial first, three did the high intensity trial first.

Appropriate analysis: 2-way ANOVA with repeated measures on both factors, i.e. trial and time.

Values for fat oxidation for each subject would be entered into the table below prior to analysis.

	Subjects	Pre-exercise (min)	Time during exercise (min)			Time during recovery (min)		
		5–10	8–10	18–20	28–30	5–10	15–20	35–40
40% $\dot{V}O_2$max	1							
	2							
	3							
	4							
	5							
	6							
70% $\dot{V}O_2$max	1							
	2							
	3							
	4							
	5							
	6							

Questions answered by the analysis:

Main effect of trial – did fat oxidation overall differ between trials?
Main effect of time – did fat oxidation change over time?
Interaction – did the pattern of change in fat oxidation over time differ between trials?

Note: The figure is for illustrative purposes and a larger number of subjects would normally be required to provide sufficient power. Other approaches to analysis are also appropriate, for example the use of summary measures.

---

of what is judged to be clinically meaningful. A statistic called the effect size[3] is sometimes also used.)

Power depends on the size of the sample, the level of significance (alpha) chosen and the error variance. Particularly when complicated, time-consuming and/or invasive measurements are proposed, it may be difficult to recruit volunteers and the sample size may be inadequate. There is then a risk in the study of not finding an effect when one is really there, i.e. a type II error. With adequate sample size, good control and accurate, complete and reliable measurements, a study will be valid. The issue of generalizability must be considered subsequently because one cannot generalize from an invalid study. The extent to which findings will apply to different populations has to be judged, based on the known or postulated mechanisms that might explain the findings. For example, numerous studies have shown that brisk walking improves fitness in middle-aged and older Caucasian women from developed countries. This activity has also been shown to elicit a sufficiently high proportion of $\dot{V}O_2$max to elicit a training effect. On the basis of these findings, it is reasonable to assume that brisk walking will have similar effects in women of this age group from other ethnic groups or from less developed countries.

Details of methods for assessment of fitness or function capacity for health-related research are beyond the scope of this book, but reference is made to a useful source in the Further Reading section at the end of this chapter.

ERROR: NATURE, SOURCES AND IMPLICATIONS

Evaluation of the validity of the findings of a study depends on the extent to which these could also be explained by chance, bias or confounding. A critical appreciation of the literature on exercise and health requires an understanding of all three sources of error. First, however, it is essential to make the distinction between precision and accuracy, both essential features of measurement. Figure 2.7 depicts these important concepts. Briefly, data are accurate if they are close to the true values and precise if the same measurement, when repeated, consistently yields similar values. Good data has to be both accurate and precise (Figure 2.7, top left); neither is sufficient alone (Box 2.3).

Random error is due to chance and leads to imprecision in measurement. It derives from several sources, including: individual biological variation; sampling error (a sample of people, rather than a population, is almost always the unit of study); and measurement error. These errors cannot be eliminated, but they can be reduced by making individual measurements as precise as possible and by increasing the size of the study. In the laboratory, precision is achieved by calibration of instruments, by making careful measurements and by increasing the number of measurements. Precise measurements are often impossible in epidemiology because it is difficult to measure physical activity or fitness and, often, health outcomes. This imprecision may be compensated by studying a large sample.

Researchers evaluate the degree to which chance variation may account for the results by calculating either the significance value (P value) or a confidence interval. Their hypothesis is accepted or rejected on the basis of these statistical tests. The P

BOX 2.3 ACCURACY AND PRECISION

- If an individual's VO_2max is measured on four occasions during one week and recorded as 25 ml kg^{-1} min^{-1}, 35 ml kg^{-1} min^{-1}, 15 ml kg^{-1} min^{-1} and 42 ml kg^{-1} min^{-1}, the measurements have low precision; they are so different that no meaningful interpretation can be placed on them – even if the average of these values is close to the true value (Figure 2.7, bottom left).
- On the other hand, repeated measurements of 34 ml kg^{-1} min^{-1}, 32 ml kg^{-1} min^{-1}, 33 ml kg^{-1} min^{-1} and 33 ml kg^{-1} min^{-1} indicate high precision, but are inaccurate if the subject's *true* VO_2max is 19 ml kg^{-1} min^{-1} (Figure 2.7, top right). This is important because the average value recorded (33 ml kg^{-1} min^{-1}) suggests that brisk walking at 4.5 METs would be very light exercise for this person (<50% of VO_2max), whereas it would actually be very vigorous (>80% VO_2max)!
- Only if repeated values are close to each other (high precision) and cluster around the true value (high accuracy), can we have confidence in the data.

Figure 2.7 Schematic representation of accuracy and precision in measurement.

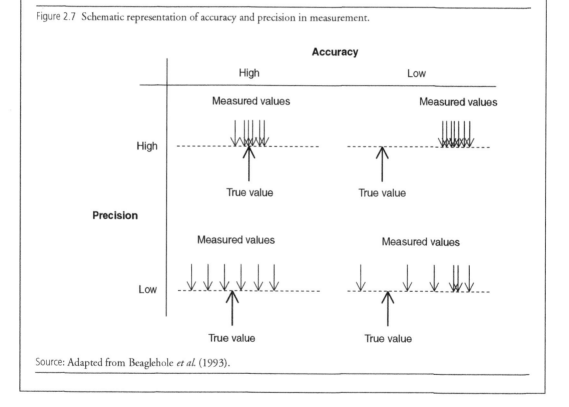

Source: Adapted from Beaglehole *et al.* (1993).

value describes the probability that the result may be due to chance alone. In medical research, investigators conventionally adopt a critical P value (α) of 0.05. This means that the probability of obtaining the observed association (or difference) is less than 5% (or 1 in 20), if the null hypothesis was in fact true. In other words, the researcher is reasonably certain that the observed data are 'unusual' enough to rule out the null hypothesis. The confidence interval is more informative and its use has increased in recent years. It gives the range within which the true magnitude of the effect lies, with a certain level of assurance. For example, among Norwegian women, physical activity equivalent to walking or bicycling for at least four hours per week has been associated with a relative risk of developing colon cancer of 0.62. The 95% confidence interval for this relative risk was 0.40–0.97, so we can be assured that, if the study were repeated 20 times on different samples, on 19 occasions the relative risk would lie between 0.40 and 0.97.

Bias is error in research design or collection of data that produces results which differ in a systematic manner from the true values. It can take many forms, but the most important are selection bias and measurement bias. Selection bias arises when the characteristics of people selected to participate in a study differ systematically from those of people who are not selected. In a laboratory study, selection bias may influence the subsequent generalizability of findings, but not its validity. In epidemiology, where associations between a putative risk factor and a health outcome are sought, selection bias threatens the validity of a study. For example, if people are asked to participate in a study of physical activity, responders are likely to differ in their exercise habits from non-responders. An investigator can also introduce bias (knowingly or unknowingly) by including people who appear more (or less) receptive to the notion that physical activity improves health rather than other potential participants. Another source of selection bias is the 'healthy worker effect'; people in employment have to be healthy enough to do their job, whereas those who are ill or disabled may often be excluded.

Systematic error in measurements is an issue in both laboratory and epidemiological studies. For example, one chemical pathology laboratory may consistently measure plasma cholesterol concentrations lower than another. This bias can be evaluated if each laboratory participating in a study analyses a portion of a 'pooled' serum sample and a correction factor is applied. Other sources of bias are more difficult to deal with. One of the most important relates to measurements that rely on human memory (e.g. consumption of coffee or of foods high in fat or, of course, participation in physical activities) and these are common in epidemiology. For example, underweight individuals tend to over-report food intake on questionnaires, while obese subjects under-report it. This error is called recall bias and is particularly important in case-control studies when individuals recently diagnosed with a disease tend to recall their past exposures with greater accuracy than controls, especially if it is widely known that the risk factor under study may be associated with that disease.

Bias is not confined to individual studies but may be evident in the literature as a whole. For example, there is a tendency for editors of journals to accept research papers reporting 'positive' findings (where the research hypothesis is supported) more readily than those who report 'negative' findings. This tendency is compounded by the fact that researchers are less likely to submit studies with negative findings for publication.

As explained early in this chapter, an epidemiological study seeks to identify an association between exposure to a designated causal (or risk) factor and a health-related outcome. Often, however, a third factor is associated both with the exposure being studied and the outcome being studied. If this third factor is unequally distributed between the exposure subgroups, it may confuse the findings. This problem is called confounding. It can even create the appearance of a cause-and-effect relationship that does not exist. For example, researchers investigating the associations between physical activity or fitness and CHD have to address the concern that people may be physically active because of some constitutional factor(s) which, in reality, is what protects them from heart disease. Another example would be studies of physical activity and colon cancer. Dietary factors can confound findings because physically active people may be more likely than sedentary people to eat a low-fat, high-fibre diet. Randomization is the best way to control the problem of confounding factors in intervention trials. In case-control and cohort studies, the problem is most commonly addressed at the analysis stage by statistical modelling to estimate the strength of associations, while controlling simultaneously for confounding variables. However, this approach cannot alter the fundamental quality of the data and confounding will inevitably introduce biases that cannot be controlled statistically.

ESTABLISHING CAUSALITY

This is an important issue because the designation of a risk factor as 'causal' is the starting point for initiating disease prevention programmes based on reducing exposure to the risk factor.

Epidemiological studies, laboratory-based studies and clinical studies all contribute evidence on physical activity and health. Assessment of the strength of this evidence involves consideration of each type of research. As noted in the previous section, large randomly-controlled intervention trials of physical activity with disease endpoints will probably never be undertaken. Epidemiological research in this area is therefore essentially observational and, because of bias and confounding, a rather blunt tool. Indeed, these two sources of error have been described as 'a plague upon the house of epidemiology' (Taubes 1995). How then does the research community assess whether physical inactivity is a causal factor for a particular health outcome? (In considering the diseases which are big public health problems in the twenty-first century, for example, heart disease, diabetes, osteoporosis, it is appropriate to talk about 'causal factors', rather than a single cause.)

Several criteria for causal significance in epidemiological studies have been proposed, and these are summarized in Box 2.4. One of the most important criteria is the strength of the association between the causal factor and the outcome. Some authorities take the view that no single epidemiological study is persuasive by itself unless the relative risk of exposure is three or more. If this were the only criterion, very few studies would indicate that physical inactivity and low fitness are causal factors for important health-related outcomes.

However, judgements on causality need also to take other aspects of the evidence into account. Two requirements must be satisfied before a causal claim is accepted: empirical demonstration of an association and a proposed underlying explanatory mechanism. Thus associations reported in epidemiological studies must be shown to be concordant with biologically plausible mechanisms. In this way, evidence from laboratory-based studies complements and extends that from epidemiology. The former demonstrate mechanisms but cannot show links with disease endpoints: the latter can

---

BOX 2.4 CRITERIA USED TO ASSESS WHETHER EPIDEMIOLOGICAL EVIDENCE IS SUFFICIENT TO CONCLUDE THAT A RISK FACTOR IS CAUSAL

- Appropriately sequenced – does the measure of level of physical activity (or fitness) precede the onset of disease?
- Plausibility – is the association consistent with other knowledge (mechanisms of action; animal studies)?
- Consistency – are findings consistent in different populations?
- Strength – what is the strength of the association between the causal factor and the effect, i.e. what is the relative risk?
- Dose-response – are increased levels of physical activity or fitness associated with a greater effect?
- Reversibility – is becoming less active or fit associated with a reduction of disease risk?
- Strong study design – are findings based on strong study designs? (The randomly controlled trial is the 'gold-standard'.)

establish links with morbidity and mortality but cannot by themselves establish causality. Reaching a conclusion on whether or not physical inactivity or low fitness may be causal factors in specific health outcomes therefore involves making judgements based on multiple lines of evidence.

Conventions for describing the strength of research evidence are now widely used, particularly among medical researchers. The convention adopted in the US was mentioned earlier (National Institutes of Health 1998). The accepted convention in the United Kingdom is the SIGN (Scottish Intercollegiate Guidelines Network) system (Petrie *et al.* 1995). Both conventions place the greatest confidence in randomly controlled trials. In the SIGN system, the highest level of evidence (Grade A, level 1a) requires meta-analysis of such trials, while Grade B evidence requires 'well-conducted clinical studies but no randomized controlled trial'; the weakest grade of evidence, Grade C, is based on 'expert committee reports or opinion ... (and) indicates absence of directly applicable studies of good quality'.

Systematic reviews in a particular area attempt to consider all aspects of all the evidence. However, this process is not straightforward. For example, searches of electronic databases (MEDLINE, PubMed) typically identify only 70–80% of relevant literature. The Cochrane Collaboration – a collaboration of international groups initiated in 1992 to review clinical areas – limit the material they review to randomized controlled trials. This approach excludes potentially valuable evidence and does not recognize that such trials do not necessarily present good data because measurements may lack accuracy and/or precision. Nevertheless, Cochrane reviews are highly regarded and the source of authoritative summaries of the strength/weakness of evidence in specific areas.

SUMMARY

- Epidemiology is the study of the distribution and determinants of health-related states or events in specified populations and the application of this study to control of health problems. It can identify risk factors but not, by itself, causality.
- Outcome measures include mortality and morbidity, but also indices of quality of life. The most accurate measure of disease frequency is the person–time incidence rate. For example, heart attacks per 1,000 person-years. These are compared between groups, yielding a relative risk that estimates the strength of an association with the risk factor under study.
- Associations may reflect the true effect of an exposure, but may have an alternative explanation, i.e. chance, bias or confounding
- In epidemiological studies, physical activity levels have most often been measured by questionnaire. This introduces bias and imprecision (misclassification) which will decrease the strength of observed associations with health outcomes. Other, more objective (but more expensive) measures involve the use of motion sensors (pedometers and accelerometers) and the doubly labelled water technique.
- It is argued that measuring physical fitness may be a more objective measure than physical activity. Fitness – as commonly measured – is, however, strongly influenced by genetic factors and difficult to measure in epidemiological studies.
- Laboratory-based studies can achieve excellent control and precision and indicate potential mechanisms. However, their outcome measures are removed from the clinical endpoints of morbidity and mortality.
- Establishing causality requires evidence from epidemiology for strong and consistent associations as well as evidence for plausible mechanisms from laboratory-based studies. These types of evidence are complementary and neither is sufficient alone. The totality of the evidence determines decisions as to causality.

STUDY TASKS

1 In epidemiology, what is considered the strongest study design and why? Discuss the reasons why this design will probably not be implemented in the study of physical activity and the risk of heart disease.
2 What is meant by confounding? Identify several factors that might be confounding factors in a case-control study of the association between the risk of colon cancer and physical activity.
3 In the Aerobics Center Longitudinal Study (a cohort study), time to exhaustion during an incremental treadmill test has been adopted as a surrogate measure of physical fitness. In this context, what are the strengths and weaknesses of this measure?
4 Table 2.3 presents data for three risk factors on the relative risk of dying over the observation period and on the population-attributable risk. Comment on the relevance of these findings for (a) the individual; and (b) public health policy.

NOTES

1 Usually it is not possible to study the entire population in which one is interested. It is therefore necessary to draw a sample and to relate its characteristics to the defined population.

2 Relative intensity may be calculated as the oxygen uptake demanded by an activity, expressed as a percentage of the individual's $\dot{V}O_2$max. For individuals with low values of $\dot{V}O_2$max, the percentage of oxygen uptake reserve ($\dot{V}O_2$max – resting oxygen uptake) demanded by a given exercise is a better measure of its relative intensity.

3 This statistic describes the size of the difference between two means, relative to the standard deviation. An effect size of 0.8 or more is usually deemed to be large; around 0.5 moderate; and 0.2 or less, small (Thomas *et al.* 2005).

FURTHER READING

Barker, D.J.P., Cooper, C. and Rose, G. (1998) *Epidemiology in Medical Practice*, 5th edn, New York: Churchill Livingstone.

Lee, I-M. (2008) ed. *Epidemiologic Methods in Physical Activity Studies*, New York: Oxford University Press.

Schriger, D.L. (2001) 'Analyzing the relationship of exercise and health: methods, assumptions, and limitations', *Medicine and Science in Sports and Exercise* 33 (Supplement): S359–63.

Thomas, J.R., Nelson, J.K. and Silverman, S.J. (2005) *Research Methods in Physical Activity*, 5th edn, Champaign: Human Kinetics.

Ward, D.S., Evenson, K.R., Vaughn, A., Rogers, A.B. and Troiano, R.P. (2005) 'Accelerometer use in physical activity: best practices and research recommendations', *Medicine and Science in Sports and Exercise* 37 (Supplement): S582–8.

Welk, G.J. (2002) *Physical Activity Assessments For Health-Related Research*, Champaign: Human Kinetics.

Knowledge assumed
Basic statistics, relative risk, population-attributable risk, basic exercise physiology

3 Physical activity and mortality

INTRODUCTION

The Norwegian epidemiologist Gunnar Erikssen asserts that 'modern day humans are dying because of a lack of physical exercise' (Erikssen 2001). In this chapter, we will examine the evidence that physical activity and physical fitness reduce the risk of dying prematurely. The studies included in this chapter are those which have addressed all-cause mortality, that is, death from any cause. Studies that have examined the link between activity/fitness and specific causes of death such as cardiovascular disease (CVD) and cancer are covered elsewhere in the book (Chapters 4 and 8, respectively, for CVD and cancer). Moreover, the studies discussed in this chapter are all epidemiological cohort studies. Therefore, they do not begin to answer the question 'why do active/fit people live longer than inactive/unfit people?' Answers to this question are provided in later chapters.

PHYSICAL ACTIVITY AND MORTALITY

Although there was some limited information linking physically active occupations to longevity in the eighteenth and nineteenth centuries, systematic study of the relationship between physical activity and longevity only began in the twentieth century. Initially, research focused on occupational activity and longevity. One such study was of US railroad industry employees. This study examined mortality rates over a two-year period (1955–6) and found lower rates among section men (classified as the most active group) compared with clerks (classified as the least active group) and switchmen (Taylor *et al.* 1962). However, there were limitations to these early studies. It was possible, for example, that the relationship between occupation and mortality risk was simply due to self-selection, that is, men who were in the process of developing chronic diseases (and therefore likely to die prematurely) might have chosen physically less demanding jobs. Also, other characteristics predictive of mortality, such as smoking, obesity and diet, were not accounted for. Moreover, leisure-time physical activity was not measured and thus there was no clear assessment of total physical activity. Nevertheless, such studies were the catalyst for future investigations with improved study designs.

In the latter half of the twentieth century, attention switched to leisure-time physical activity and the findings of several cohort studies were published in the 1980s and 1990s. The most notable of these investigations was the Harvard Alumni Health Study. This was a cohort study of men enrolled in Harvard College between 1916 and 1950. Questionnaires were used to estimate the amount of energy expended in walking, stair climbing, sports and recreational activities. One publication from this study concerned the relationship between physical activity and all-cause mortality in 16,936 men aged 35–74 years at baseline (Paffenbarger *et al.* 1986). Baseline data was collected either in 1962 or 1966. Follow-up was conducted 12–16 years later in 1978, by which time 1,413 alumni had died. The findings revealed an inverse dose–response relationship between physical activity and the risk of all-cause mortality (Figure 3.1 and Plate 2). Death rates were 25–33% lower among alumni expending 2,000 kcal week^{-1} (8,400 kJ week^{-1}) or more in weekly physical activity compared with those expending less than this amount. These findings remained significant following control for smoking, hypertension, extremes or gains in body mass and early parental death. Moreover, the inverse association between activity and mortality risk held when findings were examined within different age bands (35–49, 50–59, 60–69 and 70–84).

There was evidence in the Harvard Alumni Health Study of a slight increase in the relative risk of death in the most active group (i.e. those expending >3,499 kcal week^{-1} (14,700 kJ week^{-1})) compared with the groups expending >2,500 kcal week^{-1} but <3,499 kcal week^{-1} (Figure 3.1). This suggests that very high levels of activity may increase mortality risk slightly compared with moderate levels. This issue remains

Figure 3.1 Findings from the Harvard Alumni Health Study indicate that there is an inverse association between the amount of physical activity performed per week and the risk of all-cause mortality.

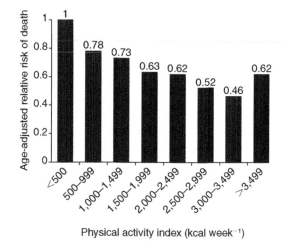

Source: Paffenbarger *et al.* (1986).
Notes: This study involved 16,936 Harvard alumni followed for 12–16 years (from 1962 or 1966 to 1978).

contentious, but it is important to note that the relative risk was still lower in the most active group compared with the groups expending <2,000 kcal week^{-1}.

A limitation of the Harvard Alumni Health Study is the use of questionnaires to assess physical activity. Questionnaires are liable to error due to inadequate or inaccurate recall. This limitation applies to all previous studies examining the association between physical activity and mortality risk. A recent study has addressed this limitation by using the gold standard method for measuring energy expenditure. In the Health, Ageing and Body Composition (Health ABC) Study (Manini *et al.* 2006) doubly labelled water was used to assess expenditure over a two-week period in 302 'high-functioning' community-dwelling older adults aged 70–82 years (Chapter 2, Box 2.2, provides a brief description of the doubly labelled water method). Participants (men and women) were divided into tertiles according to their free-living activity energy expenditure as follows: low, <521 kcal day^{-1} (2,188 kJ day^{-1}); middle, 521–770 kcal day^{-1} (2,188–3,234 kJ day^{-1}); high, >770 kcal day^{-1} (3,234 kJ day^{-1}). During an average 6.15 years of follow-up, 55 participants died and a significant association was found between objectively measured physical activity and risk of death. Death rates were two-thirds lower in the high physical activity group compared with the low physical activity group (Figure 3.2).

The findings of the Health ABC Study represent a novel and important contribution to this research field due to the objective nature of the physical activity measurements (see the accompanying editorial by Blair and Haskell (2006) for an excellent critical analysis of the study). Of note in the Health ABC Study was the very low relative risk in the high activity group (67% lower than the low activity group). This represents a stronger association than in most, if not all, previous studies, and is similar to

Plate 2 Front page of the classic paper on physical activity and all-cause mortality in Harvard college Alumni by Dr Ralph Paffenbarger *et al.* (1986).

Vol. 314 No. 10   THE NEW ENGLAND JOURNAL OF MEDICINE   605

PHYSICAL ACTIVITY, ALL-CAUSE MORTALITY, AND LONGEVITY OF COLLEGE ALUMNI

RALPH S. PAFFENBARGER, JR., M.D., DR.P.H., ROBERT T. HYDE, M.A., ALVIN L. WING, M.B.A., AND CHUNG-CHENG HSIEH, SC.D.

Abstract We examined the physical activity and other life-style characteristics of 16,936 Harvard alumni, aged 35 to 74, for relations to rates of mortality from all causes and for influences on length of life. A total of 1413 alumni died during 12 to 16 years of follow-up (1962 to 1978). Exercise reported as walking, stair climbing, and sports play related inversely to total mortality, primarily to death due to cardiovascular or respiratory causes. Death rates declined steadily as energy expended on such activity increased from less than 500 to 3500 kcal per week, beyond which rates increased slightly. Rates were one quarter to one third lower among alumni expending 2000 or more kcal during exercise per week than among less active men. With or without consideration of hypertension, cigarette smoking, extremes or gains in body weight, or early parental death, alumni mortality rates were- significantly lower among the physically active. Relative risks of death for individuals were highest among cigarette smokers and men with hypertension, and attributable risks in the community were highest among smokers and sedentary men By the age of 80, the amount of additional life attributable to adequate exercise, as compared with sedentariness, was one to more than two years. (N Engl J Med 1986; 314: 605-13.)

IMPROVED nutrition, reduced mortality from infectious diseases, and modification of some adverse personal characteristics, such as the cigarette habit, are accepted as having extended human longevity. The importance of adequate physical exercise to cardiovascular health is becoming appreciated, yet there is a longstanding debate about whether exercise also extends longevity.[1-6] To assess influences on length of life, we examined the relations of life-style elements to mortality from all causes among 16,936 Harvard alumni aged 35 to 74 who were initially free of clinically recognized coronary heart disease. Earlier studies in this population had shown that the risk of coronary heart disease was affected significantly by histories of hypertension, cigarette smoking, overweight for height, and habitual physical inactivity.[7,8] We then studied whether exercise could be shown to delay all-cause mortality in this population. The thesis that exercise does in fact add extra years to life is examined in this continuing study of ways of living and health among Harvard College alumni.

METHODS

Men who entered college in the period 1916 to 1950 were studied. Their personal and life-style characteristics (including exercise habits) during their college and post-college days were recorded, with follow-up data on influences on mortality and estimated length of life. Over three quarters of the known surviving alumni responded to mailed questionnaires that asked about specific physician-diagnosed diseases, physical activities, cigarette smoking habits, and parental diseases and death. Weekly updating of death lists by the Harvard Alumni Office provided the means to obtain death certificates and identify underlying causes of death. Fewer than 1 percent of alumni were lost to follow-up without death notification.[7,8]

From the Department of Family, Community and Preventive Medicine, Stanford University School of Medicine, Stanford; and the Department of Epidemiology, Harvard University School of Public Health, Boston. Address reprint requests to Dr. Paffenbarger at the Stanford University School of Medicine, Department of Family, Community and Preventive Medicine, Health Research and Policy Bldg., Stanford, CA 94305.

Supported by a grant (HL 24133) from the National Heart, Lung, and Blood Institute and by the Marathon Oil Foundation, the G. Unger Vetlesen Foundation, and the E.I. du Pont de Nemours Company.

Records of college physical examinations, performed early in the freshman year, and records of participation in intercollegiate (varsity) sports during years of undergraduate attendance provided measures of students' blood pressure levels, body weight and height, and athleticism. These records were examined in conjunction with data on post-college physical activities, other patterns of living, and histories of personal health and parental death, obtained by return-mail questionnaires in 1962 and 1966. Data on physical energy expenditure and personal characteristics so gathered were related to time and cause of death as reported on official death certificates between 1962 and 1978. Man-years of observation for level of energy expenditure and other characteristics under study were recorded according to single years of age for the follow-up interval of 12 to 16 years.

A total of 782 alumni who had initially reported physician-diagnosed coronary heart disease were excluded from the starting population, to reduce any selective bias toward low-level activity as a result of their disease. A separate analysis (not reported here) showed little difference between the exercise habits of this group and the other alumni, but mortality rates were higher among the patients with coronary heart disease, despite a saving effect of moderate exercise.[9] On the whole, the results of the present study would not be altered appreciably if the group with coronary heart disease had been retained. A smaller group of men with a diagnosis of cancer, stroke, or other ailments was not excluded from the starting population. Any influences of disease on their physical activity patterns, or vice versa, are inherent in the all-cause mortality findings reported here.

Alumni aged 35 to 74 years had reported by questionnaire how many city blocks they walked, how many stairs they climbed, and the types of sports they participated in and time they spent on them each week.[10] After adjustment for seasonal variation and estimates of overreporting and underreporting, the energy used for these activities was expressed in kilocalories per week. Walking seven city blocks (0.94 km or 7/12 mi) was rated as 56 kcal, and climbing 70 stairs was rated as 28 kcal; sports were classified as light (5 kcal per minute), vigorous (10 kcal per minute), or mixed (7.5 kcal per minute). A physical-activity index was computed as an estimate of energy expended in walking, climbing stairs, playing sports, yard work, and so forth.[11] When divided into ranges of less than 500, 500 to 1999, and 2000 or more kcal per week, index increments represented 15 percent, 46 percent, and 39 percent of the man-years of observation, respectively. These measures were regarded as indicators rather than absolute totals of energy expenditure, largely in leisure time.

In studying the influence of other personal characteristics as continuous variables (e.g., cigarette smoking, body weight in relation to height, and weight change since college), break points were chosen to provide three levels or categories that might reveal any gradient risk of death. Mortality rates were computed for the follow-up interval by the indirect method, using 213,716 man-years of observation for the total population as standard, with adjustment for age differ-

Figure 3.2 Association between free-living activity energy expenditure and all-cause mortality risk in the Health, Ageing and Body Composition (Health ABC) Study.

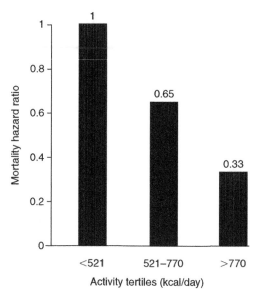

Source: Manini *et al.* (2006).

Notes: Free-living activity energy expenditure was assessed using doubly labelled water. The findings are adjusted for age, sex, race, study site, weight, height, percentage body fat, sleep duration, self-rated health, education, smoking status and history, CVD, lung disease, diabetes, hip or knee osteoarthritis, osteoporosis, cancer and depression.

the strength of the associations often observed between physical fitness and mortality risk (see below). This strong association may be related to two factors:

1 the objective and hence more accurate assessment of physical activity;
2 the fact that all physical activity was accounted for rather than just specific activities such as walking or vigorous exercise.

Thus, the energy expended in standing, ambulating around and fidgeting, i.e. what Levine *et al.* (2005) call 'non-exercise activity thermogenesis' (NEAT), was included in the Health ABC Study and this was not assessed in previous studies (see Chapter 6 for further information on NEAT). Surprisingly, self-reported physical activity was not related to mortality risk in the Health ABC Study, possibly due to misclassification exacerbated by the relatively small sample size, i.e. around 300 participants compared with close to 17,000 in the Harvard Alumni Health Study. Unfortunately, the doubly labelled water method cannot be used in very large studies due to the expense of the technique.

The findings of the Harvard Alumni Health Study and the Health ABC Study are broadly consistent with the findings from other investigations of the association between physical activity and all-cause mortality (Lee and Paffenbarger 1996 remains possibly the most comprehensive review of these studies). These investigations suggest that physically active individuals have a lower risk of dying prematurely compared with their sedentary counterparts. Thus, there is a reassuring consistency in the data. However, the studies are observational in nature and therefore do not provide proof of cause and effect for reasons outlined in the previous chapter. Nevertheless, there is other evidence supporting an association between physical activity and all-cause mortality risk, including an association between physical fitness (which is partly determined by physical activity) and all-cause mortality risk.

PHYSICAL FITNESS AND MORTALITY

The major advantage of studying physical fitness and mortality risk rather than physical activity and mortality risk is that physical fitness can be measured more objectively than self-report of physical activity. Most studies examining the association between fitness and mortality risk have used treadmill tests to give an indication of physical fitness. Often, treadmill time on a maximal exercise test has been used as a surrogate marker for VO_2max because these two variables are closely related. However, some studies have used recovery heart rate as a measure of fitness (Cole *et al.* 1999) while others have estimated exercise capacity in METs (Mora *et al.* 2003). Virtually all studies in this area have defined fitness in aerobic terms (using surrogate markers for VO_2max), although other forms of fitness such as musculoskeletal fitness have been examined (Katzmarzyk and Craig 2002).

One of the first studies to demonstrate an association between physical fitness and all-cause mortality risk was the Aerobics Center Longitudinal Study (Blair *et al.* 1989). In this study, a maximal treadmill exercise test was conducted in 10,224 men and 3,120 women, and time to exhaustion on this test was used to indicate fitness. The average period of follow-up was just over eight years, during which there were 240 deaths in men and 43 deaths in women.

Participants were classified into quintiles: quintile one contained those with the shortest treadmill times (lowest fitness); and quintile five contained those with the longest treadmill times (highest fitness). Those with the lowest fitness levels had the highest risk of death during follow-up. The lowest risk of death was seen in those with the highest fitness in men and in those in quintile four in women (Table 3.1). These trends remained after statistical adjustment for age, smoking habit, cholesterol level, systolic blood pressure, fasting blood glucose level, parental history of coronary heart disease (CHD) and follow-up interval. Blair *et al.* concluded that high levels of physical fitness appear to delay all-cause mortality primarily due to lowered rates of CVD and cancer.

In a follow-up study with a larger number of subjects, Blair *et al.* (1996) compared the strength of the association between low fitness and all-cause mortality with that of other established disease risk factors including smoking, hypertension, high cholesterol level and being overweight. In this study, low fitness was defined as the least-fit 20% of the study sample. This was based on the finding from the previous study that the greatest difference in mortality risk was between fitness quintiles one and two in both men and women (Table 3.1). After adjustment for age, examination year and all other risk factors, low fitness was associated with an equal or greater increase in mortality risk than other established risk factors in both men and women (Figure 3.3). These

Table 3.1 Physical fitness (time to exhaustion on a treadmill test) was associated with a reduction in the risk of all-cause mortality in both men and women in the Aerobics Center longitudinal Study

FITNESS GROUP	PERSON-YEARS OF FOLLOW-UP	NUMBER OF DEATHS	AGE-ADJUSTED RATES PER 10,000 PERSON-YEARS	RELATIVE RISK
Men				
1 (low)	14,515	75	64.0	3.44
2	16,898	40	25.5	1.37
3	17,287	47	27.1	1.46
4	18,792	43	21.7	1.17
5 (high)	17,557	35	18.6	1.00
Women				
1 (low)	4,916	18	39.5	4.65
2	5,329	11	20.5	2.42
3	5,053	6	12.2	1.43
4	5,522	4	6.5	0.76
5 (high)	4,613	4	8.5	1.00

Source: Blair *et al.* (1989).

findings suggest that low fitness should be considered as seriously as other established risk factors for disease.

Many other studies have confirmed the association between low levels of physical fitness and all-cause mortality risk. One example is a Californian study involving 3,679 men with CVD and 2,534 men without CVD (Myers *et al.* 2002). Exercise capacity (METs) was estimated in these men, based on the treadmill speed and incline achieved during a maximal exercise test. The average duration of follow-up was 6.2 years, during which there were 1,256 deaths. As with the Aerobics Center Longitudinal Study, the participants were divided into quintiles based on exercise capacity. The relative risk of all-cause mortality for those in the lowest quintile of fitness was four times higher than for those in the highest quintile of fitness. This finding applied both for those with CVD and for those without CVD (Figure 3.4). When these two groups were combined, every 1 MET increase in exercise capacity was associated with a 12% improvement in survival. Moreover, in both groups of subjects, exercise capacity was a stronger predictor of all-cause mortality than established CVD risk factors including hypertension, smoking and diabetes. This latter finding was confirmed in a subsequent study by the same research group (Myers *et al.* 2004).

Myers *et al.* (2002) also examined the influence of fitness on mortality risk in subgroups of participants who were at increased risk of death due to the presence of other risk factors, including a history of hypertension, chronic obstructive pulmonary disease (COPD), diabetes, smoking, obesity and hypercholesterolaemia. In all subgroups, the risk of death from any cause was approximately twice as high in subjects whose exercise capacity was below 5 METs compared with those whose exercise capacity was

Figure 3.3 Low physical fitness was associated with an equal or greater risk of all-cause mortality as other established risk factors in the Aerobics Center Longitudinal Study.

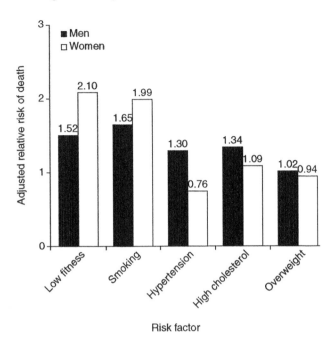

Risk factor

Source: Blair *et al.* (1996).
Notes: Low fitness: the least fit 20% of participants; smoking: current or recent smoker; hypertension: systolic blood pressure ≥140 mm Hg; high cholesterol: total cholesterol ≥6.2 mmol l⁻¹; overweight: body mass index ≥27 kg m². The relative risk of death was adjusted for age and for each of the other variables in the figure.

above 8 METs (Figure 3.5). In an editorial accompanying this study, Balady (2002) summarized its importance as follows:

> Myers *et al.* place valuable and readily applicable conclusions on the desk of the clinician. Absolute fitness levels … represent a continuum of risk – i.e., greater fitness results in longer survival. Fitness levels are important predictors of survival in persons with and without cardiovascular disease, as well as in those with specific cardiovascular risk factors.
> (p. 853)

In view of such findings, a recent study has developed a nomogram that may be used to indicate mortality risk from exercise capacity (expressed in METs) in women (Gulati *et al.* 2005). This has prompted some to argue that fitness should be a routine component of all clinical assessments (Kraus and Douglas 2005).

As with studies of physical activity, the studies of physical fitness are consistent in suggesting a protective effect of exercise. Moreover, there is also evidence of a dose–response relationship between fitness and mortality risk. However, studies of fitness are constrained by some of the limitations that apply to studies of activity, the main one being that the studies are observational. A further source of controversy is the extent to

Figure 3.4 Exercise capacity (METs) was inversely related to the risk of death in Californian men with and without CVD.

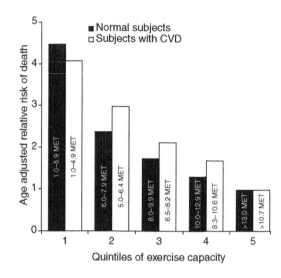

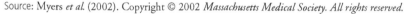

which fitness levels are determined by activity as opposed to genes. Both play a role, but which factor has the major influence within large populations is uncertain. Nevertheless, genes have an influence on other established disease risk factors, so this alone cannot detract from the importance of the fitness–mortality risk association. Moreover, changes in physical activity can have a profound effect on physical fitness (American College of Sports Medicine 1998), suggesting that individuals can modify their mortality risk by altering their activity levels and thus their fitness. Evidence to support this assertion is available in the form of studies that have examined changes in either activity or fitness to determine whether or not there is an associated change in the risk of all-cause mortality.

CHANGES IN PHYSICAL ACTIVITY AND MORTALITY

The first major epidemiological study to examine changes in physical activity and risk of all-cause mortality was the Harvard Alumni Health Study (Paffenbarger *et al.* 1993). In this study, exercise habits were assessed via a questionnaire at baseline (either 1962 or 1966) and again in 1977 in 10,269 men aged 45–84 years in 1977. These men reported being free from life-threatening disease at both observation points. Follow-up was continued until 1985 during which time 476 men died. At each observation point individuals were grouped according to: (1) their weekly physical activity levels (<2,000 kcal week^{-1} (8.4 MJ week^{-1}) versus ≥2,000 kcal week^{-1}); and (2) their participation or lack of participation in 'moderately vigorous' sports activities (defined as those requiring an intensity ≥4.5 METs) such as swimming, tennis, squash, racquetball, handball, jogging and running.

Figure 3.5 High exercise capacity was associated with a reduced risk of all-cause mortality even in the presence of established risk factors in a study of Californian men.

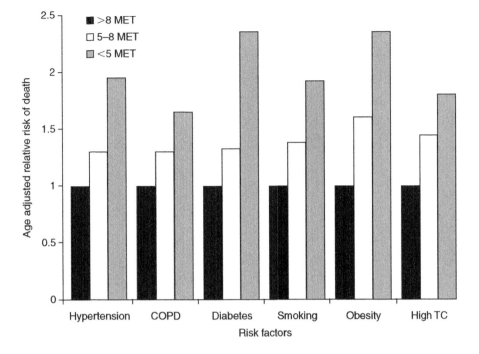

Notes: The figure shows the age-adjusted relative risk of death from any cause in subjects with various risk factors classified according to exercise capacity in METs. COPD: chronic obstructive pulmonary disease. Obesity was defined as a BMI $\geq 30 \, kg \, m^2$. High TC: high total cholesterol i.e. $\geq 5.7 \, mmol \, l^{-1}$.

The findings revealed that changes in exercise habits between observation points were associated with differences in mortality risk during follow-up. Specifically, there was a lower mortality rate in those who became more active and/or increased the intensity of their physical activity between observation points than in those who did not (Figure 3.6). These findings have been confirmed in 'older' men by the findings of the British Regional Heart Study (Wannamethee *et al.* 1998) and in 'older' women by the findings of the Study of Osteoporotic Fractures (Gregg *et al.* 2003a). Such studies provide firmer evidence to support the hypothesis that inactive people can lower their risk of dying prematurely by becoming more active. The findings of the Harvard Alumni Health Study also support the notion that 'moderately vigorous' activities such as those defined above are more effective in reducing mortality risk than 'light' activities such as 'golf, walking for pleasure, gardening and housework'. Finally, these findings suggest that past activity alone is not protective and that benefits may be lost following the cessation of regular exercise. This conclusion arises from the observation that mortality risk appears to increase in those reporting a reduction in the amount and/or intensity of physical activity between observation points (Figure 3.6).

Figure 3.6 Increases in the amount and/or intensity of physical activity over time are associated with a lower risk of all-cause mortality in comparison with the risk in those who remain sedentary.

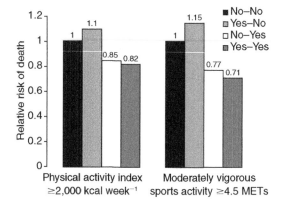

Source: Harvard Alumni Health Study (Paffenbarger *et al.* 1993).
Notes: This study involved 10,269 men assessed in 1962 or 1966 and again in 1977, and followed-up until 1985. The figure legend indicates group classifications, e.g. those in the 'no-no' group expended less than 2,000 kcal week^{-1} (8.4 MJ wk^{-1}) at both observation points.

CHANGES IN PHYSICAL FITNESS AND MORTALITY

At least two studies have examined all-cause mortality in relation to changes in physical fitness. The first of these was the Aerobics Center Longitudinal Study (Blair *et al.* 1995). This study involved 9,777 men aged 20–82 years at baseline, who completed two maximal treadmill tests between 1970 and 1989. The mean interval between treadmill tests was 4.9 years, and the mean follow-up duration after the second test was 5.1 years, during which time there were 223 deaths. For each of the treadmill tests, participants were grouped into quintiles based on treadmill time. Those in quintile one (shortest treadmill time) were classified as unfit while those in quintiles two to five were classified as fit. The age-adjusted relative risk of death was 1.0 for those who were unfit on both occasions, 0.56 for those who were unfit on the first occasion but fit on the second occasion, 0.52 for those who were fit on the first occasion but unfit on the second occasion and 0.33 for those who were fit on both occasions. This pattern – highest risk of all-cause mortality in those who were unfit on both occasions, lowest risk in those who were fit on both occasions, intermediate risk in those who were unfit on the first occasion but fit on the second occasion – held throughout all age groups (Figure 3.7). Furthermore, crude analysis within a subgroup of 1,512 men indicated that changes in fitness were related to changes in activity, providing evidence for a cause-and-effect relationship.

The association between changes in fitness and mortality risk observed in the Aerobics Center Longitudinal Study was subsequently confirmed by a smaller study involving 1,428 healthy Norwegian men (Erikssen *et al.* 1998). Collectively, studies of changes in activity/fitness provide convincing evidence that changes in activity habits

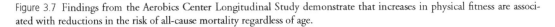

Figure 3.7 Findings from the Aerobics Center Longitudinal Study demonstrate that increases in physical fitness are associated with reductions in the risk of all-cause mortality regardless of age.

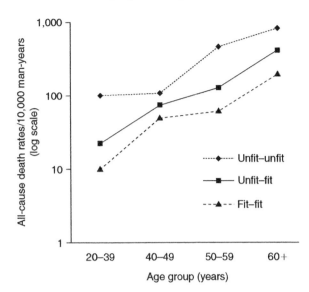

Source: Blair *et al.* (1995).
Notes: Values are plotted on a log scale. Unfit: men in quintile one of their age-specific fitness distribution; fit: men in quintiles two through to five of their age-specific fitness distribution.

have an influence on mortality risk, particularly if such changes result in an improvement in physical fitness. Thus, these studies suggest that human beings have an element of control over their own mortality. It is important to re-emphasise, however, that these studies are observational and are not proof of a cause-and-effect relationship. It is not always clear, for example, why individuals have changed their activity levels, nor is it clear to what extent overall physical activity levels (including NEAT) can be changed over the long term.

ACTIVITY, FITNESS, BODY COMPOSITION AND MORTALITY

Most of the studies discussed so far relate to initially 'healthy' individuals, although some studies have included 'healthy' and 'unhealthy' groups based on the presence or absence of disease at baseline. An issue that has been debated more recently is the extent to which exercise influences mortality risk in obese individuals irrespective of any influence on body fatness. This issue has been addressed with reference to data collected in the Aerobics Center Longitudinal Study and the Nurses' Health Study.

Lee *et al.* (1999) studied the relationship between fitness, fatness and all-cause mortality risk in 21,925 men aged 30–83 years. Body composition was measured using hydrostatic weighing, skinfold thickness or both. Physical fitness was assessed using time to exhaustion on a maximal treadmill exercise test. As in previous studies, men in the least-fit 20% of each age group were classified as unfit, and all others as fit. Men were also assigned to categories with respect to body fatness – lean, normal or obese – corresponding to <25th, 25th–<75th and ≥75th percentile scores. This resulted in the following body fatness categories: lean <16.7% body fat; normal 16.7–<25.0% body fat; obese ≥25.0% body fat. Baseline tests were completed between 1971 and 1989, and the average period of follow-up was eight years, during which there were 428 deaths.

After adjustment for age, examination year, smoking, alcohol intake and parental history of heart disease, unfit, lean men were found to have twice the risk of all-cause mortality compared with fit, obese men (Figure 3.8). Similar findings emerged in a subgroup of 14,043 men stratified according to waist circumference. Unfit men with a low waist circumference (<87 cm) had a much greater risk of all-cause mortality than fit men with a high waist circumference (≥99 cm) (Figure 3.9). These findings suggest that obese men are not homogeneous with respect to physical fitness and that obese men who are fit do not have an elevated risk of all-cause mortality. They also suggest that the benefits of leanness are restricted to those who are fit. It is important to note, however, that only 6% of the men in the lean group were classified as unfit, whereas 40% of those in the obese group were classified as unfit. Similarly, only 4% of men in the low waist circumference category were classified as unfit as opposed to 30% of men in the high waist circumference category.

Another obesity-related issue addressed by the Aerobics Center Longitudinal Study is the strength of the association between low fitness and mortality in comparison with that of other established risk factors for mortality, including CVD, diabetes, hypercholesterolaemia, hypertension and smoking (Wei *et al.* 1999b). To examine this, 25,714 men (mean age: 44 years) completed a maximal treadmill exercise test and were given a medical examination and then followed for an average of ten years, during which time there were 1,025 deaths. Of the men in this sample, 13% (3,293 men) were obese (body mass index (BMI) ≥30 kg m^2). Within this group, obese men with low fitness had more than double the risk of all-cause mortality compared with obese men not classified as such. This was comparable to, or higher than, the risk associated with other established predictors of mortality (Figure 3.10). Moreover, when the population-attributable risk (see Chapter 2) was calculated for each of these risk factors, the findings indicated that low fitness was associated with far more deaths amongst obese men than any other risk factor (Figure 3.11).

The finding that fitness is a significant predictor of mortality independent of adiposity was confirmed recently in a cohort of 2,603 adults aged 60 years and older (20% of whom were women) enrolled on the Aerobic Center Longitudinal Study (Sui *et al.* 2007). Moreover, data from the Nurses' Health Study suggest that physical activity is also associated with some protection from mortality in obese women (F.B. Hu *et al.* 2004). This study involved 116,564 nurses followed up for 24 years. In this study, high levels of physical activity appeared to ameliorate but not prevent the higher risk of death associated with obesity. As compared with women who were lean (BMI <25 kg m^2) and active (≥3.5 hours of exercise per week), multivariate relative risk of death was 1.55 for lean inactive (less than one hour per week of exercise) women, 1.91 for obese (BMI ≥30 kg m^2) women who were active and 2.42 for obese women who were inactive. Collectively, these findings suggest a complex relationship between fitness, activity and fatness. Specifically, the findings suggest that the hazards of fatness

Figure 3.8 Findings from the Aerobics Center Longitudinal Study indicate that men who are obese and fit have a similar risk of all-cause mortality compared with those who are lean and fit.

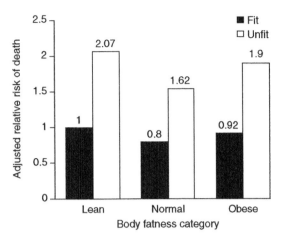

Source: Lee *et al.* (1999).
Notes: Percentage body fat values are: lean <16.7; normal 16.7–<25.0; obese ≥25.0. Unfit: men in the least-fit 20% of their respective age group; fit: all other men. Mortality risks were adjusted for age, examination year, smoking, alcohol intake, and parental history of heart disease.

Figure 3.9 Findings from the Aerobics Center Longitudinal Study indicate that fit men with a high waist circumference have a similar risk of all-cause mortality compared with fit men who have a low waist circumference.

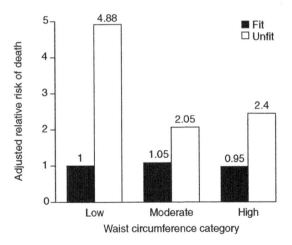

Source: Lee *et al.* (1999).
Notes: Waist circumference categories are: low <87 cm; moderate 87–<99 cm; high ≥99 cm. Unfit: men in the least-fit 20% of their respective age group; fit: all other men. Mortality risks were adjusted for age.

Figure 3.10 Amongst obese men, the association between low fitness and mortality was comparable to that of other mortality predictors in the Aerobics Center Longitudinal Study.

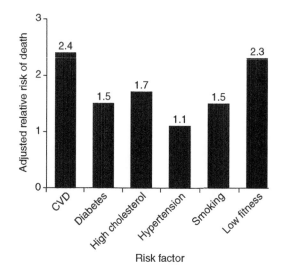

Source: Wei *et al.* (1999).
Notes: Obesity was defined as a BMI $\geq 30\,kg\,m^2$. High cholesterol: total cholesterol >6.2 mmol l^{-1}; hypertension: blood pressure >140/90 mm Hg; low fitness: least-fit 20% in each age group. Relative risks were adjusted for age and for each of the other risk factors in the figure. For each risk factor, the referent group is obese men without that risk factor.

may be limited if a certain level of activity/fitness is maintained. Moreover, the findings indicate that overweight and obese individuals may gain benefit from some exercise even in the absence of weight loss.

COMBINED HEALTHY LIFESTYLE BEHAVIOURS AND MORTALITY

The evidence discussed so far in this chapter has concerned the independent effect of activity/fitness on mortality. Some studies have examined the combined effect of what are termed 'healthy lifestyle behaviours' on mortality risk to assess the additive effect of such behaviours. One example is the Healthy Ageing: Longitudinal study in Europe (HALE) project (Knoops *et al.* 2004). This study involved over 2,300 apparently healthy men and women from 11 European countries. Participants were aged 70–90 years at baseline and were followed for an average of ten years. The study examined four healthy lifestyle behaviours:

1 Mediterranean diet (high in fruits and vegetables, legumes, nuts, seeds and grains, high in fish and low in saturated fat, meats and dairy products);
2 moderate alcohol consumption;
3 non-smoking i.e. never smoked or stopped smoking more than 15 years ago; and
4 physical activity i.e. performing at least 30 minutes of exercise each day on average.

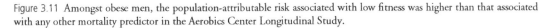

Figure 3.11 Amongst obese men, the population-attributable risk associated with low fitness was higher than that associated with any other mortality predictor in the Aerobics Center Longitudinal Study.

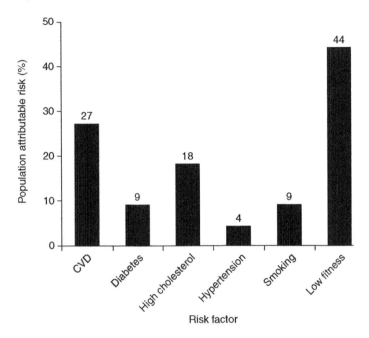

Source: Wei *et al.* (1999).

Notes: Obesity was defined as a BMI $\geq 30\,kg\,m^2$. High cholesterol: total cholesterol >6.2 mmol l^{-1}; hypertension: blood pressure >140/90 mm Hg; low fitness: least-fit 20% in each age group. Relative risks were adjusted for age and for each of the other risk factors in the figure. For each risk factor the referent group is obese men without that risk factor.

Each of the lifestyle behaviours examined in the HALE study was independently associated with deaths from all causes, as well as deaths from CHD, CVD, cancer and other causes. Mortality hazard ratios for each factor were as follows: Mediterranean diet 0.77; moderate alcohol consumption 0.78; non-smoking 0.65; physical activity 0.63. The combined effect of these factors, however, was more strongly associated with all-cause mortality with a hazard ratio of 0.35 for participants exhibiting all four healthy lifestyle behaviours (Figure 3.12). For these four factors the population attributable risk was estimated to be 60%, suggesting that if every individual in the HALE study had adopted the four healthy lifestyle behaviours examined, 60% of deaths may have been averted during the follow-up period.

The findings of the HALE study have been confirmed recently by the EPIC (European Prospective Investigation into Cancer and Nutrition)–Norfolk Prospective Population Study (Khaw *et al.* 2008). This study examined smoking habits, fruit and vegetable intake (as indicated by blood vitamin C concentrations), alcohol intake and physical activity. Once again, all four factors were independently associated with all-cause mortality but the combined effect of these factors was much stronger, indicating a four-fold higher risk of mortality in those scoring zero for healthy lifestyle behaviours compared with those scoring four. The authors concluded that 'Four health behaviours

Figure 3.12 Hazard ratios for all-cause mortality, CHD and cancer according to the number of healthy lifestyle behaviours exhibited by elderly European men and women participating in the Healthy Ageing Longitudinal study in Europe (HALE).

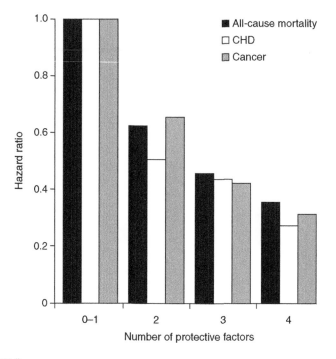

Source: Knoops *et al.* (2004).
Notes: The study population comprised 1,507 men and 832 women, aged 70–90 from 11 European countries. The healthy lifestyle behaviours examined were: Mediterranean diet, non-smoking, moderate alcohol consumption and physical activity.

combined predict a 4-fold difference in total mortality in men and women, with an estimated impact equivalent to 14 years in chronological age' (Khaw *et al.* 2008).

(Incidentally, the association between alcohol consumption and mortality is an interesting one. The general consensus appears to be of a U-shaped relationship, with non-drinkers and heavy drinkers being at increased risk. Definitions of moderate alcohol consumption vary however! In the EPIC–Norfolk study the definition of moderate alcohol consumption 1–14 units per week. For reference, a single unit is approximately 8 g of alcohol – e.g. one small glass of wine, one small glass of sherry, one single shot of spirits, or one half pint of beer).

EXERCISE AND LONGEVITY

What is the optimum amount of exercise for longevity? This is a difficult question to answer with confidence due to the difficulty in measuring physical activity accurately and to differences in the methods used to classify individuals in various studies. In some studies physical activity energy expenditure has been estimated, whereas other studies have placed individuals into discrete groups such as 'active' and 'sedentary' without reference to energy expenditure.

A review by Lee and Skerrett (2001) concluded that an energy expenditure of $4,200\,kJ\,week^{-1}$ is associated with a 20–30% reduction in the risk of all-cause mortality. This expenditure would be obtained by minimal adherence to current guidelines ('30 minutes or more of moderate-intensity physical activity on most, preferably all, days of the week'). Moreover, Lee and Skerrett found 'clear evidence' of an inverse dose–response relationship between the volume of physical activity (or level of physical fitness) and all-cause mortality rates. This suggests that the risk of dying over a given period continues to decline with increasing levels of physical activity (beyond $4,200\,kJ\,week^{-1}$) rather than displaying a threshold effect. It was also noted that this relationship has been shown in men and in women and in younger and older (≥ 60 years) subjects.

Is there an optimal intensity, duration and frequency of exercise for longevity? An analysis of data from the Harvard Alumni Health Study found that energy expended in vigorous (≥ 6 METs) but not non-vigorous (< 6 METs) activities was associated with longevity, suggesting that exercise must be 'vigorous' to be beneficial (Lee *et al.* 1995). However, caution is required regarding the interpretation of 'vigorous'. In the Harvard Alumni Health Study, vigorous activities included 'walking briskly, running or jogging, swimming laps, playing tennis, and shovelling snow'. Exercise intensity may vary greatly between these activities, all of which were classified as vigorous, and further research is needed to clarify the relationship between exercise intensity and longevity. Moreover, few if any studies have compared all-cause mortality rates in individuals matched for total energy expenditure but exercising at different durations or frequencies. Therefore, further research is also required here.

Is activity or fitness more important in determining longevity? This is another question that is difficult to answer at present. For both activity and fitness, evidence supports a dose–response relationship with all-cause mortality. This relationship appears to be stronger for fitness than for activity. In several of the studies examining fitness, mortality rates were 3–4 times lower in groups with the highest fitness compared with those with the lowest fitness. In studies of activity, the difference between groups is smaller. It is unclear, however, whether this is a genuine difference or is simply due to differences in the accuracy of measuring activity and fitness. The findings of the recent Health ABC Study (Manini *et al.* 2006) suggest that the association between activity and mortality is as strong as that between fitness and mortality. Moreover, the epidemiologist heading the Aerobics Center Longitudinal Study, Dr Steven Blair, believes that this is true also. He argues that the use of self-report questionnaires to determine physical activity levels has inevitably led to some misclassification, thus weakening associations with mortality risk. Since physical fitness is measured more objectively, there is less potential for error. In other words, Blair believes that fitness is simply a better marker for activity levels than questionnaires (Blair *et al.* 2001). Conversely, it is possible that fitness is the more important determinant of mortality risk because it reflects the combined influence of activity and genes in prolonging life. At present, there is insufficient evidence to answer this question with certainty.

How much longer can active/fit people expect to live – by avoiding premature mortality – compared with inactive/unfit people? This is another question for which there is no definitive answer. Estimates from the Harvard Alumni Health Study suggest that the amount of additional life attributable to adequate exercise, as compared with sedentariness, is two or more years (Paffenbarger *et al.* 1986). This may not sound impressive, but it is important to remember that health is about more than avoiding premature mortality. Health is also about living without illness and with the functional capacities to do things (what might be termed 'positive health') and about feeling good (well-being). This is where physical activity possibly has most to offer. In the chapters that follow, we will examine a wide variety of evidence to explain:

1   the aetiology of the major diseases/conditions that might be influenced by physical activity;
2   the associations between these diseases/conditions and physical activity/fitness; and
3   the mechanisms by which physical activity may enhance health.

SUMMARY

- Observational studies have consistently shown that physical activity and physical fitness are inversely related to all-cause mortality risk.
- The findings of these studies remain statistically significant following control for possible confounding factors, including the existence of disease and/or disease risk factors at baseline.
- Evidence is strongly supportive of a dose–response relationship and indicates that mortality rates are between 20% and 80% lower in active/fit individuals compared with inactive/unfit individuals over a defined period.
- The strength of the association between physical fitness and all-cause mortality risk suggests that it is of equal or greater importance as a mortality predictor than other established disease risk factors.
- The association between physical activity/fitness and all-cause mortality holds true for adult men and women of all ages. Most studies have been conducted in Caucasian populations from the United States and Europe, and there are limited data on other ethnic groups. There is no compelling reason, however, why this relationship should not hold true for all ethnic groups.
- Recent studies indicate that obese individuals who are physically fit have a similar risk of all-cause mortality as lean individuals who are physically fit. This suggests that physical activity may provide important health benefits for obese individuals, regardless of any influence on body fatness.
- Evidence suggests that expending $4,200 \, kJ \, week^{-1}$ ($1,000 \, kcal \, week^{-1}$) in physical activity is sufficient to lower all-cause mortality risk. Greater amounts of activity are likely to produce greater benefits. Vigorous exercise is probably more effective than non-vigorous exercise.
- Although physical activity and physical fitness are associated with the prevention of premature mortality, they do not appear to extend the natural lifespan.
- Combining physical activity with other healthy lifestyle behaviours (diet, non-smoking, moderate alcohol consumption) appears to provide greater protection from disease than activity alone.

- There are many plausible biological mechanisms to explain the association between physical activity/fitness and all-cause mortality. These will be discussed in the chapters that follow and provide strong evidence for a cause-and-effect relationship.

STUDY TASKS

1 Describe in detail the findings from one study on physical activity and one study on physical fitness. State what is novel about each study and how each study has advanced knowledge and understanding.

2 Make a list, in order of importance, of all the possible confounding factors that may preclude a cause-and-effect relationship between physical activity/fitness and all-cause mortality.

3 List the aspects of the evidence linking physical activity/fitness with all-cause mortality that are supportive of a cause-and-effect relationship.

4 Discuss the strengths and limitations of studies examining changes in physical activity/fitness and all-cause mortality risk.

5 What are the strengths and limitations of the evidence indicating that obese individuals who are fit have a similar risk of all-cause mortality as lean individuals who are fit?

6 How much exercise is required to avert premature mortality? Justify your answer with reference to the research literature.

7 Write a 500-word description of a hypothetical study which will examine the association between physical activity and all-cause mortality. What study design will you use? Which population will you study? What questions will this design allow you to answer? How will you assess physical activity levels in this study? How will the findings advance knowledge? What will be the limitations of the study?

FURTHER READING

Blair, S.N. and LaMonte, M.J. (2007) 'Physical activity, fitness, and mortality rates', in C. Bouchard, S.N. Blair, and W.L. Haskell (eds) *Physical Activity and Health*, Champaign: Human Kinetics, pp. 143–59.

Blair, S.N., Cheng, Y. and Holder, J.S. (2001) 'Is physical activity or physical fitness more important in defining health benefits?', *Medicine and Science in Sports and Exercise* 33 (Supplement): S379–99.

Erikssen, G. (2001) 'Physical fitness and changes in mortality: the survival of the fittest', *Sports Medicine* 31: 571–6.

Lee, I.-M. and Paffenbarger, R.S. (1996) 'Do physical activity and physical fitness avert premature mortality?', *Exercise and Sport Sciences Reviews* 24: 135–71.

Lee, I.-M. and Skerrett, P.J. (2001) 'Physical activity and all-cause mortality: what is the dose–response relation?', *Medicine and Science in Sports and Exercise* 33 (Supplement): S459–71.

Oguma, Y., Sesso, H.D., Paffenbarger, R.S. and Lee, I.-M. (2002) 'Physical activity and all-cause mortality in women', *British Journal of Sports Medicine* 36: 162–72.

Part II
Influence of Physical Activity on the Risk of Disease

4 Cardiovascular disease

Knowledge assumed
Basic knowledge of lipid metabolism, cardiovascular physiology and exercise physiology

INTRODUCTION

Cohort studies that started in the late 1960s discovered that, as an epidemic condition in Western countries, coronary heart disease (CHD) (the cardiovascular disease (CVD) with the highest prevalence) is largely due to environmental influences. This is not to deny the importance of genetic predisposition in modifying susceptibility. However, for most individuals, CHD is caused as much or more by 'nurture' as it is by 'nature'. One environmental influence which is related to CHD is physical activity. In the last chapter we examined evidence which showed that people who are physically active or fit are less likely to die over a defined period than those who are inactive and/or unfit. This chapter shows that one important reason for this is that individuals who are active and fit experience a lower incidence of CVD. More than 50 years after Professor Jeremy Morris' pioneering studies, the evidence that physical inactivity and low fitness are risk factors for CVD is compelling. We will now evaluate this evidence in accordance with the principles set out in Chapter 2. First, however, it is important to clarify the term CVD.

WHAT IS CVD?

CVD is the name given to a group of disorders of the heart and blood vessels (listed in Box 4.1). The disease endpoints that have been studied in relation to physical activity or fitness are CHD, stroke and hypertension. In CHD the blood flow to the myocardium is compromised because of progressive narrowing or sudden blocking of a coronary artery or arteries. A heart attack happens when blood flow to the myocardium is impaired, either because a thrombus forms or because the artery goes into spasm. The extent of the damage depends on the site of the obstruction; if flow is interrupted to a large area of the myocardium, the attack is life-threatening because the heart can no longer function as an effective pump. A stroke causes neurological damage, either because a blood vessel in the brain becomes blocked or because of a bleed into the tissues of the brain. Hypertension is the term given to abnormally high arterial blood pressure. It increases the work of the heart, damages the arterial wall and increases the possibility that a small blood vessel in the brain will rupture, causing a stroke.

Other types of CVD have been little studied in relation to exercise, but they are included in Box 4.1 for the sake of completeness. The components of the classification in Box 4.1 are not mutually exclusive. For example, heart failure is the principal manifestation of coronary atherosclerosis, heart attack, damaged valves or hypertension.

Each year more than one in three deaths in men and women in the United Kingdom are due to CVD, while in Europe as a whole over 40% of deaths in men and over 50% of deaths in women are due to CVD each year (British Heart Foundation 2007, 2008). Most of these deaths are due to CHD and stroke. CHD by itself is the single most common cause of death in the United Kingdom and Europe. In the United Kingdom, over one in five men and around one in six women die from CHD each year. In Europe, over one in five men and over one in five women die from CHD each year (Figure 4.1). CHD accounts for 1.92 million deaths in Europe each year and 101,000 deaths in the United Kingdom each year. Over the past 30 years death rates

BOX 4.1 CATEGORIES OF CVD

- Hypertension (high blood pressure).
- CHD (ischemic heart disease): this category includes angina and myocardial infarction (heart attack).
- Cerebrovascular disease (stroke): this can be due to the formation of a thrombus (blood clot), that is, a thromboembolytic or ischemic stroke, or to a bleed into the brain, that is, a haemorrhagic stroke.
- Peripheral vascular disease: this is a narrowing of peripheral arteries which compromises blood flow. This most often affects the femoral artery, causing pain on walking.
- Heart failure: the heart is unable to pump blood forward at a rate sufficient to meet the metabolic demands of the body, usually because of impaired left ventricular function.
- Rheumatic heart disease: the valves of the heart are damaged, impairing its capability to control the direction of blood flow.
- Cardiomyopathies: disorders that occur due to major structural abnormalities of the myocardium.

Figure 4.1 Percentage deaths due to CHD, stroke, other forms of CVD and all forms of CVD in men and women in the United Kingdom and Europe.

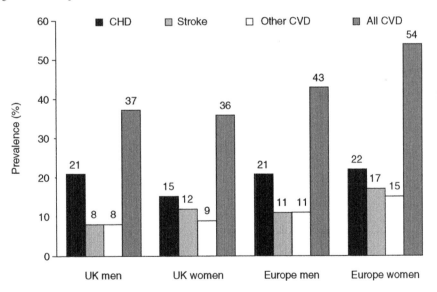

Source: Data for the United Kingdom are from the British Heart Foundation Coronary Heart Disease Statistics (2007); data for Europe are from the British Heart Foundation European Cardiovascular Disease Statistics (2008). Both may be found at: www.heartstats.org (accessed 18 March 2008).
Notes: Statistics for the United Kingdom are from the year 2005; statistics for Europe are for the latest available year.

from CHD have been falling rapidly in most Northern and Western European countries, but rising rapidly in some Central and Eastern European countries. In the United Kingdom, death rates from CHD have been falling since the late 1970s. However, morbidity from CHD appears to be increasing in the United Kingdom, particularly among older adults. Around one in four men and one in five women aged 75 and over are currently thought to be living with CHD in the United Kingdom. Moreover, due to the ageing population in the United Kingdom, one report has predicted a 44% increase in the number of CHD cases by 2031 (Majeed and Aylin 2005).

CVD is also the major cause of death in the United States. Each year the American Heart Association publishes CVD statistics for the United States. The following is a brief selection of some of the most recent findings (American Heart Association 2008): CVD accounted for 35.2% of all 2,447,910 deaths in the United States in 2005; nearly 2,400 Americans die of CVD each day – an average of one death every 37 seconds; more than 148,000 Americans killed by CVD in 2004 were <65 years of age and 32% of deaths from CVD in 2004 occurred before the age of 75 years, which is well below the average US life expectancy of 77.9 years; CHD caused one of every five deaths in the United States in 2004; in 2008, an estimated 770,000 Americans will have a new coronary attack, and about 430,000 will have a recurrent attack; about every 26 seconds, an American will have a coronary event, and about every minute someone will die from one. Each year about 780,000 people experience a new or recurrent stroke which accounts for approximately one of every 17 deaths in the United States; on average, every 40 seconds someone in the United States has a stroke.

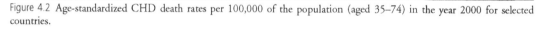

Figure 4.2 Age-standardized CHD death rates per 100,000 of the population (aged 35–74) in the year 2000 for selected countries.

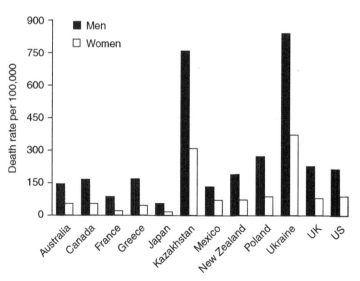

Source: British Heart Foundation Coronary Heart Disease Statistics (2007). Available at: www.heartstats.org (accessed 18 March 2008).
Notes: Observe the wide variation in rates and that CHD mortality rates are higher in males than in females in all countries displayed.

Thus, although CVD death rates have fallen in the United States in recent years, it remains a major public health issue.

World-wide, age-standardized death rates from CHD vary widely from as low as 53 per 100,000 of the male population in Japan, to as high as 867 per 100,000 of the male population in the Ukraine, a 16-fold difference (Figure 4.2). Trends over recent years vary greatly. For example, whilst the CHD death rate in Australia, Norway and the United Kingdom for men and women aged 35–74 fell by 40–50% between 1990 and 2000, it increased by over 40% in Belarus and by over 60% in the Ukraine (British Heart Foundation 2007). These strong temporal changes, within populations with (presumably) a rather stable gene pool, illustrate the important contribution from environmental factors, including physical inactivity, to the aetiology of CHD.

This chapter discusses the relationship between physical activity and fitness with CVD and risk factors for CVD. By far the most important cause of CVD is atherosclerosis and its complications.

ATHEROSCLEROSIS

Atherosclerosis begins in childhood and progresses over many decades (McGill *et al.* 2000). In a landmark study published in 1953, pathologists who conducted autopsies on US soldiers killed in the Korean War observed gross evidence of atherosclerosis in 77% of the 300 hearts examined, despite the fact that the average age of the men studied was only 22 years (Enos *et al.* 1953). A subsequent report by the same group included autopsy data on Japanese natives, and although lesions were found in 65% of cases, no plaques causing over 50% luminal narrowing were observed in young Japanese males (20–30 years old), whereas 20 such cases were found in young American men (Enos *et al.* 1955). As mentioned below, a narrowing of 45% or greater indicates a threshold for clinical symptoms related to CHD. Years later autopsy reports of US soldiers who died in the Vietnam War found that most of these young men did not have severe atherosclerosis (McNamara *et al.* 1970). The reason for this discrepancy is unclear, but some evidence of atherosclerosis was found in all of these reports, confirming that the disease process begins early in life.

The pathological hallmarks of atherosclerosis are the fatty streak (the earliest visible lesions) and the fibrous plaque (plaques are more advanced lesions that are the source of clinical symptoms). The mechanisms responsible for atherosclerosis are incompletely understood, but current models are based on the 'response to injury' hypothesis. This was proposed in the early 1970s and states that the disease begins with an injury to the lining of an artery, that is, the endothelium. The wall of normal muscular arteries consists of three orderly layers: the intima (the most 'intimate' with the blood), the media (the middle layer) and the outer adventitia. The intima – the battleground of the atherosclerotic process – comprises a single layer of endothelial cells that rests on a bed of connective tissue.

Normal endothelial cells serve critically important functions: they comprise a barrier restricting the passage of large molecules and cells; they resist thrombosis through releasing anti-clotting molecules and platelet inhibitors; they help regulate blood flow to metabolic needs by secreting vasodilator substances; and they inhibit the proliferation and migration of smooth muscle cells. Endothelial injury or dysfunction thus leads to the accumulation of molecules, especially lipids, and a proliferation of cells in the intimal layer of an artery. The intima enlarges and appears yellow and streaky to the naked eye – hence the term 'fatty streak'. Progression of atherosclerosis involves adhesion of white blood cells called monocytes to the endothelium. Once they cross the endothelium these cells become macrophages and ingest oxidized lipids, taking on a 'foamy' appearance. Macrophages and smooth muscle cells proliferate in the intima, the latter producing collagen and other molecules that increase the bulk of the lesion. This process is depicted in Figure 4.3. Molecular factors such as cytokines, growth factors and nitric oxide all play a role in the proliferation and migration of smooth muscle cells. The size of the fatty streak increases and a cap of connective tissue may cover the

Figure 4.3 Schematic representation of the early events in atherosclerosis within the innermost layer of the artery, the intima.

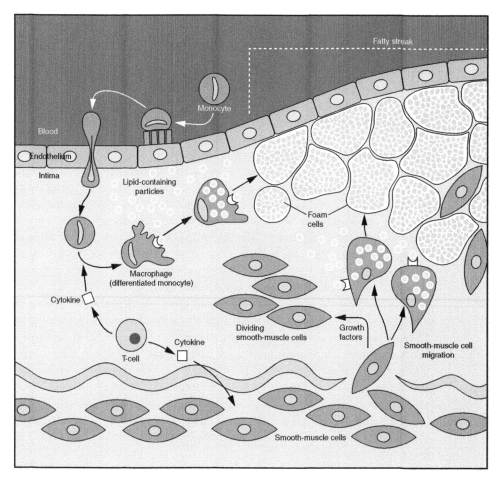

Source: Hajjar and Nicholson (1995).
Note: The media (middle layer of the artery wall) can be seen at the bottom of the diagram. Foam cells are the primary constituents of the fatty streak.

Figure 4.4 Narrowing of a coronary artery branch by a large plaque of atheroma. The consequent reduction in blood flow leads to ischemia of an area of the myocardium.

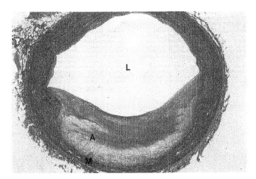

Source: Wheater *et al.* (1985).
Notes: The artery is seen in cross-section. A, atheroma; L, lumen (space inside artery); M, media.

Figure 4.5 Schematic representation of the progression of atherosclerosis from the fatty streak (depicted as a reversible process) to a clinical horizon where the ensuing ischemia leads to organ damage and symptoms develop.

Natural history of atherosclerosis

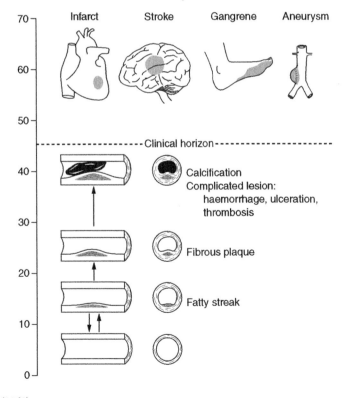

Source: McGill *et al.* (1963).

core of fat and cellular debris, forming a fibrous plaque. The site of the lesion can also become calcified, reducing the artery's elasticity.

Figure 4.4 shows the narrowing of an artery by an atherosclerotic plaque. Plaques grow gradually, and only when a lesion restricts blood flow by around 45% do symptoms develop as the tissues supplied by that artery become ischemic. This threshold is described as a 'clinical horizon' or 'clinical threshold' because the disease process then begins to limit normal functioning. Complications of atherosclerosis also derive from sudden events. For example, rupture of a vulnerable plaque is often associated with thrombus formation, leading to a heart attack or stroke. An artery wall weakened by atherosclerosis can rupture, leading to internal bleeding. Common sites of this complication include the aorta (an aneurysm) or an artery in the brain (a haemorrhagic stroke). The progression of the atherosclerotic process to the clinical horizon is shown schematically in Figure 4.5.

EPIDEMIOLOGY OF PHYSICAL ACTIVITY AND CHD

The observation that physical activity can protect against heart attack was first made in cross-sectional studies comparing incidence rates in men in a variety of occupations. Jeremy Morris *et al.* studied the drivers and conductors of London's double-decker buses. The conductors (who walked up and down stairs 11 days per fortnight, for 50 weeks of a year, often for decades) experienced roughly half the number of heart attacks and 'sudden death' due to heart attack as the drivers. Similar differences in CHD attack and death rates were found between physically active postmen (who spent 70% of their shift time walking, cycling and climbing stairs) and their sedentary colleagues who sorted the mail (Morris *et al.* 1953). The self-selection bias in such studies is obvious, however: did leaner, generally healthier men seek the more physically active jobs? Morris *et al.* subsequently published data on the waist size of the uniform trousers issued to the men – a crude measure of what is now termed central obesity (a confounding factor because of its associations with diabetes, dyslipidaemias and hypertension, all of which increase the risk of heart attack). Lean, average and portly conductors all experienced CHD rates about half those of the sedentary drivers. It appeared, therefore, that the protective effect of physical activity was independent of body fatness (at least as crudely assessed).

Occupational studies in other countries, notably those of San Francisco dockworkers (called 'longshoremen'), confirmed the protective effect of occupational work. The longshoremen ($n=6,351$), whose exercise intensity at work was categorized as light, moderate or heavy according to measurements of oxygen uptake, were followed for 22 years (Paffenbarger and Hale 1975) (the steps by which oxygen uptake measurements were converted to rates of energy expenditure are shown in Box 4.2.). Death rates of the dockworkers from CHD are shown in Figure 4.6, within ten-year age-bands. Overall, men engaged in light or moderate work were twice as likely to die from CHD as those whose work was classified as heavy. The protective effect of heavy occupational work was evident at all ages, but greatest in the oldest men. Selection bias was not a major problem because men enrolling in the industry were not allowed to choose their job assignment.

Figure 4.6 Death rates from CHD in San Francisco dockworkers between 1951 and 1972, according to intensity of physical activity at work and age at death.

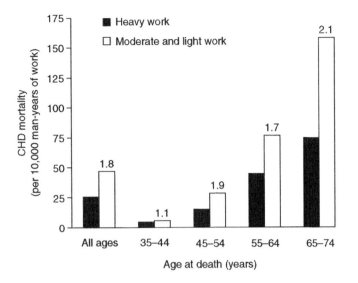

Source: Adapted from Paffenbarger and Hale (1975).
Notes: Open bars, moderate and light work at 6.3–20.9 kJ min^{-1} (1.5–5.0 kcal min^{-1}); dark bars, heavy work at 21.8–31.4 kJ min^{-1} (5.2–7.5 kcal min^{-1}). Figures over bars show relative risk, with reference group as heavy work. Difference between heavy and moderate/light work significant for all ages ($P<0.001$) and for men in all ten-year age bands ($P<0.01$) except 35–44.

By the 1960s it was clear that differences in physical activity level within populations would derive mainly from leisure-time activity – heavy occupational work was decreasing. Two large studies were thus begun, on opposite sides of the Atlantic. Morris *et al.* studied English civil servants, adopting a five-minute-by-five-minute record of how they had spent the previous Friday and Saturday as the index of leisure-time physical activity. Eight-and-a-half years later the men who reported engaging in 30 or more minutes of vigorous exercise (estimated as entailing peak rates of energy expenditure of 31.5 kJ min^{-1} (7.5 kcal min^{-1}) or more) had an incidence of CHD less than half that of their colleagues who recorded no vigorous exercise (Morris *et al.* 1980).

One of the most comprehensive data sets derives from the Harvard Alumni Study referred to in Chapter 3. The reader will recall that Paffenbarger *et al.* studied the physical activity habits of men who had graduated from Harvard University between 1916 and 1950, collating replies to questionnaires sent out in 1962 or 1966. Information was obtained not only about current physical activity, but also about participation in student sport whilst at university. Researchers found that the risk of heart attack was inversely related to total energy expenditure in physical activity over the range <2.1–8.4 MJ week^{-1} (<500–2,000 kcal week^{-1}) (Paffenbarger *et al.* 1978). As in the study of English civil servants, active men had lower risk both in the presence and in the absence of smoking, hypertension and a high body mass index (BMI), confirming that the effect of exercise is not acting through these other factors.

One finding from the Harvard Alumni Study gives a clue as to possible mechanisms. Men who participated in university sport – who might be expected to have a robust cardiovascular system – did not have a lower CHD risk unless they maintained a high level of physical activity (Figure 4.7). The finding that recent – but not past – exercise offers protection against CHD was confirmed among English civil servants. Playing vigorous sport some years earlier conferred no protection among men who did not continue to practise such exercise. Moreover, a report from the Netherlands found that light activities like walking, gardening or cycling were associated with a lower risk of acute coronary events only among men who pursued them all year round. There was no effect if these activities were seasonal (Magnus *et al.* 1979). All these findings suggest that the protection afforded by physical activity is mediated, at least in part, by some effect on the acute phases of CHD (thrombosis, vascular spasm, loss of normal heart rhythm).

In their second study of civil servants, Morris *et al.* gathered comprehensive information on possible interactions of exercise with other risk factors (Morris *et al.* 1990). They found that the protective effect of vigorous exercise was independent of family history, stature, reported attitude to healthy behaviours, cigarette smoking, BMI and sub-clinical CVD. Figure 4.8 displays death rates from CHD among men with and without these potentially confounding factors and shows that the effect of vigorous activity is consistent across subgroups. Thus, confounding by known risk factors could not account for the effects of physical activity.

During the 1970s and 1980s many other epidemiological studies of work and leisure-time physical activity were published. Almost all were of men (mainly because the

Figure 4.7 Age-adjusted rates of first heart attack in alumni reporting high (>8.37 MJ week⁻¹) and low (<8.37 MJ week⁻¹) levels of estimated gross energy expenditure in physical activity as adults, according to past participation in university sport.

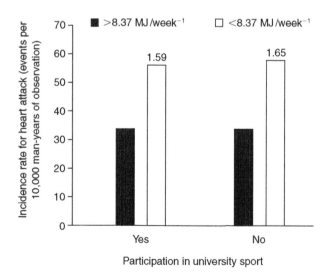

Source: Paffenbarger *et al.* (1978).
Note: Figures over bars show relative risk for the low activity group with the high activity group (>8.37 MJ week⁻¹) acting as the reference group.

BOX 4.2 ENERGY EXPENDITURE DURING EXERCISE – RELATIONSHIPS WITH OXYGEN UPTAKE

During sub-maximal exercise the majority of energy comes from the oxidation of fat and carbohydrate. The rate of oxygen uptake therefore reflects the rate of energy expenditure (metabolic rate). The exact energy expenditure per litre of oxygen depends on the proportion of fat and carbohydrate being oxidized, but if it is assumed that both contribute equally to energy metabolism, each litre of oxygen taken up is equivalent to an energy expenditure of 20.5 kJ ($\approx$5 kcal).

Examples from the epidemiology:

- Morris' studies of male English civil servants defined exercise as vigorous if the rate of energy expenditure reached peaks of $\geq$31.4 kJ min^{-1} (7.5 kcal min^{-1}). This is equivalent to an oxygen uptake of: 31.4/20.5 = 1.53 l min^{-1}.

  Question – what does this mean in terms of exercise for these men?
  Answer – metabolic rate depends on body mass. For purposes of estimating and describing exercise intensity, metabolic rate has been defined as 3.5 ml oxygen per kilogram of body mass per minute, that is, 3.5 ml kg^{-1} min^{-1} or 1 MET. If we assume that the civil servants typically weighed 78 kg, then an oxygen uptake of 1.53 l min^{-1} represents about 20 ml kg^{-1} min^{-1} or 5.7 METs. Activities such as easy cycling or doubles tennis typically demand this rate of oxygen uptake.

- In the Harvard Alumni Study, a threshold value for gross weekly energy expenditure in physical activity of 8.37 MJ (2,000 kcal) has often been used.

  Question – what does this equate to in terms that are readily understood?
  Answer – let us look at this from the point of view of, say, brisk walking. Walking briskly at 6.4 km h^{-1} (4 mile h^{-1}) demands about 4 METs, an oxygen uptake of (3.5 × 4) or 14 ml kg^{-1} min^{-1}. Assuming a body mass of 78 kg, this means 1.09 l min^{-1} and energy expenditure at a rate of (1.09 × 20.5) or 22.3 kJ min^{-1}. Thus, a total gross energy expenditure of 8.37 MJ per week is equivalent to: 8,370/22.3 = 375 minutes (6 hours and 15 minutes) of brisk walking, about 40 km (25 miles).

- In the US Nurses' Health Study, walking is expressed in MET-h week^{-1}.

  Question – the median value for nurses in the top quintile for walking was 20 MET-h week^{-1} (Manson et al. 1999). For how many hours did they walk?
  Answer – walking at a 'normal' speed of 4.8 km h^{-1} (3 mile h^{-1}) demands 3.5 METs. So, walking for one hour at this speed gives 3.5 MET-h and 20 MET-h week^{-1} means walking for 5.7 hours during a week, covering 27.4 km (17 miles).

Thus, adjectives such as 'vigorous', 'heavy' or 'moderate' do not have precise meaning in the literature. For example, much of the work activity classified as 'heavy' in Paffenbarger's studies of dockworkers (Paffenbarger and Hale 1975) would have been well below the threshold for 'vigorous' exercise adopted in the studies of English civil servants (Morris et al. 1980, 1990).

Figure 4.8 Rates of CHD per 1,000 man-years of observation in English male civil servants grouped according to the frequency of vigorous aerobic exercise: (1) most frequent; (4) least frequent. The association between vigorous aerobic exercise and low risk of CHD held across a variety of potentially confounding factors.

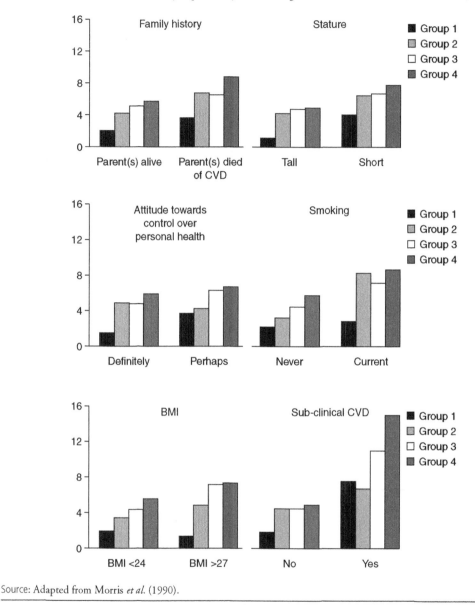

Source: Adapted from Morris *et al.* (1990).

disease incidence is so much lower in women) and the majority were from the United States. Other countries contributing to the studies were the United Kingdom, the Netherlands, Italy, Yugoslavia, Greece, Finland, Sweden, Israel and Puerto Rico. This evidence was subjected to critical review (Powell *et al.* 1987) and meta-analysis (Berlin and Colditz 1990) to provide an overall picture (meta-analysis is the statistical analysis of a collection of analytic results for the purpose of integrating the findings). About two-thirds of studies found a significant effect of exercise and, tellingly, no study found a higher risk among active people. The conclusions reached by structured review and meta-analysis were reassuringly similar: first, better studies (assessed on quality of information about both physical activity levels and cause of death) were more likely than poorer studies to report an inverse relationship between physical activity level and incidence of CHD; and, second, the relative risk of physical inactivity (median 1.9) was similar to that associated with high total cholesterol, hypertension or smoking cigarettes – all strong risk factors.

Since 1990 many more studies have been published on physical activity and CHD. What have they added that is new? First, they have provided strong evidence that the benefit is also seen in women, in older men and in more racially diverse groups. Second, they have examined the relationship between the 'dose' of exercise and the 'response' in terms of reduced risk of CHD. Evidence on this topic, crucial for the development of promoting exercise as part of a public health strategy, is discussed here, after consideration of studies of fitness.

EPIDEMIOLOGY OF FITNESS AND CHD

The difficulties of measuring physical activity were discussed in Chapter 2. Some investigators have sought to avoid these by measuring the characteristics exhibited by people who are physically active, that is, fitness, rather than the behaviour (physical activity/exercise) that leads to fitness. They argue that this reduces the chance of individuals being misclassified and, by increasing the precision of measurement, increases the likelihood that true findings will not be missed. The extent to which traditional measurements of fitness are independent of genetic factors is a matter of debate. However, some studies have found close relationships between physical activity and measures of fitness, suggesting that the environmental influence is dominant. What is certain is that information relating CHD incidence to fitness complements and extends that based on relationships with self-reported activity.

The view that fitness improves the objectivity of investigations is supported by reports that low fitness appears to be a stronger risk factor for CVD than physical inactivity. Findings from the Aerobics Center Longitudinal Study (Dallas, Texas) constitute a major part of this literature (the results of this study with respect to all-cause mortality risk are described in the previous chapter). Fitness was measured as time on a maximal treadmill test (a surrogate for $\dot{V}O_2max$) in more than 25,000 men. Steven Blair *et al.* (1996) found that the relative risk of low fitness (bottom quintile of study population versus all other men) was 1.70, a higher relative risk than often reported for physical inactivity. Based on comparisons within the same study population, the relative risk of low fitness was also higher than that observed for smoking (relative risk 1.57), systolic blood pressure $\geq 140 \, mm \, Hg$ (1.34), high cholesterol $\geq 6.2 \, mmol \, l^{-1}$ (1.65) or parental death from CHD (1.18). These estimates represent the independent risk associated with each factor as they are corrected for each other, as well as for body mass. More recently, a study of 1,294 men from Eastern Finland reported a relative risk of 3.09 for CVD-related death in those with low fitness (quartile 1: $\dot{V}O_2max$ $<27.6 \, ml \, kg^{-1} \, min^{-1}$) compared with those with high fitness (quartile 4: $\dot{V}O_2max$

Figure 4.9 Age-adjusted relative risk of CHD in US men enrolled in the Health Professionals Follow-up Study, according to overall physical activity (MET-h week⁻¹), physical activity intensity (METs), amount of running and weight lifting (both in hours per week), walking volume (MET-h week⁻¹) and walking intensity (miles h⁻¹).

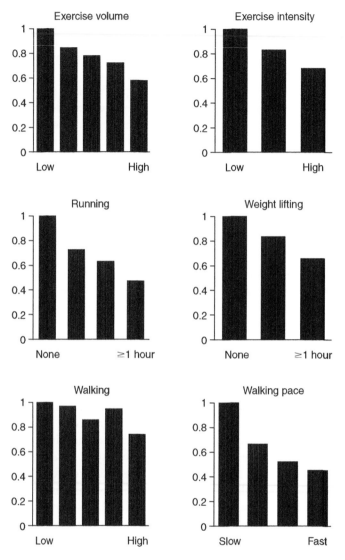

Source: Adapted from Tanasescu *et al.* (2002).
Notes: Exercise volume quintile one: 0–6.32; quintile two: 6.33–14.49; quintile three: 14.50–25.08; quintile four: 25.09–41.98; quintile five: ≥41.99 MET-h week⁻¹. Exercise intensity tertile one: 1–3.9; tertile two: 4–5.9; tertile three: ≥6 METs. Running quartile one: none; quartile two: <0.5; quartile three: 0.5–1; quartile four: ≥1 h week⁻¹. Weight lifting tertile one: none; tertile two: <0.5; tertile three: ≥1 h week⁻¹. Walking volume quintile one: 0–1.19; quintile two: 1.20–3.49; quintile three: 3.50–6.99; quintile four: 7.00–14.74; quintile five: ≥14.75 MET-h week⁻¹. Walking pace quartile one: <2; quartile two: 2–3; quartile three 3–4; quartile four: ≥4 miles h⁻¹. Displayed findings are age-adjusted relative risks, but findings remained significant in multivariate models.

$\geq 37.1\,\text{ml}\,\text{kg}^{-1}\,\text{min}^{-1}$) during an average follow-up of 10.7 years. This is one of the few studies of this nature to directly measure maximum oxygen uptake using measurements of expired air collected during exercise (Laukkanen *et al.* 2001).

Studies of fitness can make comparisons of CHD incidence among multiple ordinal fitness categories, and thus provide new information on the level of fitness below which there seems to be an important increase in risk. A few investigators have attempted to identify such thresholds, which might be important for public health policy. For middle-aged men, this is probably of the order of 8–9 METs $(28–32\,\text{ml}\,\text{kg}^{-1}\,\text{min}^{-1})$. There is little information for women, but based solely on the Aerobics Center Study, the comparable level is probably of the order of 6–7 METs $(21–25\,\text{ml}\,\text{kg}^{-1}\,\text{min}^{-1})$. The potential of popular activities like walking to elicit values at these levels will be discussed in Chapter 13.

CHANGES IN PHYSICAL ACTIVITY AND FITNESS AND CHD

All the studies referred to above used a single baseline measure of physical activity/fitness as the exposure variable. This assumes, probably wrongly in many cases, that participants' levels of physical activity or fitness are rather stable over years and leads to misclassification. Studying changes in activity or fitness between two observations several years apart increases the precision with which exposure to inactivity or low fitness is measured. It also allows the hypothesis that changing exposure is associated with a change in risk to be tested.

Several cohort studies have been able to obtain repeated measurements of activity or fitness and findings from these studies were discussed in Chapter 3 in relation to all-cause mortality. Here we examine the findings for CVD/CHD. The first of these was the Harvard Alumni Study that reported deaths from CHD in men who returned questionnaires about their activity levels in 1962 or 1966 and again in 1977. Previously sedentary men who, over this period, increased their total physical activity index to $\geq 8.4\,\text{MJ}\,\text{week}^{-1}$ had a 17% lower risk of death from CHD than those who remained sedentary (Paffenbarger *et al.* 1993). Even greater benefit was seen in the subgroup of men who took up moderately vigorous exercise at $\geq 4.5\,\text{METs}$; they had a 41% lower risk of death from CHD than those who continued to be sedentary. This difference in risk was similar to that seen among men who gave up cigarette smoking (44% lower risk than continuing smokers) or who avoided becoming overweight for their height (41% lower risk than those whose BMI increased to $\geq 26\,\text{kg}\,\text{m}^2$). Similar findings were reported among men from the British Regional Heart Study which assessed for changes in activity level at an interval of 12–14 years. In this study, the benefit of increasing physical activity was evident among men already diagnosed with CVD, as well as among healthy men (Wannamethee *et al.* 1998).

We might expect therefore that improvements in fitness would also reduce the risk of CHD. Findings from the Aerobics Center Longitudinal Study support this argument. Men who were unfit, that is, in the bottom quintile for performance on a maximal treadmill test, on one assessment but who improved their fitness when assessed five years later, had a 52% lower age-adjusted risk of CVD mortality (CHD deaths were not reported separately) than men who remained unfit (Blair *et al.* 1995).

Furthermore, men designated as fit when first assessed (quintiles two or three) but who improved their fitness so that they were in a higher quintile when reassessed, also had a 28% lower risk of CVD mortality than those who remained in quintiles two or three. These findings were independent of confounding by other risk factors at baseline or by changes in risk factors during follow-up.

Collectively, these findings strongly suggest that the relationships between fitness or physical activity and cardiovascular mortality are not due solely to hereditary factors. They also go some way to addressing concerns that low fitness and inactivity may be a consequence in some individuals of undetected, pre-existing disease. These data, from cohort studies, do not prove a causal link with reduced CVD mortality, but they strengthen the argument that, if activity or fitness improves, risk can be modified.

DOSE–RESPONSE: WHAT LEVEL OF ACTIVITY OR FITNESS CONFERS PROTECTION AGAINST CHD?

This question is important for two reasons: first, if the relationship between physical activity or fitness and the risk of CHD is causal, then there should be a graded effect – more activity/higher fitness should be associated with greater benefit; and second, public health initiatives demand an understanding of what constitutes a sufficient level of activity or fitness to confer a worthwhile decrease in risk. Only studies where several gradations of physical activity or fitness are reported can help address dose–response issues. Many studies of this nature are available for physical activity and most provide evidence of dose–response. Fewer studies are available with fitness as the exposure variable and these are mostly from the Aerobics Center Longitudinal Study. However, these are compelling in their consistency and in the steepness of the gradient across fitness groups.

A notable example of a study demonstrating dose–response effects of physical activity is the Health Professionals Follow-Up Study (Tanasescu *et al.* 2002). This study involved 44,452 US men who were followed up from 1986 to 1998. Physical activity was assessed every two years between 1986 and 1996, overcoming a limitation of many previous studies where physical activity was only assessed at baseline. Inverse dose-response relationships were found between CHD risk and the volume and intensity of physical activity, the duration and speed of walking and the duration of running and weight training (Figure 4.9). Rowing and racquet sports were also found to be associated with a lower CHD risk. These findings were confirmed in the Women's Health Initiative Observational Study (Manson *et al.* 2002), which demonstrated inverse dose–response associations between both walking and vigorous exercise and the risk of CVD in 73,743 postmenopausal women. In both of these studies the findings remained significant after control for a host of potentially confounding factors including age, BMI, alcohol intake, cigarette smoking, family history of CHD and nutrient intake.

Two papers from the Harvard Alumni Health Study provide further information regarding relationships between exercise duration and intensity and CHD risk. One examined the influence of the duration of exercise episodes, through the range <15 minutes in 15 minute increments to >60 minutes (Lee *et al.* 2000). Longer sessions of exercise did not have a different effect on the risk of CHD than shorter sessions, as long as the total energy expended was similar. The second paper examined the influence of the relative intensity of exercise (assessed using participants' ratings on the Borg scale of perceived exertion) and found a strong relationship with the risk of CHD that was independent of total energy expenditure (Lee *et al.* 2003). This ties in well with evidence from laboratory studies that the physiological 'stress' of exercise depends on the proportion of individual $\dot{V}O_2$max it demands, rather than on its intensity measured in absolute terms.

Based on the available evidence on dose–response, the conclusion may be drawn that, while moderate levels of physical activity or fitness confer a measurable decrease in the risk of CHD, more vigorous activity or higher levels of fitness confer a greater benefit. The exact shape of the relationship with risk is not known, so future epidemiological studies will attempt to describe this in more detail. Future studies may also provide greater detail on the associations between exercise and CHD risk for specific activities, e.g. running, swimming, cycling, racquet sports, etc. Currently, sufficient data is available for confident recommendations only for walking. In relation to this Morris *et al.* observed a clear inverse gradient of risk according to reported walking speed in English civil servants, with a particularly low rate of disease in men claiming to be fast walkers ($\geq 4\,\text{mile h}^{-1}$ or $6.4\,\text{km h}^{-1}$) (Morris *et al.* 1990). This finding was confirmed in both the Health Professionals Follow-up Study (Tanasescu *et al.* 2002) and the Women's Health Initiative Observational Study (Manson *et al.* 2002). A dose–response relationship between walking and CVD was also confirmed in a recent meta-analysis (Hamer and Chida 2008). Thus, it can be assumed that a walking pace of $4\,\text{mile h}^{-1}$ or greater is required for optimal protection from CHD and, within certain limits, that the greater the volume of walking the greater the protection from CHD.

ARE PHYSICAL INACTIVITY AND LOW FITNESS CAUSAL FACTORS FOR CHD?

Collectively the evidence discussed here is strongly supportive of the proposition that physical inactivity and low fitness are causative factors for CHD. However, because of the enduring problem of self-selection and because people in whom disease is developing but undetected may be more likely than others to be sedentary, epidemiological studies cannot by themselves establish causality. This limitation is nicely described in an editorial by Dr Paul Thompson who states that:

all epidemiological examinations of occupational and recreational physical activity are plagued by the possibility that people who elect vigorous lifestyles are different physiologically, emotionally, or genetically from their less active peers. Selection according to such a 'hardiness factor' can only be addressed by a clinical trial.

(Thompson 2002: p. 755)

As pointed out in Chapter 2, a randomized, controlled trial with disease endpoints as the outcome measure is not feasible. Complementary evidence that examines potential

---

BOX 4.3 FEATURES OF EVIDENCE FOR THE PROPOSITION THAT PHYSICAL ACTIVITY AND FITNESS PROTECTS AGAINST CHD

- Findings are remarkably consistent in diverse populations.
- Better studies are more likely than poorer studies to observe an inverse relationship.
- The majority of evidence is in middle-aged men, but there is some also in older men and in women.
- The relationships between CHD risk and physical activity or fitness are inverse and graded. Whether intensity and/or frequency of sessions of physical activity have separate effects over and above that of the total energy expenditure is not yet clear, although these are issues of much research interest and it appears likely that 'vigorous' exercise confers optimal protection.
- The relative risk of inactivity or low fitness is at least two.
- The majority of studies have demonstrated that they measured activity/fitness before the onset of CHD. This decreases the likelihood that participants were inactive because they had pre-clinical disease.
- The findings are not confounded by other major risk factors (hypertension – repeatedly confirmed; cigarette smoking – repeatedly confirmed; total cholesterol – less data).
- Becoming more active or fit is associated with a lower risk than remaining inactive or of low fitness.

---

biological mechanisms is therefore vital and will be described later in this chapter. The features of epidemiological evidence that can contribute towards establishing causality were explained in Chapter 2. The evidence discussed in this chapter appears to fulfil these criteria (Box 4.3).

EPIDEMIOLOGY OF PHYSICAL ACTIVITY AND STROKE

There are good reasons why the hypothesis that physical activity reduces the risk of stroke is attractive. Clear evidence links physical inactivity to CHD, and thromboembolytic stroke (ischemic stroke, the commonest type) and CHD share similar pathophysiology and risk factors (raised blood pressure, obesity, glucose intolerance, smoking).

The number of epidemiological studies examining the relationship between physical activity and stroke incidence is small compared with the numbers of studies of CHD. However, a number of comprehensive reports have been published, the majority from cohort studies. Some report a lower incidence of stroke (fatal and/or non-fatal) but the evidence lacks the consistency observed for CHD. Studies that have found an effect tend to be those with more cases and comprehensive information on physical activity (Batty and Lee 2002), but available data are insufficient to draw a conclusion.

As an example, data from the US Nurses' Health Study are shown in Figure 4.10. This figure shows total physical activity level and walking activity (both measured in MET-h per week) in relation to total stroke incidence (Hu *et al.* 2000). Data are the average of reports gathered on three occasions eight, six and two years prior to assessment of outcome and adjusted for age and for other potentially confounding factors. Two points may be made: first, the relationship is inverse, graded and statistically significant; and second, although adjustment for potentially confounding factors somewhat attenuated the risk, this remained significant. The relationship was primarily observed for ischemic stroke. For walking, the multivariate analysis adjusted for participation in vigorous exercise, so these findings can be regarded as describing the association of the risk of stroke with walking per se. By contrast with the CHD data from the same cohort referred to earlier, data were adjusted for alcohol consumption. This

Figure 4.10 Overall physical activity levels, walking activity and relative risk of stroke in 72,488 female nurses aged 40–65 years, followed from 1986 to 1992.

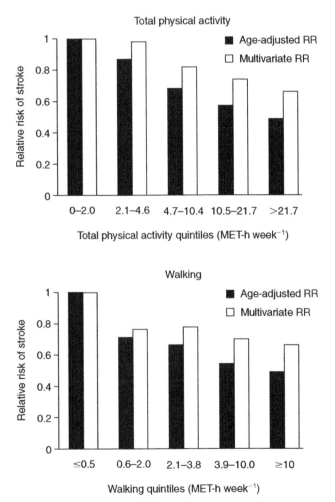

Source: US Nurses' Health Study (Hu *et al.* 2000).
Notes: Multivariate relative risks adjusted for age, smoking, BMI, menopausal status, parental history of myocardial infarction, alcohol consumption, aspirin use and history of hypertension, diabetes or hypercholesterolaemia. For walking activity the multivariate model adjusted for vigorous exercise in addition to the other factors listed above.

is because high consumption of alcohol is one of the most important risk factors for stroke, but is not a risk factor for CHD.

Few studies have allowed estimation of the separate effects (if any) of exercise intensity or frequency. One – a case-control study in Manhattan – found a significant effect of both intensity (light to moderate versus heavy) and duration (<2 h week^{-1} versus >2–<5 h week^{-1} versus ≥5 h week^{-1}) of exercise (Sacco *et al.* 1998). However, some studies show a U-shaped relationship between physical activity and the risk of stroke. This implies an increase in risk with very high levels or intensities of physical activity and warrants further study (Lee and Paffenbarger 1998).

At least two studies of fitness and stroke incidence are available. The US Aerobics Center Longitudinal Study analysed stroke mortality incidence among 16,878 men during a ten-year follow-up (Lee and Blair 2002). Compared with the least-fit 20% of men, the relative risk of stroke mortality was 0.37 in those with moderate fitness (next 40%) and 0.32 in those designated as high fitness (top 40%). The number of cases are inevitably much lower than for CHD, illustrating the difficulty of examining different types of strokes separately (it is possible that activity is not related in the same way to both thromboembolytic (ischemic) and haemorrhagic stroke). Only 32 cases of stroke mortality were documented in the Aerobics Center study, 14 in the low fitness group, 11 in the moderate fitness group and seven in the high fitness group.

The findings of the Aerobics Center Longitudinal Study were confirmed by those of the Kupio Ischemic Heart Disease Risk Factor Study in Eastern Finland. This study involved 2,011 men and an average of 11 years follow-up. Maximum oxygen uptake was determined directly in this study using a cycle ergometer test. The relative risk of stroke (all types) was 3.2 in men in the lowest quartile for fitness ($\dot{V}O_2$max <25.2 ml kg^{-1} min^{-1}, 7.2 METs) compared with those in the highest quartile ($\dot{V}O_2$max >35.3 ml kg^{-1} min^{-1}, 10.1 METs). These findings remained significant after adjustment for a variety of potentially confounding factors and the risk of low fitness was comparable to that of established risk factors for stroke, including hypertension, obesity, alcohol consumption, smoking and elevated low-density lipoprotein cholesterol (Kurl *et al.* 2003). Thus, evidence is accumulating that low levels of physical activity and physical fitness increase the risk of stroke.

RISK FACTORS FOR CVD

Evidence collected over many decades has identified several major risk factors for CVD. Identification of CVD risk factors is essential for the prevention and management of CVD. The concept of risk factors is also useful when examining the role of physical activity in CVD prevention because intervention studies can be conducted to examine the effects of exercise on CVD risk factors. As highlighted previously, randomized intervention studies examining the effect of exercise on disease endpoints (heart attack, stroke) are not feasible due to ethical and practical constraints. If it can be demonstrated that exercise positively influences CVD risk factors, this provides strong evidence that the associations between inactivity/low fitness and CVD, established through epidemiological studies, are causal. Furthermore, this would also provide strong evidence that CVD can be prevented through physical activity because

Table 4.1 Major risk factors for cardiovascular disease

MODIFIABLE RISK FACTORS	NON-MODIFIABLE RISK FACTORS
• Dyslipidaemia: elevated total cholesterol or low-density lipoprotein cholesterol concentrations, depressed high density lipoprotein cholesterol concentrations, elevated triglyceride concentrations • Hypertension • Cigarette smoking • Obesity (particularly central/abdominal obesity) • Hyperglycaemia or diabetes	• Family history: risk is increased in first degree relatives (parents, siblings and offspring) of people with premature atherosclerotic disease (men <55 years and women <65 years) • Age: higher risk in older individuals • Gender: higher risk in males than females • Ethnic background: higher risk in South Asians, although this may be due to the higher prevalence of diabetes in this group

Note: For further information on CVD risk factors and prediction models for CVD/CHD, the reader is referred to the JBS 2 (2005) guidelines and to Wilson *et al.* (1998).

Figure 4.11 Prevalence of several major CVD risk factors in men and women aged 16 and over in Great Britain/England.

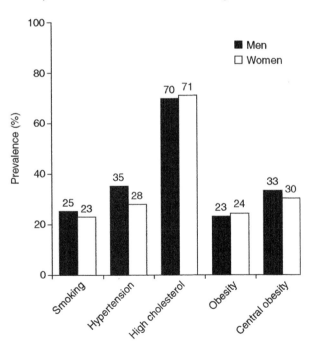

Source: British Heart Foundation (2007).
Notes: The data for smoking are for Great Britain. All remaining data are for England. Risk factor definitions: hypertension, systolic blood pressure ≥140 mm Hg and/or diastolic blood pressure ≥90 mm Hg; high cholesterol, total cholesterol ≥5 mmol l⁻¹; obesity, BMI ≥30 kg m²; central obesity, waist–hip ratio ≥0.95 for men and ≥0.85 for women.

studies have demonstrated that favourable changes in the major CVD risk factors reduce the subsequent risk of CVD.

Table 4.1 lists the major risk factors for CVD and Figure 4.11 displays the prevalence of some of these risk factors in Great Britain/England. Other, newer risk factors not listed in Table 4.1 include apolipoprotein B, small low-density lipoproteins, markers for inflammation (e.g. C-reactive protein, interleukin-6), chronic infections, thrombogenic (blood clotting) factors such as fibrinogen, homocysteine and coronary-artery calcium content. These are omitted from Table 4.1 because at present none of these factors add substantially to the prediction of CVD risk above that indicated by the 'classic' risk factors, and they do not have a clearly defined role in the clinical management of people (JBS 2 2005). Note also that physical inactivity and low physical fitness are not listed in Table 4.1. It could be argued that they should be since the evidence discussed previously indicates that low levels of physical activity and physical fitness are independently related to CVD risk. In view of this there is an argument for including activity and/or fitness assessments routinely in clinical practice. In the discussion which follows we will examine the evidence that physical activity favourably influences some of the major risk factors for CVD.

EXERCISE AND CVD RISK FACTORS

Lipids and lipoproteins

One of the major mechanisms by which physical activity may lead to a reduced risk of CVD is via an effect on lipid and lipoprotein metabolism. A detailed explanation of lipid and lipoprotein metabolism is beyond the scope of this book, and the interested reader is referred to the chapter on lipoprotein metabolism in Frayn (2003). The major lipoproteins are displayed in Figure 4.12. The main role of chylomicrons is to transport exogenous (dietary) triglyceride, whereas very low-density lipoproteins (VLDL) transport endogenous triglyceride (i.e. triglyceride which is synthesized within the liver). Together, chylomicrons and VLDL are sometimes referred to as triglyceride-rich lipoproteins since they are largely composed of triglyceride (Figure 4.12). Low-density lipoproteins (LDL) are the main carriers of cholesterol in the plasma. Elevated concentrations of all three of these lipoproteins (chylomicrons, VLDL and LDL) are atherogenic. In contrast, high concentrations of high-density lipoprotein (HDL) cholesterol protect from CVD because HDL assists in the removal of excess cholesterol from the body in a process termed 'reverse cholesterol transport'.

Many studies have demonstrated favourable effects of exercise on lipid and lipoprotein metabolism. The most consistent findings are of an increase in protective HDL cholesterol. Less consistently, reductions in total cholesterol, triglyceride, LDL and VLDL have been observed. One unique study examined HDL cholesterol in several groups of men with widely differing levels of physical activity, ranging from almost complete inactivity in those with recent spinal cord injuries to 80 miles per week of running in individuals training for the Boston marathon. The findings revealed a clear gradient in HDL-cholesterol, ranging from a mean of 0.7 mmol l^{-1} (27 mg dl^{-1}) for new spinal cord injured patients to 1.6 mmol l^{-1} (61 mg dl^{-1}) for the marathon runners

Figure 4.12 Composition of the four major lipoproteins.

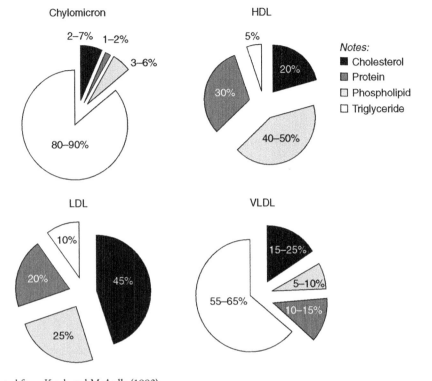

Source: Adapted from Katch and McArdle (1993).
Notes: VLDL, very-low density lipoprotein; LDL, low-density lipoprotein; HDL, high-density lipoprotein.

(Figure 4.13). Moreover, HDL cholesterol concentration was below the fifth percentile of the normal population in all of the new spinal cord injured patients (who were presumably the least active group). These findings were confirmed in a study of over 1,800 female runners which demonstrated a positive dose–response association between running mileage and HDL cholesterol concentration (Williams 1996).

More recently, well-designed randomized controlled intervention trials have shown that exercise training causes reductions in VLDL triglyceride and increases in HDL cholesterol. Relevant here is the Studies of a Targeted Risk Reduction Intervention Through Defined Exercise (STRRIDE) project (see papers by Krauss *et al.* (2002) and Slentz *et al.* (2007) and the associated editorials by Tall (2002) and Durstine and Lyerly (2007) for informative discussions on the effects of exercise on lipid and lipoprotein metabolism). In addition to demonstrating reductions in VLDL triglyceride and increases in HDL cholesterol with exercise training in previously sedentary, overweight men and women, these studies also found reductions in particularly atherogenic small LDL particles. The amount of exercise was found to be more important than the intensity of exercise for changing lipoprotein concentrations, and some of the changes were maintained during a 15-day period of detraining. Although the changes reported in the STRRIDE project occurred in the absence of major weight loss,

Figure 4.13 High-density lipoprotein (HDL) cholesterol concentrations (mmol l⁻¹) in seven groups of individuals characterized by widely different habitual physical activity levels.

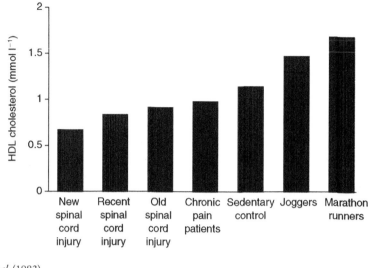

Source: LaPorte *et al.* (1983).
Note: SCI, spinal cord injury. Concentrations displayed are 50th percentile values for each group.

changes are likely to be greater if exercise reduces body mass and exercise-induced reductions in fat mass are as effective as dietary-induced reductions in modifying lipid and lipoprotein concentrations (Wood *et al.* 1988). It has been suggested that exercise is more likely to be beneficial in individuals with dyslipidaemia than in those with normal lipid/lipoprotein concentrations, but this is not always supported by the literature (Zmuda *et al.* 1998).

Aside from intervention trials, another source of indirect evidence suggesting that physical activity may be able to modify lipids and lipoproteins and hence atherosclerosis is provided from the study of the Fulani ethnic group of northern Nigeria. They are semi-nomadic people whose main occupation is cattle rearing. Their diet is very high in fat (close to 50% of total energy intake) and saturated fat (25% of total energy intake). However, their blood lipid profile is indicative of a low risk of CVD, and it has been speculated that this is due to a combination of their high physical activity level and their low total energy intake (Glew *et al.* 2001).

Do exercise-induced changes in lipoprotein metabolism result in a reduction in coronary atherosclerosis? This question is difficult to answer with certainty because few studies have addressed this issue. A study in monkeys, however, suggests that changes in lipids as a result of exercise training can reduce atherosclerosis. This study examined two groups of monkeys consuming atherogenic (atherosclerosis-inducing) diets over a two-year period. One group was maintained in a sedentary state throughout the study while the other group was trained to 'run' on a non-motorized treadmill wheel for one hour, three times per week. By the end of the study, total cholesterol was substantially elevated in both groups of monkeys and did not differ significantly between groups (mean values were approximately 15.5 mmol l⁻¹ in both groups, compared with normal values of around 2 mmol l⁻¹). However, HDL cholesterol was significantly higher and triglyceride significantly lower in the trained compared with the sedentary monkeys. Moreover, assessments of the degree of coronary artery narrowing revealed that this was much greater in the sedentary monkeys than in those who exercised (Figure 4.14). The authors concluded that 'the benefits derived from such moderate exercise for one hour three times per week in the presence of hypercholesterolaemia were less atherosclerosis in wider coronary arteries supplying a larger heart that functioned at a slower rate' (Kramsch *et al.* 1981: p. 1488).

Whether such findings apply to humans is not known with certainty. However, observational evidence suggesting that exercise ameliorates coronary atherosclerosis is available in the form of autopsy studies. An example is the case study of Clarence DeMar ('Mr Marathon') mentioned briefly in Chapter 2. DeMar was a prolific marathon runner who competed throughout his adult life. He died of cancer at the age of 70. The autopsy of his coronary arteries revealed that they were two or three times the normal diameter (Plate 3). Although there was some evidence of atherosclerosis in DeMar's arteries, no impairment of blood supply was apparent because of their large size. The question this study cannot answer is whether these large coronary arteries were the result of genetic inheritance, regular vigorous exercise or a combination of the two. The findings are consistent, however, with those of a more recent observational study indicating an association between high cardiorespiratory fitness levels and slower progression of carotid atherosclerosis in middle-aged men from Eastern Finland (Lakka *et al.* 2001).

Blood pressure

Hypertension is another major risk factor for CVD which is influenced by exercise. According to Messerli *et al.* the risk of becoming hypertensive (blood pressure

Figure 4.14 The percentage narrowing (reduction in cross-sectional area) in the coronary arteries of sedentary and physically active monkeys consuming an atherogenic diet.

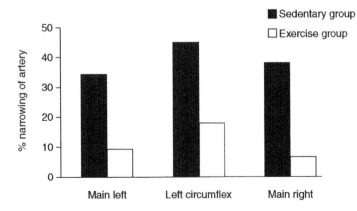

Source: Kramsch *et al.* (1981).
Note: Atherogenic diet consumed for two years. Active monkeys exercised for one hour, three times per week. Percentage narrowing was determined by histology postmortem.

Plate 3 Cross-section of the left and right coronary arteries of Clarence De Mar 'Mr Marathon'.

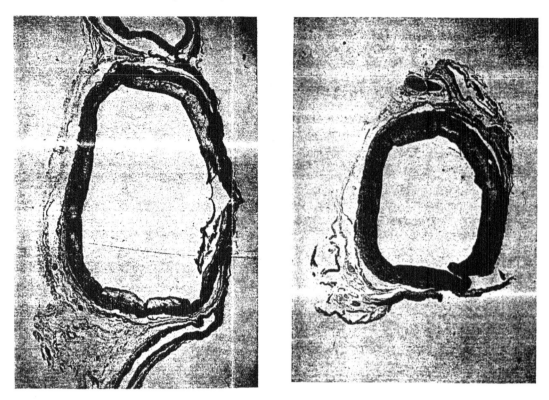

Source: Currens and White (1961).
Note: De Mar was a prolific marathon runner and following his death an autopsy of his heart revealed that his coronary arteries were 2–3 times the normal diameter. Note the large lumens and minimal atherosclerosis.

>140/90 mm Hg) during a lifetime exceeds 90% in industrialized countries (Messerli *et al.* 2007). The fact that the prevalence of hypertension increases so dramatically with age suggests that high blood pressure is an inevitable consequence of ageing. This is not the case, however, and there are reports from several groups around the world demonstrating that blood pressure does not always increase with age. One such group are the Kung Bushmen of Northern Botswana. This is an isolated group who live as hunter-gatherers all year round. In contrast to the situation in developed countries, systolic and diastolic blood pressures remain low throughout life in male and female Kung Bushmen (Figure 4.15). Several factors may explain the low blood pressure values of the Kung Bushmen, including a low salt intake, freedom from the stresses of civilization and the high levels of physical activity which are characteristic of a hunter-gatherer lifestyle.

A few cohort studies have addressed the question 'Are people who are physically active and fit less likely to develop hypertension than their inactive, unfit peers?' Among the Harvard alumni studied by Paffenbarger *et al.*, men who did not report

Figure 4.15 Systolic blood pressures for Kung Bushmen and women of Northern Botswana and men and women living in England.

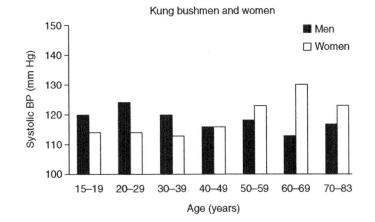

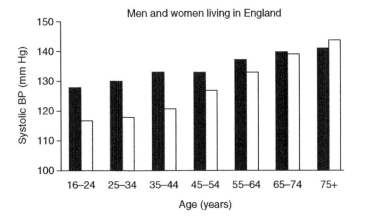

Source: Data for the Kung tribe are from Truswell *et al.* (1972). Data for Englishmen and women are for the year 2005, courtesy of the British Heart Foundation Statistics Database (2007).

engaging in vigorous sports were 35% more likely to develop hypertension during the 6–10 year follow-up than those who did (Paffenbarger *et al.* 1983). Among men and women in the Aerobics Center Longitudinal Study, individuals with low fitness (least-fit quintile) were 52% more likely than those with high fitness (most-fit quintile) to develop hypertension (Blair *et al.* 1984). Intervention studies have confirmed the blood pressure lowering effect of exercise. A meta-analysis of 54 randomized control-led trials whose intervention and control groups differed only in aerobic exercise, reported average reductions in systolic and diastolic blood pressure of 3.84 and 2.58 mm Hg respectively. Reductions were noted in hypertensive and normotensive participants and in overweight as well normal weight participants (Whelton *et al.* 2002). There is some evidence that the blood pressure lowering effect of exercise is greatest in hypertensive individuals for whom average reductions of 5–7 mm Hg may be expected (Cornelissen and Fagard 2005; Pescatello *et al.* 2004). It is important to note, however, that there are exceptions, and some studies report no benefit of exercise training for those with elevated blood pressure (e.g. Church *et al.* 2007).

Exercise has both acute and chronic effects on blood pressure, and it is now well documented that a single session of aerobic exercise causes a transient lowering of blood pressure (MacDonald 2002). This has been termed post-exercise hypotension and the effect has been shown to last for up to 22 hours in elderly hypertensive patients (Rondon *et al.* 2002). It is important to note that these responses are typical of endurance exercise. During resistance exercise, blood pressure increases sharply, mainly because the high tension generated in muscle temporarily occludes the blood vessels in muscle, increasing resistance. This is one main reason why sedentary people should increase their activity through endurance exercise before attempting sports or exercises which involve resistance work. Several mechanisms have been proposed to explain the blood pressure lowering effect of exercise, and these include reductions in total peripheral resistance due to reduced sympathetic nerve activity and increased responsiveness to vasodilators such as nitric oxide. Exercise may also invoke structural changes to arteries and veins, leading to increases in cross-sectional area and hence less resistance to blood flow. There may also be a resetting of blood pressure to a lower level via the baroreceptor reflex after exercise (Pescatello *et al.* 2004).

Endothelial function

Thus far in this section we have described evidence that exercise may assist in preventing or ameliorating dyslipidaemia and hypertension, two major risk factors for CVD. Exercise may also prevent/ameliorate CHD by exerting direct effects on myocardial perfusion, hence improving oxygen delivery. One way this may occur is through the formation of coronary collaterals, that is, accessory vessels to the main coronary vasculature that provide an increased flow of blood to the myocardial tissue. Another explanation for enhanced myocardial perfusion with exercise – one for which there is convincing evidence – is via an effect on endothelial function (Gill and Malkova 2006; Vita and Keaney 2000).

Endothelial function refers to the ability of the endothelium (the thin layer of cells lining blood vessels) to interact with vascular smooth muscle to influence blood flow. Endothelial cells exert their effects by secreting various agents that diffuse to the adjacent vascular smooth muscle and induce either vasodilation or vasoconstriction. One important vasodilator released by endothelial cells is nitric oxide. This is released continuously in the basal state, but its secretion can be rapidly increased in response to chemical stimulants such as those released during exercise. Nitric oxide secretion is also elevated in response to increases in shear stress – that is, the force exerted on the endothelium by blood flow. This would result in flow-induced arterial vasodilation and is another important mechanism for increasing blood flow when required.

Endothelial dysfunction (inability to facilitate vasodilation and therefore increase blood flow) is thought to occur in the early stages of atherosclerosis and is a trigger of

Figure 4.16 Percentage change in coronary artery luminal diameter in response to infusion of acetylcholine (7.2 µg min⁻¹).

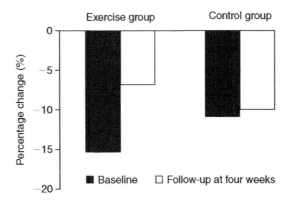

Source: Hambrecht *et al.* (2000).
Notes: Subjects were 19 patients with endothelial dysfunction as indicated by abnormal acetylcholine-induced vasoconstriction. Ten patients were assigned to exercise training, nine acted as controls. Exercise involved six, ten-minute cycling bouts daily over a period of four weeks. The exercise intensity was 80% of peak heart rate. Note that exercise training partially corrects the abnormal vasoconstriction induced by acetylcholine.

myocardial ischemia (Gielen *et al.* 2001). Cross-sectional studies have demonstrated that the coronary arteries of endurance-trained athletes have a significantly greater dilating capacity than those of inactive men (Haskell *et al.* 1993). Moreover, exercise training improves endothelium-dependent vasodilation in the coronary vessels of patients with coronary artery disease (Figure 4.16). The mechanisms responsible for exercise-induced improvements in endothelial function include an increase in the activity of nitric oxide synthase, the enzyme responsible for nitric oxide production, and an increased production of extracellular superoxide dismutase, an enzyme which prevents the premature breakdown of nitric oxide. Such effects allow for an appropriate distribution of blood to cardiac muscle at all times and represent a direct means by which exercise may aid in the prevention of CVD.

In addition to the mechanisms described in this section, there are other ways in which exercise assists in preventing CVD. Some of these are described in the chapters which follow. Physical activity has a role in the prevention and management of diabetes and obesity as discussed in Chapters 5 and 6. In addition, there is evidence indicating that exercise reduces the risk of thrombosis (Imhof and Koenig 2001) and chronic low-grade systemic inflammation (Petersen and Pedersen 2005; Smith 2001). Collectively, this evidence provides strong support for a causal relationship between physical inactivity and CVD, and hence the role of exercise in preventing CVD.

COMBINED HEALTHY LIFESTYLE BEHAVIOURS

Thus far we have been describing the evidence concerning the role of physical activity alone in preventing CVD. Some studies have investigated the association between combined healthy lifestyle behaviours and the risk of CVD. One example is the

Healthy Ageing: A Longitudinal Study in Europe (HALE) project which was discussed in the previous chapter. The main outcome of interest in this study was all-cause mortality, but the study also identified relative risks of 0.27 and 0.33 for CHD and CVD, respectively, in participants who adhered to four healthy lifestyle behaviours compared with participants who reported either none or only one of these behaviours. The healthy lifestyle behaviours examined in this study were Mediterranean diet, physical activity, non-smoking and moderate alcohol consumption (Knoops *et al.* 2004).

Another study investigating the association between CHD and lifestyle is the Nurses' Health Study. One finding from this study was that nurses who reported five low-risk factors (healthy diet, non-smoking, regular exercise, BMI <25 kg m² and moderate alcohol consumption ≥5 g day⁻¹) had an 83% lower risk of CHD (relative risk 0.17) over 14 years of follow-up compared with all other women. The population attributable risk for nurses in this group was 82%, suggesting that 82% of coronary events among nurses in the study could have been prevented if all women had been in the low-risk group (Figure 4.17). Thus, although the focus of this book is on physical activity, it is important to emphasize that a combination of healthy lifestyle behaviours is necessary for optimal protection from CVD/CHD.

EXERCISE AS THERAPY

This chapter has surveyed the evidence indicating that physical activity provides protection from CVD. It should be noted that activity and fitness are important for those who are afflicted with CVD also. The early work of Jeremy Morris *et al.* demonstrated that heart attacks were less likely to be fatal in conductors compared with drivers, suggesting that the chances of surviving a heart attack are greater in those who are active and fit (Morris *et al.* 1953). This proposition is supported by work in rats showing

Figure 4.17 Relative risk of CHD and the population attributable risk (PAR) according to lifestyle factors in 84,129 women participating in the Nurses' Health Study.

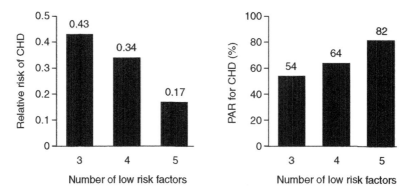

Source: Stampfer *et al.* (2000).

Note: Lifestyle factors included were: three low-risk factors, healthy diet, non-smoking and exercise (≥30 min day⁻¹); four low-risk factors, healthy diet, non-smoking, exercise (≥30 min day⁻¹) and a BMI <25 kg m²; five low-risk factors, healthy diet, non-smoking, exercise (≥30 min day⁻¹), BMI <25 kg m² and moderate alcohol consumption (≥5 g day⁻¹).

that endurance training results in improved myocardial performance during ischemia (achieved by ligation of coronary arteries) and reperfusion (Powers *et al.* 1998; Powers *et al.* 2007). In contrast to the observational evidence from epidemiological studies concerning exercise and CVD prevention, there is good evidence from randomized controlled trials confirming the effectiveness of exercise as a therapy for those who have clinical symptoms of CVD and for those who have survived a heart attack.

One area where exercise has been used extensively as a therapy is cardiac rehabilitation. Evidence for the effectiveness of exercise in this regard is provided by a meta-analysis of 48 randomized controlled trials involving 8,940 patients with CHD. The findings of this analysis revealed a 20% reduction in all-cause mortality risk and a 26% reduction in cardiac mortality in patients assigned to exercise rehabilitation compared with usual care (Taylor *et al.* 2004). These findings confirm those of previous meta-analyses and substantiate the findings of the National Exercise and Heart Disease Project (NEHDP), which observed that every 1 MET increase in work capacity was associated with an 8–14% reduction in the risk of all-cause mortality during follow-up (Dorn *et al.* 1999).

Exercise has been shown to be more effective than some surgical techniques for treating CVD. One example is a study involving 101 male patients with stable coronary artery disease who were randomly assigned to 12 months of exercise training (20 minutes of cycling each day) or to percutaneous (through the skin) coronary stenting (which involves inserting a plastic or metal mesh into an artery to reopen it or keep it open). Maximum oxygen uptake increased by 16% in the exercise training group (from $22.7 \, \text{ml} \, \text{kg}^{-1} \, \text{min}^{-1}$ at baseline to $26.2 \, \text{ml} \, \text{kg}^{-1} \, \text{min}^{-1}$ at 12 months) while remaining unchanged in those who underwent surgery ($22.3 \, \text{ml} \, \text{kg}^{-1} \, \text{min}^{-1}$ at baseline versus $22.8 \, \text{ml} \, \text{kg}^{-1} \, \text{min}^{-1}$ at 12 months). Exercise training was associated with a higher event-free survival than surgery (88% versus 70% respectively) and was cheaper. The estimated costs of delivering the exercise programme were US$3,708 per patient per year compared with US$6,086 for percutaneous coronary intervention. Notable here are the reduced costs due to rehospitalization and repeat surgery in the exercise group compared with the group who underwent surgery (Hambrecht *et al.* 2004).

The mechanisms by which exercise improves outcomes for patients with CVD are uncertain, but are thought to involve improvements in myocardial perfusion. These may result from improved endothelial function, as discussed earlier, as well as the growth of coronary collaterals within the heart (Gielen *et al.* 2001). It is also possible that exercise training may lead to reversal (regression) of coronary atherosclerosis. There is limited evidence to support this suggestion, but intervention trials involving multiple lifestyle factors (diet, exercise, stress management and smoking cessation) have shown that regression of coronary atherosclerosis is possible (Ornish *et al.* 1998).

Other areas where exercise has been proven to be effective are claudication, heart failure and hypertension. Claudication is defined as walking-induced pain in one or both legs (primarily affecting the calves) that does not go away with continued walking and is only relieved by rest (Stewart *et al.* 2002). Claudication is the primary symptom of peripheral arterial disease and seriously restricts the activity or afflicted persons. Exercise training may ameliorate the severity of claudication and increase maximal walking time by a variety of mechanisms, including improved endothelial function, vascular angiogenesis (growth of new capillaries), enhanced muscle metabolic capacity and improved walking economy. In contrast to the situation for claudication, exercise training is not widely used as a therapy for chronic heart failure, possibly because there is limited data to support its effectiveness. However, exercise can reduce the debilitating symptoms (breathlessness and fatigue) of chronic heart failure and a recent meta-analysis concluded that mortality and admission to hospital are significantly reduced after exercise training in chronic heart failure patients (ExTraMATCH Collaborative 2004).

The effects of exercise on blood pressure in normotensive and hypertensive individuals were described earlier. Exercise is a key non-pharmalogical therapy for hypertension, along with salt and alcohol restriction. Whether exercise can reduce hypertensive blood pressure values to normotensive values depends on the severity of hypertension and the amount of exercise performed. For those with mild hypertension, exercise may be sufficient to reduce blood pressure below hypertensive cut-off points, although not necessarily to normal or optimal levels (Figure 4.18, Table 4.2). The exercise prescription for the treatment of hypertension is for cardiovascular exercise to be performed 3–5 days per week at an intensity of 40–70% of $\dot{V}O_2$max. Comprehensive information concerning the role of exercise in treating hypertension is available in the American College of Sports Medicine Position Stand on exercise and hypertension (Pescatello *et al.* 2004) and in the review by Wallace (2003).

Figure 4.18 Resting arterial blood pressure values in 13 untreated patients with essential hypertension. All subjects completed three, four week trials in a random order: (1) normal sedentary activity; (2) three exercise sessions per week; (3) seven exercise sessions per week.

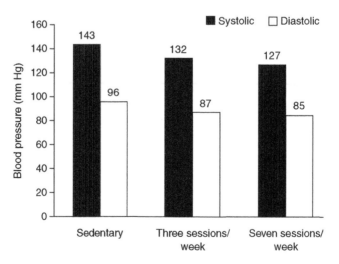

Source: Nelson *et al.* (1986).
Notes: Essential hypertension is that for which the cause is unknown. The exercise involved cycling on an electrically braked ergometer for 45 minutes per day at an intensity of 60–70% of $\dot{V}O_2$max.

Table 4.2 Blood pressure classification for adults aged 18 and older

BLOOD PRESSURE CATEGORY	SYSTOLIC BLOOD PRESSURE (mm Hg)		DIASTOLIC BLOOD PRESSURE (mm Hg)
Optimal	<120	and	<80
Normal	120–129	and	80–84
High normal	130–139	or	85–89
Stage 1 hypertension	140–159	or	90–99
Stage 2 hypertension	160–179	or	100–109
Stage 3 hypertension	≥180	or	≥110

Source: Joint National Committee on Detection, Evaluation and Treatment of High Blood Pressure (1997).

SUMMARY

- CVDs are a major cause of mortality and morbidity in developed countries and their prevalence is increasing in developing countries.
- Atherosclerosis is the major cause of CVD. It has a long clinical history and may be well progressed before symptoms occur.
- Evidence that inactivity and low fitness are strong risk factors for CHD is compelling. Both confer an increase in risk similar to that associated with smoking, hypertension and high blood cholesterol.
- Evidence that being physically active or fit reduces the risk of having a stroke is suggestive, but not as compelling as that for CHD. However, as some aetiological factors are common to these different types of CVD, benefits from activity and/or fitness are biologically plausible.
- There are many mechanisms by which physical activity may modify CVD risk, including beneficial effects on lipoprotein metabolism, blood pressure and endothelial function.
- There is strong evidence supporting the effectiveness of physical activity as a central component of cardiac rehabilitation programmes. Exercise training may be particularly effective in this regard because it enhances myocardial perfusion and hence oxygen delivery to the heart.
- Exercise is beneficial for reducing the symptoms of claudication and heart failure and may help to lower blood pressure in hypertensive individuals.

STUDY TASKS

1 Using the data in Table 4.3, calculate the relative risk of death from CHD associated with fitness. Express this first with the low fitness group as the reference category and then with the high fitness group as the reference category. As well as working out the figures, put each relative risk into words as if you were explaining the findings to someone else. In addition, explain: (a) why it is necessary to use

	NUMBER OF SUBJECTS	PERSON-YEARS OF FOLLOW-UP	NUMBER OF DEATHS	DEATH RATE PER 10,000 PERSON-YEARS*
Low fitness	5,130	46,098	112	20.70
High fitness	5,075	45,650	44	8.25

Table 4.3 Deaths from CHD over an average follow-up period of ten years

Note: *Adjusted for age.

person-years as the units for the death rate; (b) why the death rates were adjusted for age; and (c) why the person-years of follow-up are not simply ten times the numbers of subjects in each fitness group.

2 In the example given in Box 4.2 the women in the top quintile for walking in the US Nurses' Health Study completed an average of 20 MET-h of walking each week. It was estimated that this meant about 5.7 h of walking at a 'normal' pace (assumed to be 4.8 km h^{-1} or 3 mile h^{-1}). Estimate the gross weekly energy expenditure of these nurses in walking, assuming an average body mass of 60 kg.

3 In what ways could the design of epidemiological studies be improved to provide stronger evidence that physical inactivity and low fitness are causal factors for CHD? Discuss the problems that would have to be faced in seeking this information.

4 Differences in lipids and lipoproteins between exercise and control groups at the end of intervention studies are often smaller than the differences observed between trained and untrained groups in cross-sectional studies. Give three possible explanations for this.

5 Explain the term myocardial perfusion and explain three mechanisms by which exercise training may enhance this. Which of these mechanisms is most strongly supported by evidence?

6 Describe the advantages of exercise training compared with percutaneous coronary stenting for the treatment of stable coronary artery disease as indicated in the study of Hambrecht *et al.* (2004).

7 In what way is the evidence supporting the role of exercise in treating CHD stronger than the evidence indicating that regular physical activity prevents CHD?

FURTHER READING

Berlin, J.A. and Colditz, G.H. (1990) 'A meta-analysis of physical activity in the prevention of coronary heart disease', *American Journal of Epidemiology* 132: 612–28.

Booth, F.W., Chakravarthy, M.V., Gordon, S.E. and Spangenburg, E.E. (2002) 'Waging war on physical inactivity: using modern molecular ammunition against an ancient enemy', *Journal of Applied Physiology* 93: 3–30.

Gielen, S., Schuler, G. and Hambrecht, R. (2001) 'Exercise training in coronary artery disease and coronary vasomotion', *Circulation* 103: E1–6.

Pescatello, L.S., Franklin, B.A., Fagard, R., Farquhar, W.B., Kelley, G.A. and Ray, C.A. (2004)

'Exercise and hypertension: American College of Sports Medicine Position Stand', *Medicine and Science in Sports and Exercise* 36: 533–53.

Powers, S.K., Murlasits, Z., Wu, M. and Kavazis, A.N. (2007) 'Ischemia-reperfusion-induced cardiac injury: a brief review', *Medicine and Science in Sports and Exercise* 39: 1529–36.

Roberts, C.K. and Barnard, R.J. (2005) 'Effects of exercise and diet on chronic disease', *Journal of Applied Physiology* 98: 3–30.

Stewart, K.J., Hiatt, W.R., Regensteiner, J.G. and Hirsch, A.T. (2002) 'Exercise training for claudication', *New England Journal of Medicine* 347: 1941–51.

Wannamethee, G.S. and Shaper, A.G. (2001) 'Physical activity in the prevention of cardiovascular disease: an epidemiological perspective', *Sports Medicine* 31: 101–14.

5 Type 2 diabetes

Knowledge assumed
Basic human physiology and biochemistry
Basic cell physiology

INTRODUCTION

Diabetes mellitus is a disease characterized by chronic hyperglycaemia (high blood glucose concentration), as well as elevated non-esterified fatty acid (NEFA) concentrations. Over time high blood glucose and NEFA concentrations may lead to a variety of complications which impair quality of life and reduce life expectancy. On average, people with diabetes mellitus die 5–10 years before people without diabetes mellitus. The main cause of premature mortality with diabetes mellitus is cardiovascular disease (CVD) which accounts for 50% of all diabetes fatalities, and much disability. It is estimated that the lifetime risk of developing diabetes mellitus is 32.8% and 38.5% respectively in US males and females born in the year 2000 (Narayan *et al.* 2003).

There are two main forms of diabetes mellitus (henceforth simply called diabetes): type 1 diabetes and type 2 diabetes. Type 1 diabetes (referred to as insulin-dependent diabetes mellitus (IDDM) in older literature) is caused by an autoimmune destruction of the pancreatic beta cells (in the islets of Langerhans). As a result, the pancreas is unable to produce insulin and this hormone must be injected regularly to control blood glucose concentrations (insulin cannot be given orally because gastrointestinal enzymes would digest it). Type 1 diabetes usually occurs before adulthood, and for this reason is sometimes referred to as juvenile-onset diabetes. In contrast to type 1 diabetes, the defining feature of type 2 diabetes (referred to as non-insulin-dependent diabetes mellitus (NIDDM) in older literature) is unresponsiveness (insensitivity) to the effects of insulin, commonly referred to as insulin resistance. In addition to insulin resistance, the capacity of the pancreas to secrete insulin is impaired in those with type 2 diabetes, although some secretion is maintained. Type 2 diabetes usually occurs in overweight and obese adults aged 40 and over and is sometimes termed maturity-onset diabetes. However, this term is imprecise since type 2 diabetes can occur in children. Type 2 diabetes is the most common form of diabetes, accounting for 85–95% of all diabetes cases in developed countries (International Diabetes Federation 2007).

It is difficult to predict who will get type 2 diabetes. Genes are known to play a role. Studies of monozygotic (identical) and dizygotic (non-identical) twin pairs demonstrate higher concordance rates for type 2 diabetes in monozygotic twins (who share a common set of genes). Moreover, offspring whose parents are diabetic are more likely

Plate 4 Photographs of a young girl suffering from type 1 diabetes before and after treatment with insulin.

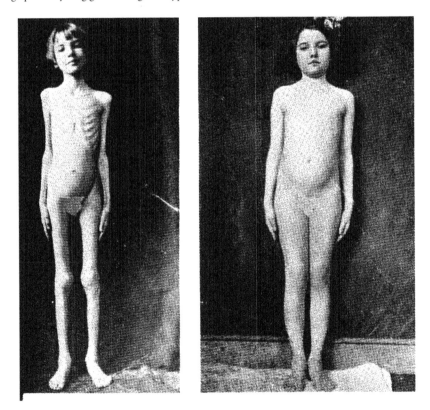

Source: Bliss (2007).
Note: This picture was taken in 1922 in the early years of insulin therapy.

to develop glucose intolerance and diabetes than offspring of non-diabetic parents. Although such findings are informative, progress in identifying the genetic variants that predispose individuals to type 2 diabetes has been slow and much remains to be learned in this regard (O'Rahilly *et al.* 2005). Furthermore, although genes may determine susceptibility to diabetes, the International Diabetes Federation (2007) estimates that up to 80% of type 2 diabetes is preventable by adopting a healthy diet and increasing physical activity.

AETIOLOGY

Although there are defects in insulin secretion in type 2 diabetes, the distinguishing feature from type 1 diabetes, as mentioned above, is insulin resistance. This means that for a given concentration of insulin, less glucose is cleared from the blood into the cells. One indication of insulin resistance is fasting hyperinsulinaemia (high blood insulin concentration) in the presence of either normal or elevated blood glucose concentrations. The most accurate (gold standard) method for determining the blood glucose response to insulin, however, is the euglycaemic clamp technique. This involves intravenous (via a vein) infusion of insulin to produce the same plasma insulin concentration in all individuals. Simultaneously, glucose is infused intravenously to obtain euglycaemia (equal blood glucose concentration). The greater the quantity of glucose required to produce euglycaemia, the more insulin sensitive (less insulin resistant) the individual.

What are the consequences of insulin resistance? As the cells become insulin insensitive their response to insulin is compromised. In the liver, glucose production continues when it should be suppressed, that is, following meals. This is due to glycogenolysis, the breakdown of glycogen to glucose, and gluconeogenesis, whereby non-carbohydrate precursors such as glycerol and amino acids are used to synthesize glucose. Although glycogenolysis and gluconeogenesis are a necessary response to fasting, they are inappropriate following meals when exogenous glucose is available. In addition to this inappropriate hepatic glucose production, glucose uptake by muscle and fat (adipocyte) cells is impaired with insulin resistance. The result is an elevation in blood glucose concentration due to both increased production and reduced removal of glucose. In the early stages of the disease an increase in blood glucose concentration due to insulin resistance is opposed by an increase in insulin secretion. This may maintain blood glucose concentration at normal levels. Over time, however, insulin resistance increases further and eventually the pancreas cannot maintain hyperinsulinaemia. Insulin secretion falls (this may be due in part to apoptosis (programmed cell death) of β cells – see Rhodes (2005) for an insightful review) and although some insulin is still present, blood glucose concentrations rise further, perhaps to $20\,mmol\,l^{-1}$ or more. Hence, there are several stages in the development of type 2 diabetes, beginning with insulin resistance and progressing to impaired glucose tolerance and then diabetes (Box 5.1).

In addition to elevated blood glucose concentrations, individuals with type 2 diabetes exhibit raised NEFA concentrations. This is also a result of insulin resistance. Since

BOX 5.1 DIAGNOSIS OF DIABETES MELLITUS

Diabetes mellitus is defined by hyperglycaemia. It may be diagnosed from either a fasting plasma glucose measurement or via an oral glucose tolerance test. The latter requires consumption of a 75 g glucose load after which blood glucose concentrations are monitored for two hours. Intermediate stages between normal and diabetic have also been established by groups such as the American Diabetes Association and the World Health Organization (WHO).

	VENOUS PLASMA GLUCOSE, MMOL L^{-1} (MG DL^{-1})	
	FASTING	120 MINUTES AFTER GLUCOSE LOAD
Normal	<6.1 (110)	<7.8 (140)
Impaired fasting glucose	≥6.1 (110) to <7.0 (126)	–
Impaired glucose tolerance	–	≥7.8 (140) to <11.1 (200)
Diabetes mellitus	≥7.0 (126)	≥11.1 (200)

Source: Expert Committee on the Diagnosis and Classification of Diabetes Mellitus (1999).

Note: In the absence of symptoms, diagnosis must be confirmed by a repeat test on a separate day.

the adipocytes have become insulin insensitive they are immune to the antilipolytic (resisting the breakdown of fat) effects of insulin. Thus, triglycerides within the adipocytes are catabolized, leading to the release of NEFAs and glycerol into the circulation. Elevated NEFA release, resulting in increased plasma NEFA concentrations, is desirable in some circumstances (e.g. during exercise or prolonged fasting). However, diabetic patients often have raised NEFA concentrations at inappropriate times (e.g. after a meal). These elevated NEFAs compromise the tissues' ability to clear glucose, thereby exacerbating insulin resistance. Some of these NEFAs are oxidized in the liver, resulting in the production of ketone bodies (ketogenesis). This can lead to a dangerous situation known as ketoacidosis, whereby an excess of ketone bodies leads to an increase in the acidity (reduction in pH) of the blood. This condition is rare in those with type 2 diabetes, however, and is one of the features that distinguish clinically between type 1 and type 2 diabetes.

Aside from the adverse effects of insulin resistance on the liver, muscle and adipose tissue, recent evidence also suggests that insulin resistance may disrupt appetite regulation within the brain (see Schwartz and Porte 2005 for an informative review). A possible mechanism involves the appetite-stimulating neurones neuropeptide Y (NPY) and Agouti-related peptide (AgRP) and the appetite-suppressing proopiomelanocortin (POMC) neurones located in the arcuate nucleus within the hypothalamus. Insulin inhibits the (appetite stimulating) NPY/AgRP neurones and stimulates the (appetite suppressing) POMC neurones, reducing appetite and promoting weight loss. Insulin resistance has the opposite effect, increasing food intake and predisposing to obesity. Obesity exacerbates insulin resistance as described below (see the section on obesity as a risk factor). In addition, NPY/AgRP neurones and POMC neurones may be linked to the liver via second order neurones, and it has been proposed that NPY/AgRP stimulation of the liver leads to increased glucose output while POMC stimulation has the opposite effect. Thus, if there is insensitivity to insulin or if insulin secretion is deficient, then inhibition of NPY/AgRP neurones may be reduced and hepatic glucose output increased (Schwartz and Porte 2005). Table 5.1 summarizes the mechanisms by which insulin resistance leads to elevated blood glucose and NEFA concentrations. Additional consequences of insulin resistance are discussed in Chapter 7.

Diabetes is associated with a variety of complications (Table 5.2). These include atherosclerosis in small (microvascular) and large (macrovascular) blood vessels, kidney problems (nephropathy), nerve problems (neuropathy), eye problems (retinopathy and cataract) and hypertension. The risk of these occurring is related to the extent and

Table 5.1 Responses to insulin in normal situations and the influence of insulin resistance on these responses

	NORMAL RESPONSE TO INSULIN	INSULIN RESISTANCE
Liver	Glucose uptake Glycogen synthesis Suppressed glycogenolysis and gluconeogenesis	Glucose release due to the lack of suppression of glycogenolysis and gluconeogenesis Triglyceride and ketone synthesis and release due to high NEFA concentrations
Muscle	Glucose uptake Glucose oxidation Glycogen synthesis	Impaired glucose uptake, oxidation and storage
Adipocytes	Glucose uptake and utilization Triglyceride synthesis Suppression of NEFA release	Impaired glucose uptake and utilization Inappropriate triglyceride catabolism due to lack of suppression via insulin Release of glycerol and NEFAs
Brain	• Appetite suppression • Possible suppression of hepatic glucose output	• Increased appetite • Possible increase in hepatic glucose output
Outcome	• Normal blood glucose and NEFA concentrations	• Elevated blood glucose and NEFA concentrations

Table 5.2 Major complications of diabetes

SITE	COMPLICATION
Brain and cerebral circulation	Cerebrovascular disease
Eyes	Retinopathy
Heart and coronary circulation	Coronary heart disease
Kidney	Nephropathy
Lower limbs	Peripheral vascular disease
Peripheral nervous system	Neuropathy
Diabetic foot	Ulceration and amputation

Source: Adapted from the International Diabetes Federation (2007).

duration of hyperglycaemia. A variety of biochemical mechanisms have been proposed to explain the adverse consequences of hyperglycaemia. These include non-enzymatic glycation (whereby glucose molecules combine with proteins, negatively affecting their function) and impaired endothelial function due to protein kinase C activation by diacylglycerol (see Frayn 2003 for further information). Good control of blood glucose concentrations lowers the risk of these complications occurring although hyperinsulinaemia, and elevated NEFA concentrations may also trigger some of the adverse consequences associated with diabetes e.g. atherosclerosis.

PREVALENCE

Diabetes is one of the most common non-communicable diseases internationally. According to the International Diabetes Federation (2007), diabetes currently affects 246 million people world-wide and is predicted to affect 380 million by 2025. In 2007 the five countries with the largest numbers of people with diabetes were India (40.9 million), China (39.8 million), the United States (19.2 million), Russia (9.6 million) and Germany (7.4 million), while the five countries with the highest diabetes prevalence amongst adults in 2007 were Nauru (30.7%), the United Arab Emirates (19.5%), Saudi Arabia (16.7%), Bahrain (15.2%) and Kuwait (14.4%). Diabetes prevalence tends to be higher in developed than developing countries, but the largest increases in diabetes prevalence are predicted to occur in developing countries. Each year approximately seven million people develop diabetes and 3.8 million deaths (6% of total global mortality) are attributable to diabetes (International Diabetes Federation 2007).

Approximately 4% of men and 3% of women in the United Kingdom currently have diagnosed diabetes. This equates to just over 1.9 million adults with diagnosed diabetes. However, estimates suggest that a further 600,000 adults have undiagnosed diabetes in the United Kingdom, giving a total of around 2.5 million adults in the United Kingdom with diabetes. Diabetes prevalence increases with age, and 10% of adults aged 75 and over in the United Kingdom have diabetes. Moreover, the prevalence of diabetes appears to be increasing. Since 1991 the prevalence of diagnosed diabetes has more than doubled for men and increased by 80% for women in the United Kingdom (British Heart Foundation 2007). Diabetes prevalence in the United Kingdom is low compared with an average prevalence of 8% in Europe (British Heart Foundation 2008) and America (Mokdad *et al.* 2003).

Although type 2 diabetes was previously considered an adult-onset disease, it is now clear that it also occurs in children and adolescents as evidenced by a growing number of reports from many countries world-wide. A review by Pinhas-Hamiel and Zeitler (2005) observed a close relation between prevalence rates of type 2 diabetes in adults and the eventual appearance of the disorder in adolescents. Thus, some of the first reports of type 2 diabetes in children and adolescents came from countries with the highest rates of adult type 2 diabetes in the world e.g. countries in the Asia-Pacific region. Another observation regarding type 2 diabetes in children and adolescents is that in many of the regions affected there has also been an increase in childhood obesity prevalence, suggesting that there is a link between obesity and type 2 diabetes in children, as is the case for adults.

▊ OBESITY AS A RISK FACTOR

Obesity, particularly abdominal obesity, appears to be the most important modifiable risk factor for type 2 diabetes. According to Rhodes (2005: p. 381), about one-third of obese individuals eventually develop type 2 diabetes. Many epidemiological studies have demonstrated an association between obesity and type 2 diabetes. Examples include the Göteborg Study in Sweden (Ohlson *et al.* 1985), the Nurses' Health Study in the US (Colditz *et al.* 1990), the US Health Professionals Follow-Up Study (Wang *et al.* 2005) and the MONICA (Monitoring Trends and Determinants on Cardiovascular Diseases) Study in Augsburg, Germany (Meisinger *et al.* 2006). In the Nurses' Health Study the elevated diabetes risk over an eight-year period ranged from 5.5 in slightly overweight women (body mass index, or BMI, ≥25–26.9 kg m²) to 60.9 in morbidly obese women (BMI ≥35 kg m²) compared with women whose BMI was <22 kg m². More recently, the Health Professionals Follow-Up Study reported that both overall obesity (assessed using the BMI) and abdominal obesity (assessed using waist circumference and waist–hip ratio) strongly and independently predict the risk of type 2 diabetes in men (Figure 5.1).

The association between obesity and type 2 diabetes is also supported by the twin trends in many countries for concurrent increases in obesity and diabetes prevalence in recent years. This is particularly apparent in the United States, where increases in

Figure 5.1 Age-adjusted relative risk of developing type 2 diabetes in the Health Professionals Follow-Up Study according to baseline waist–hip ratio, BMI and waist circumference.

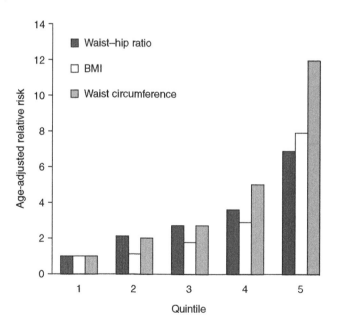

Source: Wang *et al.* (2005).
Note: Participants were 27,270 men (dentists, optometrists, pharmacists, podiatrists, osteopaths and veterinarians) followed up for 13 years. Risks were attenuated but remained significant after multivariate analysis.

obesity and diabetes prevalence have been noted for both sexes, all ages, all races, all educational levels and all smoking levels (Mokdad *et al.* 2003; Figure 5.2). If the association between obesity and type 2 diabetes represents a causal link, then weight loss in overweight and obese people should reduce the risk of type 2 diabetes. Evidence to support this proposal is available from the first Cancer Prevention Study, a 13-year prospective study of more than one million participants conducted by the American Cancer Society. One publication (Will *et al.* 2002) from this study examined the risk of developing type 2 diabetes during the 13-year follow-up in men and women who had been overweight prior to baseline (BMI ≥25 kg m^2) and who had intentionally lost weight prior to baseline (intentional weight loss was differentiated from unintentional weight loss because unintentional weight loss can be a sign of underlying disease, e.g. diabetes or cancer). The findings revealed an inverse dose–response association between weight loss and risk of developing diabetes in those who had lost weight intentionally compared with those who had not lost weight (Figure 5.3). For every 9 kg of weight lost there was an 11% lower risk for diabetes in men and a 17% lower risk for diabetes in women.

A whole variety of mechanisms have been proposed to explain how obesity might cause type 2 diabetes (for reviews see Lazar (2005) and Kahn *et al.* (2006); Rosen and Spiegelman (2006) also provide useful insights). Obesity, insulin resistance and eleva-

Figure 5.2 Prevalence of obesity (BMI ≥30 kg m^2) and diagnosed diabetes among US adults, 1991 and 2001.

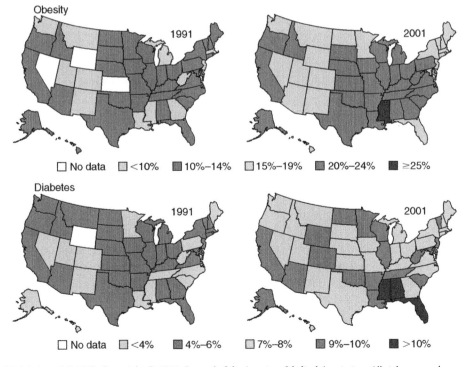

Figure 5.3 Relative risk of diabetes during 13 years of follow-up in overweight men and women who intentionally lost weight.

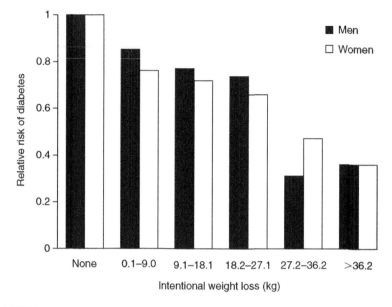

Source: Will *et al.* (2002).

Notes: Findings are from the Cancer Prevention Study and are adjusted for confounding variables. The referent categories are overweight men and women who had not lost weight. For every 9 kg of weight lost there was an 11% lower risk for diabetes in men and a 17% lower risk for diabetes in women.

tions in glucose and NEFA concentrations are all closely related. Elevations in glucose and NEFAs have a variety of metabolic effects, collectively referred to as glucotoxicity and lipotoxicity, respectively. The release of NEFAs may be the most important factor for inducing insulin resistance. Circulating NEFAs reduce adipocyte and muscle glucose uptake and promote hepatic glucose output. Elevations in NEFAs may compete with glucose for substrate oxidation, leading to the inhibition of several enzymes involved in glucose metabolism, including pyruvate dehydrogenase, phosphofructokinase and hexokinase II. Elevated NEFA concentrations may also lead to an accumulation of intracellular fatty acid metabolites such as diacylglycerol (DAG), fatty acyl-coenzyme A (fatty acyl-Co A) and ceramides (lipid molecules with structural and signalling roles), which subsequently interfere with insulin-receptor function. Chronically elevated NEFA concentrations are also thought to reduce β-cell insulin secretion due to reduced sensitivity to glucose, as well as apoptosis of islet cells.

Another mechanism by which obesity may induce type 2 diabetes relates to inflammation. Obesity is associated with elevated concentrations of inflammatory markers called cytokines. Two relevant cytokines are tumour necrosis factor alpha (TNFα) and interleukin-6. Obesity promotes secretion of TNFα and interleukin-6 from adipocytes, and these in turn stimulate the release of an intracellular signalling molecule called suppressor of cytokine signalling-3 (SOCS-3). Elevated SOCS-3 levels have been found to impair insulin signalling within cells, thus contributing to insulin resistance. Pro-inflammatory cytokines may also induce endothelial dysfunction by suppressing nitric oxide synthase, the enzyme responsible for nitric oxide production. Hence vasodilation and blood flow are compromised. Another cytokine released by adipocytes which has been implicated in the development of diabetes is adiponectin. In contrast to many other cytokines, adiponectin concentrations are decreased with obesity (large adipocytes secrete less adiponectin than small adipocytes). This may lead to insulin resistance because adiponectin is an insulin sensitizer. The decline in adiponectin with obesity may be secondary to reductions in transcription factors within cell nuclei termed peroxisome proliferator activated-receptors (PPARs).

As noted above, abdominal obesity is more closely associated with type 2 diabetes than overall adiposity. One theory to explain this is that visceral adipocytes are particularly resistant to the antilipolytic effects of insulin. Thus there is increased catabolism of triglycerides and increased release of NEFAs and glycerol into the circulation. These flow directly to the liver via the portal vein, increasing substrate availability (i.e. glycerol) for hepatic glucose production, as well as increasing the circulating level of NEFAs. It is clear from this brief discussion that a variety of complex mechanisms may explain the link between obesity and type 2 diabetes. Knowledge in this area is expanding at a rapid rate and it is likely that much more will be learned about obesity, insulin resistance and type 2 diabetes in the next few years. It would be particularly helpful if this research could identify why some obese people develop type 2 diabetes while others remain diabetes free.

PHYSICAL INACTIVITY AS A RISK FACTOR

There is a large body of evidence to support the hypothesis that environmental influences (including physical inactivity) are an important determinant of type 2 diabetes risk. Migration studies, for example, demonstrate that the prevalence of diabetes is often higher in groups who emigrate to more affluent countries compared with their compatriots who remain at 'home', suggesting a change in lifestyle is responsible. Similarly, studies of the Pima Indians (who are known to have a strong predisposition for diabetes) show that diabetes prevalence is far higher in those living an 'affluent' lifestyle in Arizona compared with those residing in Mexico and living a 'traditional' lifestyle (Ravussin *et al.* 1994). Further evidence that lifestyle changes play a role in the development of type 2 diabetes comes from trends within populations who have lived through a period of rapid economic development. An example is the city-state of Singapore, where the prevalence of diabetes increased from 2% in 1975 to 9% in 1998 (Figure 5.4).

Robust evidence concerning the relationship between physical inactivity and the risk of type 2 diabetes began to emerge in the early 1990s in the form of prospective observational studies. One of the first of these involved 5,990 male alumni of the University of Pennsylvania, followed up from 1962 to 1976. This study reported an inverse association between weekly energy expenditure in walking, stair climbing and sports activity and the risk of developing type 2 diabetes and concluded that each 500 kcal week^{-1} increment in energy expenditure was associated with a 6% lower age-adjusted risk of developing diabetes (Helmrich *et al.* 1991). Many prospective observational studies have since confirmed an association between low levels of physical

Figure 5.4 Changing prevalence of diabetes within the adult population of Singapore between the years 1975 and 1998.

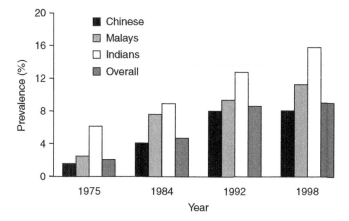
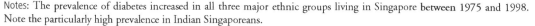

Source: Lee (2000).
Notes: The prevalence of diabetes increased in all three major ethnic groups living in Singapore between 1975 and 1998. Note the particularly high prevalence in Indian Singaporeans.

activity and increased risk of type 2 diabetes. The majority of these studies have been conducted in America. Examples include the Nurses' Health Study (Hu *et al.* 1999; Hu *et al.* 2001a), the Physicians' Health Study (Manson *et al.* 1992), the Iowa Women's Health Study (Folsom *et al.* 2000) and the Women's Health Study (Weinstein *et al.* 2004). Outside of America, similar findings have been reported in studies of Finnish men and women (Hu *et al.* 2003; Hu *et al.* 2004b), Japanese men participating in the Osaka Health Survey (Okada *et al.* 2000) and in men participating in the British Regional Heart Study (Wannamethee *et al.* 2000). In each of these studies a significant association was observed between low levels of physical activity and the subsequent risk of developing type 2 diabetes.

The largest of the studies described above was the US Nurses' Health Study. One report from this study concerned 84,941 female nurses observed over a 16-year period (1980–96). These women were free from diagnosed CVD, diabetes and cancer at baseline. Information regarding physical activity and other aspects of lifestyle was collected (via questionnaire) at baseline in 1980 and again in 1982, 1986, 1988 and 1992. From these the amount of time per week spent in moderate-to-vigorous activities (jogging, brisk walking, heavy gardening, heavy household work) requiring an expenditure of 3 METs or more was estimated. The findings revealed an inverse dose–response relationship between physical activity status and diabetes risk. Moreover, the importance of taking a holistic approach to diabetes prevention was emphasized by the finding that the relative risk of developing type 2 diabetes was only 0.1 in nurses characterized by the following combination: good diet (dietary score in upper two quintiles), low BMI (<25 kg m^2) and high physical activity levels (≥30 minutes per day of moderate-to-vigorous exercise). Based on this finding a population-attributable risk of 87% was calculated, suggesting that 87% of diabetes cases could have been avoided if all women had been in these low-risk categories (Hu *et al.* 2001a).

Collectively, epidemiological evidence linking physical inactivity with increased risk of type 2 diabetes suggests that physically active individuals have a 30–50% lower risk of developing type 2 diabetes than their sedentary counterparts (for detailed reviews of the evidence see Bassuk and Manson (2005), LaMonte *et al.* (2005b) and Jeon *et al.* (2007)). The associations between inactivity and diabetes are significant in these studies after adjustment for age and many other potentially confounding factors. In the Nurses' Health Study, for example, an inverse dose–response association was observed between physical inactivity and diabetes risk in participants with and without a parental history of diabetes (Figure 5.5), and in a Finnish study physical inactivity predicted diabetes risk in men and women with and without impaired glucose tolerance (G. Hu *et al.* 2004b). Physical inactivity also predicts type 2 diabetes risk independently of BMI, although the strength of the association is often far greater for BMI than for physical inactivity (Figure 5.6). The issue of whether physical inactivity or a high BMI is more important for diabetes risk is somewhat contentious because it may be argued that physical activity protects against type 2 diabetes by preventing obesity, and on this basis Blair and Church (2004) propose that physical activity should be a major focus of diabetes prevention programmes.

Although the findings from prospective cohort studies are consistent in reporting an inverse association between physical inactivity and diabetes risk, these studies have limitations. Assessments of physical activity are questionnaire based and therefore liable to inaccuracy, and diabetes is determined by self-report, which may lead to inaccuracy due to undiagnosed cases. Moreover, as explained in Chapter 4, observational studies cannot prove cause and effect due to the problem of self-selection. Some of these limitations are overcome by intervention studies. Such studies are labour

Figure 5.5 Multivariate relative risk of developing type 2 diabetes according to physical activity levels in women with and without a parental history of diabetes.

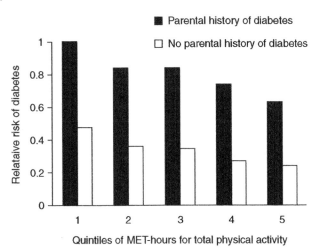

Source: Hu *et al.* (1999).
Notes: Findings are from the Nurses' Health Study. Quintile one had the lowest levels of physical activity and quintile five had the highest. The reference group is quintile one for those with a parental history of diabetes.

Figure 5.6 Relative risk of developing type 2 diabetes in the Women's Health Study according to energy expenditure (EE) levels (top panel) and BMI (bottom panel).

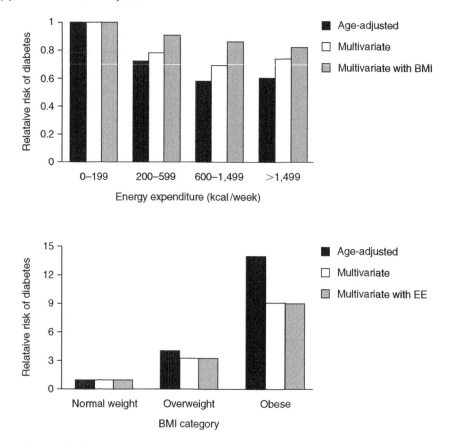

Source: Weinstein *et al.* (2004).

Notes: The multivariate relative risks have been adjusted for age, family history of diabetes, alcohol use, smoking habit, hormone replacement therapy, high cholesterol and dietary factors. Both energy expenditure and BMI are significant predictors of diabetes risk even after adjustment for each other. However, the association with diabetes risk is much stronger for BMI than for energy expenditure.

intensive and therefore involve smaller numbers than cohort studies, but they provide strong evidence that lifestyle changes can prevent the development of type 2 diabetes in high-risk individuals.

Two major intervention studies demonstrating the effectiveness of lifestyle intervention for preventing diabetes are the Finnish Diabetes Prevention Study and the US Diabetes Prevention Program. The Finnish Diabetes Prevention Study (Tuomilehto *et al.* 2001) involved 522 middle-aged (40–65 years old), overweight (BMI ≥25 kg m²) men and women with impaired glucose tolerance. Subjects were randomly allocated into either an intervention group or a control group. Subjects in the intervention group received individual counselling to help them achieve five major goals:

1   a reduction in weight of 5% or more;
2   a reduction in total fat intake to less than 30% of energy consumed;
3   a reduction in saturated fat intake to less than 10% of energy consumed;
4   an increase in fibre intake to at least 15 g per 1,000 kcal; and
5   moderate exercise for at least 30 minutes per day, totalling more than four hours
    per week.

Subjects in the control group were given oral and written information annually about diet and exercise, but no specific individualized programmes or counselling. Oral glucose tolerance tests were performed annually. The mean duration of follow-up was 3.2 years.

Despite the modest weight loss (4.2 kg), the incidence of diabetes was more than halved in the intervention group compared with the control group (11% versus 23%, respectively). Moreover, no cases of diabetes developed in individuals who were successful in attaining four or more of the goals of the intervention programme, regardless of whether these individuals were in the intervention group or the control group (Figure 5.7). Furthermore, among subjects in the intervention group who did not reach the goal of losing 5% of their initial weight, but who did achieve the goal of exercising for more than four hours per week, the odds ratio for diabetes was 0.2 (80% lower) compared with those in the intervention group who maintained a sedentary lifestyle. This suggests that even in the absence of major weight loss, exercise is effective in preventing type 2 diabetes.

The results of the Finnish Diabetes Prevention Study were confirmed by a second randomized trial conducted in the United States (Knowler *et al.* 2002). The Diabetes

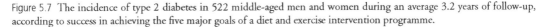

Figure 5.7 The incidence of type 2 diabetes in 522 middle-aged men and women during an average 3.2 years of follow-up, according to success in achieving the five major goals of a diet and exercise intervention programme.

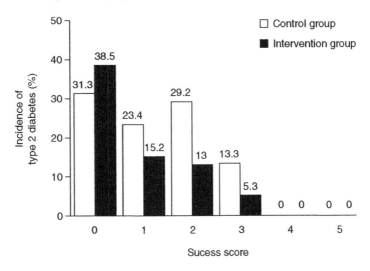

Source: Tuomilehto *et al.* (2001).
Note: Data are from the Finnish Diabetes Prevention Study.

Prevention Program was a large multi-centre trial involving 3,234 men and women with impaired fasting glucose and impaired glucose tolerance. Participants were randomly assigned to either placebo, metformin or an intensive lifestyle-modification programme with the goals of at least a 7% weight loss and at least 150 minutes of physical activity per week. The incidence of type 2 diabetes during an average follow-up of 2.8 years was 11.0, 7.8 and 4.8 per 100 person-years in the placebo, metformin and lifestyle groups, respectively. The lifestyle intervention reduced the incidence of diabetes by 58% and metformin by 31% in comparison with the placebo. The lifestyle intervention reduced the incidence of diabetes by 39% in comparison with the metformin trial. These results held across all age groups (Figure 5.8). Results were also similar in men and women regardless of ethnic group.

Aside from the Finnish Diabetes Prevention Study and the US Diabetes Prevention Program, several other studies have confirmed a benefit of lifestyle intervention in high-risk groups, including the Malmö feasibility Study (Eriksson and Lindgärde 1991), the Da Qing Impaired Glucose Tolerance and Diabetes Study (Pan *et al.* 1997), the Indian Diabetes Prevention Programme (Ramachandran *et al.* 2006) and the Multiple Risk Factor Intervention Trial (MRFIT) (Davey Smith *et al.* 2005). Of note among these studies is the non-randomized Malmö Feasibility Study, which involved a five-year intervention. Among participants with impaired glucose tolerance, 10.6% developed type 2 diabetes in the intervention group compared with 28.6% in the comparison group. This study also included 41 men with early stage type 2 diabetes, i.e. a positive result on an oral glucose tolerance test but no overt symptoms of diabetes. After five years, 54% of this group were in remission, i.e. their blood glucose

Figure 5.8 The incidence of type 2 diabetes in placebo, Metformin and lifestyle intervention groups according to age category in the US Diabetes Prevention Program.

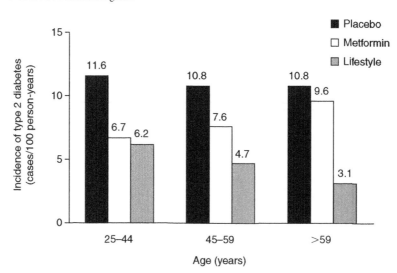

Source: Knowler *et al.* (2002).
Notes: This study involved 3,234 men and women and an average follow-up of 2.8 years. Metformin is an insulin-sensitising drug.

concentrations were no longer indicative of diabetes. A subsequent publication reported that after 12 years of follow-up, mortality rates and rates of ischemic heart disease were significantly lower in intervention than control subjects with impaired glucose tolerance. Moreover, the rates in intervention subjects with impaired glucose tolerance did not differ significantly from rates in healthy controls (Eriksson and Lind-gärde 1998).

Evidence from lifestyle interventions for the prevention or delay of type 2 diabetes in groups with impaired glucose tolerance has been subjected to systematic review and meta-analysis by Gillies *et al.* (2007). These investigators concluded that lifestyle interventions reduce the risk of diabetes by approximately 50%, and are at least as effective as drug treatment. One issue that remains to be determined is the extent to which the benefits of lifestyle intervention continue upon cessation of the programmes. Only time will answer this question, but initial follow-up findings from the Finnish Diabetes Prevention Study demonstrate a 43% reduction in the relative risk of diabetes in intervention group participants three years after the cessation of individual lifestyle counselling (Lindström *et al.* 2006). Another area of uncertainty in diabetes prevention is the relative contributions of improved diet and increased physical activity to reduced diabetes risk. Further study will be required to clarify this issue, but the important role of exercise is supported not only by the prospective observational studies of physical activity discussed earlier in this section, but also by studies examining the link between physical fitness and risk of type 2 diabetes.

LOW PHYSICAL FITNESS AS A RISK FACTOR

Several studies have examined the association between physical fitness and the risk of type 2 diabetes. One report from the Cooper Clinic in Dallas involving 8,633 initially non-diabetic men reported that those with low fitness (least-fit 20% of men based on a maximal exercise test on a treadmill – mean estimated maximal oxygen uptake, 9.3 METs) had a 1.9-fold higher risk of developing impaired fasting glucose and a 3.7-fold higher risk of developing type 2 diabetes during an average six years of follow-up than men with high fitness (the most-fit 40% of the cohort – mean maximal oxygen uptake, 13.7 METs). The association between low levels of physical fitness and increased risk of type 2 diabetes was present in younger (<45 years) and older (≥45 years) men, those with high (≥27 kg m^2) and low (<27 kg m^2) BMI, those with and without a parental history of diabetes and in those with normal and impaired fasting glucose at baseline demonstrating the independent effect of fitness (Wei *et al.* 1999a).

The findings of the Cooper Clinic in Dallas have been confirmed by a study of 5,984 Japanese men, aged 20–40 years at baseline, employed by the Tokyo Gas Company (Sawada *et al.* 2003). During a 14-year follow-up the age-adjusted relative risks of diabetes across fitness quartiles (low to high) were 1.00, 0.56, 0.35 and 0.25, and the multivariate relative risks (adjusted for age, BMI, systolic blood pressure, family history of diabetes, smoking status and alcohol intake) were 1.00, 0.78, 0.63 and 0.56. For reference, the mean values for VO$_2$max (determined using the Åstrand-Ryhming Nomogram) across fitness quartiles were 32.4, 38.0, 42.4 and 51.1 ml kg^{-1} min^{-1}).

More recently, the association between low levels of fitness and increased risk of type 2 diabetes has been confirmed in women attending the Cooper Clinic in Dallas (Sui *et al.* 2008). During a 17-year follow-up of 6,249 women aged 20–79 years and free from disease at baseline, fitness was found to be inversely related to diabetes risk in a dose-dependent manner across low, middle and high fitness levels. Relative risks were attenuated, but remained significant after control for confounding factors (Figure 5.9). Further analysis across 1 MET increments of fitness revealed that an exercise capacity of <7 METs was associated with a three-fold higher diabetes risk than an exercise capacity ≥10 METs.

An association between fitness levels and diabetes risk was also observed in the CARDIA (Coronary Artery Risk Development in Young Adults) study, which involved a 15-year follow-up of 2,029 men and 2,458 women aged 18–30 years at baseline. For those with low cardiorespiratory fitness (bottom 20% of fitness levels) the risk of developing diabetes was found to be 1.75 times higher than the risk in those with high cardiorespiratory fitness (top 40% of fitness levels) (Carnethon *et al.* 2003). Further evidence linking high fitness with low risk of diabetes is provided by a study involving selective breeding of rats across 11 generations, producing one group with high exercise capacities and another with low exercise capacities (VO$_2$max was 58% lower in the low-capacity group versus the high-capacity group). Many metabolic differences were observed between groups, including lower levels of random and fasting glucose, lower levels of triglyceride and insulin (Figure 5.10) and lower levels of NEFAs and visceral adiposity in the high-capacity rats (Wisløff *et al.* 2005). These findings are consistent with data in human patients with type 2 diabetes, demonstrating that low aerobic capacity is associ-

Figure 5.9 The association between cardiorespiratory fitness and type 2 diabetes risk in women attending the Cooper Clinic in Dallas.

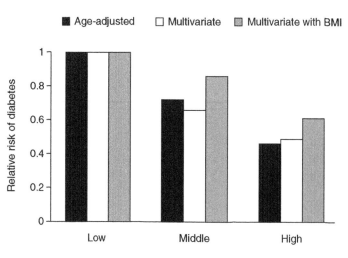

Source: Sui *et al.* (2008).

Note: Multivariate relative risks are adjusted for age, current smoking, alcohol intake, hypertension, family history of diabetes and survey response pattern.

Figure 5.10 Differences in random glucose (RG), fasting glucose (FG), triglyceride (TG) and insulin in rats selectively bred across 11 generations for low exercise capacity and high exercise capacity.

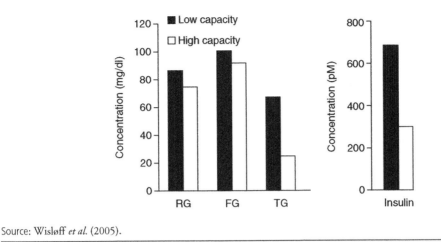

Source: Wisløff *et al.* (2005).

ated with reduced expression of genes involved in oxidative phosphorylation (Mootha *et al.* 2003).

Thus, as with physical activity, studies of fitness are consistent in indicating that low physical fitness is a risk factor for the development of type 2 diabetes. In view of this evidence, it is of interest to consider the mechanisms by which physical activity and physical fitness provide protection from type 2 diabetes.

MECHANISMS

It has long been known that inactivity has an adverse effect on glucose tolerance. For example, Lipman *et al.* (1972) found impairments in glucose tolerance in eight healthy young men following five weeks of bed rest. The impairment was less severe, however, in those permitted one hour of vigorous (70% of VO_2max) supine exercise each day. More recently, a study of masters' athletes demonstrated a loss of insulin sensitivity and glucose tolerance after a 10-day detraining period (Rogers *et al.* 1990). Such studies suggest that regular exercise can prevent the development of type 2 diabetes by maintaining glucose tolerance. This is supported by the findings of the US Diabetes Prevention Program, which observed a normalizing of glucose tolerance in 40–50% of lifestyle intervention participants (Knowler *et al.* 2002).

The beneficial effect of exercise on glucose tolerance is thought to be due, in part, to improvements in insulin sensitivity. Observational studies suggest that physical activity improves insulin sensitivity. An example is the Insulin Resistance Atherosclerosis Study conducted in Oakland, California. This study observed positive associations between overall, vigorous and non-vigorous physical activity and insulin sensitivity (assessed via an intravenous glucose tolerance test) in 1,467 men and women of African-American, Hispanic and non-Hispanic white ethnicity. Associations remained significant after adjustment for potential confounders, suggesting causation (Mayer-Davies *et al.* 1998). This has been confirmed in randomized intervention studies using either the euglycaemic clamp technique (McAuley *et al.* 2002) or an intravenous oral glucose tolerance test (Houmard *et al.* 2004). An affect has also been observed after a single session of resistance exercise (Koopman *et al.* 2005).

One elegant study demonstrating that exercise improves glucose transport into muscle and muscle glycogen synthesis employed phosphorous-31 and carbon-13 nuclear magnetic resonance spectroscopy and a hyperglycaemic-hyperinsulinaemic clamp technique (Perseghin *et al.* 1996). Ten adult children of parents with type 2 diabetes and eight normal subjects were studied before starting an exercise programme, after one session of exercise and after six weeks of exercise training. At baseline, muscle glycogen synthesis (indicated by carbon-13 concentration in the gastrocnemius muscle) was 63% lower in the offspring of diabetic parents then in normal subjects. Glycogen synthesis increased 69% and 62% after the first exercise session and 102% and 97% after six weeks of exercise training in the offspring and the normal subjects, respectively. The increment in glucose-6-phosphate during hyperglycaemic-hyperinsulinaemic clamping was lower in the offspring than in normal subjects at baseline (reflecting impaired glucose transport into muscle because glucose is converted into glucose-6-phosphate once entering muscle cells) but this increment was normalized in the offspring after one exercise session and after exercise training (Figure 5.11). These

Figure 5.11 Increased glucose transport and glycogen synthesis in normal subjects and in offspring of parents with type 2 diabetes after a single session of exercise and after six weeks of exercise training.

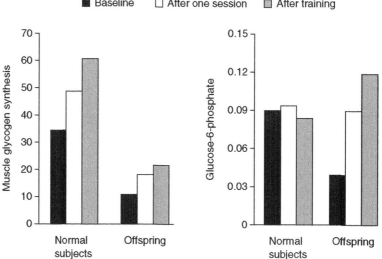

Source: Perseghin *et al.* (1996).
Notes: Glucose transport into muscle was estimated from phosphorous-31 concentrations, glycogen synthesis was estimated from carbon-13 concentrations. These were determined using nuclear magnetic resonance spectroscopy during a hyperglycaemic-hyperinsulinaemic clamp test. Units for muscle glycogen are miligram per litre of muscle per minute, units for glucose-6-phosphate are mmol l.

findings indicate that exercise increases insulin sensitivity in both normal subjects and in insulin-resistant subjects.

The mechanisms by which exercise improves glucose tolerance and insulin sensitivity are the subject of intense research, and it appears that both insulin-dependent and insulin-independent mechanisms are involved (for reviews, see Holloszy (2005), Jessen and Goodyear (2005) and Gill and Malkova (2006)). Since skeletal muscle is the major site for glucose disposal, much attention has focused on the role of the GLUT4 glucose transporter. This transporter exists within the intracellular pool, but is translocated to the cell membrane in response to both insulin and muscle contraction/hypoxia. A single bout of exercise induces an immediate increase in glucose transport, and this is thought to be due to an increase in GLUT4 translocation to the cell membrane, which occurs in response to muscle contraction/hypoxia independent of insulin. As this acute effect of exercise diminishes, it is thought to be replaced by an increase in insulin sensitivity mediated by insulin receptors within the cell membrane.

Aside from glucose transport across the cell membrane there are other responses and adaptations to exercise which may facilitate glucose and NEFA delivery and metabolism, including increased capillary density and blood flow, increased activity of enzymes involved in glucose (hexokinase, glycogen synthase) and oxidative metabolism (citrate synthase, succinate dehydrogenase) and an increase in the size and number of mitochondria (possibly due to an increased expression of the transcriptional coactivator peroxisome proliferator activator protein-γ co-activator 1α (PGC-1α)). Lowell and Shulman (2005) highlight the important role of mitochondrial dysfunction in the aetiology of type 2 diabetes. Mitochondrial defects may occur in both skeletal muscle and pancreatic β-cells, and there may be a reduction in the number of mitochondria also. This may lead to an accumulation of fatty acids (diacylglycerol and fatty acyl-Co A) within the cells, which interferes with the insulin-receptor signalling process, thereby causing insulin resistance. By increasing the size and number of mitochondria, and hence the capacity for oxidative metabolism, exercise may prevent the adverse effects related to glucotoxicity and lipotoxicity mentioned earlier.

This brief discussion has highlighted some of the major mechanisms by which exercise may enhance insulin sensitivity and glucose processing. The area is complex and there is much uncertainty regarding the precise pathways. Indeed, Dr John Holloszy, a world authority in the area, believes that it will be many decades before scientists develop a clear understanding of glucose transport and insulin sensitivity (Holloszy 2005). It is clear, however, that exercise has a beneficial effect on glucose processing. Moreover, some of the beneficial effects of exercise described in this section have been observed in those with type 2 diabetes, suggesting that physical activity may be beneficial as a therapy for type 2 diabetes. Evidence to support this proposition is examined below.

EXERCISE AS A THERAPY

In recent years many epidemiological studies have demonstrated an association between high levels of physical activity and a reduced risk of CVD and all-cause mortality in people with type 2 diabetes. These studies are usually follow-up studies to those presented in the section on physical activity and prevention of type 2 diabetes. In these large studies of initially healthy individuals, those who subsequently developed diabetes have been examined as separate groups to determine if physical activity and/or physical fitness provide any protection from the co-morbidities related to diabetes. Examples include groups from the Nurses' Health Study (Hu *et al.* 2001b), the Health Professionals Follow-up Study (Tanasescu *et al.* 2003), the National Health Interview Survey (Gregg *et al.* 2003 b), the Aerobics Centre Longitudinal Study (Wei *et al.* 2000) and a study of men and women living in Finland (Hu *et al.* 2004a). In each of these studies, higher levels of physical activity were associated with a significantly lower risk of cardiovascular and/or all-cause mortality during follow-up.

Most of the above studies specifically examined the association between walking and CVD and/or all-cause mortality. In the National Health Interview Survey it was estimated that one death per year may be prevented for every 61 people who could be persuaded to walk for at least two hours per week. The Health Professionals Follow-up Study identified an association between both the amount and speed of walking and CVD risk – those who reported walking at a very brisk pace ($\geq$4.0 mile h^{-1}) experienced an 83% lower risk of CVD than those who reported walking at an easy pace (<2.0 mile h^{-1}) even after control for CVD risk factors. Walking was also associated with a lower risk of cardiovascular events in the diabetic women observed in the Nurses' Health Study, while the findings from the study of Finnish men and women suggest that occupational, commuting (walking and cycling) and leisure-time physical activity are all associated with reduced total and CVD mortality among individuals with type 2 diabetes. Collectively, these findings suggest that walking is a particularly effective therapy for type 2 diabetes.

Physical fitness has also been shown to have an inverse, independent association with mortality and/or cardiovascular events in diabetic individuals (Church *et al.* 2004; Chacko *et al.* 2008; Kohl *et al.* 1992; Wei *et al.* 2000). In one report from the Aerobics Centre Longitudinal Study, the relative risk of all-cause mortality in men was 4.5 times higher in the least-fit quartile (mean $\dot{V}O_2$max $\leq$8.82 METs) compared with the fittest quartile (mean $\dot{V}O_2$max >11.71 METs) even after full adjustment for confounding variables, including BMI (Church *et al.* 2004). More recently a report from the ABCD (Appropriate Blood Pressure Control in Diabetes) trial has reported that a delayed heart rate recovery immediately after a peak exercise test is predictive of cardiovascular events in patients with type 2 diabetes (Chacko *et al.* 2008). A limitation of all the evidence described so far in this section is that it is observational. Exercise intervention trials with clinical endpoints in individuals with type 2 diabetes have yet to be conducted, but multifactorial interventions combining diet, exercise and pharmacotherapy have been shown to reduce cardiovascular events in those with type 2 diabetes (Gæde *et al.* 2003; Gæde *et al.* 2008).

Aside from examining clinical outcomes (i.e. CVD, all-cause mortality), some studies have investigated the effects of physical activity on markers for glucose control in people with type 2 diabetes. A key marker here is a form of glycosylated haemoglobin known as HbA1c. Glycosylation refers to the process by which sugars are chemically attached to proteins – in this case, glucose and haemoglobin, respectively. High blood glucose concentrations promote glycosylation of haemoglobin and thus elevated HbA1c concentrations in the blood (indicating poor blood glucose control over a prolonged period). Many intervention studies have examined the influence of exercise training on HbA1c in people with type 2 diabetes. One meta-analysis of 14 intervention trials (11 randomized, three non-randomized) concluded that exercise training reduces HbA1c by an amount that should decrease the risk of diabetic complications (Boulé *et al.* 2001). Another meta-analysis by the same authors reported that exercise intensity is more important than exercise volume for changes in HbA1c (Boulé *et al.* 2003). A third meta-analysis observed that both aerobic and resistance exercise training are effective for reducing HbA1c concentrations in those with type 2 diabetes and suggested that the two forms of exercise combined are most effective (Snowling and Hopkins 2006). This suggestion is supported by a randomized controlled trial involving 251 diabetic adults aged 39–70 years (Sigal *et al.* 2007). A possible explanation is that aerobic exercise induces metabolic adaptations within skeletal muscle to enhance glucose processing while resistance exercise, in addition to inducing metabolic changes within muscle, also increases muscle size and therefore glucose storage capacity.

In addition to lowering HbA1c concentration, exercise training studies have demonstrated a variety of beneficial effects for people with type 2 diabetes, including enhanced β-cell function (Dela *et al.* 2004), increased protein content of GLUT4, insulin receptor (IRS-1) and glycogen synthase (Holten *et al.* 2004), improvements in CVD risk factors such as lipids, lipoproteins and blood pressure (Cauza *et al.* 2005; Lehmann *et al.* 1995) and a reduction in the dose of prescribed medication (Castaneda *et al.* 2002). In view of such benefits, exercise guidelines have been formulated for those with type 2 diabetes (Albright *et al.* 2000; Praet and van Loon 2007). Exercise adherence remains a major issue, however, as highlighted by a finding from the Third National Health and Nutrition Examination Survey (NHANES III) that 31% of individuals with type 2 diabetes report no regular physical activity and another 38% report less than the recommended levels (Nelson *et al.* 2002).

SUMMARY

- Type 2 diabetes is a disease characterized by insulin resistance and defective insulin secretion, leading to hyperglycaemia and elevated NEFA concentrations.
- Type 2 diabetes increases the risk of CVD, which is a major cause of premature mortality in those afflicted with type 2 diabetes.
- The prevalence of type 2 diabetes is increasing in many countries and this appears to be linked to increases in the prevalence of obesity – a major risk factor for type 2 diabetes.
- Prospective observational studies demonstrate an association between low levels of physical activity and physical fitness and increased risk of type 2 diabetes.
- Lifestyle intervention programmes are effective in preventing type 2 diabetes, although the relative contributions of diet and exercise remain to be determined.
- Exercise promotes a variety of metabolic responses and adaptations which collectively improve glucose tolerance and insulin sensitivity.
- Among individuals with type 2 diabetes, high levels of physical activity and physical fitness are associated with a reduced risk of CVD and all-cause mortality.
- Exercise training reduces HbA1c concentrations in people with type 2 diabetes,

indicating improved glycaemic control and confirming the importance of exercise as a therapy for type 2 diabetes.

STUDY TASKS

1 Refer to Table 5.1 and provide a full explanation for each of the responses listed in each column.
2 Give three examples of observational evidence demonstrating an association between obesity and type 2 diabetes, and explain the mechanisms by which obesity may lead to type 2 diabetes.
3 List four prospective cohort studies which have demonstrated an association between physical activity/physical fitness and prevention of type 2 diabetes.
4 Describe the key findings of the Finnish Diabetes Prevention Study and the US Diabetes Prevention Program. What issues remain to be determined regarding the role of lifestyle intervention in preventing diabetes?
5 What mechanisms might be responsible for lowering the risk of type 2 diabetes in those who are fit and active?
6 Describe the major lines of evidence demonstrating that physical activity is an important therapy for type 2 diabetes.

FURTHER READING

Bassuk, S.S. and Manson, J.E. (2005) 'Epidemiological evidence for the role of physical activity in reducing the risk of type 2 diabetes and cardiovascular disease', *Journal of Applied Physiology* 99: 1193–204.

Frayn, K.N. (2003) 'Diabetes Mellitus' in *Metabolic Regulation: A Human Perspective*, 2nd edn, Oxford: Blackwell Science Ltd, pp. 281–99.

Gill, J.M.R. and Cooper, A.R. (2008) 'Physical activity and prevention of type 2 diabetes mellitus', *Sports Medicine* 38: 807–24.

Gill, J.M.R. and Malkova, D. (2006) 'Physical activity, fitness and cardiovascular disease risk in adults: interactions with insulin resistance and obesity', *Clinical Science* 110: 409–25.

Hawley, J.A. (2004) 'Exercise as a therapeutic intervention for the prevention and treatment of insulin resistance', *Diabetes Metabolism Research and Reviews* 20: 383–93.

Holloszy, J.O. (2005) 'Exercise-induced increase in muscle insulin sensitivity', *Journal of Applied Physiology* 99: 338–43.

Jessen, N. and Goodyear, L.J. (2005) 'Contraction signalling to glucose transport in skeletal muscle', *Journal of Applied Physiology* 99: 330–7.

LaMonte, M.J., Blair, S.N. and Church, T.S. (2005) 'Physical activity and diabetes prevention', *Journal of Applied Physiology* 99: 1205–13.

Lowell, B.B. and Shulman, G.I. (2005) 'Mitochondrial dysfunction and type 2 diabetes', *Science* 307: 384–7.

Praet, S.F.E. and van Loon, L.J.C. (2007) 'Optimizing the therapeutic benefits of exercise in type 2 diabetes', *Journal of Applied Physiology* 103: 1113–20.

Rhodes, C.J. (2005) 'Type 2 diabetes: a matter of β-cell life and death?', *Science* 307: 380–3.

Schwartz, M.W. and Porte, D. (2005) 'Diabetes, obesity, and the brain', *Science* 307: 375–9.

6 Obesity

Knowledge assumed
The energy balance equation
and components of 24-hour
energy expenditure
Basic statistics including relative
risk, confidence intervals,
correlation coefficients and
statistical power

INTRODUCTION

The topic of obesity has generated an exceptional amount of interest among the scientific community, the media and the public recently. A vast amount has been written on the subject and much has been learned about the causes and consequences of obesity. Despite this accumulation of knowledge, there remain many uncertainties regarding how best to prevent and manage obesity, and there is disagreement within the literature regarding the scale and seriousness of the issue. According to James (2008), for example, 'The epidemic of obesity took off from about 1980 and in almost all countries has been rising inexorably ever since' (p. 336). Haslam *et al.* are more emphatic, stating:

The obesity epidemic in the United Kingdom is out of control, and none of the measures being undertaken show signs of halting the problem, let alone reversing the trend. The United States is about 10 years ahead in terms of its obesity problem, and it has an epidemic of type 2 diabetes with obesity levels that are rocketing.

(Haslam *et al.* 2006: p. 640)

In stark contrast are the views of Campos *et al.*, who state: 'In our view the available scientific data neither support alarmist claims about obesity nor justify diverting scarce resources away from far more pressing public health issues' (Campos *et al.* 2006). According to these authors there is limited evidence for a widespread obesity epidemic, and they go further in stating: 'Except at true statistical extremes, high body mass index is a very weak predictor of mortality, and may even be protective in older populations' (Campos *et al.* 2006: p. 56). Consistent with this are the views of Basham and Luik (2008), who argue that 'much of the data on overweight people and obesity are limited, equivocal, and compromised in terms of extent and the reliability of the measurements and the populations sampled' (Basham and Luik 2008: p. 244).

In this chapter we examine a variety of topics relating to obesity, including the definition of obesity, how obesity develops and the prevalence and health risks of obesity. After this the two major issues of the chapter are discussed:

1   evidence that physical inactivity causes obesity; and
2   the role of exercise in the management of obesity.

The final section of the chapter outlines exercise recommendations for weight control. Not covered in this chapter is the issue of childhood obesity. Information on this topic is covered in Chapter 10. By the end of the current chapter the reader should appreciate that obesity is a complex condition and despite the abundance of information on the topic many uncertainties remain.

DEFINITION

Haslam *et al.* (2006, p. 640) define obesity as 'excess body fat accumulation with multiple organ-specific pathological consequences'. Implicit within this definition is the link between excess body fat and ill-health which will be examined later in this chapter. The most frequently used method for assessing obesity is the body mass index (BMI). This is calculated by dividing weight (in kilograms) by height (in meters) squared. Values between 18.5 and 24.9 kg m^2 are used to indicate healthy weight, values above 25 kg m^2 indicate overweight and values above 30 kg m^2 indicate obesity. One often-cited limitation of the BMI is its inability to distinguish between muscle and fat. However, although in trained athletes a high BMI may be due to an unusually large muscle mass, according to Han *et al.* (2006), athletic training rarely increases the BMI above 32 kg m^2. Thus, in most individuals, high BMI values indicate high levels of body fat.

In recent years the simple measure of the waist circumference has been adopted as an indicator of obesity. Many studies indicate that the waist circumference is a better

Table 6.1 Classification of overweight and obesity by BMI, waist circumference, and associated disease risk (i.e. type 2 diabetes, hypertension and cardiovascular disease)

		RISK RELATIVE TO NORMAL WEIGHT AND WAIST CIRCUMFERENCE	
	BMI (kg m²)	MEN <102 cm, WOMEN <88 cm	MEN ≥102 cm, WOMEN ≥88 cm
Underweight	<18.5	Not increased	Not increased
Normal	18.5–24.9	Not increased	Increased
Overweight	25.0–29.9	Increased	High
Obesity (class I)	30.0–34.9	High	Very high
Obesity (class II)	35.0–39.9	Very high	Extremely high
Extreme obesity (class III)	≥40.0	Extremely high	Extremely high

Source: Adapted from data from the US National Institutes of Health by Han *et al.* (2006).

Note: 102 cm = 40 inches, 88 cm = 35 inches.

indicator of health risk than the BMI. According to Han *et al.* (2006) the waist circumference is as good an indicator of total body fat as BMI or skinfold thickness, and is the best anthropometric predictor of visceral fat, i.e. fat within the abdominal cavity. Table 6.1 provides criteria for overweight and obesity together with waist circumference cut-off points and the associated disease risk.

As we shall see, uncertainty remains as to exactly how accurately the BMI cut-off points given in Table 6.1 identify the health risks associated with obesity. There is also debate regarding the extent to which BMI cut-off points can be applied across different ethnic groups. This issue was addressed for Asian populations by the World Health Organization (WHO) in 2004, which found that the cut-off point for observed risk varies from 22 kg m² to 25 kg m² in different Asian populations. The report suggested that a cut-off point as low as 23 kg m² may be useful as a 'health action point' in Asian populations (WHO expert consultation 2004). Also problematic is the issue of BMI cut-off points in children. This is discussed in Chapter 10.

AETIOLOGY

Obesity appears to be the result of a chronic imbalance between energy intake and energy expenditure such that energy intake exceeds energy expenditure over a prolonged period (Frayn 2003). Put simply, the intake of energy from food exceeds daily energy expenditure and hence energy storage and weight gain result. Perhaps the clearest example of the influence of food intake (or lack of it) on body mass is provided by a study of an obese 27-year-old man who fasted under medical supervision for 382 days (Figure 6.1). His weight at the beginning of this period was 207 kg (32.5 stone) and by the end of this period his weight was reduced to 82 kg (13 stone). Moreover, five years after undertaking the fast, the man's weight remained relatively depressed at around 89 kg (14 stone).

Figure 6.1 Weight loss in a 27-year-old male patient who fasted under medical supervision (as an outpatient) for 382 days.

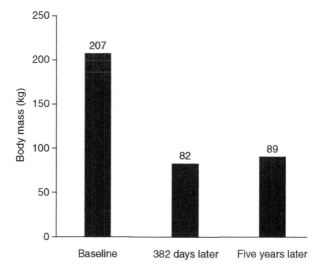

Source: Stewart *et al.* (1973).
Note: Vitamin supplements were given daily throughout the fast. In the latter stages of the fast potassium and sodium supplements were provided. Non-caloric fluids were allowed *ad libitum*. 'Evacuation' (excretion) was infrequent in the latter stages of the fast, with 37–48 days between stools. Apparently, the patient experienced no ill-effects from prolonged fasting.

This example clearly demonstrates that energy intake influences weight status. As we shall see later in this chapter, changes in energy expenditure also influence weight status. This is not to suggest that obesity is simply a matter of poor willpower leading to gluttony and laziness. The situation is more complex than this and some of the factors that determine energy intake and energy expenditure appear to be outside of our conscious control. In addition, attempts to modify body weight by reducing food intake may be met with metabolic alterations which oppose weight loss.

A clear example of metabolic alterations during dieting is provided by a study which was published in the *Lancet* in 1969. In this study George Bray subjected six 'grossly' obese women (body mass range 135–209 kg) to a 24-day liquid formula diet providing a very low energy intake of 450 kcal/day. This diet resulted in a weight loss of 10.3 kg, but over half of this decrease occurred during the first eight days of the diet, with a reduced rate of weight loss after this time. This reduced rate of weight loss was linked to a 15% decrease in energy expenditure (assessed using indirect calorimetry) between the beginning and end of the diet period (Bray 1969). These findings were confirmed and extended by those of a more recent study which demonstrated that 24-hour energy expenditure is reduced during a diet-induced body mass loss of 10% and increased during a period of overfeeding to increase body mass by 10% (Figure 6.2). These findings (which were observed in obese and non-obese subjects) led the authors to conclude that compensatory changes in energy expenditure may explain the poor long-term efficacy of treatments for obesity (Leibel *et al.* 1995).

It is clear from the evidence discussed above that alterations in body mass influence metabolic rate, and it is of interest to ask if the reverse is true also, i.e. do changes in

Figure 6.2 Change in 24-hour energy expenditure (EE) (expressed in kilocalories per kilogram of fat-free mass (FFM) per day) after periods of weight loss and weight gain in obese and non-obese subjects.

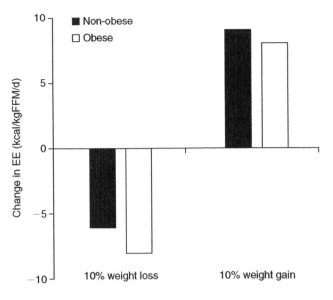

Source: Leibel *et al.* (1995).

Notes: Energy expenditure was measured by indirect calorimetry and doubly labelled water. Observe that the changes in energy expenditure oppose the maintenance of a body weight that is different from the usual (initial) weight, suggesting that long-term maintenance of weight loss or weight gain may be difficult.

metabolic rate influence body mass? In particular, is there evidence to support the commonly held assumption that a low metabolic rate causes obesity? Here we must distinguish between the overall daily metabolic rate, i.e. 24-hour energy expenditure, and the resting metabolic rate (RMR). Twenty-four hour energy expenditure is made up of three components namely:

1   RMR;
2   the thermic effect of feeding; and
3   the energy expenditure due to physical activity.

A variety of study designs have been used to assess whether or not a low RMR is a cause of obesity. Cross-sectional studies have examined RMR in obese versus lean individuals, in non-obese individuals at risk of obesity (by virtue of having obese parents) compared with non-obese individuals not perceived to be at risk of obesity and in formerly obese individuals who have lost weight compared with individuals who have never been obese. Longitudinal studies have also examined whether a low RMR at baseline is associated with weight gain at follow-up. In most cases these studies indicate that a low RMR is not a cause of obesity. A notable exception is the longitudinal study of Ravussin *et al.* (1988), which found an association between low RMR and weight gain over a four-year follow-up period. Contrary to initial expectations, most studies indicate that RMR is higher in obese versus lean individuals due to the elevated fat-free mass and fat mass associated with obesity. RMR does not tend to differ between lean individuals 'at risk' or 'not at risk' of obesity or in obese individuals who have lost weight compared with individuals who have never been obese and most longitudinal studies have failed to identify a low RMR as a cause of weight gain or obesity (Hill and Wyatt 1999).

Since a low RMR has been ruled out as a cause of obesity for most individuals, it appears that an imbalance between food intake and physical activity is responsible. Exactly why this imbalance occurs is the topic of intense research, and much has been learnt in recent years regarding a variety of hormones which influence food intake and energy expenditure. One prominent example is the adipocyte hormone, leptin, which is discussed in the section on genetics and obesity. In addition to leptin, a variety of gut hormones are now known to influence appetite, food intake and in some cases energy expenditure (for reviews see Badman and Flier (2005) and Murphy and Bloom (2006)). These include (but are not limited to) cholecystokinin (CCK), ghrelin, glucagon like peptide 1 (GLP1), oxyntomodulin, pancreatic polypeptide (PP) and peptide YY (PYY).

Ghrelin is unique among the hormones listed above because it is the only one which stimulates appetite; the others are all satiety signals. Ghrelin gets its name from its first known action of stimulating growth hormone release. Ghrelin concentrations rise

Figure 6.3 Changes in energy intake and energy expenditure (EE) in 15 overweight men and women after oxyntomodulin administration.

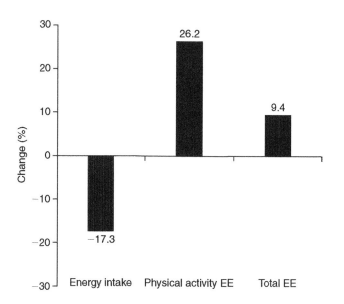

Source: Wynne *et al.* (2006).
Notes: The study was a randomized double-blind cross-over trial. Oxyntomodulin was self-administered subcutaneously three times per day over a four-week period. Injections were performed prior to meals. Energy intake was assessed during a 'study meal'. Energy expenditure was measured using indirect calorimetry and combined heart rate and movement monitoring over a 24-hour period.

prior to meals, suggesting that it plays a role in initiating food intake. This has been confirmed by studies demonstrating increased food intake after intravenous administration of ghrelin in humans (Druce *et al.* 2005; Wren *et al.* 2001). Interestingly, ghrelin concentrations are very low in morbidly obese patients who have undergone gastric bypass surgery (in which most of the stomach and duodenum are bypassed by surgical anastomosis) and this possibly contributes to the weight loss associated with the procedure (Cummings *et al.* 2002).

The hormones that act as satiety signals are important for terminating feeding. Prominent among these hormones is PYY. PYY levels rise sharply after meals, reducing food intake by modifying appetite circuits within the hypothalamus. Intravenous administration of PYY has been shown to lower weight gain in rabbits (Silenco *et al.* 2006), while research in humans has demonstrated that obese individuals have lower endogenous PYY levels than non-obese individuals and that their PYY response to feeding is blunted, suggesting that defective PYY secretion may play a role in the development of obesity (Batterham *et al.* 2003). Another interesting satiety hormone is oxyntomodulin. One study of overweight and obese humans found that oxyntomodulin injections reduced energy intake during a 'study meal' and increased 24-hour energy expenditure (Figure 6.3) while another study by the same group observed a 2.3 kg weight loss over four weeks in overweight and obese individuals who self-administered oxyntomodulin three times each day (Wynne *et al.* 2005). These findings suggest that oxyntomodulin has potential as an anti-obesity therapy.

GENETIC INFLUENCE

It is clear that genes contribute to the development of obesity. An excellent illustration of this is provided by a Danish adoption study. In this study, Stunkard *et al.* (1986b) compared the BMI of 540 adult adoptees with that of their biological and adoptive parents. Ninety per cent of the adoptees had been placed in their adoptive homes within the first year of life. The study found a clear relationship between the weight class of the adoptees and that of their biological parents, but no relationship between the weight class of the adoptees and that of their adoptive parents (Figure 6.4). This suggests that genes are a strong determinant of body fatness and that childhood family environment has less influence. Another study from the same group (Stunkard *et al.* 1986a) demonstrated high concordance rates among monozygotic (identical) twins for height, weight and BMI both at 20 years old (intra-pair $r=0.91$, 0.85 and 0.81, respectively) and after 25 years of follow-up ($r=0.88$, 0.74 and 0.67 respectively).

Although the findings of Stunkard *et al.* demonstrate the influence of genes on body composition, this does not mean that obesity is inevitable in certain individuals or that the environment is unimportant for the development of obesity. Obesity results from an interaction between genes and the environment. Famine and/or high levels of physical activity may prevent the expression of any genetic tendency towards fatness. A good example of the interaction between genes and food intake is provided by a study of overfeeding in monozygotic twins (Bouchard *et al.* 1990). In this study, 12 pairs of male monozygotic twins were overfed by 353 MJ (84,000 kcal) over a 100-day period. Men gained an average of 8.1 kg in weight, but the range of weight gain varied from

Figure 6.4 The association between the BMI of adopted children and that of their biological parents (left panel) and their adoptive parents (right panel).

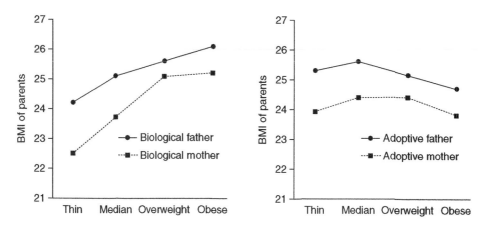

Note: The BMI of the adopted children is strongly associated with that of their biological parents, but shows no association with that of their adoptive parents, indicating a strong genetic effect.

Figure 6.5 Weight gain (left panel) and visceral fat gain (right panel) in 12 pairs of monozygotic male twins after 100 days of overfeeding.

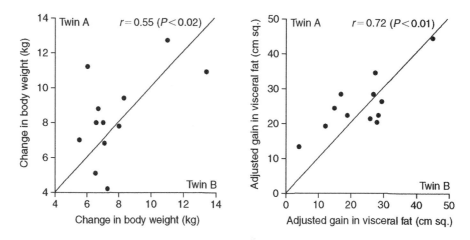

Notes: Visceral fat gain was adjusted for the gain in total fat mass. The data suggest a moderate effect of genes for weight gain with overfeeding and a strong effect for visceral fat gain.

4.3 kg to 13.3 kg. Moreover, there was a significant relationship between weight gains within twin pairs, indicating a genetic influence on weight gain. This influence was more pronounced when examining gain in visceral fat (Figure 6.5). These findings demonstrate that genes influence an individual's susceptibility to weight gain through overeating. As we shall see later in this chapter, genes also influence the amount of weight loss that occurs with exercise.

BOX 6.1 LEPTIN AND OBESITY

The word 'leptin' is derived from the Greek word 'leptos', meaning 'thin'. Leptin is an adipocyte-derived hormone which acts on the hypothalamus to suppress appetite and increase energy expenditure. As fat cells increase in size, they secrete more leptin to stabilize or reduce food intake and oppose further weight gain. Individuals with defective *ob* genes do not produce leptin, and as a consequence their appetites are not suppressed. This results in overeating and obesity. In such individuals, leptin therapy is highly effective in reversing weight gain. In one report concerning a nine-year-old leptin-deficient girl, subcutaneous leptin injections led to a 16.4 kg reduction in body mass (from 94.4 kg to 78 kg) over a 12-month period (Farooqi *et al.* 1999). Another report demonstrates that leptin therapy is equally effective in leptin-deficient adults (Figure 6.6). Defects in leptin secretion are very rare, however, and most obese individuals exhibit high rather than low leptin concentrations. This suggests insensitivity to leptin, possibly due to a defect in leptin receptors.

Figure 6.6 The influence of leptin replacement therapy on body mass, fat mass, fat-free mass and percentage body fat in three obese, leptin-deficient adults over a period of 18 months.

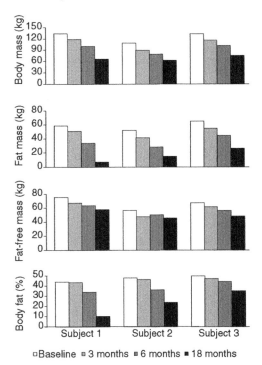

Source: Licinio *et al.* (2004).
Notes: At the time the study was conducted the subjects were 'the only three adults identified to date who have genetically based leptin deficiency'. Leptin was administered daily over an 18-month period causing a marked reduction in food intake (assessed by self-report) and an increase in physical activity (assessed using accelerometers). One of the subjects had type 2 diabetes at baseline. This was 'resolved' by the end of the study.

Although a genetic influence on obesity is clear, much remains to be learned regarding the mechanisms by which genes predispose to obesity. In most individuals, obesity is likely to be a polygenic disorder caused by interactions between a variety of genes controlling energy intake and energy expenditure. Few of these genes have been identified, although some monogenic causes of obesity have been discovered. Most notable among these is a defect in the *ob* gene responsible for leptin production (Box 6.1; Figure 6.6). Another example involves defective melanocortin-4 receptors (MC4R). Stimulation of the MC4R by α-melanocyte-stimulating hormone (α-MSH) causes decreased food intake and increased energy expenditure and defects in the MC4R lead to overeating and obesity. Such defects are rare according to Korner and Aronne (2003), who estimate that 1–5% of humans with a BMI >40 have mutations in MC4R. Other known monogenic causes of obesity are also rare. Moreover, genetic factors alone cannot explain the change in obesity prevalence that has occurred in recent decades.

PREVALENCE

One of the reasons that there is so much interest in the field of obesity is because its prevalence appears to be increasing throughout the world. Citing data from the WHO's Global Database on Body Mass Index, Jeffery and Sherwood (2008) reveal that obesity prevalence varies from 0.7% to 78.5% among countries, and that rates of obesity have roughly tripled in countries such as Japan, Brazil, England and the United States over the last 20–30 years. According to Andrew Prentice 'the obesity pandemic originated in the US and crossed to Europe and the world's other rich nations before, remarkably, it penetrated even the world's poorest countries especially in their urban areas' (Prentice 2006: p. 93).

In the United States, temporal changes in height and weight (and hence BMI) among the population have been monitored by the National Health and Nutrition Examination Survey (NHANES) programme. Data from these surveys reveal that the mean BMI ($kg\,m^2$) of American men increased from 25.1 to 27.9, while that of American women increased from 24.9 to 28.2 between the first survey in 1960–2 and the fourth survey in 1999–2002 (Table 6.2). According to Flegal (2006), these BMI changes are equivalent to an average weight gain in excess of 7 kg since 1976–80 for American men and women of average heights. When these data are used to identify the prevalence of obesity (BMI $\geq 30\,kg\,m^2$) they reveal an increase from approximately 14.5% in 1976–80 to approximately 30% in 1999–2000 (Blair and LaMonte 2006).

Table 6.2 Mean BMI values for men and women living in the United States across four NHANES programme periods from 1960–2 to 1999–2002

	1960–2	1976–80	1988–94	1999–2002
Men	25.1	25.6	26.8	27.9
Women	24.9	25.3	26.6	28.2

Source: Flegal (2006).

These trends have led some researchers to speculate that the steady rise in life expectancy in the United States during the last two centuries may come to an end in the present century (Haslam and James 2005; Olshansky *et al.* 2005).

Consistent with trends in the United States, the prevalence of obesity in England increased from 7% to 23% in men and from 12% to 24% in women between 1986/7 and 2004 (Figure 6.7). Moreover, data collated by the British Heart Foundation (2007) show that the prevalence of obesity is high in many countries throughout the world as demonstrated in Figure 6.8. Surveys also indicate that the prevalence of obesity has increased among children and adolescents in many countries (see Chapter 10).

There has been some dispute about the scale and seriousness of the issue of obesity, with some academics arguing that the obesity epidemic has been exaggerated (Basham and Luik 2008) and that this represents a 'moral panic' (Campos *et al.* 2006). Some of the controversy is due to the use of the word 'epidemic', but this word does appear to be justified based on BMI data from numerous surveys conducted world-wide (see Flegal (2006) for an informative discussion of this issue). Aside from questioning prevalence data, Basham and Luik (2008) and Campos *et al.* (2006) have also questioned the extent to which obesity increases the risk of morbidity and mortality. This issue is examined in the next section.

Figure 6.7 Prevalence of obesity (BMI >30 kg m²) among adults (aged 16–64 years) in England between 1986/7 and 2004.

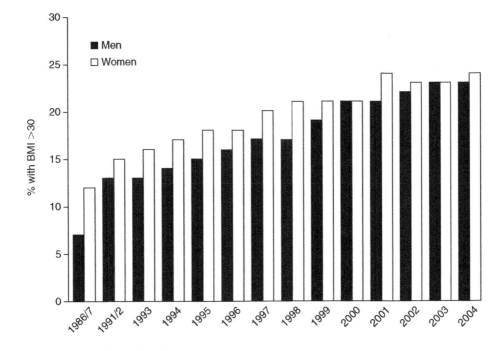

Source: British Heart Foundation (2007).

Figure 6.8 Prevalence of obesity (BMI ≥30 kg m²) in the year 2002 for adults (aged 15 and over) in selected countries world-wide.

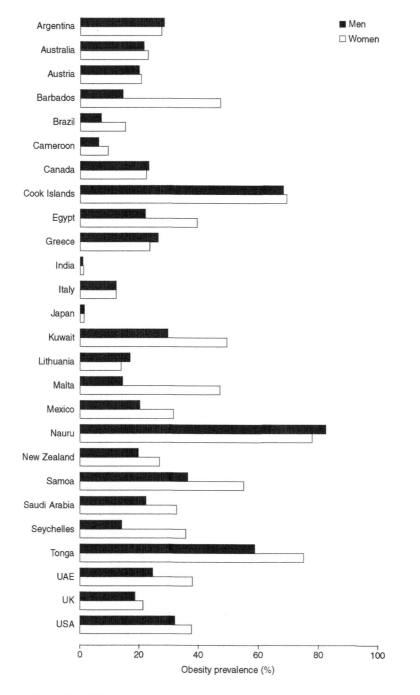

Source: British Heart Foundation (2007).
Note: UAE, United Arab Emirates

HEALTH RISKS

Obesity increases the risk of a variety of health outcomes, most notably type 2 diabetes and, to a lesser extent, cardiovascular disease (CVD) and cancer. Care should be taken, however, not to exaggerate the risks of obesity, and in particular care should be taken to distinguish between the risks of overweight (BMI 25–<30 kg m²) and mild obesity (BMI ≥30 kg m²) versus the risks of severe (morbid) obesity (BMI ≥40 kg m²). To take one example, James (2008, p. 336) states that an optimum population BMI is about 21 kg m², but data from many studies conflict with this. One study of American men and women, for example, reported that the optimal BMI, associated with the greatest longevity, is approximately 23–25 for whites and 23–30 for blacks (Fontaine *et al.* 2003). The same study observed that severe obesity (BMI >45) in young adults (aged 20–30 years) is associated with a 13-year reduction in life expectancy in men and an 8-year reduction in women, but such dramatic reductions would not apply to the large number of marginally obese individuals.

A further illustration of the conflicting evidence in this area is provided by the findings of some recent studies, all published in highly respected journals. Two papers appearing in the *New England Journal of Medicine* in 2006 concluded that both overweight and obesity increased the risk of death. One of these studies involved a 12-year follow-up of 1.2 million Korean men and women (Jee *et al.* 2006). The other involved up to ten years of follow-up of over 500,000 American men and women (Adams *et al.* 2006). In contrast are the findings of Flegal *et al.* (2005), published in the *Journal of the American Medical Association* relating to data from NHANES. Obesity was associated with 112,000 excess deaths in the United States. This was much lower than a previous estimate of 280,000, based on data from five prospective US cohort studies (Allison *et al.* 1999). Moreover, being overweight was not associated with excess mortality in the study of Flegal *et al.* (2005).

More recently, Flegal *et al.* (2007) have published a follow-up study examining cause-specific mortality using data from NHANES. In this report being overweight was associated with significantly *decreased* mortality from non-cancer, non-CVD causes, but not associated with cancer or CVD mortality. Obesity was associated with significantly increased CVD mortality, but not associated with cancer mortality or with non-cancer, non-CVD mortality. Consistent with these findings are the findings of a systematic review of 40 studies (250,000 individuals) published in the *Lancet* observing the *lowest* risk of death in overweight individuals (i.e. lower than normal weight individuals) while the risk of death was not elevated in obese individuals compared with those of 'normal' BMI (Romero-Corral *et al.* 2006).

The inconsistencies reported here are used not to dispute that obesity has adverse consequences for health. Obesity is associated with an increased risk of developing type 2 diabetes, CVD (Wild and Byrne 2006) and some types of cancer (McMillian *et al.* 2006; Reeves *et al.* 2007) as well as certain other conditions (Haslam *et al.* 2006). Figure 6.9 displays some of the elevated health risks of obesity. The strong association between obesity and type 2 diabetes was addressed in the previous chapter. Part of the reason for the decline in mortality from obesity reported in the United States may be improvements in medical care. This suggestion is supported by the observation that the prevalence of CVD risk factors has declined in obese individuals in the United

Figure 6.9 Prevalence of various health conditions according to weight status in men and women from the United States.

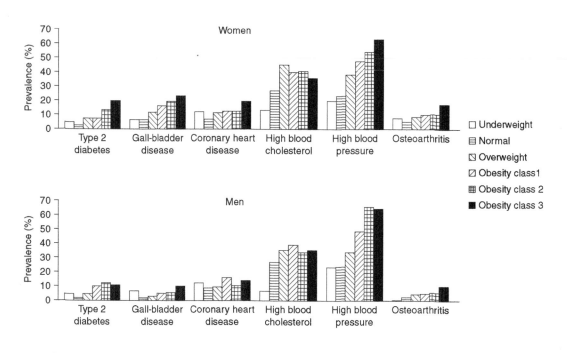

Source: Must *et al.* (1999).

Notes: The sample size was 7,689 for women and 6,987 for men. Observe in particular the high prevalence of hypertension and that in most cases there is evidence of dose–response.

States over the past 40 years, possibly due to increases in lipid-lowering therapy and antihypertensive medication (Gregg *et al.* 2005). Moreover, although there have been declines in obesity-related mortality in the United States, obesity-related disability has increased (Alley and Chang 2007).

There is uncertainty, however, regarding the extent to which overweight (as currently defined, i.e. BMI 25–<30 kg m^2) increases the risk of disease and mortality. For mild obesity the increase in the relative risk of diseases such as CVD and cancer, although significant, is often small. For example, in the Million Women Study (Reeves *et al.* 2007) which involved 1.2 million UK women, obesity was associated with a two- to three-fold increase in the risk of cancers of the endometrium and oesophagus, but for all cancers combined the increase in risk was just 12% (i.e. relative risk equal to 1.12). Although significant, this represents a rather small increase in absolute risk of cancer for any given individual, a point which is often absent from scientific and media reports describing the association between obesity and disease risk. (For readers wishing to explore this issue further Rifkin and Bouwer's (2007) book, *The Illusion of Certainty*, provides an excellent starting point.)

Some of the uncertainty about the link between obesity and health may be resolved by studies examining markers for abdominal obesity. Several large studies of this nature have been published recently. One was a case-control study examining the association between obesity and risk of myocardial infarction in 27,000 participants from 52 countries (Yusuf *et al.* 2005). Only a 'modest' association was observed between BMI and myocardial infarction risk, and this association was not significant after adjustment for potentially confounding factors. In contrast, waist-to-hip ratio (a marker for abdominal obesity) showed a graded and 'highly significant' association with myocardial infarction, leading to the suggestion by some that the BMI is 'obsolete' as a marker for obesity (Kragelund and Omland 2005). Other recent studies have confirmed that abdominal obesity is associated with type 2 diabetes, CVD, cancer and all-cause mortality (Balkau *et al.* 2007; Zhang *et al.* 2008). Such findings will lead to improved identification of the risks associated with obesity, but the prediction of these risks remains an imperfect science.

PHYSICAL INACTIVITY AS A RISK FACTOR

Low levels of physical activity and high levels of food intake are thought to be the driving force behind the increasing prevalence of obesity. Keith *et al.* (2006) label diet and exercise as the 'Big Two' explanations for the obesity epidemic while proposing that a variety of additional environmental influences may play a role including increased sleep debt, reduced variability in ambient temperature (due, for example, to central heating which reduces the need for thermogenesis) and decreased smoking prevalence (smoking has thermogenic and appetite suppressing effects and smokers tend to weigh less than non-smokers). In this section we will examine evidence from a variety of sources which indicates that low levels of physical activity predispose individuals to obesity. Much of the evidence supports a link between inactivity and obesity, but there are important limitations to this evidence which will be highlighted.

Cross-sectional studies have identified an association between low levels of physical activity and increased risk of obesity. In most of these studies questionnaires have been used to assess physical activity levels. One example is a study examining physical activity levels of over 15,000 men and women from 15 member states of the European Union. This study found an inverse association between leisure-time physical activity and BMI and a positive association between the amount of time spent sitting and BMI. Odds ratios for obesity (BMI >30 kg m^2) were 0.52 for those who were most active in leisure time versus those who were least active, and 1.61 for those who spent more than 35 hours per week of their leisure time sitting down compared with those who spent less than 15 hours sitting (Martínez-González *et al.* 1999). Consistent with these findings are those of the FINRISK study conducted in Finland (Lahti-Koski *et al.* 2002). This study involved four independent cross-sectional surveys conducted at five-year intervals between 1982 and 1997. Altogether, 24,604 randomly selected men and women participated in the surveys. Inverse associations were found between activity levels in leisure time and the risk of obesity and also between the amount of time spent walking or cycling to work and the risk of obesity (Figure 6.10).

An obvious limitation of cross-sectional studies is their inability to distinguish between cause and effect. Prospective and retrospective studies address this issue to some extent by assessing the association between physical activity levels and weight change over time. One example is a report from the VITamins And Lifestyle (VITAL)

Figure 6.10 Association between time spent walking or cycling to work and the risk of obesity (BMI >30 kg m²) in Finnish men and women participating in the FINRISK studies.

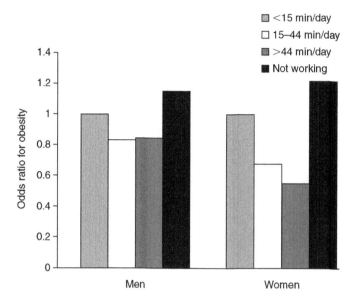

Source: Lahti-Koski *et al.* (2002).
Notes: Data are from four cross-sectional surveys conducted in 1982, 1987, 1992 and 1997 involving 26,604 men and women aged 25–64. A clear negative association between active commuting and risk of obesity is evident in women, but the pattern is less clear in men.

study involving over 15,000 adults from Washington State in the US (Littman *et al.* 2005). This study found high levels of physical activity, including common activities carried out at a moderate intensity, such as walking, were associated with lower weight gain over time (Figure 6.11). These findings are supported by reports from the Cancer Prevention Study in the United States (Kahn *et al.* 1997) and from a study conducted in Finland (Haapanen *et al.* 1997). Moreover, a report from the US Health Professionals Follow-up Study has extended these findings by demonstrating an association between high levels of physical activity and a reduced risk of weight gain over time (Koh-Banerjee *et al.* 2003). However, some studies have failed to identify an association between baseline physical activity levels and subsequent weight gain (Williamson *et al.* 1993) while other cross-sectional (Williams and Pate 2005) and prospective (Williams and Wood 2006) studies indicate that although physical activity attenuates the weight gain associated with ageing, it does not prevent it completely.

One of the limitations of questionnaire-based assessments of physical activity is that they are susceptible to inaccuracy in recall and reporter bias. This limitation can be addressed using the doubly labelled water technique for measuring total energy expenditure (see Box 2.2). This technique has been used to study physical activity levels in a group called 'Pima Indians', who are known to be genetically predisposed to obesity and type 2 diabetes. One group of Pima Indians resides in the Sierra Madre Mountains in Mexico and is reported to lead a 'traditional lifestyle'. Another group

Figure 6.11 Weight change after age 45 in men and women aged 53–57 years, according to physical activity levels (MET-h week⁻¹) over the previous ten years.

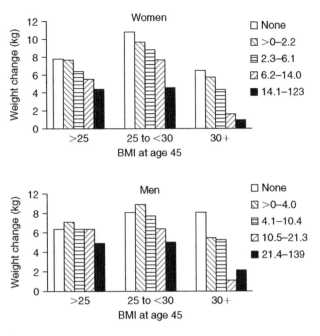

Source: Littman *et al.* (2005).

Notes: Subjects were 15,000 adults living in Washington State in the United States, enrolled on the VITamins And Lifestyle (VITAL) study. Physical activity was assessed retrospectively using a questionnaire. Weight change was adjusted for age at baseline (i.e. 53–57 years), weight at age 45, education, energy intake, smoking and weight change between ages 30 and 45 years.

resides in Arizona and have apparently adopted a 'typical North American lifestyle'. A cross-sectional study conducted by Esparza *et al.* (2000) found that physical activity levels were significantly higher in the Mexican versus the US Pima Indians (Table 6.3), leading the researchers to conclude that high levels of physical activity in combination with a diet low in fat and high in fibre may protect the Mexican Pima Indians from obesity and type 2 diabetes, which is far more prevalent in the Pima Indians living in Arizona.

Longitudinal studies employing the doubly labelled water technique have confirmed that low levels of physical activity are an important predisposing factor for weight gain. One such study involved 61 pre-menopausal American women assessed before and after a one-year period of no intervention (Weinsier *et al.* 2002). Energy expenditure in physical activity was estimated by deducting sleeping energy expenditure and the energy expenditure involved in metabolizing meals from total energy expenditure. Subjects were classified as weight maintainers or weight gainers at the end of the study year. Maintainers exhibited far higher physical activity energy expenditure than gainers, both at baseline (2,937 kJ/day versus 2,054 kJ/day) and at follow-up (2,841 kJ/ day versus 1,954 kJ/day). Similarly, Roberts *et al.* (1988) reported that total energy

Table 6.3 Physical characteristics, energy expenditure values and physical activity levels in Mexican Pima Indians and US Pima Indians (mean ± SD)

	MEXICAN PIMA INDIANS (17 FEMALE/23 MALE)	US PIMA INDIANS (17 FEMALE/23 MALE)
Age (years)	36.6 ± 11.4	37.2 ± 12.4
Height (cm)	163 ± 9	166 ± 7
Weight (kg)	66.5 ± 12.6	92.8 ± 22.4
Fat (%)	29 ± 10	41 ± 10
Fat mass (kg)	16.7 ± 6.7	33.5 ± 14.1
RMR (kcal/day)	1,529 ± 223	1,881 ± 327
TEE (kcal/day)	3,010 ± 722	2,940 ± 514
TEE (kcal/kgFFM/day)	3,156 ± 415	2,805 ± 415
PAL	1.97 ± 0.34	1.57 ± 0.16

Source: Esparza *et al.* (2000).

Notes: RMR: resting metabolic rate; TEE: total energy expenditure; FFM: fat-free mass; PAL: physical activity level. TEE was measured using doubly labelled water. PAL was calculated as the ratio of TEE (kcal/kgFFM/day) to RMR. Age, height and TEE (kcal/day) did not differ significantly between groups. All other differences are significant ($P<0.004$ to $P<0.0001$).

expenditure (assessed at three months of age using doubly labelled water) was 20% lower in infants who became overweight between birth and one year than in infants who remained lean.

Another objective method for assessing physical activity involves the use of devices such as accelerometers and inclinometers. These can be attached to the body to provide movement counts, as well as estimates of movement speed and body position, e.g. standing versus lying down. Such devices were used in a novel study by James Levine *et al.* (2005), which monitored activity patterns in ten lean subjects and ten obese subjects over a period of ten days. During this time, researchers collected 25 million data points from each volunteer and they observed that obese individuals spent more time sitting and less time standing and moving around than lean individuals (Figure 6.12).

As with other cross-sectional studies, the study of Levine *et al.* (2005) cannot determine whether decreased physical activity caused obesity or whether obesity lead to reductions in physical activity. The former suggestion is supported, however, by the finding that posture allocation did not change in obese individuals after weight loss or in lean individuals after weight gain. Importantly, both the lean and the obese individuals participating in this study described themselves as 'couch potatoes' and the differences in activity levels were not due to differences in deliberate exercise, but rather to differences in the energy expended in daily activities such as sitting, standing, walking and talking. Levine *et al.* labelled this 'non-exercise activity thermogenesis' (NEAT). They suggest that NEAT may be biologically determined and they estimate that it may vary between people by up to 2,000 kcal/day (8.4 MJ/day). They conclude that 'the obesity epidemic may reflect the emergence of a chair-enticing environment to which those with an innate tendency to sit, did so, and became obese' (Levine *et al.* 2006: p. 729).

Figure 6.12 Time allocation for different postures for ten obese and ten lean sedentary subjects.

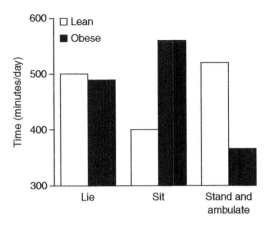

Source: Levine *et al.* (2005).

Notes: Posture allocation was assessed using inclinometers and accelerometers to capture data on body position and motion 120 times each minute over a ten-day period. Compared with obese individuals, lean individuals spent significantly more time standing and moving around, and significantly less time sitting. Both groups described themselves as 'couch potatoes', suggesting that high levels of non-exercise activity thermogenesis (NEAT) may protect from obesity.

Recently, James Levine's research group have provided further evidence implicating physical inactivity with weight gain and obesity. Once again they used inclinometers and accelerometers attached to lean and obese men and women (their average age was 39 years), but this time they focused specifically on free-living walking activity before and after an eight-week period of overfeeding (4.2 MJ/day) during which subjects gained an average of 3.6 kg in weight (2.8 kg gain in fat mass). One key finding from the study was that lean subjects walked 3.5 miles per day more than obese subjects both before and after overfeeding. Equally important, however, was the finding that average free-living walking speed was reduced without any compensation in walking duration. This resulted in a significant decrease in daily walking distance in both lean and obese subjects, suggesting that progressive increases in weight are associated with progressive decreases in walking distance, which are likely to exacerbate weight gain over time (Levine *et al.* 2008).

Some studies have attempted to identify which is more important in determining obesity: physical inactivity or overeating. One frequently cited example is the paper entitled 'Obesity in Britain: gluttony or sloth?' by Andrew Prentice and Susan Jebb. This paper revealed that changing patterns of car ownership and television viewing (used as surrogate markers for physical inactivity) mirrored changes in obesity prevalence in Britain, whereas changes in energy and fat intake were unrelated to changes in obesity prevalence (Figure 6.13). This led the authors to conclude that 'modern inactive lifestyles are at least as important as diet in the aetiology of obesity and possibly represent the dominant factor' (Prentice and Jebb 1995: p. 437).

In contrast to the findings of Prentice and Jebb, data collected in the NHANES programme in the United States indicate that between 1971 and 2000 average energy

Figure 6.13 Temporal trends in diet (left) and activity (right) in relation to obesity in Britain.

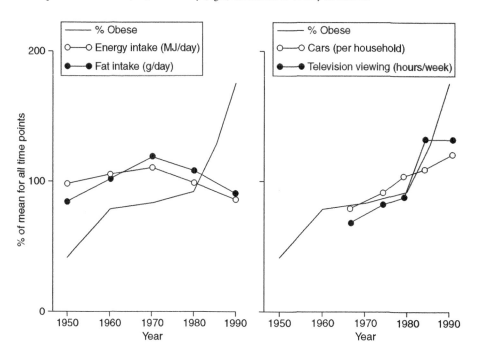

Source: Reproduced from 'Obesity in Britain: gluttony or sloth?', Prentice, A.M. and Jebb, S.A., *British Medical Journal* 311: 437–9., page 439, (1995) with permission from BMJ Publishing Group Ltd.
Notes: Data for diet are from the National Food Survey; data for BMI are from the Office of Population Censuses and Surveys and historical surveys; data for television viewing and car ownership are from the Central Statistical Office.

intake increased from 2,450 kcal/day to 2,618 kcal/day in men and from 1,542 kcal/day to 1,877 kcal/day in women. This suggests that diet played a prominent role in the increased obesity prevalence occurring in the United States during these years (Morbidity and Mortality Weekly Report 2004). In addition, recent work examining energy expenditure trends over time using doubly labelled water suggests that physical activity levels have not declined since the 1980s, a time when there were rapid increases in obesity prevalence in Europe and North America, indicating that physical inactivity may not be a major explanation for the changes in obesity prevalence observed since the 1980s (Westerterp and Speakman 2008). Unfortunately, all of the studies reported here have their limitations. Physical activity levels may not be strongly correlated with car ownership and television viewing; dietary surveys are subject to recall bias and doubly labelled water data collected from relatively small groups of subjects may not be representative of the general population. In view of this, the relative contributions of diet and physical inactivity to obesity remain uncertain and they may differ between different individuals and within the same individual over time.

It is clear from the preceding discussion that evidence can be found to implicate low levels of physical activity with the development of obesity. However, all of the studies described here are observational and confounding by other factors and reverse causality cannot be ruled out as explanations for the association between physical inactivity and obesity. Nicholas Wareham *et al.* (2005) recently reviewed the evidence concerning physical activity and obesity prevention and they concluded that low levels of activity are only weakly associated with future weight gain. They point out that randomized clinical trials are essential for determining more clearly the role of physical activity in preventing obesity. Unfortunately, they found only six clinical trials published since 2000 which have addressed this issue, and for various methodological reasons the conclusions of these trials are uncertain. Thus, further study is required before definitive statements can be made regarding the role of physical activity in preventing obesity.

EXERCISE AS THERAPY

Many studies have examined the effectiveness of exercise, either alone or in combination with diet, as a therapy for overweight and obesity. It is important to note from the outset when discussing the therapeutic effects of exercise for obesity that obesity, as defined by the BMI, is a heterogeneous condition. This means that the role and effectiveness of exercise are likely to vary depending on the severity of obesity. For individuals whose BMI is just above $30 \, kg \, m^2$, exercise may be sufficient to produce meaningful weight loss, whereas surgery may be the only option for achieving significant weight loss for those with a BMI of $60 \, kg \, m^2$ or more, although diet and exercise would still form important components of an overall therapeutic strategy in such individuals.

Several studies have demonstrated that large amounts of weight loss are possible when exercise is the sole or main form of intervention. One example is a study of 32 obese Bulgarian women who lost an average of 12.4 kg after a 45-day exercise training programme while consuming normocaloric diets (Hadjiolova *et al.* 1982). Another example is a study of 197 young obese men undergoing basic military training in Singapore. The subjects in this study were divided into three groups based on their initial percentage body fat as follows: 24–<30% fat, 30–<35% fat and ≥35% fat. At the end of the 20-week training period average weight loss was 10.7 kg, 13.1 kg and 16.1 kg, respectively, for each group (Lee *et al.* 1994). These findings in Bulgarian women and Singaporean men are not typical. They demonstrate what can be achieved in highly controlled environments with very large amounts of exercise (the Bulgarian women exercised for about ten hours per day and expended 1.51–1.55 MJ per day).

A more representative example of the effectiveness of exercise intervention is provided by the Midwest Exercise Trial. This study involved a 16-month intervention in previously sedentary, overweight and moderately obese men and women aged 17–35 years. Participants were encouraged to exercise on five days each week with a target energy expenditure of 8.4 MJ/week and they were allowed to consume food ad libitum throughout the study. By the end of the study men in the intervention group had lost an average of 5 kg. There was no weight loss in women in the intervention group, but the exercise intervention did prevent a 3 kg weight gain which occurred in women in the control group (Donnelly *et al.* 2003). Findings such as these have led some to conclude that exercise without dietary restriction is an effective strategy for reducing obesity (Ross *et al.* 2000). It seems clear from the literature, however, that a combination of diet and exercise is likely to be most effective for achieving weight loss (Avenell *et al.* 2006).

Examples of well-controlled studies demonstrating significant weight loss after combined diet and exercise programmes come mainly from America (Andersen *et al.* 1999; Jakicic *et al.* 1999; Jakicic *et al.* 2003; Jeffery *et al.* 2003). These studies clearly show that exercise volume is a crucial factor determining the amount of weight lost. In one study by Jakicic *et al.* those performing more than 200 minutes of exercise per week (close to 30 minutes per day) lost 13.1 kg after 18 months, whereas those performing 150–200 minutes of exercise per week lost 8.5 kg, and those performing less than 150 minutes of exercise per week lost only 3.5 kg (Figure 6.14). There is also evidence to show that some individuals will experience a greater amount of weight loss than others despite an equal dose of exercise and that this difference is partly determined by genetic factors (Figure 6.15).

The data in Figure 6.15 indicate that as well as inducing weight loss, exercise also reduces visceral (intra-abdominal) adipose tissue in men. This has been confirmed in women as well (Irwin *et al.* 2003). Reductions in intra-abdominal fat may occur in the absence of weight loss, but greater reductions are likely when there is concurrent weight loss (Ross and Janssen 2007) and this is most likely when diet and exercise are combined. Plate 5 displays magnetic resonance images of subcutaneous and visceral adipose tissue before and after diet and exercise intervention. These clearly illustrate that reductions occur in both adipose tissue regions.

Despite the positive findings described above, studies consistently indicate that long term maintenance of weight loss is difficult. In a systematic review of randomized clinical trials comparing diet-and-exercise interventions with diet-alone interventions,

Figure 6.14 Dose–response relationship between weekly exercise duration and weight loss in 148 overweight and obese women participating in an 18-month weight-control programme.

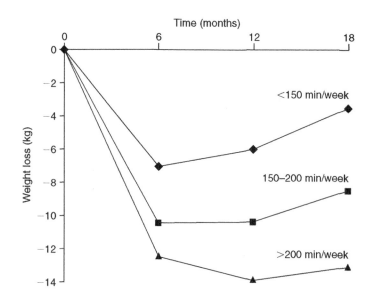

Source: Jakicic *et al.* (1999). Copyright © 1999 *Journal of the American Medical Association. All rights reserved.*
Note: The weight-control programme included reductions in energy and fat intake as well as exercise intervention.

Figure 6.15 Genetic influence on exercise-induced weight loss as indicated by changes in body weight (left panel) and visceral fat (right panel) in seven pairs of male monozygotic twins after a 244 MJ energy deficit induced by exercise over a 93-day period.

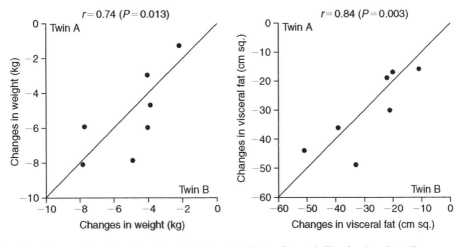

Source: Reprinted by permission from Macmillan Publishers Ltd: Obesity Research (Bouchard *et al.* 1994).

Curioni and Lourenço (2005) observed that combined diet-and-exercise interventions produced greater initial weight loss (13 kg versus 9.9 kg) and greater sustained weight loss after one year (6.7 kg versus 4.5 kg) than diet-only interventions, but in both cases almost half of the initial weight loss is regained after one year. Nevertheless, Wing and Phelan (2005) point out that approximately 20% of overweight people in the general population are successful at long-term weight loss maintenance. In the United States the National Weight Control Registry (NWCR) has been used to study people who are successful at long-term maintenance of weight loss. One report from this registry provided information on 629 women and 155 men who had lost an average of 30 kg and maintained a minimum weight loss of 13.6 kg (30 lbs) for five years (14% of registry members had lost 45.4 kg (100 lb) or more). The factors common among these individuals were low energy intakes (5,778 kJ/day), low fat intakes (24% of energy from fat) and high energy expenditures (11,830 kJ/week) through physical activity (Klem *et al.* 1997). These findings demonstrate that long term weight loss maintenance is possible if individuals remain motivated to maintain lifestyle change.

Long-term maintenance of weight loss may be aided by pharmacotherapy. Three drugs are currently approved for the management of obesity. These are orlistat, sibutramine and rimonabant (Table 6.4). These drugs are generally associated with modest weight loss (<5 kg), but some studies have shown that combined pharmacotherapy and lifestyle intervention (including physical activity) can be particularly effective. Wadden *et al.* (2005), for example, noted average one-year weight losses of 5.0 kg for sibutramine alone, 6.7 kg for lifestyle modification alone and 12.1 kg for combined intervention. Also, nearly twice as many subjects in the combined therapy group as in the monotherapy groups lost 10% or more of their initial weight. Similarly, orlistat has been shown to reduce weight regain after conventional dieting (Hill *et al.* 1999), while

Plate 5 Magnetic resonance images in the lumbar spine for a man and a woman before and after a 16-week programme of diet and exercise.

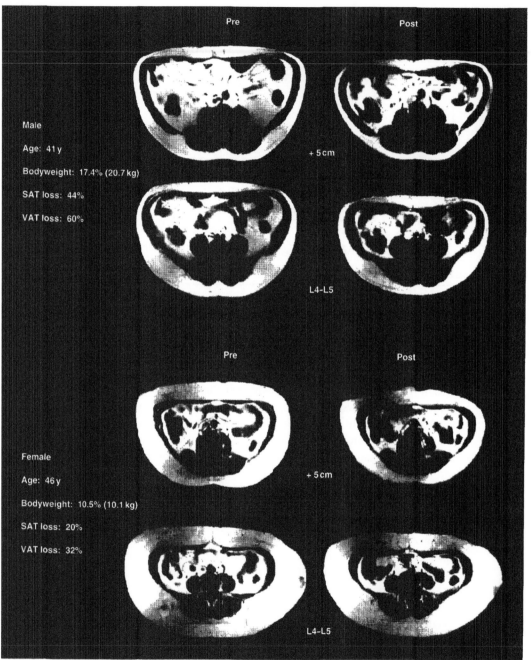

Source: Ross (1997).
Notes: The scans are taken at the lumbar level L4–L5 and 5 cm above this. The diet and exercise programme resulted in a mean weight loss of 11 kg. Adipose tissue is shown in white. SAT, subcutaneous adipose tissue; VAT, visceral adipose tissue. Note the reductions in SAT and VAT indicated by the reduced amount of whiteness in the post intervention scans.

Table 6.4 Drugs licensed for obesity management

DRUG NAME	MECHANISM	MEAN WEIGHT LOSS	OTHER BENEFITS	POSSIBLE ADVERSE EFFECTS
Orlistat	Intestinal lipase inhibitor. Inhibits the breakdown of fat.	2.9 kg (2.5–3.2 kg). Average across 16 trials.	Reduced risk of diabetes, improved TC and LDL-C concentrations. Improved BP and glycaemic control in patients with diabetes.	Gastrointestinal side effects and slightly lowered HDL-C concentrations.
Sibutramine	Inhibits the re-uptake of noradrenalin and serotonin at receptor sites that affect food intake.	4.2 kg (3.6–4.7 kg). Average across ten trials.	Improved HDL-C and TG concentrations.	Dry mouth, dizziness, nausea, constipation, headaches, depression and raised BP.
Rimonabant	Cannabinoid-1 receptor antagonist. (Stimulation of cannabinoid-1 receptors in the brain promotes eating.)	4.7 kg (4.1–5.3 kg). Average across four trials.	Improved HDL-C and TG concentrations. Improved BP and glycaemic control in patients with diabetes.	Dizziness, nausea, diarrhoea, anxiety and depression.

Source: Compiled from Rucker *et al.* (2007) and Lean and Finer (2006)

Notes: Numbers in parenthesis indicate 95% confidence intervals. TC: total cholesterol; LDL-C: low density lipoprotein cholesterol; BP: blood pressure; HDL-C: high-density lipoprotein cholesterol; TG: triglyceride.

the non-energy-containing fat-replacer olestra provides a non-pharmalogical method of reducing energy and fat intake (Hill *et al.* 1998) which may be combined with exercise to assist weight loss.

As well as reducing weight and body fat, exercise may be important as a therapy for some of the co-morbidities associated with obesity. The effectiveness of exercise for reducing the risk of type 2 diabetes in overweight and obese adults was addressed in the previous chapter. There is also evidence to suggest that exercise training may reduce the risk of CVD in overweight and obese individuals. For example, aerobic exercise training has been shown to reduce triglyceride concentrations in overweight and obese adults (Kelley *et al.* 2005), although this is not always the case (Snyder *et al.* 1997). Cross-sectional studies indicate that the association between obesity and CVD risk is stronger than that between physical inactivity (Mora *et al.* 2006) or physical fitness (Christou *et al.* 2005) and CVD risk, suggesting that physical activity can reduce but not prevent the excess risk of CVD associated with obesity. This suggestion is supported by findings from the prospective Danish Diet, Cancer and Health study which observed that overweight and obesity were associated with a higher risk of acute coronary events among both active and inactive individuals, although the risk was lower in active individuals (Jensen *et al.* 2008).

In the section on health risks of obesity earlier in this chapter, it was highlighted that severe obesity increases the risk of premature death and it is therefore of interest to ask whether weight loss in obese individuals will reduce the risk of premature death. Data from studies of bariatric (weight loss) surgery are available to answer this question. Systematic review and meta-analysis of papers on bariatric surgery has demonstrated that diabetes, hyperlipidaemia, hypertension and obstructive sleep apnoea are 'resolved' in the majority of patients who undergo weight loss surgery (Buchwald *et al.* 2004), suggesting benefits for mortality. This has been confirmed in two recent studies, one conducted in Sweden (Sjöström *et al.* 2007), the other in the United States (Adams *et al.* 2007), both demonstrating lower long-term mortality rates in severely obese subjects who have undergone weight loss surgery than in severely obese

Table 6.5 Hazard ratios and 95% confidence intervals of total mortality between 1982 and 1999 by intention to lose weight in 1975 and weight change between 1975 and 1981

INTENTION TO LOSE WEIGHT (AND WEIGHT CHANGE)	HAZARD RATIO	CONFIDENCE INTERVAL	P VALUE
Yes (loss)	1.87	1.22–2.87	0.004
Yes (stable)	0.84	0.49–1.48	0.56
Yes (gain)	0.93	0.55–1.56	0.78
No (loss)	1.17	0.82–1.66	0.40
No (stable)	1.00	N/A	N/A
No (gain)	1.58	1.08–2.30	0.018

Source: Adapted from Sørensen *et al.* (2005).

Notes: The subjects were overweight men and women without co-morbidities. Hazard ratios are adjusted for sex, age, BMI, hypertension, smoking, alcohol drinking, physical activity, life satisfaction, work status and income. Note that, contrary to expectations, the highest risk of death occurred in those who intended to lose weight and lost weight.

individuals who have not undergone such surgery. Unfortunately, data concerning non-surgical weight loss and mortality are inconsistent and there is even data to suggest that intentional weight loss is associated with increased mortality risk in overweight individuals without co-morbidities (Table 6.5). This demonstrates once again that obesity is a complex condition, and in many respects knowledge of this condition remains incomplete.

PHYSICAL ACTIVITY RECOMMENDATIONS

Notwithstanding the uncertainties highlighted in this chapter, physical activity guidelines are required for those wishing to use exercise to avoid weight gain or to facilitate weight loss. Unfortunately, there is uncertainty here also. Hill *et al.* (2003) estimate that affecting energy balance by as little 0.42 MJ/day (100 kcal/day) (by a combination of diet and exercise) may be sufficient to prevent weight gain in most of the population. In contrast, the UK Department of Health (2004) recommends 45–60 minutes of exercise per day (5.25–7 hours per week) to avoid obesity.

The American College of Sports Medicine guidelines (Donnelly *et al.* 2009) recommend 150–250 minutes per week (2.5–4+ hours per week) of moderate-intensity exercise for preventing weight gain. These are lower than the UK Department of Health targets for avoiding obesity, although the American College of Sports Medicine recommendations state that greater amounts of physical activity (>250 minutes per week) will result in greater weight loss. An alternative recommendation for weight loss comes from Levine *et al.* (2006) who state that obese individuals could reverse their condition if they expended an additional 1.5 MJ/day (350 kcal/day) in NEAT (equivalent to standing and ambulating for an additional 2.5 hours each day).

There is general agreement that people who have been obese and lost weight may require greater amounts of exercise than those who have never been obese. The UK Department of Health (2004) recommends 60–90 minutes of exercise per day for those wishing to avoid regaining lost weight, a view endorsed by other experts in the field (Jakicic and Otto 2005; Hill and Wyatt 2005). The reader will by now appreciate that there will be variability in the response to these guidelines between individuals.

SUMMARY

- Obesity is defined as an excess of body fat to the point that health is endangered.
- Obesity is most commonly determined using the body mass index, with a value of 30 kg m^2 or more representing obesity. Elevated waist circumference is another useful marker for obesity.
- Obesity develops due to an imbalance between energy intake and energy expenditure. Genes appear to play a major role in determining an individual's susceptibility to obesity.

- The prevalence of obesity has increased in many countries around the world over the last few decades.
- Obesity, particularly severe obesity, increases the risk of premature mortality, type 2 diabetes, CVD, some forms of cancer and osteoarthritis. The extent to which overweight increases the risk of these outcomes is less certain.
- Observational evidence from a variety of sources suggests that physical inactivity is associated with the development of obesity, but there is a lack of evidence from intervention trials regarding the role of exercise in preventing obesity.
- Exercise can be effective in the management of obesity, particularly for those with mild obesity. Exercise is most effective when combined with diet.
- Weight regain is common among those who have lost weight through diet and exercise, but long-term maintenance of weight loss is possible in highly motivated individuals who maintain healthy dietary and exercise habits.
- Recommendations suggest that 45–60 minutes of exercise per day is required to prevent obesity and 60–90 minutes of exercise per day is required to prevent weight regain in formerly obese individuals, but there will be individual variation in the response to these doses of exercise.

STUDY TASKS

1 List the cut-off points for underweight, normal weight, overweight and obesity classes I, II and III. Identify waist circumference cut-off points indicative of increased health risks for men and women.

2 Highlight the health risks of obesity and discuss why there is some uncertainty regarding the health risks of being overweight.

3 Discuss evidence from three studies which indicate a genetic influence on suscepti-bility to obesity.

4 Discuss the findings of three studies which have demonstrated an association between physical inactivity and the risk of obesity. Highlight the methods used and state what is novel about each study. Then explain the strengths and limitations of the findings from each study.

5 With reference to research literature, write a one-page objective commentary regarding the role of exercise as a therapy for obesity. This commentary should discuss both the short-term and long-term effects of exercise.

6 Identify three drugs that may be used in the management of obesity. What amount of weight loss would you expect to see with each drug? List the advantages and dis-advantages of each drug.

7 Make a brief list of exercise recommendations:

a for the prevention of weight gain;
b for weight loss; and
c for the prevention of weight regain in formerly obese individuals.

What factors may determine an individual's response to these guidelines?

FURTHER READING

Avenell, A., Sattar, N. and Lean, M. (2006) 'ABC of obesity: management: part 1 – behaviour change, diet, and activity', *British Medical Journal* 333: 740–3.

Blair, S.N. and LaMonte, M.J. (2006) 'Commentary: current perspectives on obesity and health: black and white, or shades of grey?', *International Journal of Epidemiology* 35: 69–72.

Campos, P., Saguy, A., Ernsberger, P., Oliver, E. and Gaesser, G. (2006) 'The epidemiology of over-weight and obesity: public health crisis or moral panic?' *International Journal of Epidemiology* 35: 55–60.

Donnelly, J.E., Blair, S.N., Jakicic, J.M., Manore, M.M., Rankin, J.W. and Smith, B.K. (2009) 'Appropriate physical activity intervention strategies for weight loss and prevention of weight regain in adults', *Medicine and Science in Sports and Exercise* 41: 459–71.

Frayn, K.N. (2003) 'Energy Balance and Body Weight Regulation' in *Metabolic Regulation: A Human Perspective*, 2nd edn, Oxford: Blackwell Science Ltd, pp. 300–19.

Han, T.S., Sattar, N. and Lean, M. (2006) 'ABC of obesity: assessment of obesity and its clinical implications', *British Medical Journal* 333: 695–8.

Hill, J.O., Wyatt, H.R., Reed, G.W. and Peters, J.C. (2003) 'Obesity and the environment: where do we go from here?', *Science* 299: 853–5.

Kim, S. and Popkin, B.M. (2006) 'Commentary: understanding the epidemiology of overweight and obesity: a real global public health concern', *International Journal of Epidemiology* 35: 60–7.

Levine, J.A., Vander Weg, M.W., Hill, J.O. and Klesges, R.C. (2006) 'Non-exercise activity thermo-genesis: the crouching tiger hidden dragon of societal weight gain', *Arteriosclerosis, Thrombosis, and Vascular Biology* 26: 729–36.

Ross, R. and Janssen, I. (2007) 'Physical activity, fitness, and obesity', in Bouchard, C., Blair, S.N. and Haskell, W.L. (eds) *Physical Activity and Health*, Champaign: Human Kinetics, pp. 173–89.

Wareham, N.J., van Sluijs, E.M.F. and Ekelund, U. (2005) 'Physical activity and obesity prevention: a review of the current evidence', *Proceedings of the Nutrition Society* 64: 229–47.

7 Metabolic syndrome

Knowledge assumed
Actions of insulin
Basics of fat and carbohydrate metabolism
Cardiovascular physiology

INTRODUCTION

So far risk factors for cardiovascular disease (CVD) have been discussed individually in relation to the effects of physical activity (see Chapter 4). However, some risk factors tend to cluster together. These include dyslipidaemia (specifically, high triglycerides and low high-density lipoprotein (HDL)-cholesterol), impaired glucose regulation or diabetes, obesity (particularly visceral obesity) and hypertension. The phrase 'cluster together' means that these risk factors coexist more commonly than would be expected by chance. For example, diabetes and obesity are twice as common among people with hypertension as among those with normal blood pressure. As a combination, risk

Figure 7.1 Relative risk for CHD in people with increasing numbers of metabolic risk factors. Data from Framingham Offspring Study.

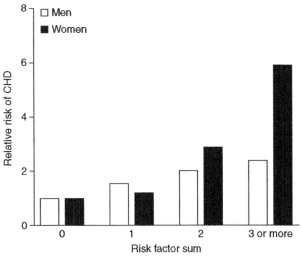

Source: Adapted from Wilson *et al.* (1999).

factors become much more powerful predictors of disease. Data from the Framingham Offspring Study[1] shows that clusters of three or more factors increased the risk of coronary heart disease (CHD) more than two-fold in men and nearly six-fold in women (Figure 7.1).

This clustering of risk factors is important for at least three reasons: first, it suggests the existence of a common aetiology; second, it makes it difficult to treat people because drugs are designed to target one pathology, not several; and third, (as the reader will realize) physical activity may be an especially attractive preventive and/or therapeutic intervention if it is beneficial for more than one component of the cluster.

A group of symptoms or abnormalities that occur together, making a pattern, are called a syndrome. The name most commonly given to the constellation of disturbances identified above and associated with elevated risk for CVD and type 2 diabetes is 'metabolic syndrome'.

DEFINITION AND PREVALENCE

While the concept of the metabolic syndrome has existed for at least 80 years, it is only since 1998 that attempts have been made to develop an internationally recognized definition. Details of two widely used sets of criteria with which to identify individuals with the syndrome are presented in Table 7.1. It is important to realize that both are intended to be simple tools with which clinicians can assess patients to improve their management, rather than a comprehensive list of the metabolic derangements associated with the metabolic syndrome.

Table 7.1 Clinical definitions of the metabolic syndrome

US NATIONAL CHOLESTEROL EDUCATION PROGRAM ADULT TREATMENT PANEL III (2001)	INTERNATIONAL DIABETES FEDERATION (2005)
Three or more of the following:	Central obesity: waist circumference*
Central obesity: waist circumference >102 cm (men), >88 cm (women)	≥94 cm (men), ≥80 cm (women) plus any two of the following:
Raised triglycerides: ≥1.7 mmol l^{-1}	• Raised triglycerides: >1.7 mmol l^{-1}
Low HDL-cholesterol: <1.0 mmol l^{-1} (men), <1.3 mmol l^{-1} (women)	• Low HDL-cholesterol: <1.03 mmol l^{-1} (men), <1.29 mmol l^{-1} (women)
Raised blood pressure: ≥135/85 mm Hg	• Raised blood pressure: systolic ≥130 mm Hg, diastolic ≥85 mm Hg
Raised fasting plasma glucose: ≥6.1 mmol l^{-1}	• Raised fasting plasma glucose: ≥5.6 mmol l^{-1}

Notes: Full details of the rationale and criteria adopted by these two expert panels available in National Institutes of Health (2001) or www.nhlbi.nih.gov/guidelines/cholesterol/index.htm and Alberti *et al.* (2006) or www.idf.org/home/index.cfm?unode=1120071E-AACE-41D2-9FA0-BAB6E25BA072.
* Values are for white people of European origin. Different cut-off points were identified for other ethnic groups.

Over the past two decades there has been a striking increase world-wide in the number of people with the metabolic syndrome, associated with the twin global epidemics of obesity and diabetes. Prevalence estimates differ according to the criteria adopted. As with any syndrome (and recognized in the definitions presented in Table 7.1), not all features are always present in the same individual. Available data using the US Adult Treatment Panel III criteria show wide variation in prevalence in both sexes, from 8% (India) to 24% (United States) in men and from 7% (France) to 43% (Iran) in women (Cameron *et al.* 2004), with average values in developed countries typically 20–25% of normal-weight adults. A much larger proportion of obese persons, around two-thirds, exhibit core features of the syndrome. Prevalence is highly age-dependent, increasing for example in the United States from 7% in those aged 20–29 years to 44% in 60–69-year-olds. On the other hand, the metabolic syndrome is now evident also in children, particularly obese children.

There appears to be a genetic predisposition to the metabolic syndrome among some ethnic groups. For example, prevalence is higher among Mexican-Americans than among non-Hispanic whites. In the United Kingdom, the high prevalence of CHD and type 2 diabetes among immigrants from the Indian subcontinent may be attributable to the metabolic syndrome.

CAUSAL FACTORS

The common 'cause' of the metabolic syndrome is a subject of considerable controversy. It has been argued that its defining feature is insulin resistance (Reaven 1988) and that the clustering of the components that make up the metabolic syndrome occurs only in insulin-resistant persons. Indeed, the term 'insulin resistance syndrome' has often been employed, in appreciation of this hypothesis.

An alternative view is that abdominal obesity, because it leads to the development of insulin resistance, is the primary causative component. The International Diabetes Federation, by considering this to be the one essential criterion, appear to assign to this abnormality a central aetiological role. Ectopic (wrongly placed) fat in the liver has also been proposed as a critical determinant of the insulin resistance associated with the metabolic syndrome. Survey data shows that an increase in liver fat content predicts type 2 diabetes, independently of obesity. Whatever the mechanisms that lead to its development, there is a strong argument that a reduction in sensitivity to insulin plays a fundamental role in the multifarious derangements that characterize the metabolic syndrome.

CHARACTERISTIC ABNORMALITIES

Insulin affects many diverse metabolic processes and, as sensitivity to its actions is reduced, these are impaired. Thus many of the abnormalities that characterize the metabolic syndrome – summarized in Box 7.1 – typify insulin-resistant states. The links between insulin resistance and the major syndrome features are explained below, insofar as they are understood.

Glucose intolerance

In people who are glucose intolerant there are deficiencies in insulin's ability to mediate glucose uptake and metabolism in muscle and adipose tissue, and in its ability to suppress glucose production by the liver and kidney (see Chapter 5 for further details). Therefore the blood glucose concentration rises and insulin is released in greater quantities from the pancreas. Some people can maintain this and avoid becoming diabetic, exhibiting higher than normal responses of both glucose and insulin to a standard oral glucose test. In others, the ability of the islets of Langerhans to sustain high rates of insulin production begins to fail and type 2 diabetes develops.

BOX 7.1 ABNORMALITIES ASSOCIATED WITH INSULIN RESISTANCE AND THE METABOLIC SYNDROME NOT INCLUDED IN DIAGNOSTIC CRITERIA

- Diabetes or impaired glucose tolerance
- Hyperinsulinaemia
- Atherogenic dyslipidaemia, e.g. high levels of Apolipoprotein B and C-III, small dense LDLs
- High level of postprandial lipaemia
- Prothrombotic factors, e.g. high fibrinogen, high viscosity
- High levels of markers for inflammation
- Microalbinuria[*]
- High uric acid[†]
- Non-alcoholic fatty liver disease
- Endothelial dysfunction

[*] Abnormally high albumin in urine indicative of vascular damage to glomeruli of kidney.
[†] Abnormally high uric acid in blood resulting from defects in insulin action on renal tubular reabsorption of uric acid.

Dyslipidaemia

Insulin exerts multiple influences on lipid metabolism that affect plasma lipoprotein variables. Collectively, they promote the uptake and storage of fatty acids in adipose tissue, inhibit their mobilization from adipose tissue and decrease secretion of very low-density lipoproteins (VLDL) from the liver. Plate 6 illustrates these influences schematically. When insulin resistance develops, its normal effects are impaired, leading to high plasma concentrations of triglycerides – one of the important diagnostic criteria for the metabolic syndrome.

Because insulin coordinates metabolism during the hours after a meal, the consequences of resistance to its effects on lipid metabolism are seen most clearly during the postprandial period. In insulin-resistant people, not only are fasting triglycerides higher, but the postprandial rise in triglycerides is also exaggerated and prolonged. Chylomicrons and VLDL circulate for longer, facilitating exchange of triglycerides in their core with HDL and LDL. This depletes HDL of cholesterol and leads to triglyceride-poor VLDL that are degraded to small dense LDL. This combination of lipid abnor-

Plate 6 Influence of insulin on lipid metabolism to promote lipid synthesis and storage.

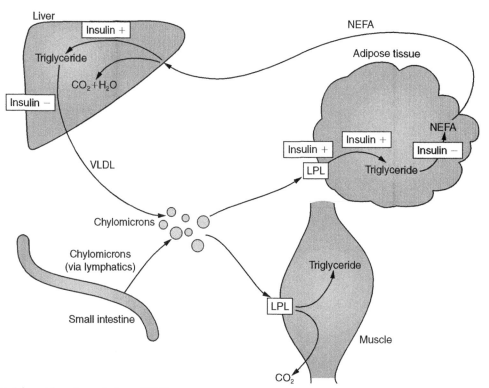

Source: Adapted from figures in Frayn (2003).
Note: LPL, lipoprotein lipase; Insulin +, insulin stimulates; Insulin –, insulin inhibits; NEFA, non-esterified fatty acids; VLDL, very low-density lipoproteins.

malities confers a high level of cardiovascular risk and is sometimes called the 'atherogenic lipoprotein phenotype'. Since people are non-fasting for most of the day, atherosclerosis may be regarded as a postprandial phenomenon.

Hypertension

Insulin-resistant states are consistently associated with hypertension. However, this is nowhere near as easy to explain as the association between insulin resistance and disordered lipid metabolism. Several potential mechanisms have been advanced. Three are explained briefly here. First, hyperinsulinaemia enhances renal sodium retention by increasing reabsorption in the distal tubules of the kidney. Plasma volume expands, leading to an increase in blood pressure. Second, insulin resistance increases sympathetic nervous activity that may be expected to increase blood pressure via an increase in total peripheral resistance. Third, hyperinsulinaemia creates a growth-promoting milieu that may induce vascular smooth muscle hypertrophy, perhaps in resistance vessels. This would also increase blood pressure through an increase in peripheral resistance.

Obesity

Nearly half the variation in insulin sensitivity amongst individuals is accounted for by variations in body fat content, even within relatively normal ranges of the body mass index (BMI). Thus, nearly all subjects who are obese have poor insulin sensitivity, even if they are apparently healthy. Weight reduction lowers the risk of type 2 diabetes and, in persons already affected by the disease, can improve insulin sensitivity and glucose tolerance. Thus over-fatness and insulin resistance are closely linked. The argument goes like this: excessive flux of non-esterified fatty acids from an enlarged adipose tissue mass impairs glucose uptake and utilization in muscle through the action of the glucose–fatty acid cycle; glucose uptake is then lower than expected for a given insulin concentration, i.e. sensitivity to insulin is reduced.

Another mechanism by which obesity may be linked to insulin resistance involves elevation of cytokines (inflammatory markers). (Both mechanisms were described in more detail in Chapter 5.)

However, the regional accumulation of adipose tissue in the visceral depot is a more reliable predictor than total body mass per se of the risk of CVD and type 2 diabetes. The reasons for this are not fully understood, but visceral adipocytes are particularly resistant to suppression of lipolysis by insulin. The portal vein drains visceral adipose tissue. Thus, in insulin-resistant states the liver is exposed to high concentrations of NEFAs and glycerol (a gluconeogenic precursor); hepatic glucose production is increased, while systemic glucose uptake is reduced because plasma NEFA concentrations remain high all day.

Figure 7.2 compares plasma responses of glucose and insulin to an oral glucose challenge in men with low or high levels of visceral adipose tissue, with similar levels of overall obesity. Both responses were significantly higher in men with high visceral obesity, showing that this exaggerates hyperglycaemia and hyperinsulinaemia (and by inference insulin resistance).

Figure 7.2 Differences in postprandial responses of glucose, insulin and triglycerides between men with either high or low levels of visceral obesity, matched for total fat mass.

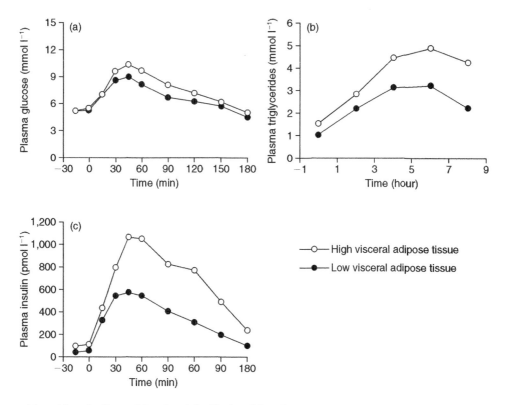

Sources: Adapted from Pouliot *et al.* (1992) and Couillard *et al.* (1998).

Note: Plasma concentrations of glucose (panel (a)) and insulin (panel (b)) after 75 g glucose tolerance test; plasma triglyceride concentration (panel (c)) after a mixed meal (64%, 18% and 18% of energy from fat, carbohydrate and protein, respectively).

Other manifestations

Insulin resistance is accompanied by many other metabolic and vascular abnormalities. These include: endothelial dysfunction that impairs the capability of blood vessels to respond to changes in blood flow; microalbinuria that indicates vascular damage affecting the glomeruli of the kidney; and the presence of prothrombotic factors. Further abnormalities are suggestive of a chronic, systemic low-grade inflammatory state now known to be associated with CVD and type 2 diabetes. Among these is an increased plasma concentration of tumour necrosis factor-α, a cytokine that originates largely in adipose tissue. Indeed, it has been suggested that TNF-α plays a direct role in the metabolic syndrome.

PHYSICAL ACTIVITY AND FITNESS IN RELATION TO THE METABOLIC SYNDROME

Insulin resistance is a key feature of the metabolic syndrome. Skeletal muscle is the body's largest insulin-sensitive tissue and the major influence on whole-body responsiveness to insulin. Conversely, insulin resistance resides largely in skeletal muscle. It is therefore logical to propose that physical activity may decrease the risk of developing the metabolic syndrome and/or have a therapeutic role in its management. This latter statement is supported by evidence from a prospective study that all-cause mortality is more than twice as high in unfit men with the metabolic syndrome than in fit men with the syndrome (Katzmarzyk *et al.* 2004).

The preventive potential of physical activity may be particularly cogent for two reasons: first, the metabolic abnormalities that comprise the syndrome may be present for up to ten years before they are detected; and second, there is evidence that physical activity has favourable effects on blood pressure, lipoprotein metabolism and body fatness above and beyond those mediated through changes in insulin sensitivity (see Chapters 4 and 5). These have already been discussed individually, so consideration here is restricted to evidence about physical activity or fitness and the metabolic syndrome as an entity.

Associations with physical activity levels

A substantial number of cross-sectional studies have tested the hypothesis that the metabolic syndrome is less prevalent in people who are active, compared with their inactive counterparts. Most have attempted to control for known confounding factors. Almost all studies report that higher levels of physical activity are associated with a lower prevalence of the metabolic syndrome in men and women and many have found a dose–response relationship.

For example, in the Kuopio Ischemic Heart Disease Risk Factor study, Finnish men who engaged in moderate or vigorous activity (≥ 4.5 METs) in their leisure time for less than one hour per week were 60% more likely to have the metabolic syndrome than those who engaged in such activity for three or more hours per week, even after adjustment for confounders (Lakka *et al.* 2003). There was a dose–response relationship for minutes of total activity or moderate/vigorous activity, but not low-intensity activity (Figure 7.3). This finding, together with indications from other studies, suggests that the intensity of activity may be important.

Findings from prospective studies undertaken to examine this issue and evidence for a beneficial effect of physical activity on the likelihood of developing the metabolic syndrome are not as consistent as those from cross-sectional studies. In one of the few available studies, the cohort of Finnish men referred to above were followed for four years (Laaksonen *et al.* 2002). Researchers found that men engaging in more than three hours per week of moderate or vigorous activity in their leisure time were only half as likely as sedentary men to have the metabolic syndrome, even after adjustment for potentially confounding factors. On the other hand, some studies have found that measures of activity did not predict the development of the syndrome.

Figure 7.3 Odds ratios for having the metabolic syndrome according to categories of leisure-time physical activity in middle-aged men. A dose–response relationship was evident for total activity and for moderate/vigorous activity but not for low-intensity activity.

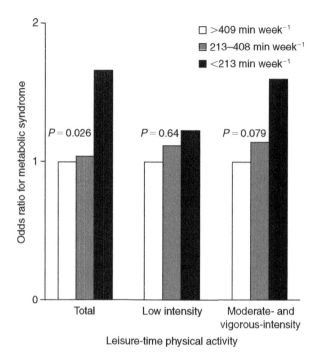

Source: Lakka *et al.* (2003).
Note: Subjects were 1,069 participants in the Kuopio Ischemic Heart Disease Risk Factor Study. Data adjusted for age category, smoking, alcohol consumption and socio-economic status.

Physical fitness and metabolic syndrome

A substantial body of evidence from cross-sectional studies shows that there is a significant, inverse relationship between fitness and the prevalence of the metabolic syndrome. As with studies of physical activity, a dose–response relationship between measures of these two variables is a rather consistent finding. The Aerobics Center Longitudinal Study has provided data on two aspects of fitness – aerobic fitness and muscular strength – in a large cohort of men (Jurca *et al.* 2004). Both measures were inversely and independently associated with the prevalence of the metabolic syndrome. A clear dose–response relationship was evident in both cases (Figure 7.4). Subsequent six-year follow-up confirmed that men in the highest category for muscular fitness were around 40% less likely to develop the metabolic syndrome than men in the lowest category (Jurca *et al.* 2005), supporting the proposition that strength – as well as aerobic fitness – may protect against the metabolic syndrome.

Most of the small number of prospective studies have noted that participants who had higher levels of aerobic fitness were less likely to develop the metabolic syndrome than those who exhibited lower levels. The Aerobics Center Longitudinal Study

Figure 7.4 Prevalence of metabolic syndrome according to level of muscular strength and cardiorespiratory fitness.

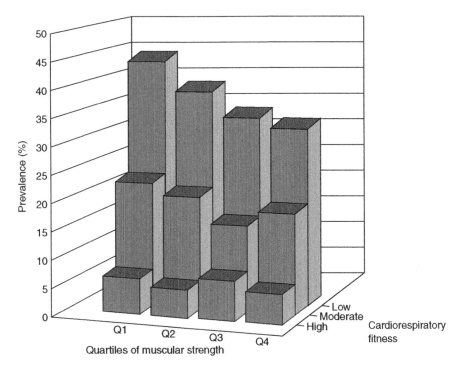

Source: Jurca *et al.* (2004).
Note: Data from the Aerobics Center Longitudinal Study. The prevalence of the metabolic syndrome was inversely related to muscular strength within the moderate and low cardiorespiratory categories and inversely proportional to cardiorespiratory fitness within each muscular strength quartile.

reported data for 9,007 American men and 1,491 women (LaMonte *et al.* 2005a). In both sexes, there was a significant, inverse relationship across tertiles of aerobic fitness (Figure 7.5). These findings are in line with those from the Kuopio Ischemic Heart Disease Risk Factor study, with an important exception; in the US study the relationships remained significant even after adjustment for the number of components of the metabolic syndrome evident at baseline, but this was not the case in the Finnish study.

Sedentary behaviours and metabolic syndrome

One way to evaluate inactivity is to measure parameters that describe sedentary behaviour. Several cross-sectional studies have shown that the prevalence of the metabolic syndrome increases in relation to the amount of time spent watching television or using a computer. These include studies of representative samples of men and women in the United States and Australia. In the US study, people who watched television for four or more hours per day were twice as likely to have the metabolic syndrome as those who watched for less than one hour per day (Ford *et al.* 2005). Moreover, there

Figure 7.5 Incidence of metabolic syndrome according to category of cardiorespiratory fitness in men and women.

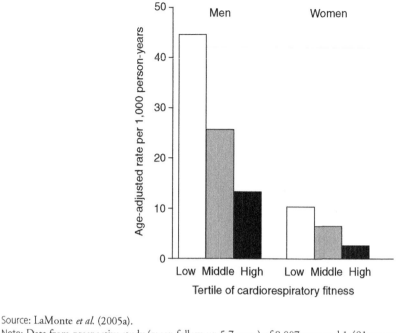

Source: LaMonte *et al.* (2005a).
Note: Data from prospective study (mean follow-up 5.7 years) of 9,007 men and 1,491 women.

was a significant positive dose–response relationship between the amount of sedentary behaviour and the prevalence of the metabolic syndrome (Ford and Li 2006). Similar findings were reported for the Australian study: men and women who watched television for more than 14 hours per week were 1.5 times as likely and twice as likely, respectively, to have the metabolic syndrome compared with those who watched for half this time (Dunstan *et al.* 2005).

EXERCISE AND POSTPRANDIAL EVENTS

As explained above, many of the abnormalities of the metabolic syndrome can be linked to the impairment of events during the postprandial period. Repeated exaggerated episodes of postprandial lipaemia lead to low HDL-cholesterol and a preponderance of small, dense LDL. High levels of postprandial lipaemia are a characteristic of obesity, particularly the abdominal type (Figure 7.2). When triglycerides are high, blood has an increased propensity to clot, there are detrimental effects on endothelial function and systemic inflammation is increased. Therefore the influence of exercise on postprandial events is a topic of research interest, although there is a paucity of evidence from people known to have the metabolic syndrome. Evidence is most extensive for disturbances to lipoprotein metabolism, but research looking at non-lipid disturbances is in progress.

Early studies found that endurance-trained athletes show a lower postprandial rise in triglycerides after a high-fat meal than do sedentary controls (Figure 7.6). However, if trained people go just 2.5 days without training they experience a marked increase in postprandial triglycerides. Therefore their characteristically low response to dietary fat is due, at least in part, to the fact that they have always exercised recently.

Consistent with this hypothesis, a single session of aerobic exercise has been shown to attenuate both hypertriglyceridaemia and impairment of endothelium-dependent micro-vascular function after a high-fat meal. Figure 7.7 presents data from a repeated-measures laboratory study in lean middle-aged men and in men with central obesity (Gill *et al.* 2004). On one occasion the men walked briskly for 90 minutes at 50% $\dot{V}O_2$max in the afternoon before eating the test meal for breakfast the following morning (exercise); in the control situation they refrained from all exercise the day before the test meal (control). Postprandial triglycerides were reduced by about 25% with prior exercise and the postprandial impairment of endothelial function was attenuated by 15–20%. Post-prandial hyperinsulinaemia was significantly reduced only in the obese men.

The energy expenditure of a session of exercise is an important determinant of its effects on postprandial lipaemia, as shown by a study in which exercise intensity was 'traded' for duration (Tsetsonis and Hardman 1996). Postprandial lipaemia was meas-ured on three mornings, again in a repeated-measures design. These were: after two days with minimal activity (control); after a 90-minute walk at 60% $\dot{V}O_2$max the previous afternoon; and after walking for twice as long at half the intensity (Figure 7.8). Prior exercise reduced postprandial lipaemia by nearly one-third, irrespective of its intensity. Much less is known about the influence of resistance exercise on

---

Figure 7.6 Plasma triglyceride responses to a meal containing fat (approximately 70 g) and carbohydrate in endurance-trained and untrained men who were matched for age, height and weight.

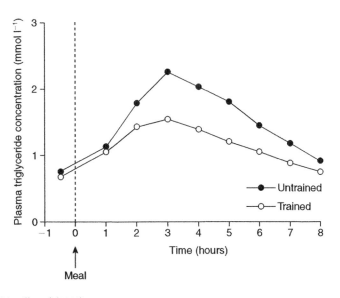

Source: Redrawn from Merrill *et al.* (1989).

Figure 7.7 Influence of prior exercise on postprandial responses of plasma triglycerides (top panel) and insulin (bottom panel) in lean men (left panel) and centrally obese men (right panel).

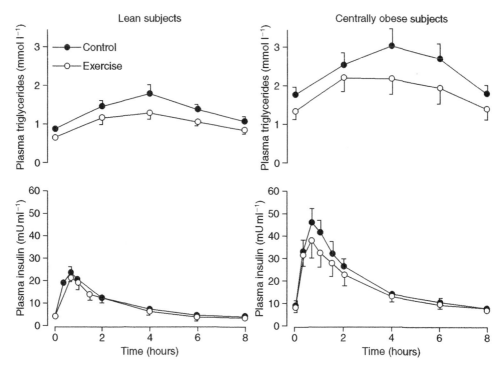

Source: Gill *et al.* (2004).
Note: Middle-aged men walked for 90 minutes at ~50% V̇O₂max during the afternoon before the exercise trial. Data are mean and SEM.

postprandial lipaemia than about aerobic exercise; there are reports that this is reduced, unchanged or even increased.

The mechanisms by which prior exercise reduces postprandial lipaemia are incompletely understood, but must involve enhanced clearance of triglyceride and/or a reduced rate of entry into the circulation. Hydrolysis by the enzyme lipoprotein lipase (LPL) is the rate-limiting step in triglyceride clearance. Exercise increases LPL in skeletal muscle, with maximal increases in LPL mRNA occurring around four hours post-exercise, a timeframe consistent with maximal attenuation of triglyceride concentrations following a session of exercise (Seip *et al.* 1995). A second mechanism may be reduced hepatic VLDL secretion; prior exercise might alter the hepatic partitioning of fatty acids, enhancing their oxidation so that fewer are available for synthesis and secretion as triglycerides in VLDL.

Exercise-induced changes to LPL also exert an important influence on energy balance and thus body fat levels. This enzyme is effectively a 'gate-keeper', governing the proportion of fatty acids from triglyceride-rich lipoproteins taken up into muscle versus adipose tissue. The ratio of its activities in adipose tissue/muscle has been reported to increase nine-fold when endurance-trained athletes interrupted their train-

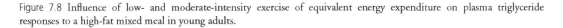

Figure 7.8 Influence of low- and moderate-intensity exercise of equivalent energy expenditure on plasma triglyceride responses to a high-fat mixed meal in young adults.

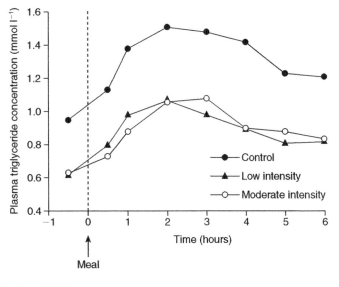

Source: Tsetsonis and Hardman (1996).

ing for two weeks (Simsolo *et al.* 1993). Thus, inactivity favours storage of fatty acids in adipose tissue. By contrast, regular exercise favours oxidation of dietary fatty acids in skeletal muscle and, because fat balance largely determines energy balance (discussed in Chapter 6), this may oppose weight gain. Thus, the enhancement of LPL activity by exercise nicely illustrates its diverse but interrelated effects on features of the metabolic syndrome.

PREVENTION

Both a Western diet (high in fat and refined carbohydrates) and physical inactivity increase the risk of developing the metabolic syndrome. Lifestyle change is therefore an attractive preventive approach. Given the high prevalence of the syndrome, and the rising incidence world-wide of some of its core components, this is important.

Physical activity is likely to be most effective when it involves high levels of energy expenditure on most days of the week. The frequency of activity is important to maintain low plasma triglycerides and maximize blood pressure-lowering effects. Of course, increasing physical activity also involves risks (discussed in Chapter 12) that need to be considered alongside benefits. Orthopaedic problems are a real concern because the individuals at risk of developing the metabolic syndrome carry excess weight. Moreover, this makes it difficult for them to expend sufficient energy in physical activity without suffering fatigue.

PHYSICAL ACTIVITY AS THERAPY?

As mentioned in the introduction to this chapter, pharmacological therapy for patients with the metabolic syndrome is complex because drugs target individual pathologies and may have neutral or even negative effects on other syndrome features. For example, treatment with diuretics reduces blood pressure, but also increases total cholesterol; treatment with beta-blockers reduces blood pressure but leads to a decrease in HDL-cholesterol. Thus, the overall benefit for CVD risk is not always clear. An alternative strategy may be to prescribe drugs that improve insulin sensitivity, on the premise that this is the central causal feature of the metabolic syndrome. Whatever approach is adopted, multiple drug regimens are invariably necessary, and these are difficult to adhere to, particularly for older people. Finally, all drugs have side effects that have to be set against their benefits. Physical activity, with its multiple beneficial effects on syndrome features, is thus an attractive alternative or complementary therapeutic measure, particularly when accompanied by weight loss.

Evidence from intervention studies that shows the importance of physical activity for core abnormalities associated with the metabolic syndrome (discussed in Chapters 4, 5 and 6). For example, randomized, controlled trials have now shown that dietary change and increased physical activity are effective in preventing the development of type 2 diabetes in individuals who are overweight and have impaired glucose tolerance.

By comparison, there are few studies of the therapeutic value of activity for people who already have the metabolic syndrome. One involved 105 participants in the HERITAGE Family Study in Canada diagnosed with this syndrome using the NCEP ATPIII criteria; after 20 weeks of supervised aerobic training, 32 of these individuals were no longer classified as having the metabolic syndrome because of changes to one or more of its core features (Katzmarzyk *et al.* 2003). Flow-mediated dilatation – impaired in the metabolic syndrome – has also been reported to be improved in patients who trained for 12 weeks, compared with randomly allocated controls (Lavrencic *et al.* 2000). So, while there is some evidence for the efficacy of physical activity in treating the metabolic syndrome, this is an area of active research interest.

The fact that experimental studies in individuals who already exhibit the metabolic syndrome are few and far between is an important weakness in the rationale for physical activity as therapy. It is also possible that genetic factors predisposing to the syndrome may limit the efficacy of physical activity in modifying its abnormalities, at least in some populations, but little is known.

SUMMARY

- The metabolic syndrome is the name given to a cluster of risk factors for CVD. Physical inactivity, obesity and genetic make-up probably interact with dietary factors to explain its high prevalence in developed countries. Its importance is that it helps to identify individuals who are at high risk of type 2 diabetes and CVD.
- The defining causal feature of the syndrome is controversial.

- Syndrome abnormalities include: hyperinsulinaemia, high triglycerides, low HDL-cholesterol, hypertension, obesity (particularly of the abdominal type), non-alcoholic fatty liver disease and probably endothelial dysfunction and systemic inflammation.
- Physical inactivity, low fitness and sedentary behaviours are associated with increased prevalence of the metabolic syndrome in cross-sectional and prospective studies.
- Prevention is important; by the time the metabolic syndrome is identified in an individual, its features have been established for a long time.
- Lipid and non-lipid disturbances during the postprandial period are important abnormalities that are attenuated by physical activity.
- Physical activity has a preventive – and probably a therapeutic – role in ameliorating multiple syndrome features.

STUDY TASKS

1 Explain why the metabolic syndrome is a public health problem world-wide.
2 List the key abnormalities that comprise the metabolic syndrome.
3 What types of epidemiological evidence show that physical inactivity or low fitness is associated with increased risk for the metabolic syndrome? In which category is evidence most convincing and why?
4 Explain why increasing physical activity is a particularly attractive preventive measure against the metabolic syndrome.
5 Explain the effects of a session of exercise on subsequent postprandial lipoprotein metabolism.

NOTE

1 This study followed the children of participants in the original Framingham Study – one of the first cohort studies conceived to gain insight into the causes of CHD.

FURTHER READING

Buemann, B. and Tremblay, A. (1996) 'Effects of exercise training on abdominal obesity and related metabolic complications', *Sports Medicine* 21: 191–212.

Eckel, R.H., Grundy, S.M. and Zimmet, P.Z. (2005) 'The metabolic syndrome', *Lancet* 365: 1415–28.

Eriksson, J., Taimela, S. and Koivisto, V.A. (1997) 'Exercise and the metabolic syndrome', *Diabetologia* 40: 125–35.

Ford, E.S. and Li, C. (2006) 'Physical activity or fitness and the metabolic syndrome', *Expert Review of Cardiovascular Therapy* 4: 897–915. Online, available at: www.future-drugs.com/doi/abs/10.1586/14779072.4.6.897 (accessed 21 April 2007).

Gill, J.M.R. and Malkova, D. (2006) 'Physical activity, fitness and cardiovascular disease risk in adults: interactions with insulin resistance and obesity', *Clinical Science* 110: 409–25.

8 Cancer

Knowledge assumed
Simple cell biology, including the
role of nucleic acids
Basic anatomy and systems
physiology
Basic measures in epidemiology

INTRODUCTION

Cancer has afflicted humans throughout recorded history. The origin of the word
'cancer' has been credited to Hippocrates (460–370 BC) who used the terms 'carcinos'
and 'carcinoma' to describe tumours. In Greek these words refer to a crab, most likely
because the finger-like spreading projections from a cancer called to mind the shape of
a crab. Carcinoma is the most common type of cancer.

Cancer is not one disease, but a set of diseases characterized by unregulated cell
growth leading to invasion of surrounding tissues and spread to other parts of the
body. It is a leading cause of morbidity and mortality, accounting for around

one-quarter of all deaths in developed countries such as the United States, the United Kingdom, Australia and Canada, where the lifetime risk of developing cancer is around one in three. Moreover, cancer is becoming an increasingly important factor in the global burden of disease – the World Health Organization (WHO) estimates that the number of new cases annually will rise from ten million in 2000 to 15 million by 2020. Plate 7 shows examples of four different kinds of cancer.

The role of environmental factors in cancer causation is illustrated by the enormous geographical differences in incidence world-wide. For example, Australia has an incidence of skin cancer that is 155 times higher than that in Japan. These differences cannot be explained fully by genetic factors, as studies of migrants have shown. For example, the incidence of stomach cancer is much higher in Japan than in Hawaii, while the incidence of breast cancer is lower. When Japanese people migrate to Hawaii, their incidence rates for these two cancers move towards the rates in the indigenous population (Figure 8.1). Second-generation migrants experience rates even closer to those of the host country, presumably because they have been exposed for longer than their parents to the environmental factors that prevail in the host country. Contrary to public perception, therefore, some risk factors for cancer can be changed and some cancers prevented. For instance, of the seven million deaths from cancer world-wide in 2001, an estimated 35% have been attributed to nine potentially modifiable risk factors, including physical inactivity (Danaei *et al.* 2005).

Plate 7 Main types of cancer – cancer can originate almost anywhere in the body.

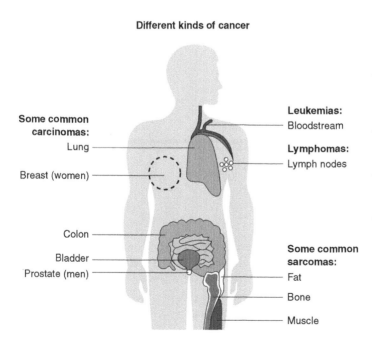

Different kinds of cancer

Some common carcinomas:
Lung

Breast (women)

Colon

Bladder

Prostate (men)

Leukemias:
Bloodstream

Lymphomas:
Lymph nodes

Some common sarcomas:
Fat

Bone

Muscle

Carcinomas, the most common types of cancer, arise from the cells that cover external and internal body surfaces. Lung, breast and colon are the most frequent cancers of this type.

Sarcomas are cancers arising from cells found in the supporting tissues of the body such as bone, cartilage, fat, connective tissue and muscle.

Lymphomas are cancers that arise in the lymph nodes and tissues of the body's immune system.

Leukemias are cancers of the immature blood cells that grow in the bone marrow and tend to accumulate in large numbers in the bloodstream.

Source: US National Cancer Institute website at www.cancer.gov.

Figure 8.1 Typical patterns of change in cancer incidence among migrant populations: breast and stomach cancer in Japanese migrants to Hawaii.

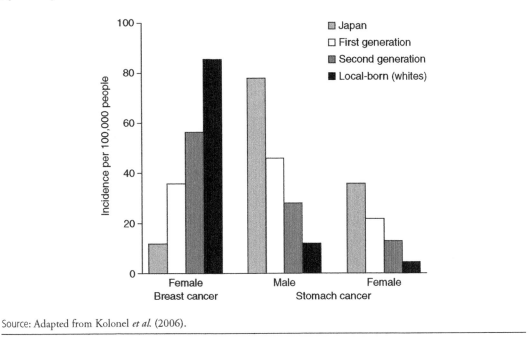

Source: Adapted from Kolonel *et al.* (2006).

Although a role for energy balance in cancer causation was advanced almost three centuries ago, it was not until the mid-1980s that researchers began to ask whether physical activity – the main contributor to inter-individual differences in energy expenditure – influences the risk of cancer. The extent, consistency, strengths and limitations of the available evidence will be discussed later, but first it is necessary to understand a little more about carcinogenesis (the process by which cancers are generated) and how tumours develop.

CARCINOGENESIS

Normal body cells grow, divide and die in an orderly fashion. After the early years of life, most cells reproduce only to replace those that have died, through injury or illness for example. Cells somehow know (through intercellular signalling) when there are enough new cells to repair an injury and they then stop reproducing. In fact, human cells seem to be pre-programmed to reproduce up to a maximum of 50–60 times. Normal cells also have a natural ability to stick together in the right place; this property, called cell adhesion, is derived from molecules on the surface of the cell and ensures the integrity of tissues and organs. If a cell becomes detached from its proper place, if it becomes too old or if its genes are badly damaged it will 'commit suicide' so that these faults are not passed on to daughter cells. This self-destruction is called apoptosis.

BOX 8.1 DIFFERENCES BETWEEN NORMAL CELLS AND CANCER CELLS

Normal cells:	Cancer cells:
• Reproduce themselves exactly • Stop reproducing at the right time • Stick together in the right place (cell adhesion) • Self-destruct if they are damaged (apoptosis) • Become specialized or mature	• Carry on reproducing • Do not obey signals from neighbouring cells • Can become detached from the primary tumour and travel to other parts of the body • Do not become specialized, but stay immature • Do not die if they move to another part of the body

---

Box 8.1 lists some important ways in which cancer cells differ from normal cells. Cancer cells do not stop reproducing, they go on doubling. Moreover, instead of dying in an orderly way, cancer cells self-destruct more slowly than they reproduce, so their numbers continue to increase until a lump, called a tumour, is formed. As it grows, a tumour invades and destroys surrounding tissues. Its centre gets farther and farther from blood vessels in the area. By interacting with normal cells, the cancerous cells promote the development of new blood vessels, thereby ensuring an adequate supply of oxygen and nutrients and promoting further growth.

One of the most troublesome characteristics of cancer cells is that they travel to other sites in the body, where they begin to grow and replace normal tissue. This process, called metastasis, occurs because cancer cells can lose the molecules on their surface that keep normal cells in the right place. Cancer cells travel in the bloodstream or lymph vessels and stop at the first place they get stuck. In the bloodstream this is the next capillary bed they encounter – often in the lungs because venous blood from most organs goes next through these capillaries.

What initiates carcinogenesis?

Cells become cancerous because of damage to their DNA – the nucleic acid that is the basis of the genetic code. Genes direct the activities of every cell, but when mutations (damage to a gene or loss of a gene) occur, vital control systems are lost.

Abnormalities of three different types of genes are important in making a cell cancerous:

• Genes that encourage the cell to multiply (most cells only multiply to repair damage, for example after a wound). If these genes, called oncogenes, become abnormal, they tell the cell to multiply all the time.
• Genes that stop the cell multiplying and act as a brake to the oncogene's accelerator. If one of these genes becomes damaged, the cell may carry on and on multiplying – it becomes immortal.
• Genes that repair other damaged genes. If these genes are damaged, other muta-

tions are not repaired but replicated during the process of cell division and inherited by all subsequent daughter cells.

How do mutations arise?

Fortunately, it is not easy for a normal cell to turn into a cancer cell. Although DNA is continuously exposed to damaging agents from within as well as outside the body, damage to DNA is normally repaired efficiently so that mutations are not inherited by daughter cells. In cancer cells, the damaged DNA is not repaired.

Mutations can happen by chance when a cell is reproducing, but this often leads the cell to self-destruct; or, cells carrying a mutation may be recognized as abnormal by the immune system and killed. Thus, most pre-cancerous cells die before they can cause disease and only a few develop into a cancer. Moreover, carcinogenesis results from the accumulation of errors in the genetic code and it can take a long time before enough mutations happen for a cell to become cancerous (this is why cancers are more common in older people – there has been more time to be exposed to carcinogens and more time for errors to happen when cells reproduce).

Something that damages the genetic machinery of a cell and makes it more likely to be cancerous is called a carcinogen. People can inherit damaged DNA, but fewer than 15% of all cancers are familial. Most often, a person's DNA becomes damaged by exposure to some environmental factor – chemicals, radiation or viruses. For some cancers, initiating agents have been clearly identified. These include lung cancer (tobacco smoke) and leukaemia (ionizing radiation), but it is difficult to define initiating agents in cancers of the colon, prostate and breast. Natural events such as free radical generation may be the driving force for these common cancers.

Once carcinogenesis has been initiated, proliferative signals could derive from exogenous factors such as diet, viral infection or hormones (contraceptive pill, hormone replacement therapy for example) or endogenous factors. Cancer is therefore a

---

BOX 8.2 ESTABLISHED RISK FACTORS FOR SOME OF THE MAIN CANCERS

- Age – the single most important factor.
- Presence of genes that increase susceptibility. For example, genes (named BRCA1 and BRCA2) have been identified for breast cancer.
- Impaired immune function – those with problems of the immune system, for example AIDS, are more likely to get some forms of cancer.
- Diet – diets high in fat, meat, salt and alcohol increase the risk of some cancers. (Diets high in fruit and vegetables are protective against several common cancers.)
- Agents in the day-to-day environment – for example, tobacco smoke, sun, natural and man-made radiation, workplace hazards, asbestos.
- Viruses encountered – viruses can help to cause some cancers. This does not mean that cancer can be caught like an infection, but that a virus can cause genetic changes in cells that make them more likely to become cancerous. Examples include hepatitis B virus (liver cancer) and human papilloma virus (cancer of cervix).

multi-factorial disease. There is no single cause for any one cancer. For example, tobacco smoke contains potent carcinogens – smoking 20–30 cigarettes per day increases the risk of lung cancer 40-fold – but not everyone who smokes gets lung cancer, so other factors must be at work. Epidemiology has provided clues as to factors that increase the risk of developing some cancers (Box 8.2). Research accumulated over the past 25 years now strongly suggests that physical inactivity is a risk factor for some cancers. The data suggest that the relationship between physical activity level and cancer differs according to the site of the cancer. For this reason, the following sections deal separately with site-specific cancers.

PHYSICAL ACTIVITY AND COLORECTAL CANCER

The colon, or large intestine, forms a rectangle in the abdominal cavity that frames the tightly packed small intestine. Its main function is to store waste material until it is eliminated from the body. By contrast, the rectum, which links the colon to the anus, is empty except when the urge to defecate is initiated. Risk factors for colorectal cancer that are widely recognized include family history, high meat consumption, low intake of vegetables, high body mass index (BMI), smoking and alcohol consumption.

Colorectal cancer is the most commonly investigated cancer in relation to physical activity. Some studies present data describing cancers of the colon and rectum collectively, others report data for these two sites separately. It is now clear that findings differ according to site, so combining data in a single outcome measure may obscure real relationships. For this reason, the following discussion deals separately with colon and rectal cancer.

At least 50 observational studies[1] have investigated whether physical activity is associated with the risk of colon cancer. These studies have been conducted in many countries in North America, Europe, Asia, Australia and New Zealand, but overwhelmingly in white people. Around 80% have reported a large and statistically significant reduction in risk among the most physically active men and women. The consistency of these findings across occupational and leisure-time activity, different study designs (cohort, population-based case-control, hospital-based case-control) is all the more remarkable because methods of assessing physical activity have often been quite crude. When comparing the most active subjects with the least active, the median relative risk across all studies is 0.7, indicating a 30% reduction in risk. Overall, the evidence that physical activity has a preventive role in colon cancer has been assessed as 'convincing' according to criteria developed by the World Cancer Research Fund and the American Institute for Cancer Research.

In marked contrast to findings for colon cancer, there is general agreement across studies that there is no association between physical activity and the risk of cancer of the rectum. Across all studies the median relative risk comparing the most with the least active subjects is 1.0. This probably accounts for the fact that studies combining colon and rectal cancers have tended to find weaker relationships with physical activity than those reporting findings for colon cancer alone.

The initial associations between physical activity and colon cancer were derived from observations that people involved in active occupations were less likely to develop colon cancer than those in sedentary occupations. These studies, published in the mid-1980s, stimulated further investigations not only of occupational activity, but also of leisure-time and total physical activity. There are several indications that high levels of physical activity maintained over a long period confer the strongest protection.

For example, one large case-control study assessed energy expenditure, based on reported intensity and duration of activities at home, leisure and work for (1) the referent year, (2) ten years ago and (3) (for older participants) 20 years ago (Slattery *et al.* 1997). These researchers obtained data for 2,073 cases and a similar number of controls. Lack of a lifetime history of vigorous leisure-time activity was associated with an increased risk for colon cancer in men (odds ratio 1.63, 95% CI 1.14–2.67) and in women (odds ratio 1.59, 95% CI 1.21–2.10).

Long-term activity was also evaluated prospectively in the Harvard Alumni Study. (The reader will recall that this study obtained detailed information on leisure-time activity, as well as on walking and stair climbing.) Those men who were highly or moderately active at several assessments had half the risk of developing colon cancer, compared with those who were not (relative risk 0.50, 95% CI 0.27–0.93) (Lee *et al.* 1991). Physical activity assessed at any single time period did not show a protective effect.

There is some evidence for a dose–response relationship between physical activity and colon cancer risk. For example, in the US Nurses' Health Study (a cohort study of more than 120,000 female nurses which began in 1976) there was a significant association between level of leisure-time physical activity and the risk of colon cancer (Martínez *et al.* 1997) (Figure 8.2). Overall, of the studies with at least three levels of physical activity, more than half reported data indicative of an inverse dose–response.

Figure 8.2 Relative risk of colon cancer according to level of leisure-time physical activity in the US Nurses' Health Study.

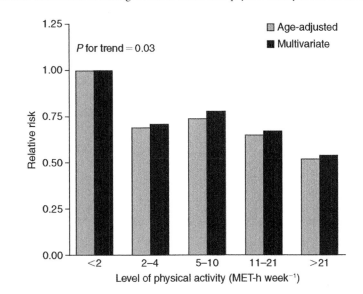

Source: Martínez *et al.* (1997).
Note: Multivariate analysis adjusted for age, cigarette smoking, family history, BMI, postmenopausal hormone use, aspirin use, intake of red meat and alcohol consumption.

How much activity is needed to lower the risk of colon cancer? In the Harvard Alumni Study men who reported activities expending at least $4.2\,MJ\,week^{-1}$ (approximately 2.5 hours of moderate activity) had a significantly lower risk (Lee *et al.* 1991). However, among men in the Health Professionals Follow-Up Study, risk was only reduced among those in the top quintile of physical activity, who expended a median of $46.8\,MET\text{-}h\,week^{-1}$, or approximately 12 hours per week of moderate activity (Giovannucci *et al.* 1995). In the Nurses' Health Study, women participating in 21 $MET\text{-}h\,week^{-1}$ of activity experienced a 50% reduction in risk, compared with women in the least active group (Figure 8.2). This is equivalent to around five hours of moderate-intensity physical activity. Yet another study found that only men and women who reported engaging in activity amounting to at least 60 minutes per day of vigorous activity experienced a significantly lower risk (Slattery *et al.* 1997). Based on these data, it appears that at least 30–60 minutes a day of moderate-to-vigorous activity are needed for a significant reduction in the risk of colon cancer.

How do we know that it is the physical activity itself that is protecting people from colon cancer, rather than other health behaviours? The issue of confounding is an important one because physically active people tend to eat healthy diets (e.g. less red meat, more fibre) and are less prone to being overweight than their sedentary peers. However, studies that have adjusted for known confounding factors have found that the associations between colon cancer risk and level of physical activity were not materially altered. For example, in the Health Professionals Follow-up Study, physically active men were more likely to use multivitamins than inactive men and had lower intake of saturated fat, higher intakes of fibre, lower prevalence of smoking and lower BMI. After controlling for all these risk factors, as well as for aspirin use and family history, the protection associated with physical activity was reduced somewhat, but only from 56% to 47% (Giovannucci *et al.* 1995). Thus, it can be concluded that activity is not merely a marker of a healthier lifestyle, but exerts an independent protective effect against colon cancer.

Energy balance as a whole seems to be associated with the risk of cancer. This may be illustrated from the findings of a large US case-control study. In addition to estimating energy expenditure in physical activity, researchers measured BMI (a crude measure of energy storage) and energy intake. Either a high BMI or a high energy intake was associated with a significant increase in the risk of colon cancer (by 94% and 74%, respectively). The most interesting finding, however, emerged when the interactions between physical activity, energy intake and BMI were examined (Table 8.1). At high levels of physical activity, the risk of colon cancer was not significantly

Table 8.1 Risk of colon cancer in people with high energy intake and high BMI		
ACTIVITY STATUS	ODDS RATIO	95% CI
Low physical activity	3.35	2.09–5.35
High physical activity	1.28	0.81–2.03

Source: Slattery *et al.* (1997).

Note: Risk estimates were adjusted for confounding factors. Referent group: people who were active, consumed low levels of energy and had low BMI.

influenced by BMI or energy intake. Among people with low levels of physical activity, two things changed: (1) BMI became a more important indicator of risk; and (2) the risk associated with a high energy intake increased. (This is an example of 'effect modification', that is, the effect of one exposure differs according to the level of another.) This finding suggests that the influence of physical activity on the risk of colon cancer may be mediated through systemic metabolic effects related to energy balance. This possibility is discussed later in the section on potential mechanisms.

PHYSICAL ACTIVITY AND BREAST CANCER

The evidence for an association between physical activity and female breast cancer, although neither as strong nor as consistent as that found for colon cancer, is also regarded as 'convincing'. At least 57 observational studies have been published on this topic. Overall, the data support an inverse relationship between physical activity levels and the risk of breast cancer. Comparing the most active subjects with the least active, the median relative risk (controlled for potential confounding) is 0.8, indicating a 20% reduction in risk.

What type of activity and how much is associated with reduction of the risk of breast cancer? More than half of the studies that measured only occupational activity and 70% of those that measured only leisure-time activity have found a lower risk in the most active women. However, when *total* activity (i.e. occupational, leisure time and, in one instance, household activity) has been measured, studies have *consistently* found a lower risk in the most active women. This suggests that total activity – regardless of context – is what matters. (Measuring either occupational or leisure-time activity alone inevitably probably leads to misclassification and weakens associations.)

A few studies have attempted to measure physical activity comprehensively. One in particular deserves mention because the methodology shows the researchers' appreciation of the complexity of the relationship between physical activity and breast cancer. Friedenrich *et al.* obtained information about lifetime total physical activity (including variables of intensity, frequency and duration) from childhood until the referent year in 1,233 cases and 1,237 controls drawn from the general population (Friedenreich *et al.* 2001). The greatest risk reductions were observed for activity sustained throughout the lifetime (Figure 8.3) and for activity done between menopause and the referent year, suggesting that the protective effect of physical activity is greater for postmenopausal than for premenopausal women. The findings of a major cohort study, the Women's Health Study, are consistent with this suggestion. These researchers found a significant inverse trend between physical activity and breast cancer risk among postmenopausal but not premenopausal women (Lee *et al.* 2001a).[2] On the other hand, another large well-designed cohort study of Norwegian women found that physical activity was associated with greater risk reductions in premenopausal than in postmenopausal women (Thune *et al.* 1997). The interrelationships between physical activity, breast cancer risk and menopausal status thus require further investigation.

The 'dose' of physical activity required for breast cancer risk reduction can be estimated from studies that have provided sufficient detail on the activity level at which risk decreases were observed. The prospective Nurses' Health Study (Rockhill *et al.*

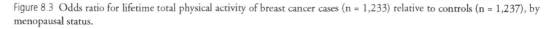

Figure 8.3 Odds ratio for lifetime total physical activity of breast cancer cases (n = 1,233) relative to controls (n = 1,237), by menopausal status.

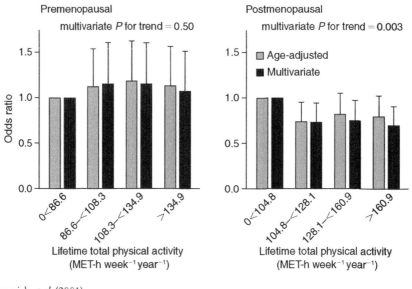

Source: Friedenreich *et al.* (2001).

Note: Left panel, premenopausal women; right panel, postmenopausal women. Multivariate analyses corrected for age and seven other potentially confounding factors.

1999) is one of fewer than 20 such studies. Figure 8.4 shows the risk of breast cancer in women who reported increasing levels of activity – measured as MET-h week^{-1}. The data are a cumulative average of reports obtained at two-year intervals over a 14-year period, and so represent long-term habits of activity/inactivity. There was a significant trend towards lower risk among more active women; women with an average of seven or more hours of moderate or vigorous activity per week had a nearly 20% lower risk of breast cancer than those in the least active group. In this study there was no evidence that vigorous activity was more likely than moderate activity to reduce risk. Other estimates of the level of activity associated with significantly lower rates of breast cancer have included, for example, exercising at least 3.8 hours per week (primarily vigorous exercise) (Bernstein *et al.* 1994) and exercising to keep fit for at least four hours per week (Thune *et al.* 1997). Overall, available data suggest that a total of around 25 MET-h week^{-1} (equivalent to 30–60 minutes per day of moderate-to-vigorous-intensity activity) is probably needed for the reduction of breast cancer risk (International Agency for Research on Cancer 2002), similar to that observed for colon cancer.

Could confounding factors explain the finding that physical activity reduces the risk of breast cancer? Besides age, important risk factors for breast cancer include: family history, benign breast disease, variables which reflect exposure to oestrogens, high energy intake, high intake of fat and – for postmenopausal breast cancer, obesity or adult weight gain. Several of these could distort the estimated effect of physical activity. All the major studies of physical activity have controlled for potentially confound-

Figure 8.4 Relative risk for breast cancer according to level of physical activity between 1980 and 1994 among women who were aged 30–55 in 1976.

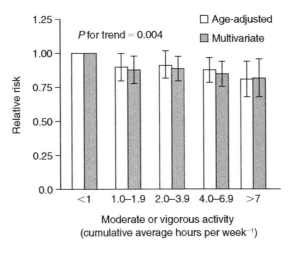

Source: Rockhill *et al.* (1999).

ing factors, including obesity and those related to exposure to oestrogens. This does not materially alter the risk reduction associated with high levels of physical activity, as can be seen by comparing age-adjusted and multivariate analyses in the prospective in the Canadian case-control study referred to earlier (Figure 8.3) or in the Nurses' Health Study (Figure 8.4).

PHYSICAL ACTIVITY AND OTHER CANCERS

In addition to breast and colon cancer, the associations of physical activity with several other common cancers have been investigated. These include cancers of the prostate, endometrium, ovary, lung and pancreas. Of these, the most extensive body of evidence is available for prostate cancer.

The main risk factors for prostate cancer are age, race and family history – all non-modifiable. However, because rates for this cancer increase among migrants who move from areas of low incidence to areas of high incidence, lifestyle factors are also implicated. At least 36 epidemiological studies on physical activity and prostate cancer are available, all from developed countries. The median relative risk across all studies, comparing the most active men with the least active, is 0.9. Around one-quarter of studies found no association and several have found an increased risk in physically active men. Thus, studies are inconsistent in their findings and, if there is a reduction in risk, it is probably modest. These conclusions also hold if only the studies with the best measures of activity are considered.[3] For example, two reports from the Harvard Alumni cohort yielded conflicting findings (Lee *et al.* 1992; Lee *et al.* 2001b). One explanation could be confounding due to higher levels of screening for early detection of prostate cancer among physically active, more health-conscious men.

The results of 18 epidemiological studies on endometrial cancer are rather consistent, with an average risk reduction of 30% in active women. Most have taken into account other known risk factors, including age, body mass, adiposity and reproductive and menstrual factors, so it is unlikely that these associations are due to confounding (Cust *et al.* 2007). Thus physical activity probably protects against cancer of the endometrium.

A majority of approximately 20 studies of lung cancer have found a significantly reduced risk of lung cancer in men with the highest activity levels, and four studies found evidence for a dose–response relationship. It is therefore possible that physical activity is linked to a reduced risk of lung cancer. A major concern in relation to this body of evidence, however, is the capability of researchers to control adequately for confounding by cigarette smoking. Nearly 20 studies of physical activity and pancreatic cancer have been published but, although there is evidence for a lower risk with higher levels of activity, this is rather inconsistent.

Other cancers that have been studied for an association with physical activity include ovarian cancer, testicular cancer, kidney cancer, bladder cancer and haemopoietic cancers. Available data are, however, inadequate to justify drawing a conclusion regarding any of these sites.

MECHANISMS

There is clearly an effect of physical activity on cancer, as shown by the summary of the extent and quality of the epidemiological evidence presented in Table 8.2.

However, the studies included in this table are all observational and overwhelmingly in Caucasian populations from Europe and North America. (No reports are available from clinical trials that have the occurrence of cancer as an outcome.) Evidence for biologically plausible mechanisms which could explain these associations would strengthen the argument that physical inactivity is a causal factor in the development of cancer. Several such mechanisms have been proposed; these may be divided into systemic mechanisms that could pertain to several types of cancer and site-specific mechanisms.

Systemic mechanisms

Systemic mechanisms include changes in circulating levels of metabolic hormones, alteration of body fat and possibly enhanced immune function. One of the most important metabolic hormones, insulin, is clearly influenced by exercise – as discussed in Chapter 5. Insulin has a general anabolic role, stimulating net protein synthesis. For this reason, hyperinsulinaemia constitutes a growth-promoting milieu that may facilitate carcinogenesis. Elevated blood insulin concentrations have been associated with increased risk of breast cancer, and individuals with colon cancer have been reported to have a higher-than-expected incidence of the metabolic syndrome – which is characterized by hyperinsulinaemia (Chapter 7). Exercise enhances insulin sensitivity and reduces plasma concentrations of this hormone. It may therefore contribute to its protective effect against cancers.

Table 8.2 Summary of epidemiological evidence on the association between physical activity and cancer

CANCER SITE	NUMBER OF STUDIES		STRENGTH OF ASSOCIATION	DOSE-RESPONSE	BIOLOGICAL PLAUSIBILITY	OVERALL LEVEL OF EVIDENCE
	COHORT	CASE-CONTROL	MEDIAN RELATIVE RISK			
Colon	21	29	0.7	Yes – reported in more than half of studies that have three or more levels of activity	Yes, several hypotheses	Convincing
Breast	28	29	0.8 premenopause, 0.7 postmenopause	Yes – reported in three-quarters of studies that have three or more levels of activity	Yes, several hypotheses	Convincing/probable for postmenopausal, limited evidence for premenopausal
Endometrium	7	11	0.7	Insufficient data	Yes, a few hypotheses	Probable
Prostate	22	14	0.9	Insufficient data	Yes, some hypotheses	Possible
Pancreas	12	6	Inconsistent	Insufficient data	Yes, at least two hypotheses	Possible, limited evidence
Lung	15	6	women 0.5, men 0.8	Insufficient data	None plausible	Possible, limited evidence

Sources: Friedenreich (2001); Lee and Oguma (2006); Cust *et al.* (2007); and World Cancer Research Fund (2007).

Note: More than 40 studies have looked for a possible association between physical activity and a number of other cancers, including ovarian cancer, testicular cancer, kidney cancer, bladder cancer and haematopoietic cancer. For none of these sites is there sufficient evidence to draw a conclusion.

High levels of insulin-like growth factors (IGFs) and low levels of the proteins to which they are bound in the bloodstream have been associated with an increased risk of colorectal, breast, prostate and lung cancers. IGFs are peptide hormones that are synthesized in direct response to growth hormones. As their name implies, they have insulin-like actions in that they stimulate cell turnover in most body tissues. IGFs are down-regulated by increased production of their binding proteins, which can occur with physical activity. Thus, IGFs may link physical activity to decreased cancer risk.

Alterations to adiposity may represent a major pathway through which activity influences the risk of obesity-related cancers, such as postmenopausal breast cancer, endometrial cancer and colorectal cancer. Postmenopausal weight, weight gain and abdominal adiposity have all been associated with breast cancer risk. Thus, physical activity may decrease cancer risk through improved weight regulation (Chapter 6). Men and women who are physically active have only slightly higher energy intake than their sedentary peers but are leaner, suggesting that net available energy is lower in active people. This would fit with findings in animals that energy intake restriction inhibits carcinogenesis. A reduction in the highly metabolically active abdominal fat mass – particularly visceral fat – may be of particular importance because rather small (<2 kg) decreases in visceral fat have important beneficial effects on insulin sensitivity.

The body's innate immune system has the potential to destroy tumour cells and prevent tumour growth. So, if immune surveillance is impaired, malignant cells are more likely to survive and the risk of some cancers increases. For example, patients with AIDS are at increased risk of developing lymphomas. Effects of endurance exercise on immune function have been described (Klarlund Pedersen and Hoffman-Goetz 2000). The relationship with intensity and/or volume of activity appears to be J-shaped, with the lowest risk among individuals who undertake regular moderate exercise (over-training and/or intense competition leads to immunosuppression). The hypothesis is that there exists a level of physical activity that results in enhanced immune function, leading to a reduced risk for cancer. Moderate-intensity exercise leads to increases in the number and/or activity of macrophages and natural killer cells. Both types of cell are involved in early recognition of tumour cells and in defence against tumour spread. There are, however, two weaknesses in the argument that effects on immune function contribute to a reduced risk of cancer in physically active people: first, the majority of human cancers are insensitive to control through the innate immune system; second, the evidence that immune function is enhanced above ordinary levels through moderate exercise is scant and beset with methodological problems.

Site-specific mechanisms

Sex hormones have powerful mitogenic and proliferative effects, and therefore are important in the aetiology of reproductive cancers. Cancers of the breast, prostate, testes and endometrium are all related to lifetime exposure to endogenous sex steroid hormones. For example, measures that reflect a high level of exposure to oestrogens, for example, early menarche, late menopause or an increased number of ovulatory cycles, increase a woman's risk for breast cancer. In contrast, women with irregular menses (thus reduced progesterone and oestradiol) have only half the risk of breast cancer as women with regular cycles. In men, a strong linear trend of increasing risk of prostate cancer with increasing plasma concentrations of testosterone has been observed.

Participation in exercise may therefore reduce the risk of hormone-related cancers by lowering concentrations of sex hormones. Young women who participate at a high level in vigorous sports such as gymnastics, ballet and endurance running have late menarche and exhibit a high incidence of primary and secondary amenorrhoea (Loucks 1996). Many have irregular, often anovulatory, menstrual cycles, the prevalence of which increases with the volume of training. However, the majority of the physical activity recorded in observational studies of cancer is not vigorous, and less is known about the extent to which this might be associated with menstrual dysfunction. For this reason, data from two US cohorts (reported as one study) are important. In one, total physical activity and vigorous recreational activity were both positively related to cycle length. In the other, vigorous exercise during a given cycle was associated with an increase in the length of that cycle (Sternfeld et al. 2003). Researchers have also compared ovarian steroids in college-age women who engaged in moderate leisure-time exercise (running 20–30 km week^{-1}, plus gymnastics, tennis or dancing) and in BMI-matched sedentary controls (Broocks et al. 1990). The recreational athletes had substantially lower concentrations of oestrogens. These studies both support the view that it is not only high-intensity, high-volume training that disrupts menstrual function.

These observational studies are now supported by a small number of randomly controlled intervention trials of the influence of physical activity on risk factors for breast cancer, specifically oestrogen concentrations and metabolism. For example, in previously sedentary, postmenopausal women aged 50–75, who exercised over 12 months for an average of 170 minutes per week (walking and stationary cycling), levels of oestrone, total and free oestradiol were all reduced, compared with controls who remained sedentary (McTiernan et al. 2004). The effect was limited to women who lost ≥2% body fat, suggesting that these changes were mediated by changes in adiposity. This mechanism might be of particular importance in relation to postmenopausal breast cancer; after the menopause, oestrogens continue to be produced, mainly in fat cells, through the peripheral conversion of adrenal androgens. Thus, loss of body fat or avoidance of weight gain will lead to lower oestrogen exposure.

It has been postulated that, in men, reduction of androgen levels by physical activity could explain the lower risk of prostate cancer. Some, but not all, studies have found lower circulating concentrations of androgens in endurance-trained men, elite marathon runners for example, than in sedentary controls, even after taking BMI into account. There is no evidence, however, that regular activity at a more moderate intensity, such as regular walking, leads to lower levels.

The influence of exercise in reducing concentrations of sex steroid hormones may be enhanced through decreased bioavailability. These hormones are carried in the blood, bound to a plasma protein, sex hormone-binding globulin. It is the free (unbound) hormone that binds to receptors within the cytoplasm of the target cell. In both sexes, physical activity is associated with an increase in sex hormone-binding globulin, thereby decreasing unbound levels of oestrogens/androgens and reducing endogenous exposure to the active hormones. Moreover, triglycerides displace oestradiol from its tight binding to sex hormone binding globulin. Physically active people

Figure 8.5 Changes in bowel transit time in runners and controls.

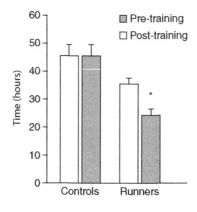

Source: Cordain *et al.* (1986).
Notes: Runners trained for six weeks, three 30-minute sessions per week. Controls remained sedentary. * values for runners significantly different pre- versus post-training. $P<0.05$. No between-group differences reported.

have low plasma concentrations of triglycerides (see Chapter 7), and this also would reduce their exposure to sex hormones.

One mechanism that might help to explain the lower incidence of colon cancer in physically active people involves bowel transit time. When individuals begin a running programme, bowel transit time may be reduced (Figure 8.5), decreasing the opportunity for carcinogens to have contact with bowel mucosa (Cordain *et al.* 1986). This would fit with findings that physical activity protects against cancer of the colon but not the rectum – which is only intermittently in contact with carcinogens in faecal matter. The evidence for an effect on colonic motility is limited, however, and mostly relates to running – an activity that may have unique effects associated with repeated regular impacts. A further limitation is that, although stool bulk is a good (inverse) correlate of colorectal cancer risk, transit time is not a well-established risk factor. Another mechanism by which activity influences colon cancer risk might involve changes to prostaglandins (local signalling molecules). The level of leisure-time physical activity has been reported to be inversely related to the concentration of prostaglandin E2 (Martínez *et al.* 1999), which increases the rate of colonic cell proliferation and decreases colonic motility.

POPULATION-ATTRIBUTABLE RISK

Four types of cancer – lung, breast, colorectal and prostate cancer – account for over half of cancer deaths in developed countries. Moreover, their incidence increases greatly with economic development. As underdeveloped countries become more urbanized, therefore, these cancers will become an even more important cause of death world-wide.

Population-attributable risks[4] for inactivity have been estimated as 13–14% for colon cancer and 11% for postmenopausal breast cancer (International Agency for

Research on Cancer 2002). These estimates should be largely independent of body weight because most of the studies providing estimates of relative risk have adjusted for BMI. However, if part of the benefit of physical activity is through improved weight maintenance, they will underestimate the impact of inactivity – and hence the potential for prevention.

A specific example provides an indication of the potential for cancer prevention through increasing the physical activity level in a population. Researchers took the distribution of activity in the Health Professionals Follow-up Study (Giovannucci *et al.* 1995) and modelled the effect of adding three hours of walking to all participants. They found that this would be expected to lead to a 17% decrease in the incidence of colon cancer (Colditz *et al.* 1997).

PHYSICAL ACTIVITY IN CANCER SURVIVORS

Cancer treatments are increasingly effective for improving survival. The population of long-term cancer survivors – approximately 9.8 million in the United States – continues to grow. These treatments – typically involving one or more of surgery, radiotherapy and drugs – clearly have adverse effects and physical activity has been proposed as a non-pharmacological intervention to combat these. Despite an increase since the mid-1990s in research to address its efficacy, few data are available regarding the effects of physical activity on health outcomes among people who have or have had cancer.

The literature on interventions involves mainly, but not exclusively, studies of breast cancer. Cardiorespiratory fitness is improved both during and after treatment for cancer, and symptoms and side effects may be attenuated. Most studies have involved aerobic exercise, but resistance training is likely to be more effective for men with prostate cancer because the adverse effects of drug regimens for this cancer include reductions in muscle strength and bone mass.

It is not possible to draw a conclusion on whether or not physical activity can alter the progression of cancer. The large US Nurses' Health Study reported findings on breast cancer mortality risk according to reported level of physical activity (Holmes *et al.* 2005). There was a significant, inverse relationship between MET-h of activity and the risk of death, with the greatest protection in those who performed the equivalent of walking for 3–5 hours per week. The association was particularly apparent among women with hormone-responsive tumours, suggesting a possible hormonal mechanism. Further research will undoubtedly seek to confirm or question these findings, and will also need to address concerns for the safety of exercise interventions in cancer survivors.

SUMMARY

- Cancer is a major cause of morbidity and mortality. Over half of cancer deaths are accounted for by cancers of the lung, breast, large bowel and prostate. Risk factors vary by tumour site.

- Carcinogenesis involves disruption of the orderly fashion in which normal body cells grow, divide and die.
- Increasing levels of physical activity are associated with reductions in the risk of several site-specific cancers. Evidence, predominantly in Caucasians, is strongest for cancers of the colon and breast.
- There is some evidence for dose–response relationships between the level of activity and the risk of colon and breast cancer, but these are not well described. At least 30–60 minutes per day of moderate to vigorous activity may be needed for optimal reduction in risk of cancers of the colon and breast.
- Potential systemic mechanisms which might influence the risk of cancer include: changes to metabolic factors, in particular insulin; avoidance of weight gain; and improved immune surveillance.
- Hypothesized site-specific mechanisms include: for cancers of the reproductive system, a decrease in exposure to sex steroid hormones; for colon cancer, a decrease in bowel transit time.

STUDY TASKS

1 What are the possible explanations for the wide differences between countries in the incidence rates for specific cancers? Which seem most tenable and why?
2 How do cancer cells differ from normal cells? Explain how these characteristics lead to the development of a tumour.
3 Briefly describe the mechanisms by which high levels of physical activity may influence the risk of colon cancer.
4 Explain why a high proportion of epidemiological studies of breast cancer have used the case-control design. Give one example of such a study, describing the important features of methodology and the main findings.
5 Why is confounding an important problem for researchers conducting epidemiological studies of colon cancer? How do researchers tackle this problem? Can confounding explain the inverse relationship between level of activity and risk for this cancer?

NOTES

1 Case-control studies comprise a greater proportion of this literature (and that on other cancers), than of literature on coronary heart disease and diabetes; the reason is that the incidence of site-specific cancers is much lower, so it is difficult with a cohort study to obtain sufficient cancer cases to obtain sufficient statistical power to detect effects.
2 These two studies illustrate why so many studies in this area have used a case-control design. Lee *et al.* followed a cohort of 39,322 healthy women to obtain 411 breast cancer cases, one-third of the number studied by Friedenreich *et al.* in their case-control study, and even then had limited statistical power to detect small effects.
3 The relationship between CHD and physical activity has been shown to be strongest when only the better studies (based on quality of methodology, particularly in measuring activity) were considered.
4 For explanation of this statistic see Chapter 2, Measures of health-related outcomes.

FURTHER READING

American Cancer Society website: www.cancer.org/docroot/CRI/CRI_2_5x.asp?dt=72.

Cancer Research UK website: http://info.cancerresearchuk.org/cancerandresearch/learnaboutcancer.

Irwin, M.L. (2006) 'Randomized controlled trials of physical activity and breast cancer prevention', *Exercise Sports Science Reviews* 34: 182–93.

McTiernan, A. (ed.) (2006) *Cancer Prevention and Management Through Exercise and Weight Control*, Boca Raton: CRC Press.

Rogers, C.J., Colbert, L.H., Greiner, J.W., Perkins, S.N. and Hursting, S.D. (2008) 'Physical activity and cancer prevention: pathways and targets for intervention', *Sports Medicine* 38: 271–96.

Slattery, M.L. and Potter, J.D. (2002) 'Physical activity and colon cancer: confounding or interaction?', *Medicine and Science in Sports and Exercise* 34: 913–19.

Thune, I. (2001) 'Physical activity and cancer risk: dose–response and cancer, all sites and site-specific', *Medicine and Science in Sports and Exercise* 33 (Supplement): S530–50.

World Cancer Research Fund (2007) 'Food, nutrition, physical activity, and the prevention of cancer: a global perspective. Second expert report. Chapter 5. Online, available at: www.dietand-cancerreport.org/downloads/chapters/chapter_05.pdf (accessed 16 January 2008).

9 Skeletal health

Knowledge assumed
Basic anatomy of the
musculoskeletal system
Simple physiology of the
endocrine system
Basic biomechanical principles

INTRODUCTION

The skeleton provides physical support and protection for internal organs and, through the actions of muscles, enables movement. It also acts as a reservoir for minerals, particularly calcium. The structure of bone confers 'strength with lightness', so that transporting the skeleton around is not a metabolic burden. As people age, bone strength decreases and bones become more fragile, with an increased propensity to fracture. Low muscle strength and poor balance in elderly people compound this problem by increasing the likelihood of a fall that may precipitate a fracture.

This chapter reviews the evidence concerning the role of physical activity in skeletal health. Knowledge of the anatomy of bone – as an organ and as a tissue – helps us to understand how different types of activity affect its load-bearing competence. The first section therefore provides revision of the basic anatomy of bone and some aspects of its physiology.

BIOLOGY OF BONE

An adult has 10–12 kg of bone, a dynamic tissue with high metabolic activity. It comprises organic material, an inorganic matrix and a small amount of water. The organic component is mainly collagen. The inorganic component is almost all hydroxyapatite, a mineral composed of calcium and phosphate. Bone is not a homogeneous tissue, however, and these components are organized in different ways in cortical and trabecular bone.

Cortical bone is dense and 'ivory-like', properties well-suited to its functions of support and protection. It forms the external part of the long bones and is thickest in the shaft, where it encloses a cavity filled with yellow, fatty marrow (Plate 8). Towards the ends of a long bone, this cavity is replaced by trabecular bone – also called

Plate 8 Structure of a long bone.

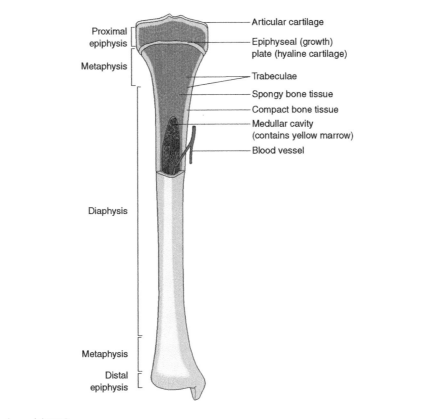

Source: Carola *et al.* (1992).

cancellous or 'spongy' bone. Trabecular bone is much less dense than cortical bone and is made up of a lattice of thin, calcified struts (trabeculae) that form along the lines of greatest stress. Different types of bone predominate at different skeletal sites, according to the functional requirements. For example, trabecular bone makes up 40% of vertebrae but only 1% of the mid-radius.

The outer surface of cortical bone, facing the soft tissue, is the periosteum. Facing the medullary cavity (and covering the trabeculae of trabecular bone) is the endosteum. In both types of bone, cells lining the endosteum are metabolically active and much involved in bone formation and resorption. Trabecular bone has a particularly high metabolic rate – its open structure allows bone marrow, blood vessels and connective tissue to be in contact with the endosteum.

Bone cells regulate bone metabolism and confer adaptive potential by responding to various environmental signals. There are three types of cells: osteoblasts, osteocytes and osteoclasts. Osteocytes are mature cells embedded within small cavities in bone. Their main role is to activate bone turnover and regulate extracellular calcium. Osteoblasts produce bone matrix and build new bone, whilst osteoclasts remove old bone. The activities of these two types of cell are closely coupled during bone remodelling. Even after growth has ended, the skeleton is in a continuous state of remodelling, and between 1% and 10% of skeletal mass is remodelled each year. This process, which takes place in cycles lasting 3–5 months, enables the maintenance of serum calcium levels, the repair of microfractures and fatigue damage that bone sustains daily and confers bone's adaptive potential.

The events of the remodelling cycle are shown schematically in Figure 9.1. Osteoclasts are abundant at the surfaces of bone undergoing erosion and secrete enzymes that create an acid environment to resorb (digest) old bone, creating a cavity. After a delay, osteoblasts fill this cavity with a volume of new bone that then undergoes remineralization. Bone resorption initiates bone formation and, under most circumstances, restores lost bone. However, as age advances, less new bone is formed than is resorbed in each remodelling site, leading to bone loss and structural damage. It follows that, in older people, increased turnover enhances age-related bone loss.

The remodelling process is influenced by hormones that regulate plasma calcium, that is, parathyroid hormone, vitamin D and, to a lesser extent, calcitonin. Parathyroid hormone acts to raise plasma calcium levels; it stimulates bone resorption, enhances calcium absorption from the gut and reduces urinary calcium excretion. Vitamin D is converted in the skin from a precursor; the main action of its metabolites, which behave as hormones, is to stimulate the absorption of ingested calcium. It must also be concerned with calcification of the bone matrix, as vitamin D deficiency gives rise to rickets in children and osteomalacia in adults. Secretion of calcitonin increases when plasma calcium is elevated. Its main effect is to inhibit the activity of osteoclasts, reducing resorption so that less calcium is released into the plasma.

Other hormones influence calcium metabolism, although they are not involved in the regulation of plasma calcium. The most important of these is oestrogen, which helps to conserve bone mass by limiting bone resorption and turnover. It also increases intestinal calcium absorption and reduces urinary calcium excretion, both bone-conserving effects. Oestrogen withdrawal therefore results in an increase in the intensity of remodelling, accelerating bone loss.

Figure 9.1 Remodelling cycle in trabecular bone: (a) inactive surface; (b) resorption by osteoclasts; (c) final resorption cavity; and (d) formation.

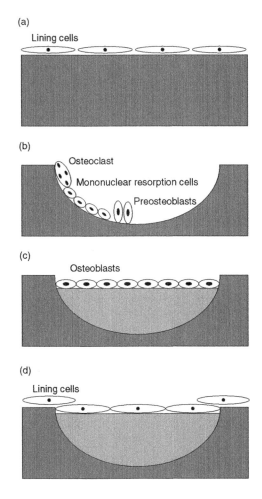

(a)

Lining cells

(b)

Osteoclast

Mononuclear resorption cells

Preosteoblasts

(c)

Osteoblasts

(d)

Lining cells

Source: Khan *et al.* (2001).

Bone strength

The strength of bone reflects the integration of two main features: bone quality and bone density. Quality refers to architecture, turnover and damage accumulation (e.g. microfractures). Bone density determines about 70% of bone strength. It depends on mineral content and is measured by imaging techniques, the most common of which are: dual energy X-ray absorptiometry (DXA); quantitative ultrasound; and quantitative computerized tomography (CT). The principles of these techniques, which measure different properties of bone, are explained in Box 9.1. DXA measurements of bone mass explain 80–90% of the variance in the breaking strength of bone and, at a group level, are quite good at predicting fracture risk. Ultrasound techniques are relatively new and so the evidence related to their potential to predict fracture risk is less extensive.

BOX 9.1 MEASURES OF THE STRUCTURAL PROPERTIES OF BONE

Dual energy X-ray absorptiometry

DXA uses X-ray beams of two distinct energy levels to distinguish the relative composition of bone and non-bone compartments of the body. The measurements are based on the degree to which the X-ray beam is attenuated by the tissues. Two measures are derived: bone mineral content – the total grams of bone mineral within a measured region of bone; and bone mineral density* (BMD) – the grams of bone mineral per unit of bone area scanned. Bone mineral content is highly dependent on bone size, thus a larger person will have a greater value than a smaller person. When bone strength is increased through changes in size as well as in mineral content (as might be the case for physical activity during growth), BMD alone would not detect this, so these two measures are complementary.

- The main limitation of DXA is that, although it measures all bone within a given area, it does not assess bone architecture nor does it differentiate between trabecular and cortical bone.
- Advantages of DXA include the low level of radiation exposure and its accuracy and precision. Scans take as little as five minutes and can measure bone at clinically relevant sites.

Quantitative ultrasound

Two ultrasound transducers (transmitter and a receiver) are positioned on each side of the tissue to be measured (usually the calcaneus, but sometimes the tibia or radius). Measurements reflect the nature and extent of the distortion of a short burst of variable-frequency ultrasound pulse as it passes through bone.

- Limitations include doubts about how well measurements made at the calcaneus reflect the characteristics of bone at the common sites of fracture.
- Advantages are that ultrasound measurements reflect bone architecture as well as bone mineral. They are also cheaper than DXA, can be used outside the laboratory and do not involve exposure to ionizing radiation.

Quantitative computed tomography

This technique uses X-rays to create an image of specific thin layers through the body that are built up to provide a measure of the density of bone. It measures bone mineral content, BMD and axial cross-sectional area.

- The advantage of this technique is that it can measure the type of bone present, as well as size, shape and bone mass.
- Limitations include difficulties in making measurements at the femoral neck and poorer precision, relative to DXA. This technique also involves higher exposure to radiation than DXA and is more expensive.

* This use of the term density is not technically correct; in physics, density is defined as mass per unit volume. The quotient of bone mineral content and area gives a two-dimensional picture and is therefore often described as an *areal density*.

Figure 9.2 Schematic representation of changes in BMD over the life-span. Peak bone mass, attained in early adulthood, is 30–40% higher in men than in women.

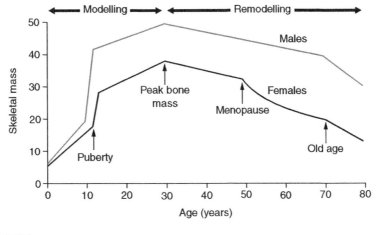

Source: Birdwood (1996).

Bone mass increases during growth and reaches a peak towards the end of the second decade. Peak rates of bone accrual are about 20% greater in boys than in girls so that, from puberty onwards, bone mass is greater in men than in women. Bone mass remains fairly stable until about 50 years of age, when progressive loss begins (Figure 9.2). In women, the rate of bone loss accelerates sharply at the menopause to about 10% per decade, levelling off to about 3% per decade after age 75. Some women lose as much as 30% of bone mass by age 70.

Twin and family studies show that differences in bone size, shape and BMD are largely (50–85%) attributable to genetic factors. However, lifestyle factors are also important determinants of adult bone structure. For example, inadequate intake of calcium impairs bone accrual during growth and leads to bone loss in adults. The potential of the mechanical loading of bone during physical activity to influence its structure will be of particular interest to the reader.

Adaptation to load-bearing

Bone is deposited in relation to the load it must bear. It is this principle that makes it biologically plausible that exercise strengthens bone and attenuates bone loss; with greater loading, the load-bearing capacity of bone increases – and vice versa. The strains (deformations) produced during loading stimulate an adaptive response in bone that is determined by the magnitude, rate and distribution of strains, as well as the number of repetitions (strain cycles). It derives from bone cells in the region where the strains are experienced and is thus described as a 'local response to local loading'. The mechanisms by which bone cells recognize changes in loading and initiate an osteogenic response are still being unravelled but, somehow, many cells behave in a coordinated fashion to achieve the modelling and remodelling necessary to adjust bone strength to the loads it must bear.

The general principles governing the response of bone to load bearing were established through *in vivo* experiments with the turkey ulna and subsequently supported by studies in other species, including humans. Disuse results in an increase in remodelling activity that is dominated by resorption and consequent loss of bone. Immobilization and space flight, for example, both lead to net bone loss (astronauts typically lose as much bone mass in the proximal femur in one month as postmenopausal women on Earth lose in one year). Conversely, when loading-induced strain exceeds 'normal' strains at a particular skeletal site, new bone is added, increasing bone strength. Oestrogen receptor-α in osteoblasts and osteocytes appears to mediate this response.

Bone's response to an overload in the number of strain cycles to which it is exposed appears to 'saturate' quickly, suggesting that many repetitions of a given strain stimulus confer no additional advantage to that achieved by a few. However, any unusual distribution of strain enhances the osteogenic response at a given strain magnitude (both observations have implications for the type of physical activity likely to exert optimal effect on bone).

OSTEOPOROSIS: DEFINITION, PREVALENCE AND CONSEQUENCES

Osteoporosis (literally meaning 'porous bones') is a skeletal disorder characterized by low bone mass and microarchitectural deterioration of bone tissue, with a consequent increase in fragility and susceptibility to fracture (Figure 9.3). Diagnosis relies on measurements of BMD at the hip as a proxy measure of bone strength. The World Health Organization (WHO) operationally defines osteoporosis as bone density 2.5 standard deviations below the mean for young white adult women, based on DXA scan results. Osteopenia (low BMD not reaching a threshold for diagnosis of osteoporosis) is identified when BMD is 1–2.5 standard deviations below this mean.

Figure 9.3 Osteoporotic changes in lumbar vertebrae. The strong vertebral bodies of (a) early adult life lose much of their structure and become prone to crush fractures as weight-bearing capacity diminishes (b).

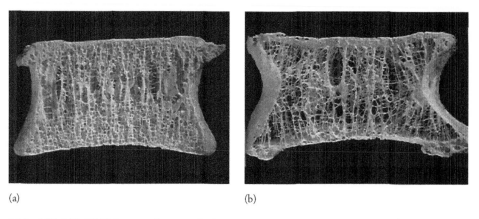

(a)   (b)

Source: L Mosekilde MD, DMSci, personal communication.

The public health issue is primary osteoporosis – which often follows menopause in women as the rate of bone loss accelerates and occurs later in life in men (secondary osteoporosis is a result of medical conditions, diseases or medications). Bone loss with ageing is, however, not the only contributing factor to primary osteoporosis. Suboptimal bone growth in childhood and adolescence (see Chapter 10) is as important to its development as bone loss in middle and old age.

Osteoporosis is second only to cardiovascular disease (CVD) as a leading health care problem world-wide. The WHO estimates that one in three women and one in eight men over age 50 risk having an osteoporotic fracture during their lifetime. These fractures cause disability, loss of independence and loss of quality of life. Their financial, physical and psychosocial consequences significantly affect the family and the community, as well as the individual. Osteoporotic fractures are a major contributor to medical care costs in many regions of the world. Moreover, the social burden associated with osteoporotic fractures is bound to increase, especially in industrialized countries, as the population ages (see Chapter 1).

Osteoporotic fractures

Almost all types of fracture are increased in patients with low BMD, but the most vulnerable skeletal sites are those where trabecular bone predominates. The greater metabolic rate of this type of bone means that it responds more quickly than cortical bone to changes in environmental influences, internal or external. In women, loss of circulating oestrogen (and its bone-conserving effects) around the menopause is the most important cause of bone loss. Box 9.2 shows risk factors for osteoporosis.

BOX 9.2 RISK FACTORS FOR PRIMARY OSTEOPOROSIS

Strongest risk factors
Female sex
Age greater than 60 years
Family history of osteoporosis

Other important risk factors
Caucasian or Asian origin
Untreated premature menopause
Low body mass index (BMI)
History of secondary amenorrhoea for more than one year
Smoking
Eating disorder
Low calcium intake
Low vitamin D levels (lack of sunlight and/or low dietary intake)
Sedentary lifestyle (particularly during adolescence) or conditions associated with prolonged immobility
Alcohol abuse
History of fracture as adult

The most common sites of osteoporotic fractures are the hip, the vertebrae and the wrist. Bone loss is an important predisposing factor, but fractures are often the result of a fall. The incidence of hip fractures rises exponentially with age. Since women have lower BMD than men, live longer, experience more bone loss and have more falls, more than three-quarters of these disabling fractures occur in women. Half of the patients who fracture their hip cannot walk independently afterwards, and many will move from the community to a nursing home. Seventeen per cent of 50-year-old white women and 6% of 50-year-old white men will have a hip fracture during their lifetime (the risk for black people is much lower). The number of hip fractures world-wide is expected to increase to 6.3 million in 2050 (from 1.7 million in 1990).

Vertebral crush fractures result in loss of weight-bearing competence of the vertebral bodies. Like hip fractures, they occur more often in women than in men. Most are precipitated by routine everyday activities. The associated loss of height can be considerable and gives rise to secondary problems because abdominal and thoracic organs are compressed, leading to chronic, disabling pain and deformity.

In perimenopausal women, the wrist is the most common site of fracture. Wrist fractures are usually associated with a fall, typically outdoors and often in icy weather. Few patients are completely disabled by a wrist fracture, but fewer than half experience a satisfactory return to function.

Treatments for osteoporosis

Treatment focuses on agents that reduce bone loss. The first-line treatment is usually one of the bisphosphonates – drugs that are potent inhibitors of bone turnover. Calcium supplementation also decreases the risk of hip fracture (24% reduction with 1,000 mg day^{-1}) but is associated with maintenance, rather than gain, of skeletal mass. Vitamin D supplementation may also be helpful, as deficiency of this vitamin is not uncommon among the frail elderly living in institutions, probably because of inadequate exposure to sunlight. Calcitonin reduces bone resorption by inhibiting osteoclastic activity and may have a role to play in reducing vertebral fractures. Oestrogen is not recommended because the associated increase in breast cancer, stroke, thrombotic events and CVD outweigh its skeletal benefit.

PHYSICAL ACTIVITY AND BONE STRENGTH

Two main factors determine whether or not an individual develops osteopenia or osteoporosis – their peak bone mass as a young adult and the rate of bone loss they experience as they age.

Studies in animals consistently show that growing bone has a substantially greater capacity to add new bone than does mature bone. Therefore, childhood and adolescence probably represent a 'window of opportunity' for interventions aimed at reducing the risk of osteoporosis in later life: high peak bone mass is associated with reduced risk of osteoporotic fractures later in life. Evidence on the effects of physical activity and exercise on skeletal health in children is presented in Chapter 10.

The response to exercise-related bone loading, like other environmental stimuli, may be mediated by individual genetic variability. Polymorphisms of the vitamin D receptor gene and of the gene coding for oestrogen receptor-α have both been studied for interaction with structural parameters at different skeletal sites. To date, however, there is no consensus as to the nature of such interactions, or indeed whether or not they exist.

Premenopausal women and men

Cross-sectional studies have consistently reported that athletes have higher bone mineral than inactive controls, especially at the skeletal sites specifically loaded in their sport. Most have looked at premenopausal women, although similar findings are available also for men, postmenopausal women and children.

For example, researchers in Finland employed quantitative computed tomography to compare a range of structural variables at different skeletal sites between female athletes and non-athlete controls (Nikander *et al.* 2006). The national-level athletes studied were volleyball players, hurdlers, racket games players, soccer players and swimmers. As expected, the athletes' bone mass at the loaded sites was substantially higher than controls. In addition, the weight-bearing bones of the athletes (swimmers excluded) had larger diaphysis, thicker cortices and somewhat denser trabecular bone than controls, and the bones of their arms were generally larger in cross-sectional area. Joint moments resulting from the action of muscles involved during specific movements were estimated and the researchers concluded that the osteogenic response was related to both muscle action and impact loading in the lower limb. By contrast, in the shafts of the arm bones the structural characteristics were attributable to the estimated joint moments. Thus, loading-induced additional bone mass in athletes builds mechanically strong and appropriate bone structures that relate to the nature of the loading.

Studies comparing athletes with non-athletes, while useful indicators of the optimal osteogenic response to mechanical loading, cannot control for bias or confounding. For example, self-selection bias is inevitable (people with strong bones may tend to take up sport). Potential confounding factors include differences in lifestyle (healthy nutrition and avoidance of smoking in athletes) or physical activity history during childhood and adolescence. Alternative experimental designs that take care of some of these factors are: side-to-side comparisons in racket games players where only one limb is exposed to impact in the sport; and intervention studies where changes in exercisers can be compared with changes in controls.

Another study from Finland constitutes an example of the first of these designs (Kontulainen *et al.* 2003). These researchers compared side-to-side differences in indices of bone strength, again derived using peripheral quantitative tomography, in the humeral shaft of 64 female tennis and squash players and 27 controls matched for age, height and weight. To examine the influence of age at which differential loading of the arm bones began, the players were divided into two groups; 'young starters' had started playing at or before menarche, while 'old starters' had started playing at least one year after menarche. Among old starters, side-to-side differences in indices of bone strength were significantly greater than in controls (Figure 9.4), confirming that loading augments the mature skeleton in a site-specific manner. However, the young starters' side-to-side differences were generally twice as large as those in the old starters,

Figure 9.4 Side-to-side differences of bone variables at the humeral shaft of female tennis and squash players, according to age of starting training, and age-matched controls.

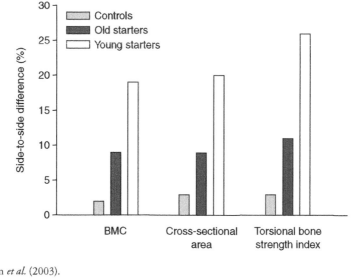

Source: Kontulainen *et al.* (2003).
Note: Values are means for 36 young starters, 28 old starters and 27 controls.

indicating a particularly potent effect on bone during the pubescent years (Figure 9.4). In both groups of players, the structural adaptation of the humerus was attributable to an enlarged cortical area, indicating that the loaded humerus seemed to have grown periosteally.

Controlled intervention trials of bone-loading in previously sedentary premenopausal women have typically found small (1–3%) increases in BMD, compared with controls. Interventions have included jogging, strength training, weight lifting, aerobics and high-impact jumping activities that can create ground reaction forces up to six times body weight. The main findings from one large, well-designed study are shown in Figure 9.5 (Heinonen *et al.* 1996). Sedentary women aged 35–45 were randomly assigned to either a training group or a control group. Women in the training group did progressive high-impact exercises (jumping and step exercises) three times per week for 18 months. BMD was measured using DXA, with careful attention to precision and accuracy, both of which can be difficult to achieve over a long observation period. At the skeletal sites loaded by the exercise regimen, BMD increased more in exercisers than in the controls. For example, a mean increase of 1.6% (95% confidence interval 0.8–2.4) was seen at the femoral neck.

A handful of studies suggest that exercise-induced benefits for bone start to disappear after cessation of training but, 3.5 years after the end of the high-impact exercise intervention described above, the gains in BMD achieved were maintained, relative to controls (Kontulainen *et al.* 2004). In addition, the greater side-to-side differences in BMC of the humerus of female racquet sport players (compared with controls) persisted after four years of retirement (Kontulainen *et al.* 1999). Thus, participation in high-impact activities may have lasting advantages for skeletal health.

Figure 9.5 Percentage change over 18 months at different skeletal sites in sedentary women aged 35–45.

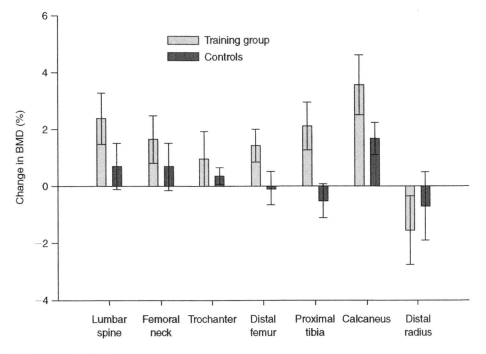

Source: Heinonen *et al.* (1996).
Note: Women in the training group (*n* = 39) did progressive, high-impact exercises three times per week. Controls (*n* = 45) were asked to maintain pre-trial levels of physical activity. Data are mean and 95% CI.

Far fewer studies have been conducted in men than in women (because their risk of osteoporosis is lower) but their findings are broadly similar. Cross-sectional comparisons of athletes and controls have found significantly higher BMD in athletes at skeletal sites loaded in their sports. Side-to-side differences in the BMC of the arm bones have been reported to be 13–25%, depending on the site measured, compared with differences in controls of only 1–5% (Kontulainen *et al.* 1999). Several of the small number of controlled exercise intervention studies in men have found small (2–3%), but significant, gains in BMD. The general conclusion from meta-analysis of published studies is that exercise can improve or maintain BMD in men.

Postmenopausal women

Can healthy older women reduce their risk of fracture through increasing their physical activity? Many prospective, controlled trials have addressed this question. The topic is complex, however, because of potential interactions with hormone replacement therapy (oestrogen may facilitate the osteogenic effect of physical activity); because bone loading is a site-specific effect; and because a variety of exercise interventions have been used.

Strength training or high-impact loading have often been the exercise regimens of choice, based on the principles governing the osteogenic response to bone-loading.

Two well-designed studies are described here as examples. In a year-long randomized intervention trial, Nelson *et al.* studied postmenopausal white women aged 50–70 (Nelson *et al.* 1994). None were taking hormone replacement therapy. Exercising women did high-intensity strength training for 45 minutes, two days per week. The major muscle groups attached to the bones of the lumbar spine and the hip were trained with exercises at 80% of one repetition maximum, using the principle of progressive overload. Compared with controls, the women who trained gained strength, as well as total body BMC and BMD at the lumbar spine and femoral neck. The benefit of training, that is, relative to controls who lost bone, for BMD was 2.8% and 3.4%, respectively.

Using a randomized, controlled design, researchers compared the effects of high-impact activities (jogging, running, stair-climbing) or strength training on BMD in previously sedentary postmenopausal women (Kohrt *et al.* 1997). The women who trained did so for 45 minutes, three or four times per week for 11 months, and dietary supplementation ensured that all women ingested sufficient calcium. Both exercise programmes achieved a 1–2% increase in BMD at the lumbar spine, but only the impact-loading programme augmented BMD at the femoral neck (Figure 9.6).

Figure 9.6 Comparison of impact loading and resistance training on BMD in postmenopausal women.

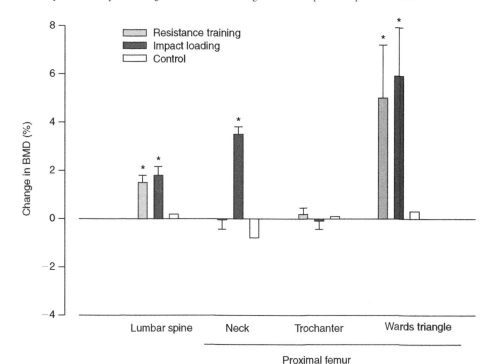

Source: Kohrt *et al.* (1997).
Note: Percentage change at the lumbar spine and at three different sites at the hip. Ward's triangle is a defined area of the proximal femur. Bars are SE. Different from change in control group. $*P < 0.05$, $*P < 0.01$.

After more than a decade of research on this topic, it can be concluded that a variety of types of exercise can preserve bone mass in older women. Specifically, meta-analyses have concluded that exercise regimens 'prevented or reversed' around 1–3% of bone loss per year at both the lumbar spine and femoral neck in postmenopausal women (Kelley 1998; Wolff *et al.* 1999). 'Prevented' in this context means that in a number of studies a *decrease* in BMD in controls contributed to the benefit of exercise, assessed as the difference in response over time between exercisers and controls.

Thus, exercise intervention in older women can maintain bone mineral or attenuate the rate of loss, but does not serve to add substantial amounts of new bone (Kelley and Kelley, 2006). An interesting methodological point is that the effects of exercise reported for non-randomized controlled trials have been almost twice as high as those for randomized controlled trials, giving an indication of the importance of confounding introduced by non-random allocation of subjects to groups (Chapter 2).

PHYSICAL ACTIVITY AND FRACTURE RISK

Evidence from prospective studies suggests that physical activity is associated with a lower risk of hip fracture. For example, in a cohort of more than 60,000 postmenopausal women from the Nurses' Health Study, active women who reported at least $24\,MET\text{-}h\,week^{-1}$ of physical activity had a 55% lower risk than sedentary women reporting less than $3\,MET\text{-}h\,week^{-1}$ (Feskanich *et al.* 2002). There was evidence for a dose–response relationship – the risk for hip fracture was 6% less for each increase in activity of $3\,MET\text{-}h\,week^{-1}$. Among women who did no other exercise, walking for at least four hours per week was associated with a 41% lower risk for hip fracture than among those who walked for less than one hour per week. This observation is interesting because it suggests that low-intensity weight-bearing activity like walking may reduce fracture risk, even though minimal changes in BMD would be expected. It is supported by at least one other study that found a 30% lower risk of hip fracture among women who walked regularly for exercise, compared with women who did not walk regularly (Cummings *et al.* 1995).

A handful of prospective studies have examined risk factors, including physical inactivity, for vertebral fractures. In 3.7 years of follow-up of more than 5,800 American women aged 65 or over who had no fracture when enrolled, low physical activity (walking less than one block or doing less than one hour of household chores per day) was associated with a 60% increase in the risk of first vertebral fracture (Nevitt *et al.* 2005). At the other end of the spectrum, participating in recreational activity at high or moderate intensity at least once a month halved the risk for fracture at this site. Interestingly, these effects were independent of BMD, showing that other exercise-related factors are important determinants of fracture risk.

Risk for falls

The lower risk for hip and vertebral fractures among active individuals may reflect a decrease in falls. Nearly all hip fractures involve falls – usually from a standing height or less. Falls also play a role in vertebral fractures, although this is more limited.

Intrinsic risk factors include poor levels of muscle strength, range of motion, balance, gait and reaction time – all of which might be improved through regular exercise. Systematic review and meta-analysis of randomized clinical trials that aimed to prevent falls in older adults found that exercise interventions that included balance, leg strength, flexibility and/or endurance training reduced the risk of falling (Chang *et al.* 2004).

One large study of falls in 1,090 people over 70, living at home in Australia, is described here as an example. Researchers examined the potential of three different interventions to reduce falls (Day *et al.* 2002).

These were designed to improve: strength and balance through exercises; home hazard management; and vision. Interventions were implemented singly and in all combinations, allocating subjects randomly to one of eight equal-sized groups (one was control, no intervention).

Exercise, either alone or in combination with other interventions, conferred a significant decrease in the risk of a fall. The exercise regimen adopted by the subjects was modest, one hour per week of supervised exercises for 15 weeks, supplemented by twice weekly home exercises for the remainder of the 18-month trial.

However, it is important to recognize that many extrinsic risk factors for falling that prevail in nursing homes, poor vision for example, or use of sedatives, would not be expected to be improved by exercise. Moreover, for older people living in the community, becoming more active may actually increase the opportunity for falling.

PHYSICAL ACTIVITY IN PREVENTION AND MANAGEMENT OF OSTEOPOROSIS

Pharmacological therapy in patients with established osteoporosis cannot restore lost bone, highlighting the need actively to pursue possibilities for prevention. To decrease her life-long risk of fracture, a woman must maximize peak bone mass, maintain this through middle-age and attenuate the rate of loss of bone after the menopause. In the later decades of life, she must try to decrease the risk of falls. Intakes of calcium and vitamin D are, of course, also important for skeletal health. A daily dietary intake of 1,000 mg calcium is advised, with (for adults over 65) 400 IU of vitamin D.

To achieve these aims, a life-long habit of weight-bearing exercise is clearly important. Its effects are particularly potent during growth, when gains in BMD of 5–10% are possible. For optimal effect, mechanical loading should expose multiple skeletal sites to high and varied strains through high-impact and/or heavy-resistance exercises. Whether bone gain during growth can be maintained during adulthood if the level of activity declines is not clear.

In women, premenopause and postmenopause, the benefit of exercise for BMD is around 1%. How important, clinically, is this? Estimates suggest that an increase in BMD of this magnitude could, if maintained, result in a 10% decrease in fracture risk. This is clearly worthwhile, but the overall benefit may be even greater if exercises to improve balance reduce the risk of falls. In practice, two issues limit the implementation of targeted bone-loading exercises as a strategy to reduce fracture risk, particularly in older women. These are: (1) poor compliance with high-impact exercises; and (2) the associated risk of injury.

For these reasons researchers have examined the potential of simple, everyday aerobic exercise to limit age-related bone loss. For example, in one randomly controlled trial, women aged 52–53 followed a programme of walking, stair climbing, cycling and jogging (55–75% $\dot{V}O_2$max), 3–4 times per week for 18 months (Heinonen *et al.* 1998). These aerobic exercisers avoided the loss of BMD at the femoral neck that was seen in the control group.

Physical activity clearly has a preventive role in osteoporosis, but its therapeutic effectiveness in women with a clinically defined condition is still being explored. Vertebral fractures invariably leads to exaggerated kyphosis. This posture not only increases the risk of falling, but also causes severe back pain. Strengthening back extensor muscles and engaging in dynamic posture training can help these patients on both counts. These interventions may also decrease depression and improve the quality of life.

For patients who have had a hip fracture, there is strong evidence that exercise programmes can improve strength and mobility, but it is not known whether these improvements are sufficient to prevent falls and further fractures in this high-risk group. Nevertheless, it can be argued that exercise is the only single therapy that can simultaneously ameliorate low bone mineral density, augment muscle mass, promote strength gain, and improve dynamic balance – all of which are independent risk factors for fracture.

PHYSICAL ACTIVITY AND OSTEOARTHRITIS

Osteoarthritis – the most common form of arthritis – is characterized by degenerative and sometimes hypertrophic changes in the bone and cartilage of joints (most frequently fingers, knee, hips and spine) and a progressive wearing down of opposing joint surfaces, leading to distortion of joint positioning. The disease is disabling and impairs the quality of life. Over the age of 50, about eight out of ten people are affected, and numbers are expected to rise over time as the population ages and because of the increasing prevalence of obesity.

Epidemiological studies have demonstrated that participation in sports that involve high-intensity, acute, direct joint impacts and/or twisting and torsional types of stress appear to increase the risk for osteoarthritis. This risk correlates with the intensity and duration of exposure. To put it into perspective, however, the risk for osteoarthritis associated with sport is less than that associated with a history of trauma or overweight. Occupational activity can also lead to joint stress and an increased in risk for developing osteoarthritis. One common factor is that both types of activity have a higher risk of joint injuries – a known risk factor for arthritis.

On the other hand, participation in moderate types and amounts of aerobic activity, including sports that cause minimal joint impact and torsional loading, confers little, if any, risk of osteoarthritis. Indeed, some level of 'ordinary' activity is necessary for joint health (immobilization is associated not only with loss of muscle and bone, but also with connective tissue stiffness and other effects associated with impairment of joint function). One review concluded that 'exercise pursued with a goal of health improvement' had a favourable effect on pain and function in sedentary patients with osteoarthritis of the knee and should be performed between one and three times per week (Vignon *et al.* 2006).

Exercise is thus increasingly regarded as a key component of the management of osteoarthritis. Comprehensive interventions that include aerobic exercise (usually walking) and/or resistance exercise to strengthen quadricep muscles, pain management and education result in moderate improvements in measures of disability, physical performance (e.g. six-minute walking distance, stair-climbing, getting in and out of a car) and perception of pain. Exercise does not worsen the disease, provided that it does not predispose to trauma, and is relatively safe. For example, only 2% of participants had serious musculoskeletal injuries related to exercise in the 18-month long US Fitness, Arthritis and Seniors Trial (Ettinger *et al.* 1997). More experimental evidence about the influence (beneficial and detrimental) of exercise on joint structure and cartilaginous tissue is needed.

Chronic low back pain – often associated with osteoarthritis – causes a great amount of suffering, loss of productivity and independence, and its prevalence is increasing. Heavy physical work is one of the predisposing factors for low back pain but, paradoxically, exercise is now regarded as a first line therapy for sufferers. Based on a review of randomly controlled trials, exercise is deemed to be 'slightly' effective in decreasing pain and improving function in adults with chronic low back pain, particularly among those whose pain leads them to seek healthcare (Hayden *et al.* 2005). On the other hand, exercise therapy appears to be no better than other conservative treatments – or no treatment – for an acute episode of back pain.

SUMMARY

- Bone is a dynamic tissue that responds to changes in the internal or external environment. Functional loading is the most important influence on bone remodelling.
- Strain rate and an unusual strain distribution are important determinants of the site-specific osteogenic effects of mechanical loading.
- Bone mass increases during growth and reaches a peak towards the end of the second decade. It then remains fairly stable until about 50 years of age when progressive loss begins. Age-related loss of bone can lead to osteopenia and osteoporosis, compromising strength and increasing the risk of fracture.
- The potential of exercise to augment bone mineral in the mature skeleton is clear but small. In premenopausal women its effect is mainly conservation of bone, although specific bone-loading exercise can lead to modest bone accrual. In older women its effect is to reduce the rate of bone loss.
- Women with a physically active lifestyle, including walking for exercise, have a lower risk of osteoporotic fracture of the hip and maybe of the spine.
- Many fractures are caused by falls. Exercise can decrease the risk of falls through improving balance, strength and maybe neuromuscular coordination.
- Participation in sports involving high-intensity impacts or torsional types of stress increases the risk for osteoarthritis. On the other hand, moderate amounts and intensities of exercise have a favourable effect on pain and function in patients with osteoarthritis of the knee.

STUDY TASKS

1 Describe the basic principles that govern the effect of mechanical loading on bone.

2 Identify the common sites of osteoporotic fracture and suggest specific exercises that might be expected to elicit an osteogenic response at each of these sites.

3 Explain why the age-related rise in hip fractures occurs 5–10 years later in men than in women. How might exercise alter the risk of this fracture even if it does not increase BMD?

4 Explain as fully as possible why studies of athletes who play racquet games are so informative in the context of the influence of exercise on BMD.

FURTHER READING

Beck, B. and Snow, C.M. (2003) 'Bone health across the lifespan: exercising our options', *Exercise and Sport Sciences Reviews* 31: 117–22.

Kannus, P., Uusi-Rasi, K., Palvanen, M. and Parkkari, J. (2005) 'Non-pharmacological means to prevent fractures among older adults', *Annals of Medicine* 37: 303–10.

Khan, K., McKay, H., Kannus, R, Bailey, D., Wark, J. and Bennell, K. (2001) *Physical Activity and Bone Health*, Champaign: Human Kinetics.

Kohrt, W.M., Bloomfield, S.A., Little, K.D., Nelson, M.E. and Yingling, V.R. (2004) 'Physical activity and bone health: ACSM position stand', *Medicine and Science in Sports and Exercise* 36: 1985–96.

Wallace, B.A. and Cumming, R.G. (2000) 'Systematic review of randomized trials of the effect of exercise on bone mass in pre- and postmenopausal women', *Calcified Tissue International* 67: 10–18.

Part III
Physical Activity in Youth and Old Age

10 Children's health

Knowledge assumed
Basic exercise physiology
Basic knowledge of growth and
development
Basic knowledge of statistics

INTRODUCTION

Thus far this book has examined the relationship between physical activity and health in adults, although the issue of health in children was mentioned in the Introduction and briefly in several other chapters. In this chapter we focus on studies that have examined the relationship between physical activity and health in children. The health outcomes examined are obesity, type 2 diabetes, cardiovascular disease (CVD) and bone health. As is the case with adults, the majority of studies in children are observational and although intervention trials have been conducted, few of these are randomized controlled trials.

One issue that should be remembered when discussing children's health is that differences in maturation may confound the findings of studies where only chronological age is assessed. Another issue is the extent to which physical activity in childhood influences health in later life. Most studies of physical activity and children's health have examined associations between physical activity in childhood and risk markers for disease in childhood because disease itself is rare in children. However, some studies have attempted to examine the relationship between physical activity in childhood and health in adulthood. Such studies require long-term follow-up periods, and even then the endpoints are often risk factors rather than disease. In this chapter we will distinguish between studies focusing on exercise and health in childhood and those examining exercise in childhood and health in adulthood.

Where possible, in this chapter a distinction is made between childhood (the period before puberty) and adolescence (the period from the beginning of puberty until adulthood). At times, however, the terms 'children' and 'childhood' will be used in the general sense to mean the entire period between birth and adulthood. This chapter begins by examining physical activity and physical fitness levels in children and adolescents.

PHYSICAL ACTIVITY AND PHYSICAL FITNESS

The difficulties inherent in accurately quantifying physical activity levels were addressed earlier in this book, and these difficulties also apply to studies involving children. In recent years accelerometers have been a popular tool for examining physical activity levels in children, but other methods such as survey data and doubly labelled water have also been employed. Regardless of the method used, the literature is fairly consistent in suggesting that physical activity levels are low in children living in developed countries and that physical activity levels have declined in children in recent years. In the United States, for example, approximately half of all schoolchildren walked to school in 1969 and 87% of those living within 1 mile of school walked or bicycled. In contrast, fewer than 15% of children and adolescents used active modes of transportation in 2004 (Morbidity and Mortality Weekly Reports 2005). Parental fears of the dangers of traffic and crime were two of the explanations thought to be responsible for this decline. A similar trend has been noted in Australia as mentioned in the introductory chapter, and it is likely that this trend has occurred in many other developed countries.

In the United Kingdom, physical activity levels have been measured in Scottish children living in Glasgow using a combination of accelerometry and doubly labelled water. The findings suggest that three-year-old children spend 79% of their time in sedentary behaviour and only 2% of their time in moderate-to-vigorous physical activity. For five-year-old children the figures were 76% and 4% respectively. The investigators concluded that 'modern British children establish a sedentary lifestyle at an early age' (Reilly et al. 2004). Consistent with these findings are those of the Avon Longitudinal Study of Parents and Children (ALSPAC) birth cohort study involving 5,595 children from the county of Avon in the southwest of England (Riddoch et al. 2006). Once again, accelerometry was used to measure physical activity levels in counts per minute. The study observed that only 2.5% of children (5.1% for boys, 0.4% for girls) met internationally recognized recommendations for physical activity in children (defined as at least 60 minutes of moderate-to-vigorous (≥ 4 METs) physical activity daily).

Some studies have attempted to identify which factors predict children's physical activity levels. Mattocks et al. (2008), for example, in another report from the

ALSPAC study found that parents' physical activity during pregnancy and early in the child's life showed a modest association with the physical activity of the child at age 11–12. Similarly, a birth cohort study set in Pelotas, southern Brazil, found that physical activity at age four (based on maternal report) was a significant predictor of physical activity in adolescence (Hallal *et al.* 2006). Some studies have examined the relationship between the mode of transport to school and overall physical activity levels in children and adolescents. Alexander *et al.* (2005), for example, again using accelerometers, found that among adolescents (aged 13–14) living in the Edinburgh area, walking to and from school was associated with higher overall moderate-to-vigorous physical activity throughout the day, compared with travelling by car, bus or train. In contrast, a study of five-year-old children also employing accelerometry found that being driven to school does not affect overall physical activity (Metcalf *et al.* 2004). A possible explanation for this discrepancy is the different age groups studied.

A common and consistent finding in longitudinal studies is that physical activity declines from childhood to adolescence. A recent example is the National Institute of Child Health and Human Development Study of Early Child Care and Youth Development (Nader *et al.* 2008). This study observed steep physical activity declines in young people between the ages of nine and 15 (Figure 10.1). Similarly, the National Heart, Lung, and Blood Institute Growth and Health Study observed substantial declines in physical activity from the ages of nine or ten to the ages of 18 or 19 years in black and white girls living in America (Figure 10.2). Predictors of declines in physical activity among black girls, white girls or both included lower levels of parental education, higher body mass index (BMI), pregnancy and cigarette smoking (Kimm *et al.* 2002).

Figure 10.1 Mean minutes of moderate-to-vigorous physical activity per day in boys and girls followed from ages 9–15 years.

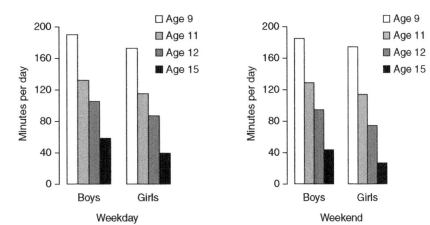

Source: Nader *et al.* (2008).
Notes: Data are from 1,032 participants (517 boys, 515 girls) in the 1991–2007 National Institute of Child Health and Human Development Study of Early Child Care and Youth Development. Moderate-to-vigorous physical activity was defined as a sum of time spent in moderate (3.0–5.9 METs), vigorous (6.0–8.9 METs) and very vigorous (>9 METs) physical activity estimated from accelerometer data.

Figure 10.2 Median values for physical activity scores in 1,166 white girls and 1,213 black girls in the United States. Participants were enrolled in the National Heart, Lung, and Blood Institute Growth and Health Study from the ages of 9 or 10 to the ages of 18 or 19 years.

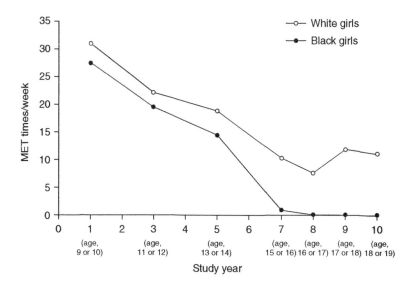

Notes: Scores exclude activities performed in physical education classes at school. The units here (MET-times per week) are unusual and take no account of the duration of each session of activity. Girls reported the number of occasions on which they participated in specific sports/activities over the previous year. Researchers computed the score by multiplying an estimate of the metabolic equivalent (MET) by the reported weekly frequency and the fraction of the year during which it was performed. Typical values are: bicycling one or two times per week for 52 weeks of the year, 8.0 MET-times per week; and swimming three or more times per week for 13 weeks of the year, 4.5 MET-times per week.

Some studies have focused on the association between physical activity and physical fitness in children and adolescents. One novel study compared physical activity and physical fitness characteristics in Old Order Mennonite children from Ontario, Canada (a group living a traditional agrarian lifestyle) with characteristics in children living in urban and rural Saskatchewan, Canada. The findings revealed that Old Order Mennonite children tended to be leaner, stronger and more active than urban and rural dwelling children living a contemporary Canadian lifestyle (Tremblay *et al.* 2005). These findings suggest that activity influences fitness in children, a finding supported by the low, but significant, correlations observed in cross-sectional studies between $\dot{V}O_2max$ and total activity ($r = 0.23$ for boys, $r = 0.23$ for girls, both $P<0.05$) as well as $\dot{V}O_2max$ and time spent in vigorous activity ($r = 0.32$ for boys, $r = 0.30$ in girls, both $P<0.05$) (Dencker *et al.* 2006).

In some studies with adults, high physical fitness appears to offer greater protection from disease than high physical activity. This suggests that it may be more important to focus on physical fitness levels in children and adolescents than physical activity levels. Matton *et al.* (2006) observed a better tracking of fitness than activity between youth and adulthood in Flemish females, while one recent study involving 15,621 English children (aged 9–11) reported a decline in cardiorespiratory fitness (assessed using the 20-metre multi-stage shuttle run test) between 1998/9 and 2003/4. Findings such as these often lead to calls for increases in the amount of physical education included within the school curriculum. While logic would suggest that this would increase children's overall physical activity levels (and possibly increase physical fitness), in practice this is not always the case. One study observed that the total amount of physical activity (measured by accelerometers) done by primary school children does not depend on how much physical education is timetabled at school, because children in schools with low amounts of timetabled physical education compensate by being more active outside of school (Mallam *et al.* 2003) (Figure 10.3).

Figure 10.3 Mean physical activity done by children at three primary schools.

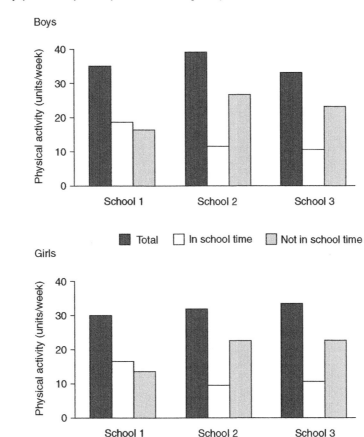

Source: Reproduced from 'Contribution of timetabled physical education to total physical activity in primary school children: cross sectional study', Mallam, K.M. *et al.*, *British Medical Journal* 327:592–593 page 592, (2003) with permission from BMJ Publishing Group Ltd.
Notes: Activity was measured during waking hours for seven days using accelerometers in 215 children (120 boys and 95 girls aged 7.0–10.5 years) from three schools with different sporting facilities and opportunity for physical education in the curriculum. School one was a private school with nine hours of physical education (PE) in the curriculum each week. School two was a village school offering 2.2 hours of timetabled PE each week, while school three was an inner-city school offering 1.8 hours of PE each week. Despite these differences, the overall physical activity levels of the children did not differ between schools.

Another study observed that a five-fold variation in timetabled physical education explained less than 1% of the total variation in physical activity (Wilkin *et al.* 2006). Having said this, a recent systematic review of controlled trials concluded that there is strong evidence that school-based interventions with the involvement of the family or community and multi-component interventions can increase physical activity in adolescents (van Sluijs *et al.* 2007).

OBESITY

One obvious concern related to low levels of physical activity in children and adolescents is that it predisposes them to obesity. Figure 1.1 highlighted the increasing prevalence of obesity in English boys and girls in recent years, a finding confirmed in several studies (Chinn and Rona 2001; Lobstein *et al.* 2003; Stamatakis *et al.* 2005). An increasing prevalence of childhood obesity has also been noted in the United States (Eckel *et al.* 2005; Ogden *et al.* 2006) and in many other developed and developing countries (Cole 2006; Gorden-Larsen and Popkin 2006; Speiser *et al.* 2005). In Chapter 6 the health risks of obesity in adults were discussed, and these same health risks are also associated with obesity in childhood and adolescence (Daniels *et al.* 2005; Regan and Betts 2006; Reilly and Wilson 2006).

As in studies of adults, BMI is a popular tool by which to diagnose obesity in children and adolescents, although there is variation in the cut-off points used to indicate obesity. One approach has been to establish the BMI for each age which would predict a BMI of 25 (overweight) or 30 (obese) in adulthood (Cole *et al.* 2000) (Table 10.1). This same approach has also been used to draw up guidelines for thinness in children and adolescents (Cole *et al.* 2007). Another approach has been to use a given BMI percentile to indicate overweight and obesity, often the 85th and 95th percentiles,

Table 10.1 Cut-off points for BMI for overweight and obesity by sex between 11 and 18 years, defined to pass through BMI of 25 and 30 kg m² at age 18

| | BMI 25 kg/m² | | BMI 30 kg/m² | |
AGE (YEARS)	MALES	FEMALES	MALES	FEMALES
11	20.6	20.7	25.1	25.4
12	21.2	21.7	26.0	26.7
13	21.9	22.6	26.8	27.8
14	22.6	23.3	27.6	28.6
15	23.3	23.9	28.3	29.1
16	23.9	24.4	28.9	29.4
17	24.5	24.7	29.4	29.7
18	25.0	25.0	30.0	30.0

Source: Cole *et al.* (2000).

Note: See Cole *et al.* (2000: p. 1242) for a more extensive table, providing BMI cut-off points in 0.5-year increments from age 2–18.

Figure 10.4 Percentage of US children and adolescents (aged 2–19 years) above selected BMI cut-off points based on the reference population of the US Centers for Disease Control and Prevention 2000 growth charts.

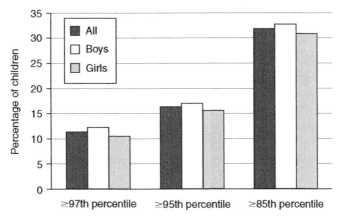

Source: Ogden *et al.* (2008).
Note: A BMI above the 85th percentile indicates that a child is overweight, a BMI above the 95th percentile indicates obesity and a BMI above the 97th percentile indicates severe obesity.

respectively. This approach was used in a recent study in the United States (Ogden *et al.* 2008), which indicated a prevalence of 15% and 30% for overweight and obesity, respectively, among American children and adolescents (Figure 10.4).

The obvious limitation of the BMI, that it does not discriminate between lean and fat mass, applies in children as it does in adults. Despite this limitation, the BMI has been shown to correlate highly with dual energy X-ray absorptiometry estimates of body fatness in adolescents (Steinberger *et al.* 2005) and is considered to be an acceptable, albeit imperfect, tool for diagnosing obesity in children (Must and Anderson 2006; Reilly 2006a). For those who have access to accurate methods for determining body fatness in children, body fat reference curves are available for the diagnosis of 'underfat', 'normal', 'overfat' and 'obese' (McCarthy *et al.* 2006). Waist circumference may prove to be another effective method for diagnosing the risks of obesity (particularly central obesity) in children and adolescents (McCarthy *et al.* 2003).

As is the case in adults, interplay between genetic and environmental factors is responsible for childhood obesity. Many studies have observed that obesity often runs in families and that children who have obese parents are at greater risk of obesity themselves (Garn and Clark 1976). This, of course, could be explained by both genetic and environmental factors. Reilly *et al.* (2005) observed an obesity odds ratio of 10.44 for seven-year-old children if both of their parents were obese. These investigators also examined the influence of a period termed the 'adiposity rebound' on the subsequent risk of obesity in children. After an increase in the first year of life, BMI falls until the age of about 4–6 years, after which it increases again. This increase in BMI is called the adiposity rebound. Reilly *et al.* (2005) observed an obesity odds ratio of 15 in seven-year-old children who had experienced a very early (by 43 months) BMI or adiposity rebound. These findings are consistent with those of a systematic review which identified 'being big or growing fast' during infancy (defined as the first two years of life) as risk factors for obesity at any age after infancy (Baird *et al.* 2005).

Many studies have indicated that obesity in childhood and adolescence increases the risk of obesity in adulthood (Whitaker *et al.* 1997; Figure 10.5), although not all obese children become obese adults (Funatogawa *et al.* 2008) and extreme thinness in childhood may also be a risk factor for obesity in adulthood (Wright *et al.* 2001). Long-term follow-up studies have demonstrated that obesity during childhood and adolescence is related to a variety of adverse health outcomes in adulthood, particularly CVD (Baker *et al.* 2007; Must *et al.* 1992). This has led to predictions that heart disease rates will increase in young and middle-aged adults in the future, causing substantial morbidity and mortality (Bibbins-Domingo *et al.* 2007).

Although there is a strong genetic influence on childhood adiposity (Wardle *et al.* 2008), there is also evidence that physical inactivity plays a role. Cross-sectional studies have demonstrated an inverse association between physical activity levels and markers for adiposity, such as the BMI. One study set in a large urban high school in Houston, Texas observed that physical activity levels (assessed by ankle actigraphy) in overweight (BMI ≥95th percentile on CDC 2000 BMI charts) female adolescents were 10% lower than normal-weight (BMI <85th percentile) adolescents. Moreover, in those considered at risk of overweight (BMI ≥85th percentile but <95th percentile) physical activity levels were 6% lower than normal-weight girls (Sulemana *et al.* 2006). In the European Youth Heart Study (Ruiz *et al.* 2006) vigorous-intensity (>6 METs) physical activity, but not moderate or overall physical activity, was associated with lower body fat in 780 children aged 9–10 years, while a study involving 2,859 Spanish adolescents found that high levels of cardiorespiratory fitness (predicted VO_2max) and low participation in sedentary activities (less than two hours per day) were associated with lower abdominal obesity as measured by waist circumference (Ortega *et al.* 2007).

Figure 10.5 Odds ratio for obesity in young adulthood (defined as 21–29 years of age) according to obesity in childhood and adolescence.

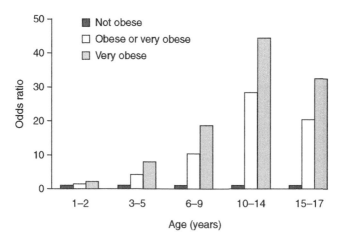

Source: Whitaker *et al.* (1997).

Notes: Findings are from a retrospective study of 854 subjects born in Washington State between 1965 and 1971. Childhood obesity was defined as a BMI at or above the 85th percentile for age and sex, and obesity in adulthood as a mean BMI at or above 27.8 for men and 27.3 for women. Note that obese children under the age of three years are at low risk for obesity in adulthood, but among older children obesity is an increasingly important predictor of adult obesity.

It is important to highlight that some studies have failed to detect a relationship between physical activity levels and obesity. One study comparing obese and non-obese adolescents found no differences in total energy expenditure or activity-related energy expenditure (assessed using doubly labelled water), although total physical activity levels assessed using accelerometry were lower in obese than normal-weight adolescents (Ekelund *et al.* 2002). Another cross-sectional study used doubly labelled water to examine physical activity levels in 6–8-year-old children who were classed as either high risk or low risk for obesity by virtue of the obesity status of their parents. No difference in physical activity levels was observed between the groups (Rennie *et al.* 2005). Consistent with this are the findings of the Stockholm Weight Development Study which observed that variation in physical activity (assessed using a self-report questionnaire) explained <4% of the adiposity variation in 445, 17-year-old adolescents, and even this small relation was only found in males (Ekelund *et al.* 2005).

Prospective studies examining the relationship between physical activity and adiposity over time in children and adolescents have also produced conflicting findings. A study by Kimm *et al.* (2005) involving 1,152 black girls and 1,135 white girls followed from ages 9–10 to 18–19 years observed that higher levels of physical activity during adolescence were related to smaller increases in BMI and adiposity (Figure 10.6). However, Kettaneh *et al.* (2005), albeit in a smaller study, found that girls with the highest level of physical activity at baseline experienced the highest adiposity gain from baseline to follow-up. Parsons *et al.* (2006), when examining data from the 1958 British cohort, found some evidence that physical activity reduces BMI gain from adolescence to mid-adulthood in females, but found an inconsistent relationship for males.

Figure 10.6 Mean difference for BMI (left panel) and sum of skinfold thickness (right panel) in female adolescents classed as active or inactive and followed longitudinally over ten years.

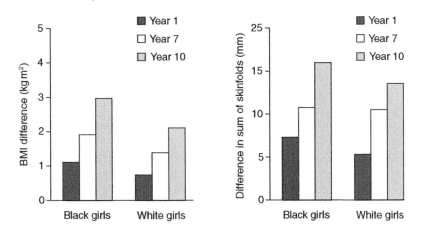

Source: Kimm *et al.* (2005).
Notes: Subjects were 1,152 black and 1,135 white girls from the United States, who were followed up prospectively from ages 9 or 10 to 18 or 19 years. Physical activity was assessed using a habitual activity questionnaire (HAQ). Mean values for BMI and sum of skinfold thickness were higher in the inactive girls throughout the study period and between group differences increased over time.

A variety of intervention programmes have been devised and tested in an attempt to prevent obesity in children and adolescents. These have met with mixed results. Robinson (1999) conducted a randomized, controlled trial which aimed to reduce television, videotape and video game use in two public elementary schools in San Jose, California and found this intervention to be effective in reducing age-related gains in BMI and adiposity. Similarly, a randomized trial conducted in Turku, Finland which involved individualized dietary and lifestyle counselling, provided twice a year since infancy, was effective in decreasing the prevalence of overweight by age ten (Hakanen *et al.* 2006). In contrast, a cluster, randomized, controlled trial conducted in Glasgow, Scotland observed no affect of an enhanced physical activity programme on the BMI values of nursery school children aged four (Reilly *et al.* 2006).

Several review papers have been published recently, evaluating the evidence that intervention programmes can prevent obesity in children and adolescents. One of these concluded that it is possible to prevent obesity in children and adolescents through school-based programmes which combine dietary and exercise intervention (Flodmark *et al.* 2006). Another came to similar conclusions, but highlighted that an increased prevalence of underweight has also been observed following an intervention programme and recommended that greater attention be given to the possible adverse outcomes of intervention programmes (Doak *et al.* 2006). Finally, a review of systematic reviews concluded that although 'the evidence base on childhood obesity prevention has increased markedly in recent years [it] remains extremely limited, and no successful, high-quality, generalizable interventions presently exist' (Reilly 2006b: p. 219).

In addition to its role in preventing obesity, physical activity has also been included as a key component of weight management programmes in children and adolescents. One example is the 'Bright Bodies' programme conducted at the Yale Pediatric Obesity Clinic in New Haven, Connecticut. A randomized, controlled trial examining the programme found it to have beneficial effects on body composition and insulin resistance in overweight children aged 8–16, and the effects were sustained up to the end of observation at 12 months (Savoye *et al.* 2007). Another recent study found that behavioural skills maintenance (focusing on weight loss strategies) and social facilitation maintenance (focusing on social support) improved the effectiveness of standard weight loss programmes in overweight and obese 7–12-year-olds, although the effects waned over time (Wilfley *et al.* 2007).

The lipase inhibitor Orlistat has also been used in combination with diet, exercise and behaviour therapy in the treatment of adolescent obesity. A randomized, controlled trial found that this combination led to a statistically significant improvement in weight management in obese adolescents compared with a placebo over a one-year period (Chanoine *et al.* 2005). Recent reviews concerning the effectiveness of exercise training (either alone or in combination with dietary therapy) for treating overweight and obesity in children and adolescents have concluded that exercise does not consistently decrease body weight or BMI, but that an aerobic exercise prescription of 155–180 minutes per week of moderate-to-high-intensity aerobic exercise is effective for reducing body fat in overweight children and adolescents (Atlantis *et al.* 2006; Watts *et al.* 2005).

TYPE 2 DIABETES

The link between obesity and type 2 diabetes was discussed in Chapter 5, and the emergence of type 2 diabetes in children and adolescents was also highlighted here. Obesity is the most potent modifiable risk factor for type 2 diabetes and is thought to be fuelling the rising prevalence of this disease in children and adolescents. Pinhas-Hamiel and Zeitler (2005) observe that before 1990 there were only two reports in the literature of type 2 diabetes in children and adolescents, whereas there were 53 reports between 2000 and 2003. According to these authors, in 1990 less than 3% of all cases of new-onset diabetes in American children and adolescents were type 2 diabetes, but by 2004 type 2 diabetes accounted for 45% of new-onset cases among adolescents. Pinhas-Hamiel and Zeitler (2005) go on to document a rising prevalence of type 2 diabetes in children and adolescents in many countries including Japan, Taiwan, Singapore, Hong Kong, Thailand, New Zealand, Argentina, America and Canada.

The prevalence of type 2 diabetes is particularly high in certain minority groups such as the Pima Indians in the United States, and those of Pakistani, Indian or Arabic origin in the United Kingdom (Pinhas-Hamiel and Zeitler 2005). Drake *et al.* (2002) were apparently the first to report type 2 diabetes in white adolescents living in England. They identified four individuals (three females, one male) aged 13–15, each of whom was obese (BMI ranging from 32.7 to 40.6 kg m^2). These authors predicted that type 2 diabetes would become increasingly common in children and adolescents living in the United Kingdom. This prediction is supported by a report from Aylin *et al.* (2005) documenting a 54% increase in the number of new type 2 diabetes cases in children and adolescents in England from 213 to 328 between 1996–7 and 2003–4 (Figure 10.7).

More recently a report by Haines *et al.* (2007) has confirmed that there is a rising incidence of type 2 diabetes in children in the United Kingdom. This report again highlights that children from ethnic minorities are at particularly high risk, in this case children of black and South-Asian origin. Of those diagnosed with type 2 diabetes,

Figure 10.7 Hospital admission rate for children aged 0–18 years, admitted to English hospitals with obesity and type 2 diabetes.

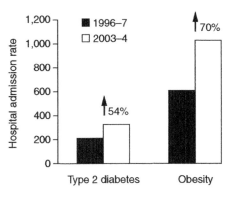

Source: Aylin *et al.* (2005).

95% were overweight and 83% were obese, while 84% had a family history of type 2 diabetes (Haines *et al.* 2007). It is important to emphasize, however, that although rates have increased, type 2 diabetes remains a relatively infrequent disease in young people, with rates of 17.0–49.4 per 100,000 person-years documented among 15–19-year-old minority groups in the United States (Writing Group for the SEARCH for Diabetes in Youth Study Group 2007).

Cross-sectional studies have identified a link between obesity and the insulin-resistance syndrome (a risk marker for type 2 diabetes) in children and adolescents. One example is a study involving 103 obese (BMI >95th percentile) children and adolescents (aged 2–18) living in the United Kingdom. One-third of these individuals were found to have the insulin-resistance syndrome (obesity, abnormal glucose homeostasis, hypertension and dyslipidaemia), although none had type 2 diabetes (Viner *et al.* 2005). Another study conducted in the Yale Pediatric Obesity Clinic between 1999 and 2001 detected impaired glucose tolerance in 25% of 55 obese children (4–10 years old) and 21% of 112 adolescents (11–18 years old). Type 2 diabetes was identified in 4% of the obese adolescents. Similarly, a study of 4,902 adolescents aged 12–19 who participated in the National Health and Nutrition Examination Survey 1999–2002 found that weight status was 'by far' the most important determinant of insulin resistance determined by the homeostasis model assessment (HOMA) (an estimate of insulin resistance derived from fasting glucose and insulin levels) (Lee *et al.* 2006). Thinness in infancy and an early adiposity rebound have also been related to impaired glucose tolerance in young (26–32 years old) adults (Bhargava *et al.* 2004).

Clearly, physical activity has the potential to assist in the prevention of type 2 diabetes in children and adolescents by virtue of its effect on body composition. However, there are no trials testing the effectiveness of physical activity in this regard and it would be difficult to prove that exercise can prevent type 2 diabetes in children and adolescents due to the relatively low number of individuals who develop the disease, i.e. huge numbers would be required for such a study. Nevertheless, findings from the National Health and Nutrition Examination Survey have demonstrated that high levels of physical activity (assessed by questionnaire) and cardiovascular fitness (predicted VO_2max) are significantly and positively associated with insulin sensitivity in male adolescents (Imperatore *et al.* 2006). Furthermore, the European Youth Heart Study found that total, moderate and vigorous physical activity (assessed by accelerometry) was inversely correlated with insulin resistance (assessed using homeostasis model assessment) in 613 Swedish adolescents (Rizzo *et al.* 2008). These findings suggest that regular physical activity could make a contribution to the prevention of type 2 diabetes in children and adolescents.

CVD

Although the clinical horizon for CVD occurs in middle age (see Figure 4.5), there is evidence that the disease begins in childhood (McGill *et al.* 2000). In view of this it is of interest to assess whether physical activity in childhood can slow the development of the disease. Typically, studies addressing this question have examined risk factors for CVD (e.g. blood pressure and blood lipids) rather than directly assessing atherosclerosis or clinical outcomes since these are rare in children and adolescents. A variety of cross-sectional studies have observed an association between low levels of physical activity and/or physical fitness and elevations in risk factors for CVD, including the metabolic syndrome (Steele *et al.* 2008). Examples include the European Youth Heart Study (Andersen *et al.* 2006; Ruiz *et al.* 2007), the National Health and Nutrition Examination Survey (Carnethon *et al.* 2005) and the Québec Family Study (Eisenmann *et al.* 2005a).

One analysis from the European Youth Heart Study involved 1,732 randomly selected 9-year-old and 15-year-old children from Denmark, Estonia and Portugal. A risk factor score was calculated for each child based on systolic blood pressure, triglyceride, total cholesterol/high-density lipoprotein cholesterol, insulin resistance, sum of four skinfolds and aerobic fitness. Physical activity was assessed using accelerometry. Subjects were divided into quintiles based on their physical activity and the lowest three quintiles were all observed to have an elevated risk factor profile. Since the mean time spent above 2,000 counts per minute (equivalent to walking about $4\,km\,h^{-1}$) in quintile four was $116\,min\,day^{-1}$ in 9-year-old children and $88\,min\,day^{-1}$ in 15-year-old children, the authors concluded that children and adolescents should perform more than one hour per day of moderate-intensity physical activity to avoid a clustering of CVD risk factors (Andersen *et al.* 2006).

In the National Health and Nutrition Examination Survey (Carnethon *et al.* 2005), low levels of physical fitness (bottom 20% of the sample for predicted VO_2max) were related to a variety of CVD risk factors including obesity, hypercholesterolaemia and the metabolic syndrome (Figure 10.8). Findings from the Québec Family Study

Figure 10.8 Age- and race-adjusted odds of having CVD risk factors in female and male US adolescents aged 12–19 years with low (versus moderate or high) fitness status, NHANES 1999–2002.

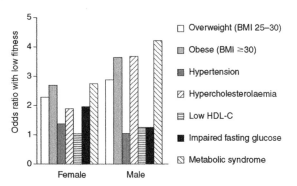

Source: Carnethon *et al.* (2005).
Notes: The participants were 3,110 adolescents participating in the National Health and Nutrition Examination Survey. (NHANES) Low fitness was defined as <20th percentile. BMI, $kg\,m^2$; HDL, high-density lipoprotein cholesterol. Hypercholesterolaemia was defined as a total cholesterol level >$5.2\,mmol\,l^{-1}$ ($200\,mg\,dl^{-1}$); impaired fasting glucose was defined as a glucose level >$5.6\,mmol\,l^{-1}$ ($100\,mg\,dl^{-1}$). The metabolic syndrome was identified in adolescents with three or more of the following: triglycerides ≥$1.4\,mmol\,l^{-1}$ ($110\,mg\,dl^{-1}$), HDL-C ≤$1.0\,mmol\,l^{-1}$ ($40\,mg\,dl^{-1}$), waist circumference ≥ the sex-specific 90th percentile, fasting glucose level >$5.6\,mmol\,l^{-1}$ ($100\,mg\,dl^{-1}$), hypertension >90th percentile of systolic or diastolic blood pressure by age, sex and height.

(Eisenmann *et al.* 2005a) also demonstrate an association between low levels of physical fitness and CVD risk markers (blood pressure, blood lipids and blood glucose) while a recent publication from the European Youth Heart Study (Ruiz *et al.* 2007) observed that low levels of physical activity (assessed using accelerometry) were related to elevations in markers for low-grade inflammation (C-reactive protein, fibrinogen, complement factors C3 and C4), again suggesting that physical activity may ameliorate the development of CVD in childhood.

A few prospective observational studies have examined the relationship between physical inactivity in childhood/adolescence and CVD risk in adulthood. One interesting example is a study conducted in Dunedin, New Zealand involving approximately 1,000 individuals born in 1972–3. These individuals were monitored at regular intervals up to age 26. Television viewing (a surrogate marker for physical inactivity and poor diet) was assessed during childhood and adolescence. The findings revealed an association between high amounts of television viewing in childhood and adolescence and overweight, poor fitness, elevated cholesterol and smoking in adulthood (Figure 10.9). The authors concluded that excessive television viewing might have long-lasting adverse effects on health and that children's television viewing should be limited to between one and two hours per day, or ideally less than one hour per day (Hancox *et al.* 2004).

Figure 10.9 Prevalence of selected CVD risk factors at age 26 years according to the mean hours of television viewing per weekday between the ages 5 and 15.

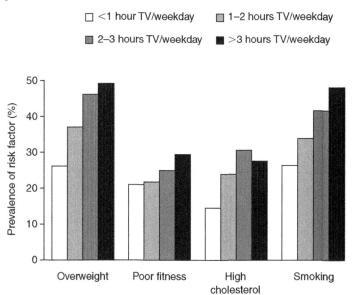

Source: Hancox *et al.* (2004).
Notes: Subjects were 1,000 individuals born in Dunedin, New Zealand in 1972–3 and monitored at regular intervals up to age 26 years. Information was obtained on television viewing at ages 5, 7, 9, 11, 13, 15 and 21 years. Between ages 5 and 11 years, parents were asked how much time study members spent watching television. At ages 13, 15 and 21 years, study members provided the information themselves. The trend was significant for each risk factor: overweight (BMI $\geq 25 \, \text{kg m}^2$), $P=0.0001$; lowest quartile for $\dot{V}O_2$max (adjusted for bodyweight and sex), $P=0.0432$; raised total cholesterol ($>5.5 \, \text{mmol l}^{-1}$), $P=0.0321$; smoking (current smoker), $P=0.0002$.

The Aerobics Centre Longitudinal Study is one of the few studies that has examined prospectively the relationship between adolescent (mean age of 15.8 years) fitness and CVD risk factors in adulthood (mean age of 26.6 years). Although there was an association between adolescent cardiorespiratory fitness and fatness in adulthood in this study, there was no association between adolescent cardiorespiratory fitness and adult cholesterol, blood pressure and glucose levels (Eisenmann *et al.* 2005b). In contrast, findings from the Coronary Artery Risk Development in Young Adults (CARDIA) Study observed that poor cardiovascular fitness in young adulthood (age 18–30) was associated with a two-fold increase in the risk of developing hypertension, diabetes and the metabolic syndrome over 15 years of follow-up (Carnethon *et al.* 2003).

Several prospective studies have attempted to identify whether adolescent physical activity or physical fitness is more important as a determinant of CVD risk in adulthood. Relevant studies include the Amsterdam Growth and Health Longitudinal Study (Twisk *et al.* 2002), the Northern Ireland Young Hearts Project (Boreham *et al.* 2002), the Danish Youth and Sports Study (Hasselstrøm *et al.* 2002) and the Leuven Longitudinal Study on Lifestyle, Fitness and Health (Lefevre *et al.* 2002). The general consensus among these studies is that adolescent physical fitness is associated with a healthy CVD risk profile later in life, although this may be partly mediated by body fatness. Physical activity in youth was not associated with a healthy CVD risk profile in later life, although this may be partly explained by the difficulty in accurately measuring physical activity.

Intervention studies have been conducted in children and adolescents with the aim of modifying CVD risk. Dr Thomas Rowland, a leading expert in the field of paediatric exercise physiology, states that 'improving physical activity levels – even to the extent of exercise training – is unlikely to alter CVD risk factors in normotensive, lean youth with normal serum lipid levels' (Rowland 2007: p. 264). He goes on to state; however, that exercise intervention can be effective in those with elevated body fat, blood lipids or blood pressure. A good example of the effectiveness of exercise in this regard is the Obeldicks intervention programme conducted in Germany (Reinehr *et al.* 2006). This programme involved exercise, diet and behaviour therapy which provoked beneficial changes in BMI, systolic blood pressure, low-density lipoprotein cholesterol and insulin in obese children and adolescents aged 6–14 (Figure 10.10). Exercise training has also been shown to improve arterial function in children with CVD risk factors (Fernhall and Agiovlasitis 2008).

BONE HEALTH

In a recent commentary McKay and Smith state that 'well designed childhood physical activity programs are likely critical for preventing osteoporosis in mature adults' (McKay and Smith 2008: p. 980). Another recent review argues that 'it is increasingly accepted that osteoporosis is a paediatric disease' (Vicente-Rodríguez 2006: p. 561) while Bass (2000) asserts that the prepubertal and peripubertal (around puberty) years are a unique stage of growth when the skeleton may be most responsive to exercise. This viewpoint is supported by the findings from animal studies which illustrate

Figure 10.10 Values for BMI and selected CVD risk markers in 174 obese children (age 6–14 years) and 49 control children (37 obese, 12 normal weight) at baseline (0 y), at the end of one year of intervention (1 y) and one year after the end of intervention (2 y).

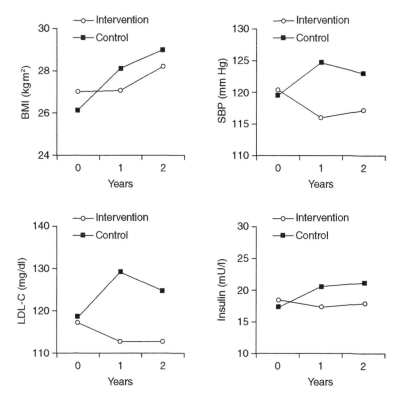

Source: Reinehr *et al.* (2006).
Notes: Abbreviations: BMI, body mass index; SBP, systolic blood pressure; LDL-C, low-density lipoprotein cholesterol. Obesity was defined as a BMI >97th percentile. The one-year intervention programme involved 'exercise, nutrition education and behaviour therapy including the individual psychological care of the child and his or her family'. There was a significant interaction effect for BMI (P=0.013), SBP (P=0.002) and insulin (P=0.008). The interaction effect for LDL-C (P=0.059) approached significance.

greater structural and material adaptations of growing bone to exercise than in adult bones (Forwood 2008).

Cross-sectional studies provide strong evidence that physical activity during childhood and adolescence is an excellent stimulus for increasing bone mineral density (BMD). The limitations of cross-sectional studies are overcome to some extent in bone health research by the observation of individuals who play racquet sports. In these individuals the non-playing arm acts as a control and BMD in this arm is compared with BMD in the playing arm to provide an indication of the effects of exercise. Using this model Haapasalo *et al.* (1998) studied BMD (using dual energy X-ray absorptiometry – see Chapter 9) in 91 7–17-year-old female tennis players and 58 healthy female controls. Pubertal status was assessed (by visual inspection) so that comparisons could be made at each stage of pubertal development. In the tennis players, BMD differences between the playing and non-playing arms were significant at all Tanner stages, with the mean difference ranging from 1.6% to 15.7%. In control subjects the differences were much smaller, ranging from –0.2% to 4.6%. The differences between playing and non-playing limbs in the tennis players became very clear around the time of the adolescent growth spurt (Tanner stage 3) and, in the lumbar spine, at Tanner stage 4. In a non-loaded site (the non-dominant distal radius), no significant differences were found in BMD between the players and the controls at any Tanner stage.

Another notable cross-sectional study examined side-to-side differences in bone mineral content (BMC) (see Box 9.1 for the distinction between BMC and BMD) in 105 Finnish national-level female tennis and squash players (mean age of 27.7 years) and 50 age-matched healthy female controls (Kannus *et al.* 1995). Compared with controls, the players had a significantly larger side-to-side difference at every measured site (proximal humerus, humeral shaft, radial shaft, and distal radius). The key finding of the study, however, was that side-to-side differences were 2–4 times greater in players who had started their playing careers before or at menarche than in those who started playing more than 15 years after menarche (Figure 10.11). This clearly suggests that physical activity before and around the time of puberty is particularly effective for increasing BMC.

A variety of intervention studies have confirmed the effectiveness of exercise for increasing BMD and/or BMC in children and adolescents (Macdonald *et al.* 2007;

Figure 10.11 The mean playing-to-non-playing arm difference in the bone mineral content of the humeral shaft in 105 Finnish national-level female tennis and squash players (mean age 27.7 years) and 50 age-matched healthy female controls.

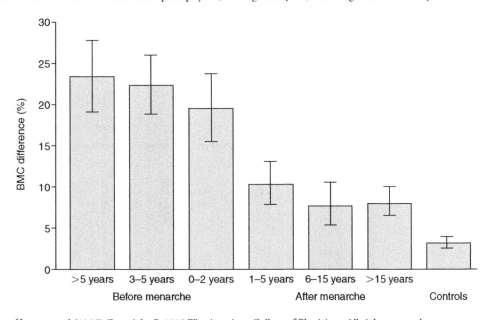

Source: Kannus *et al.* (1995) Copyright © 1995 The American College of Physicians. All rights reserved.
Note: Values are percentage difference of bone mineral content between arms displayed according to the biological age at which training was started, that is, according to the starting age of playing relative to the age at menarche. n = 105 racket sports players, n = 50 controls. Bars represent the 95% CIs.

McKay *et al.* 2005; Weeks *et al.* 2008; Yu *et al.* 2005). These studies indicate that exercise must be weight bearing, with several studies demonstrating the particular effectiveness of jumping (Macdonald *et al.* 2007; McKay *et al.* 2005; Weeks *et al.* 2008). Relatively small amounts of such exercise (a few minutes several days a week) may be effective in building bone. It should be noted, however, that one study has reported an increased risk of fracture in children who perform vigorous physical activity, presumably because they are more likely to fall (Clark *et al.* 2008). Recent studies have gone beyond mere measures of BMD or BMC by using quantitative computed tomography (see Box 9.1) to assess changes in bone structure more precisely, and hence give a better indication of changes in bone strength with exercise (Macdonald *et al.* 2007; McKay and Smith 2008). Some intervention studies have also demonstrated that a combination of exercise and calcium supplementation is more effective for increasing BMD/BMC in children than either intervention alone (Bass *et al.* 2007; Courteix *et al.* 2005).

Some studies have attempted to assess the extent to which exercise-induced increases in BMC/BMD persist post-intervention. The recently published study of Gunter *et al.* (2008) is an excellent example. This study involved a seven-month jumping intervention in prepubertal children (boys and girls, mean age of 7.6 years) and follow-up for eight years. The intervention participants had a 3.6% greater total hip bone mass than controls immediately after the intervention and a 1.4% greater hip bone mass than controls after eight years (both significant). The authors concluded that

Figure 10.12 BMD expressed as z-scores at weight bearing (femoral neck and legs) and non-weight bearing (arm) sites in active and retired soccer players.

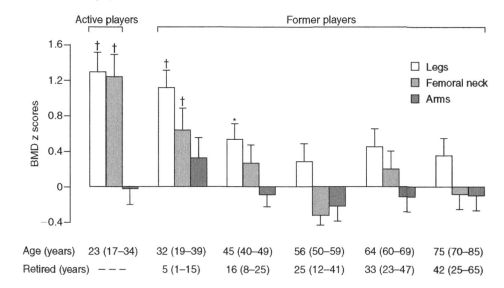

Source: Reprinted from the *Lancet*, 355: 469–70, Karlsson, M.K. *et al.*, 'Exercise during growth and bone mineral density and fractures in old age', page 470, Copyright 2000, with permission from Elsevier.
Notes: Values are mean (range). *$P<0.05$; †$P<0.01$ for difference between soccer players and controls. Note that there are apparent benefits to BMD 10–20 years beyond the active careers of soccer players, but these benefits do not appear to last into old age.

short-term high-impact exercise undertaken in early childhood has sustained benefit. It is still uncertain, however, whether such benefits will reduce the risk of fractures in later life. A study of active and retired soccer players indicates that although former soccer players may retain increased BMD in the legs and femoral neck for up to 20 years after retirement, they are not at lower risk of fracture in old age (Karlsson *et al.* 2000; Figure 10.12). Collectively, these findings suggest that although exercise in youth has undoubted benefits for bone health, exercise in adulthood is necessary to optimize these benefits.

A recent review of randomized and non-randomized controlled trials concludes that the optimal exercise programme for enhancing bone mineral accrual in children remains to be determined (Hind and Burrows 2007). In the absence of definitive evidence, the American College of Sports Medicine Position Stand on Physical Activity and Bone Health provides useful guidelines for children and adolescents (Kohrt *et al.* 2004). These guidelines are displayed in Table 10.2. Sports and activities involving

Table 10.2 Exercise recommendations for enhancing bone mineral accrual in children and adolescents

Mode	Impact activities, such as gymnastics, plyometrics, and jumping, and moderate intensity resistance training; participation in sports that involve running and jumping (soccer, basketball) is likely to be of benefit, but scientific evidence is lacking
Intensity	High, in terms of bone-loading forces; for safety reasons, resistance training should be <60% of one-repetition maximum
Frequency	At least three days per week
Duration	10–20 minutes (twice per day or more may be more effective)

Source: American College of Sports Medicine Position Stand on Physical Activity and Bone Health (Kohrt *et al.* 2004).

Plate 9 Sports and activities involving impact forces such as gymnastics and jumping are particularly beneficial for bone health in children.

Source: Photos courtesy of Mr James Smith.

impact forces such as gymnastics and jumping are highlighted as being particularly beneficial (Plate 9). Chapter 13 contains further information on exercise recommendations for children and adolescents.

SUMMARY

- Many children and adolescents exhibit low levels of physical activity and there is a significant decline in physical activity during the transition from childhood to adolescence.
- Physical activity and physical fitness are related in children and adolescents, although correlations are often low.
- There is evidence that physical activity levels can be increased in children and adolescents through school-based programmes which involve the family and/or the community.
- The prevalence of obesity among children and adolescents has increased in many countries in recent years.
- Some studies have observed that physical activity and adiposity are inversely related in young people, although this is not a universal finding.
- Physical activity has a role to play in the prevention and management of obesity in children and adolescents, but evidence to support effective interventions is limited.
- Although an increased prevalence of type 2 diabetes has been reported among children and adolescents in recent years (a trend which may be related to increases in obesity prevalence) absolute rates of type 2 diabetes remain low in children.
- High levels of physical activity are positively associated with insulin sensitivity and negatively associated with insulin resistance in children and adolescents.
- High levels of physical activity and physical fitness are related to healthy CVD risk factor profiles in children and adolescents and exercise training may lead to favourable changes in CVD risk factors in children who exhibit unhealthy profiles.
- There is good evidence that physical activity, particularly high-impact activity, is effective for promoting bone growth and strength in children and adolescents. This effect may last well into adulthood but is unlikely to reduce the risk of fracture in old age unless some physical activity is maintained.

STUDY TASKS

1 Explain the various methods used to assess physical activity in children and adolescents. What is the basis for stating that many children and adolescents lead sedentary lives?
2 Discuss the methods used to assess obesity in children and adolescents and explain the advantages and disadvantages of each method.
3 Give examples of studies observing a relationship between physical inactivity and adiposity in children and adolescents, and highlight the strengths and limitations of these studies.
4 Discuss the findings of one study linking physical activity with low levels of CVD

risk and one study linking physical fitness with low levels of CVD risk in children and adolescents. Describe as clearly as possible what can be concluded from these studies and what questions remain to be answered.

5 Discuss the research evidence that childhood may provide a unique opportunity for developing bone mass and strength. What exercise prescription would you recommend for optimizing bone mineral accrual in children and adolescents?

FURTHER READING

Atlantis, E., Barnes, E.H. and Fiatarone Singh, M.A. (2006) 'Efficacy of exercise for treating overweight in children and adolescents: a systematic review', *International Journal of Obesity* 30: 1027–40.

Doak, C.M., Visscher, T.L.S., Renders, C.M. and Seidell, J.C. (2006) 'The prevention of overweight and obesity in children and adolescents: a review of intervention programmes', *Obesity Reviews* 7: 111–36.

Fernhall, B. and Agiovlasitis, S. (2008) 'Arterial function in youth: window into cardiovascular risk', *Journal of Applied Physiology* 105: 325–33.

Flodmark, C.E., Marcus, C. and Britton, M. (2006) 'Interventions to prevent obesity in children and adolescents: a systematic literature review', *International Journal of Obesity* 30: 579–89.

Forwood, M.R. (2008) 'Physical activity and bone development during childhood: insights from animal models', *Journal of Applied Physiology* 105: 334–41.

Ortega, F.B., Ruiz, J.R., Castillo, M.J. and Sjöström, M. (2008) 'Physical fitness in childhood and adolescence: a powerful marker for health', *International Journal of Obesity* 32: 1–11.

Pinhas-Hamiel, O. and Zeitler, P. (2005) 'The global spread of type 2 diabetes mellitus in children and adolescents', *Journal of Pediatrics* 146: 693–700.

Rowland, T.W. (2007) 'Physical activity, fitness and children', in C. Bouchard, S.N. Blair and W.L. Haskell (eds) *Physical Activity and Health*, Champaign: Human Kinetics, pp. 259–70.

Vicente-Rodríguez, G. (2006) 'How does exercise affect bone development during growth?', *Sports Medicine* 36: 561–9.

Watts, K., Jones, T.W., Davis, E.A. and Green, D. (2005) 'Exercise training in obese children and adolescents: current concepts', *Sports Medicine* 35: 375–92.

11 Ageing

Knowledge assumed
Basic exercise physiology

INTRODUCTION

Chapter 1 highlighted that an improvement in life expectancy is leading to an increase in the total number of older people world-wide. This trend is expected to continue into the foreseeable future and brings challenges for society. As described in several earlier chapters, the prevalence of many diseases (e.g. heart disease, diabetes, cancer and osteoporosis) and disease risk factors (e.g. hypercholesterolaemia, hypertension and obesity) increases with age. Thus, although people are living longer, many are burdened with disease or disability in the latter stages of their lives. Moreover, lifestyle and the ability to live independently may be impaired even in individuals free from disease due to a reduction in functional capacities (e.g. strength, endurance and flexibility) which limits their ability to perform everyday tasks, such as rising from a chair, getting into and out of a bath, climbing a flight of stairs or crossing a road in the time allotted at pedestrian crossings.

Aside from declines in physical fitness and mobility, ageing is also associated with a decline in cognitive function and, in severe cases, dementia. Evidence is accumulating to suggest that physical activity may ameliorate age-related declines in cognitive function and reduce the risk of dementia. In this chapter we will examine how ageing leads to a decline in functional capacities in humans and the extent to which this can be offset by frequent exercise. We will also assess evidence that remaining active into old age reduces the risk of mental infirmity and disease. Collectively, the evidence surveyed here suggests that regular physical activity helps older adults to maintain their independence and hence a good quality of life.

DECLINE IN FUNCTIONAL CAPACITIES

The effect of ageing on physical fitness is clearly demonstrated by examining the UK age group records for the marathon. Beyond age 35–40 years, marathon run time increases gradually in men and women until age 70. This increase is equivalent to approximately 1% per year in men and 2% per year in women between the ages of 35–40 and 70. Beyond age 70 the decline in performance is more dramatic, averaging nearly 4.4% per year for men and 10% per year for women between the ages of 70 and 90. These observations are consistent with findings from the US Masters Swimming Championships, which also reveal a steep decline in performance beyond age 70 in both men and women (Tanaka and Seals 1997). The above examples are based on the few individuals who maintain heavy training/competition, indicating an affect of age per se rather than physical inactivity. Age-related declines in sporting performance are due to declines in various aspects of physiological function and these will be examined in the following sections, beginning with maximum oxygen uptake.

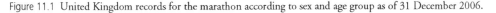

Figure 11.1 United Kingdom records for the marathon according to sex and age group as of 31 December 2006.

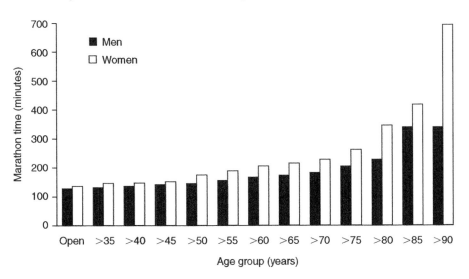

Source: Great Britain Athletics UK All-Time lists. Online, available at: www.gbrathletics.com/uk (accessed 1 November 2008).

Many studies have documented a decline in $\dot{V}O_2$max in ageing humans, and this is the main physiological factor underlying the decrease in endurance performance with age (Åstrand *et al.* 1997; Fitzgerald *et al.* 1997; Hawkins and Wiswell 2003; Pollock *et al.* 1997; Trappe *et al.* 1996). The approximate rate of decline in $\dot{V}O_2$max is 1% per year or 10% per decade from the age of 25 onwards, although this varies depending on several factors, including physical activity levels. Continual hard training may be able to prevent any decline in $\dot{V}O_2$max until the late 30s, and individuals who continue exercising into old age retain higher $\dot{V}O_2$max values than those who stop training or remain untrained. Figure 11.2 illustrates the decline in $\dot{V}O_2$max from age 25 to 75 using cross-sectional data from athletes who continue training and from untrained healthy persons. Also included are data from three groups of older track athletes assessed on three occasions over a period of 20 years. The data show that $\dot{V}O_2$max values were better maintained in the high- and moderate-intensity training groups than in the low-intensity training group.

There is some evidence that the decline in $\dot{V}O_2$max with age is primarily due to an impaired efficiency of skeletal muscle to extract oxygen, at least within the 20–50-year-old range. This is indicated by the findings from a recent follow-up of the classic Dallas Bed Rest and Training Study (McGuire *et al.* 2001a; McGuire *et al.* 2001b). In the original study (in 1966), five healthy 20-year-old men were assessed: (1) at baseline; (2) after three weeks of bed rest; and (3) after eight weeks of intensive dynamic exercise training. Follow-up was performed 30 years later (in 1996) when the men were 50 years old. During this 30-year period the men had maintained varying levels of activity. Absolute $\dot{V}O_2$max values were 12% lower ($2.9\,l\,min^{-1}$ versus $3.3\,l\,min^{-1}$)

Figure 11.2 Cross-sectional data demonstrating the decline in $\dot{V}O_2$max with age in untrained healthy persons and in athletes who continue to train. Also included are 20-year follow-up data from older track athletes who continued to train at either a high, moderate or low intensity.

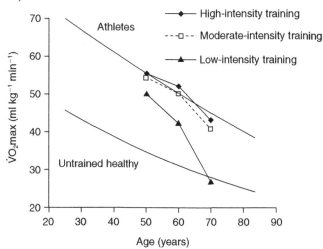

Source: Adapted from Pollock *et al.* (1997). Used with permission of The American Physiological Society.
Note: The lines for 'athletes' and 'untrained healthy persons' represent average values obtained in many groups of athletes and untrained persons of different ages.

and relative $\dot{V}O_2$max values were 28% lower (31 ml kg^{-1} min^{-1} versus 43 ml kg^{-1} min^{-1}) at age 50 compared with age 20. Although maximal heart rate had declined at follow-up, maximal cardiac output remained unchanged due to an increase in maximal stroke volume. Thus, the decline in $\dot{V}O_2$max was entirely due to a 15% reduction in the maximal difference between the oxygen content of arterial and mixed venous blood (a$-\bar{v}O_2$ diff.). In other words, this study indicates oxygen supply is not compromised with age, rather the ageing process impairs the ability of skeletal muscle to extract and/ or utilize oxygen. In contrast, cross-sectional data suggest that a reduced maximum heart rate is the main factor responsible for the decline in $\dot{V}O_2$max in masters athletes compared with young athletes (Heath *et al.* 1981).

What causes the reduction in oxygen extraction/usage with age? This is not known for certain, but there are several likely causes. A large portion of the age-associated decline in $\dot{V}O_2$max in non-trained individuals is due to the loss of muscle mass observed with advancing age (Fleg and Lakatta 1988). Moreover, a 20-year follow-up study of distance runners has documented a decrease in type I and type II muscle fibre areas, as well as a decrease in skeletal muscle oxidative capacity as indicated by lower activity of the enzyme succinate dehydrogenase (Trappe *et al.* 1995). Ageing also results in decreases in the synthesis rates of muscle proteins, specifically of myosin heavy chain and mitochondrial proteins, as well as decreases in mitochondrial DNA and RNA (Nair 2005). Such changes would lead to reductions in adenosine triphosphate (ATP) production rate and hence the capacity for maximal exercise.

Muscular strength is another key functional capacity which declines with age. In the Framingham study 40% of women aged 55–64, 45% of women aged 65–74 and 65% of women aged 75–84 years were unable to lift 4.5 kg (Jette and Branch 1981). Cross-sectional and longitudinal data indicate that muscle strength declines by approximately 15% per decade in the sixth and seventh decade, and about 30% thereafter (Mazzeo *et al.* 1998). An example of the decline in muscle strength with age is illustrated in Figure 11.3. These data are from a cross-sectional study of 45–78-year-old men and women. Muscle strength was determined using an isokinetic dynamometer. Note that ageing is associated with impaired muscle strength in both men and women (Frontera *et al.* 1991). When the data in Figure 11.3 were expressed per kilogram of muscle mass the differences between the age groups became smaller and there was no significant difference between the strength of males and females. This supports the hypothesis that the decline in muscle strength with age is largely due to a decline in muscle mass (a condition termed 'sarcopenia'). Such declines have been demonstrated in longitudinal studies documenting declines in muscle cross-sectional area (assessed using computerized tomography) over time (Frontera *et al.* 2000).

The reductions in maximum oxygen uptake and muscle strength are the most notable and possibly the most debilitating effects of ageing, but many other aspects of physiological function decline with age, including lung function (vital capacity and forced expiratory volume), resting metabolic rate (largely due to the reduction in fat-free mass) and flexibility (Mazzeo *et al.* 1998; Skelton and Dinan-Young 2008). Impaired balance and gait are additional hazards of ageing and these are significant risk factors for limited mobility and falls in the elderly (Daley and Spinks 2000). Moreover, many people gain weight as they age and this may further impair general mobility. A nice example of the weight gain typical with age is provided by data from the

Figure 11.3 Decline in isokinetic muscle strength ($60° s^{-1}$) of the knee extensors of the dominant side in men and women.

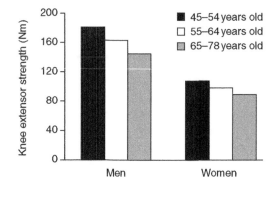

Source: Frontera *et al.* (1991).

Figure 11.4 Weight (top panel) and percentage body fat (bottom panel) in 1966 and 1996 in five individuals who participated in the Dallas Bedrest and Training Study in 1966 and a follow-up study 30 years later in 1996.

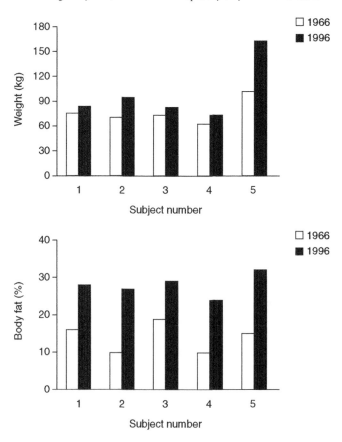

Source: McGuire *et al.* (2001a).
Note: The average age of the subjects in 1966 was 20. Body fat percentage was determined by underwater weighing.

five individuals who participated in the Dallas Bed Rest and Training Study described earlier. The body mass and percentage body fat of these individuals in 1966 and 1996 are illustrated in Figure 11.4, which demonstrates increases in both variables for all five subjects (McGuire *et al.* 2001a).

The extent to which the decline in physical characteristics is a result of ageing per se rather than a decline in physical activity is a matter of debate. It is well recognized that physical activity levels decline with age, as highlighted in the first chapter of this book (Figure 1.6). This decline is not peculiar to humans and occurs across a wide range of nonhuman species, including rodents, nematodes (microscopic worms), houseflies, fruit flies, monkeys and dogs (Ingram 2000). Based on these findings it would appear that at least some of the decline in physical activity with age has a biological basis. In humans, however, some of the age-related decline in physical activity may be due to environmental factors, implying that reductions in fitness, balance and mobility with age may be partly due to disuse rather than ageing per se. If this is true then physical activity and exercise training may counteract declines in physical function or even enhance physical function in older adults. In the next section we examine the evidence that various aspects of physiological function can be improved in older individuals who engage in exercise training.

EXERCISE TRAINING AND FUNCTIONAL CAPACITIES

Exercise training can profoundly influence functional capacity in older individuals. As an example we may again refer to the UK age group records for a marathon. The UK record for a marathon for men aged over 70 is 3 hours and 58 seconds, while for the women it is 3 hours 48 minutes and 14 seconds (Great Britain Athletics UK All-Time lists, available at: www.gbrathletics.com/uk). These are remarkable performances, and the average 25-year-old male or female would have difficulty in matching them. These performances are possible due to a combination of genetic makeup and continual hard training. Evidence shows, however, that even untrained older adults can adapt and benefit from exercise training.

Cardiovascular fitness and muscular strength are the two most well-studied functional capacities in older adults. A noteworthy study of cardiovascular fitness involved 16 previously untrained men and women aged 70–79 years old (Hagberg *et al.* 1989). These individuals followed a 26-week endurance-training programme involving walking and slow jogging. Sessions were conducted three times per week. Exercise intensity range was 50–70% of $\dot{V}O_2$max during the first half of the programme and increased to 75–85% of $\dot{V}O_2$max during the second half of the programme. This resulted in an 18% increase in $\dot{V}O_2$max expressed in absolute units (1.88 l min^{-1} versus 1.59 l min^{-1}) and a 20% increase in $\dot{V}O_2$max expressed in relative units (27.1 ml kg^{-1} min^{-1} versus 22.5 ml kg^{-1} min^{-1}). In practical terms an increase of this nature would translate into a 1 mile h^{-1} increase in comfortable walking speed. Moreover, these data demonstrate that men and women retain the ability to respond to exercise training during their eighth decade of life, while another study observed a 15% increase in $\dot{V}O_2$max in women who were in their ninth decade of life (i.e. women aged 79–91) after 24 weeks of exercise training (Malbut *et al.* 2002).

A further study demonstrating that $\dot{V}O_2$max remains trainable in older individuals is the follow-up to the Dallas Bed Rest and Training Study referred to in the previous section (McGuire *et al.* 2001a; McGuire *et al.* 2001b). The reader will recall that the original study (conducted in 1966) examined aspects of physiological function prior to and following three weeks of bed rest, and then again after eight weeks of training. In the follow-up study, conducted 30 years later (in 1996), cardiovascular responses to sub-maximal and maximal exercise were examined prior to and following a six-month endurance-training programme. This programme resulted in a significant improvement in $\dot{V}O_2$max, such that post-training values ($1\,min^{-1}$) in 1996 were similar to pre-bed rest values in 1966 (Figure 11.5). The investigators concluded that three weeks of bed rest at age 20 had a more profound effect on $\dot{V}O_2$max than did three decades of ageing. Furthermore, 100% of the age-related decline in $\dot{V}O_2$max was reversed by a six-month endurance-training programme. However, no subject achieved the same $\dot{V}O_2$max attained after training 30 years earlier. This study clearly demonstrates the combined effects of ageing and physical inactivity on $\dot{V}O_2$max.

The increase in $\dot{V}O_2$max post-training in the follow-up to the Dallas Bed Rest and Training Study was primarily the result of peripheral adaptation, with no improvement in maximal oxygen delivery. Maximal heart rate was decreased post-training compared with pre-training in 1996, but maximal cardiac output remained unchanged due to an increase in maximal stroke volume. The maximal $a-\bar{v}O_2$ diff. increased by 10% however, and this was the key factor for the increase in $\dot{V}O_2$max in the 50-year-old men (McGuire *et al.* 2001b). Another study has reported that increases in $\dot{V}O_2$max with endurance exercise are due to increases in both stroke volume and maximal

Figure 11.5 Maximum oxygen uptake in five male subjects prior to and following training in 1966 and again in 1996. Subjects were 20 in 1966.

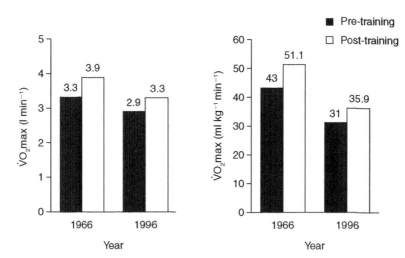

Source: Adapted from McGuire *et al.* (2001b).

Note: The post-training $\dot{V}O_2$max attained in 1996 was the same as the pre-training $\dot{V}O_2$max attained in 1966 when expressed in $1\,min^{-1}$. This was not the case when values were expressed in $ml\,kg^{-1}\,min^{-1}$ because the subjects were $19\,kg$ heavier post-training in 1996 compared with pre-training in 1966 ($96\,kg$ versus $77\,kg$).

a−v̄O$_2$ diff. in older men, while in older women O$_2$ extraction is more important (Spina *et al.* 1993).

Several factors could be responsible for an improvement in maximal a−v̄O$_2$ diff. following endurance training in older individuals. These include increases in capillary density and oxidative enzyme activity. Cross-sectional findings support such mechanisms (Coggan *et al.* 1990) as do training studies. In one study, 60–70-year-old men and women participated in a prolonged period (9–12 months) of endurance training involving walking/jogging at 80% of maximal heart rate for 45 minutes per day, four days per week (Coggan *et al.* 1992). Needle biopsy samples of the lateral gastrocnemius (calf) muscle obtained before and after training revealed significant increases in capillary density (Figure 11.6) and several enzymes associated with oxidative metabolism, including succinate dehydrogenase, citrate synthase and β-hydroxyacyl-CoA dehydrogenase (Table 11.1). A significant increase in the percentage of type IIa muscle fibres, together with a significant decrease in the percentage of type IIb muscle fibres, was also noted post-training in this study. These are the same changes qualitatively as those seen in young adults. Such changes would enhance stamina/resistance to fatigue. Furthermore, these changes demonstrate that the skeletal muscle of older men and women retains its ability to adapt to endurance training (Russ and Kent-Braun 2004).

As well as retaining its ability to adapt to endurance training, skeletal muscle also retains its ability to adapt to strength training in older adults. Cross-sectional comparisons demonstrate skeletal muscle hypertrophy in strength trained individuals (Plate 10). Exercise training studies confirm that adaption is possible after relatively brief periods of training. This is demonstrated by a study involving 12 previously untrained men aged 60–72 who completed a 12-week strength-training programme (Frontera *et al.* 1988). Training was conducted three days per week at an intensity of 80% of one-repetition maximum. Three sets of eight repetitions were completed for the knee

---

Figure 11.6 Increased capillary density in the gastrocnemius muscles of 60–70-year-old men and women following a 9–12 month period of endurance training.

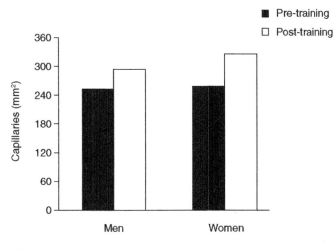

Source: Coggan *et al.* (1992).

Table 11.1 Increased oxidative enzyme activities (mol kg protein⁻¹ h⁻¹) in the gastrocnemius muscles of 60–70-year-old men and women following a 9–12-month period of endurance training

	MALES		FEMALES	
	PRE-TRAINING	POST-TRAINING	PRE-TRAINING	POST-TRAINING
Succinate dehydrogenase	1.11	1.83	0.76	1.05
Citrate synthase	2.97	3.83	2.21	2.58
β-hydroxyacyl-CoA dehydrogenase	5.95	8.45	5.29	7.19

Source: Coggan *et al.* (1992).

Note: The standard unit for enzyme activity is μmoles min⁻¹ g wet weight. Values in the table should be multiplied by a factor of three to give an approximate conversion to the standard unit. This assumes that muscle contains 20% protein (wet weight).

Plate 10 Computerized tomography scans of the upper arms of three 57-year old men of similar body weights.

Untrained | Swim-trained | Strength-trained

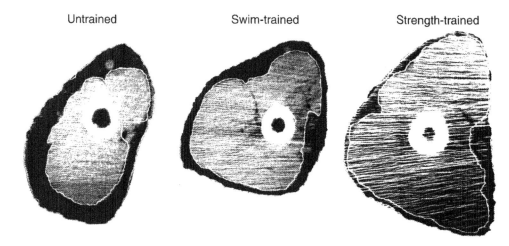

Source: Wilmore and Costill (2004).
Note: The scans show bone (the dark centre surrounded by the white ring), muscle (the striated grey area), and subcutaneous fat (dark perimeter). Note the enlargement of the triceps muscle in the swim-trained man and both the biceps and triceps muscle in the strength-trained man.

---

extensors and knee flexors on each training day. The findings demonstrated a progressive increase in muscle strength in both the knee flexors and knee extensors over the 12 weeks of the programme (Figure 11.7). Alongside the increase in strength, there was an increase in quadriceps muscle cross-sectional area as determined by computerized tomography scans (Figure 11.8). This muscle hypertrophy was in turn due to an increase in both type I and type II muscle fibre area. These findings have been confirmed in several other studies which collectively illustrate that older men and women experience similar strength gains as younger individuals after resistance training (Mazzeo *et al.* 1998; Skelton and Dinan-Young 2008). Such gains could have important implications for the daily living activities of elderly people. The ability to rise unaided from a low chair or toilet, for example, is dependent on quadriceps strength.

Figure 11.7 Improvements in strength (one-repetition maximum) of the knee extensors and knee flexors in men aged 60–72 years following a 12-week strength-training programme.

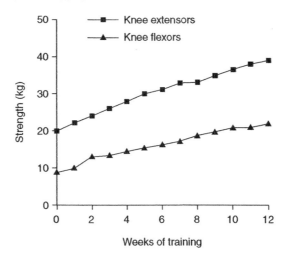

Source: Frontera *et al.* (1988). Used with permission of The American Physiological Society.

Figure 11.8 An increase in the cross-sectional area of the quadriceps muscles of the right and left legs following a 12-week strength-training programme in 12 men aged 60–72.

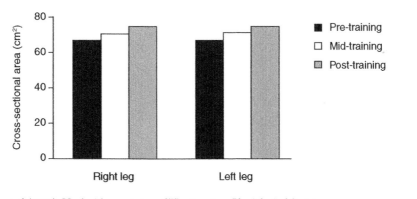

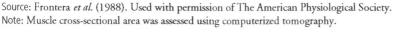

Source: Frontera *et al.* (1988). Used with permission of The American Physiological Society.
Note: Muscle cross-sectional area was assessed using computerized tomography.

Strength training may help preserve quadriceps strength, allowing elderly individuals greater independence.

Exercise training has been recommended for older individuals for a variety of reasons beyond any effects on $\dot{V}O_2$max and muscle strength. It has been proposed that exercise training will increase energy expenditure in the elderly, thus combating the increase in body fatness that often accompanies ageing. However, the evidence to support this suggestion is sparse and some studies have shown that any increase in energy expenditure due to exercise training in elderly people is nullified by a compensatory decrease in energy expenditure at other times of the day, so that total daily energy expenditure remains unchanged (Morio *et al.* 1998).

Other areas where exercise training may be beneficial for the elderly are postural stability and flexibility. Postural stability refers to the ability of an individual to retain balance, which is directly related to the risk of falling among older adults. Flexibility refers to the range of motion of single or multiple joints, and this affects the ability to perform specific tasks. There is evidence supporting the use of exercise as a means of improving postural stability and flexibility in older individuals (Mazzeo *et al.* 1998; Skelton and Dinan-Young 2008). Finally, the benefits of exercise described in this section are not limited to older adults who are already fit and healthy; exercise training is effective for improving functional capacities even in 'frail' older people, as demonstrated by the findings of a recent systematic review (Chin A Paw *et al.* 2008).

EXERCISE, AGEING AND INDEPENDENT LIVING

The decreases in functional capacities noted above have important implications for the ability to perform many activities of daily living. In one report, for example, less than 1% of pedestrians (5 out of 989) aged 72 or older had a normal walking speed sufficient to cross a street in the time typically allotted at pedestrian crossings (Langlois *et al.* 1997). Unfortunately, decreases in functional capacities (walking speed, quadriceps strength, joint flexibility) often go unnoticed until a threshold is reached when a person has difficulty performing a particular task, e.g. crossing a road in time, getting up from a low chair, climbing a stair, opening the cap on a jar, putting socks on, etc. This results in a loss of independence and an inability to participate fully in life. As might be expected, the number of people reporting that they are unable to perform one or more activities of daily living increases with age (Daley and Spinks 2000).

The level of proficiency in performing everyday tasks is related to the risk of disability. This was demonstrated in a four-year follow-up study involving non-disabled older persons living in Iowa (Guralnik *et al.* 1995). Lower-extremity function was assessed by measuring standing balance, walking speed and the time taken to stand from a chair and sit back down. These measures were found to be highly predictive of subsequent disability.

Evidence from cohort studies indicates that a regularly active lifestyle may slow the decline in mobility performance (Spirduso and Cronin 2001). One example is the Longitudinal Aging Study Amsterdam (Visser *et al.* 2002). This was a three-year follow-up study involving 2,109 men and women initially aged 55–85. Mobility performance was assessed using two tests: (1) the time taken to walk 6 metres; (2) the time taken to stand up and sit down five times from a kitchen chair. Physical activity was assessed using an interviewer-administered questionnaire. After three years there was a decline in total physical activity (measured either as hours day^{-1} or kcal day^{-1}) and mobility performance, which declined for 46% of the sample. Sports participation and a higher level of total physical activity, walking or household activity at baseline were associated with a smaller decline in mobility. Continuation of physical activity over time was also associated with a smaller decline in mobility.

Similar findings have emerged from cross-sectional studies. For example, a study of

619 healthy 70-year-old people in the city of Gothenburg, Sweden found that those who took a daily walk of at least 30 minutes had a significantly better climbing capacity (ability to climb a 40 cm high box without use of a handrail) than subjects who walked less (Frändin *et al.* 1991). Obviously these cross-sectional and cohort studies do not prove causality, but intervention studies suggest a causal relationship as will be discussed in the next section.

Longitudinal studies in older adults strongly suggest that physical activity reduces the risk of morbidity and mortality from disease. An interesting recent example is a study involving 538 runners and 423 controls aged 50 and older who were followed for 21 years (Chakravarty *et al.* 2008). All subjects were healthy at baseline. Disability was assessed by the Health Assessment Questionnaire Disability Index (HAQ-DI). Scores on this index were higher in controls than runners at all time points (indicating greater difficulty in performing certain tasks). Scores increased with age in both groups, but to a lesser degree in runners. At 19 years, 15% of runners had died compared with 34% of controls. Runners were also significantly less likely to suffer from cardiovascular disease (CVD), coronary heart disease (CHD), stroke, cancer or neurological illness than controls (Figure 11.9).

The findings of Chakravarty *et al.* (2008) are supported by those of prospective studies. A cohort study in Washington, Seattle, for example, examined the risk of CVD hospitalizations in older adults (men and women aged 65 and over) and found that walking more than four hours per week was associated with a reduced risk of hospitalization over a 4.2-year follow-up period (Figure 11.10). These findings indicate

Figure 11.9 Ratio of rate of deaths in runners to rate of deaths in healthy controls aged 50 or older at baseline and followed annually for 21 years.

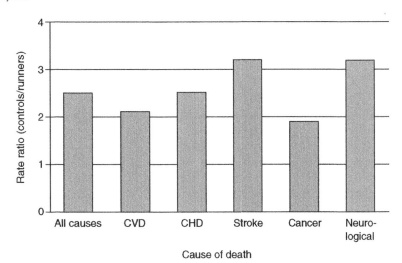

Source: Chakravarty *et al.* (2008).
Notes: *n* = 538 members of a nationwide running club in the United States and 423 healthy controls from northern California. Rate ratios were calculated as deaths per 100,000 person-years in controls/deaths per 100,000 person-years in runners. Abbreviations: CVD, all cardiovascular disease; CHD, coronary heart disease. In each case the rate ratio is significantly higher in the controls than the runners.

Figure 11.10 Relative risk of hospitalization due to CVD in men and women initially aged 65 according to the amount of walking performed each week.

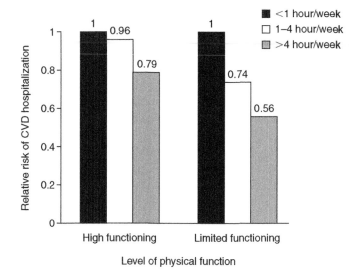

Source: LaCroix *et al.* (1996).
Note: Follow-up lasted for 4.2 years. Level of physical function was determined using a seven-point scale measuring limitations in physical tasks ranging from vigorous activities to self-care activities.

that a sustained programme of walking may help to prevent CVD events (LaCroix *et al.* 1996). More recently a study involving 3,075 community-dwelling adults aged 70–79 observed that long-distance corridor walk performance was inversely related to CVD risk over a 4.9-year period (Newman *et al.* 2006).

In addition to maintaining physical function, regular exercise may also help to prevent age-related declines in cognitive function. In one report from the Nurses' Health Study leisure-time physical activity was assessed biennially, beginning in 1986 through to 2001 using questionnaires. Cognitive function was measured twice, approximately two years apart by means of telephone assessments. Cognitive function assessments included tests of general cognition, verbal memory, category fluency (participants were asked to name as many animals as they could in one minute!) and attention. Higher levels of physical activity were associated with better cognitive performance and less cognitive decline (Figure 11.11). Women in the highest physical activity quintile had a 20% lower risk of cognitive impairment than women in the lowest physical activity quintile. Higher levels of walking were also significantly related to higher cognitive function (Weuve *et al.* 2004). Similar findings have been reported recently from the Canadian Study of Health and Aging, which involved 8,403 people followed over five years (Middleton *et al.* 2008).

If physical activity is effective in preserving cognitive function, this suggests that it may assist in the prevention of mental disorders such as dementia, which is characterized by deterioration in mental ability resulting in memory loss, confusion and general intellectual decline. Observational evidence is available to support this suggestion. One example is the Honolulu–Asia Aging Study (Abbott *et al.* 2004) which reported that

Figure 11.11 Mean differences in change in cognitive function scores by quintiles of physical activity for 18,766 US women aged 70–81, participating in the Nurses' Health Study.

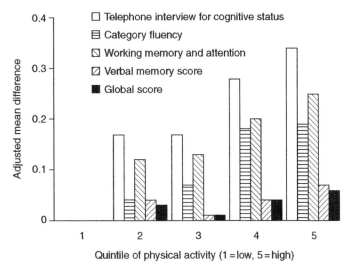

Source: Weuve *et al.* (2004).

Notes: The least active group has been used as the reference group with scores in the other groups expressed in relation to the least active group. Positive scores indicate a reduced level of cognitive decline. Trends are significant for each of the five factors displayed. Verbal memory score averages performance in immediate and delayed ten-word recalls and immediate and delayed East Boston Memory Tests. Global score averages performance on all cognitive tests. Mean differences are adjusted for age and many other potentially confounding variables.

walking <0.25 miles/day was associated with a 1.8-fold excess risk of dementia and Alzheimer's disease (a form of dementia resulting from a gradual degeneration of brain cells) compared with walking >2 miles/day (Figure 11.12). Other observational studies have identified a similar association including the Canadian Study of Health and Aging (Lindsay *et al.* 2002) and a Swedish study indicating that people in their late 40s and early 50s who exercised for half an hour at least twice a week had a 50% lower risk of dementia in later life than those who were less active during midlife (Rovio *et al.* 2005).

Can regular physical activity delay the ageing process? There is some evidence to support this idea, although it is observational and thus falls short of proving cause and effect. A recent report published in the *Archives of Internal Medicine* assessed the association between leisure-time physical activity and leukocyte telomere length in 2,401 twin volunteers (2,152 women and 249 men) from the UK Adult Twin Registry (Cherkas *et al.* 2008). Telomeres are pieces of DNA at the end of chromosomes. They protect the chromosomes from damage, but every time the cell divides telomeres shorten. Telomere length can therefore be used as an index of biological age – longer telomeres indicating a lower biological age. Cherkas *et al.* (2008) found that higher levels of leisure-time physical activity were associated with longer telomeres, suggesting an anti-ageing effect of exercise (Figure 11.13). The study authors observed that inactive subjects may be biologically older by ten years than more active subjects. Genetic factors are a possible confounding factor in this study, but the researchers addressed

Figure 11.12 Unadjusted and age-adjusted incidence of dementia and Alzheimer's disease according to distance walked per day in 2,257 physically capable men aged 71–93 in the Honolulu-Asia Aging Study.

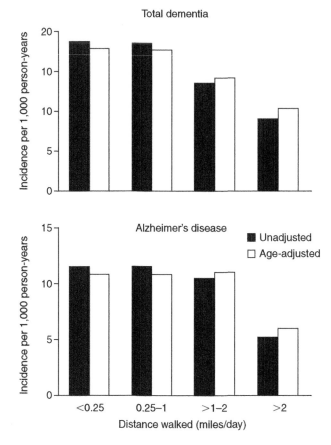

Source: Abbott *et al.* (2004).
Notes: Distance walked was assessed from 1991 to 1993. Dementia was based on neurological assessment at two repeat examinations (1994–6 and 1997–9).

this issue by comparing leukocyte telomere length in monozygotic and dizygotic twin pairs discordant for physical activity. The relationship between telomere length and physical activity remained significant in this analysis, suggesting that genetic factors are not responsible for the differences in telomere length between active and inactive individuals.

Aside from the evidence described so far in this chapter, there is also evidence that regular physical activity can reduce the risk of falls and fractures in older adults. Some of this evidence was highlighted in Chapter 9. Other potential benefits of exercise for older adults include social and emotional benefits which help in preventing isolation and reducing the risk of depression (Mazzeo *et al.* 1998; Young and Dinan 2005). Studies in older adults also suggest that physical activity (Knoops *et al.* 2004; Manini *et al.* 2006) and physical fitness (Willcox *et al.* 2006) are associated with a reduced risk of premature mortality. A limitation of all of the evidence discussed in this section,

Figure 11.13 Association between mean leukocyte telomere length and leisure-time physical activity levels in middle-aged men and women.

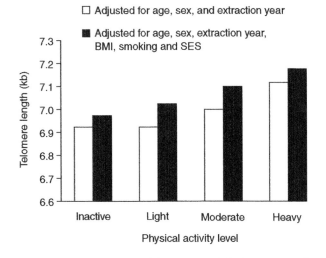

Source: Cherkas *et al.* (2008). Copyright © 2008 *Journal of the American Medical Association. All rights reserved.*
Notes: The subjects were 2,401 white twins (2,152 women and 249 men) from the UK Adult Twin Registry. The sample comprised 167 monozygotic twin pairs, 915 dizygotic twin pairs and 237 unpaired twins). Physical activity levels were assessed using questionnaires. The 'extraction year' refers to the year of DNA extraction and was used to account for leukocyte telomere length measurement differences between batches. Abbreviations: kb, kilobases; BMI, body mass index; SES, socioeconomic status.

however, is that it is observational and therefore does not provide proof of cause and effect. In the final section of this chapter we review the findings of some notable intervention trials which have examined the impact of exercise training on various aspects of fitness and health in older adults.

INTERVENTION TRIALS OF PHYSICAL ACTIVITY IN THE ELDERLY

Several intervention trials have been conducted to assess the extent to which exercise training can enhance the ability to perform activities of daily living in elderly men and women. Some of these trials have been conducted in very elderly individuals living in nursing homes, others have assessed community-dwelling elderly persons. Although the findings are not unanimous, several intervention studies show that exercise training, particularly resistance/weight training, can help to restore physical function, thus improving quality of life and the ability for independent living.

The importance of leg-strength for walking endurance was clearly demonstrated by a randomized intervention trial conducted in healthy elderly persons aged 65–79. Exercise intervention involved a 12-week resistance-training programme. This programme consisted of three sets of eight repetitions of seven exercises on three days per week. Resistance was initially set at 50% of one-repetition maximum, but was increased to 80% of one-repetition maximum by week nine. This programme led to a significant improvement in leg strength and walking endurance at 80% of baseline VO_2max (Figure 11.14). VO_2max was unaltered by the training programme (Ades *et al.* 1996). Improvements in walking endurance have also been demonstrated in nursing home residents (>80 years of age) following a 12-week programme of supervised daily walking performed at a self-selected pace (MacRae *et al.* 1996).

The potential of resistance training to counteract physical frailty has also been demonstrated in a randomized controlled trial involving 100 very elderly people (mean age of 87 years; age range of 72–98 years) resident in a nursing home (Fiatarone *et al.* 1994). Participants in the exercise intervention group followed a high-intensity (80% of one-repetition maximum) ten-week progressive-resistance training programme

Figure 11.14 A 12-week weight-training programme has been shown to improve leg strength (one-repetition maximum) and walking endurance (time to exhaustion at 80% of VO_2max) in healthy elderly persons aged 65–79.

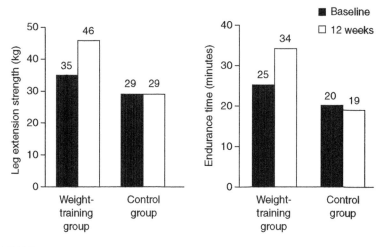

Source: Ades *et al.* (1996).

Table 11.2 Percentage change (mean ± SEM) in muscle strength, walking speed, stair-climbing power and thigh muscle cross-sectional area in frail nursing home residents (mean age of 87 years, age range of 72–98 years) after a ten-week resistance exercise training programme

	CONTROL GROUP ($n=26$)	EXERCISE GROUP ($n=25$)
Muscle strength	3±9	113±8
Walking speed	–1±4	12±4
Stair-climbing power	4±7	28±7
Thigh muscle area	–2±2	3±2

Source: Fiatarone *et al.* (1994).

Notes: The exercise programme targeted the hip and knee extensors and was conducted at 80% of one-repetition maximum. Three sessions were conducted each week and each session lasted for 45 minutes. Muscle strength of the hip and knee extensors was assessed using a dynamic concentric one-repetition maximum test. Walking speed was measured over a 6.1 m course. Stair-climbing power was calculated using a four-riser staircase with banisters. Thigh muscle cross-sectional area was quantified using computed tomography.

(three sessions per week) targeting the hip and knee extensors. This programme increased muscle strength, walking speed, stair-climbing power and thigh muscle cross-sectional area (Table 11.2). There was also an increase in spontaneous physical activity in the resistance-training group (assessed using activity monitors worn around both ankles). Over the same period there were small but significant reductions in walking speed and thigh muscle cross-sectional area in non-exercising participants. The authors concluded that 'high-intensity resistance exercise training is a feasible and effective means of counteracting muscle weakness and physical frailty in very elderly people' (Fiatarone *et al.* 1994: p. 1769).

Intervention programmes with older adults have also been conducted to examine the effects of exercise on disease or risk factors for disease. In one example, exercise training (three times per week for six months) in combination with dietary therapy was found to be effective in decreasing body weight, waist circumference, plasma glucose, serum triacylglycerol, systolic and diastolic blood pressure, C-reactive protein and interleukin 6 (the latter two being markers for inflammation) in obese (body mass index (BMI) $\geq 30\,\mathrm{kg\,m^2}$) older adults (aged ≥ 65 years). These findings suggest that the risk of CVD and type 2 diabetes was lowered in the intervention participants (Villareal *et al.* 2006). Another recent six-month intervention trial reported that exercise in combination with calorie restriction was effective in reducing two 'biomarkers of longevity' (fasting insulin level and body temperature) in overweight (BMI $25-<30\,\mathrm{kg\,m^2}$) men and women, as well as reducing DNA damage. If such changes were maintained over the long term they have the potential to attenuate the ageing process, although further study is required to confirm this (Heilbronn *et al.* 2006).

The link between physical inactivity, cognitive function, dementia and Alzheimer's disease was mentioned in the previous section, and in view of this link randomized controlled trials have been conducted to assess the potential benefits of exercise training for mental health. One recent example is an intervention conducted in Perth, Western Australia between 2004 and 2007 (Lautenschlager *et al.* 2008). This study involved 170 volunteers who reported memory problems but did not meet criteria for dementia. Participants were randomly allocated to an education and usual care group or to a six-month home-based programme of physical activity. The main outcome measure was change in Alzheimer Disease Assessment Scale-Cognitive Subscale (ADAS-Cog) scores (possible range 0–70) over 18 months. Participants in the intervention group improved 0.26 points and those in the usual care group deteriorated 1.04 points on the ADAS-Cog at the end of the six-month intervention. After 18 months participants in the intervention group improved 0.73 points compared with 0.04 points in the usual care group. The authors concluded that physical activity provoked a modest improvement in cognition in adults with subjective memory impairment. Another randomized controlled trial conducted in the United States found that exercise training in combination with behavioural management improves physical health and depression in patients with Alzheimer's disease (Teri *et al.* 2003).

The findings from intervention studies such as the ones described here demonstrate that exercise training offers a valuable means of maintaining functional capacities and mobility throughout the adult lifespan. This in turn should help to minimize the risk of disease, disability and premature death; improve quality of life and enhance the capacity for independent living. With these ends in mind, exercise recommendations have been formulated specifically for older adults (e.g. Nelson *et al.* 2007; Young and Dinan 2005). Some of these recommendations are discussed in Chapter 13.

SUMMARY

- Functional capacities decline with age. Most noteworthy amongst these are $\dot{V}O_2$max and muscle strength. Flexibility, balance and general mobility also decline with age, and there are changes in body composition, most notably a decline in muscle mass and an increase in percentage fat.
- Loss of muscle mass is a major reason for the decline in muscle strength with age. It may also explain a large portion of the decline in $\dot{V}O_2$max.
- Some of the decline in functional capacity with age is due to inactivity rather than a genuine effect of ageing. Age group records for a variety of sports indicate that individuals who remain active are capable of very high levels of physical performance into their eighth decade of life.
- The body retains it ability to adapt to exercise training throughout life. Adaptations shown to occur in older individuals after a period of exercise training include increases in $\dot{V}O_2$max, skeletal muscle oxidative enzyme activity, skeletal muscle capillarization, muscle mass, muscle fibre area and muscle strength.
- The decline in functional capacities associated with ageing eventually impairs mobility and the ability to perform activities of daily living. This leads to a loss of independence and quality of life.
- An active lifestyle can help to counter the age-related decline in functional capacities and mobility. This reduces the risk of disease, disability and hospitalization, and allows individuals to retain their independence. Resistance training is particularly effective in this regard.
- Along with declines in physical ability, cognitive function also declines with age and the risk of dementia is increased. Physical activity is associated with a lower risk of dementia and Alzheimer's disease in older adults, and there is some evidence that exercise intervention can enhance cognitive function in people who are at increased risk of dementia and Alzheimer's disease.

STUDY TASKS

1 Describe the major changes in functional capacities associated with ageing. What evidence is there to suggest that some of these changes are due to disuse rather than ageing?
2 Discuss the possible physiological mechanisms that might underlie a decline in $\dot{V}O_2$max with age. What evidence is there to support a role for these mechanisms in the age-related decline in $\dot{V}O_2$max?
3 Make a list of everyday tasks that older individuals may have difficulty in performing due to a decline in: (a) $\dot{V}O_2$max; (b) leg strength; and (c) flexibility.
4 Describe as fully as possible why resistance training may be particularly beneficial for older individuals.

5 Discuss evidence from observational and intervention trials that physical activity is beneficial for physical and mental health in older adults.

6 What evidence is available to suggest that physical activity can slow the ageing process? How convincing is this evidence?

FURTHER READING

Chin A Paw, M.J.M., van Uffelen, J.G.Z., Riphagen, I. and van Mechelen, W. (2008) 'The functional effects of physical exercise training in frail older people: a systematic review', *Sports Medicine* 38: 781–93.

Daley, M.J. and Spinks, W.L. (2000) 'Exercise, mobility and aging', *Sports Medicine* 29: 1–12.

DiPietro, L. (2007) 'Physical activity, fitness, and ageing', in C. Bouchard, S.N. Blair and W.L. Haskell (eds) *Physical Activity and Health*, Champaign: Human Kinetics, pp. 271–85.

Hawkins, S.A. and Wiswell, R.A. (2003) 'Rate and mechanism of maximal oxygen consumption decline with aging', *Sports Medicine* 33: 877–88.

Mazzeo, R.S., Cavanagh, P., Evans, W.J., Fiatarone, M., Hagberg, J., McAuley, E. and Startzell, J. (1998) 'American College of Sports Medicine Position Stand: exercise and physical activity for older adults', *Medicine and Science in Sports and Exercise* 30: 992–1008.

Russ, D.W. and Kent-Braun, J.A. (2004) 'Is skeletal muscle oxidative capacity decreased in old age?', *Sports Medicine* 34: 221–9.

Skelton, D.A. and Dinan-Young, S.M. (2008) 'Ageing and older people', in J. Buckley (ed.) *Exercise Physiology in Special Populations*, Edinburgh: Churchill Livingstone Elsevier, pp. 161–223.

Young, A. and Dinan, S. (2005) 'Activity in later life', *British Medical Journal* 330: 189–91.

Part IV
Physical Activity

Risks and Opportunities

12 Hazards

Knowledge assumed
Basic anatomy and physiology of
the cardiovascular,
musculoskeletal and female
reproductive systems
Principles of immune function
and cells involved

INTRODUCTION

Physical activity can be hazardous as well as beneficial to health. Jogging, walking and cycling inevitably increase exposure to the risk of injury through collisions with vehicles and falls. Cycling is particularly hazardous. In the United Kingdom, more than 1,300 cyclists were killed or seriously injured on the roads in 2005, which was 4% of all road accident fatalities. Around 540,000 injuries incurred during cycling are treated every year in US departments of emergency medicine, and nearly 800 people die; about one-third of these injuries are to the head and two-thirds of deaths are attributable to traumatic brain injury. Rather fewer injuries are incurred during swimming, but deaths do occur from drowning in swimming pools, mainly among young children.

A number of other negative outcomes from exercise have been documented. Prolonged exercise in the heat can lead to hyperthermia, particularly if fluid intake is insufficient, and even to electrolyte imbalance. Hypothermia can be experienced by those engaging in water sports, hill-walking and even marathon running (deep body temperature can fall in individuals who cannot maintain a speed of walking or running sufficient to match heat production to heat loss). Rhabdomyolisis (sporadic appearance in blood of abnormal levels of myoglobin) has been reported among endurance runners engaged in high volume training. There may be an increased likelihood of osteoarthritis in individuals who engage over many years in sports involving a lot of high impacts and/or torsional loading of joints. There are also reports of exercise 'dependence' – a craving for leisure-time activity that results in uncontrollable excessive exercise behaviour that manifests in psychological and/or physiological symptoms. Criteria to define 'how much is too much' and the development of more objective measures are needed, however, before this area of research yields secure findings.

Specific hazards are, of course, associated with physical activity for people with existing disease. Exercise can lead to hypoglycaemia in diabetics who take insulin or hypoglycaemic agents because it increases the rate of glucose uptake into muscle. Asthma may be precipitated by exercise – running in cold weather is a particularly potent trigger. In urban environments, air contains small amounts of gases and particulates other than its normal constituents. The increased ventilation of the lungs during exercise increases exposure to this pollution and may exacerbate respiratory problems in asthmatics. Even in healthy people, ozone and sulphur dioxide impair lung function.

Thus, while the incidence of serious health problems among people who engage in physical activity at a moderate intensity in moderate amounts is very low, participation in vigorous exercise or sports can be hazardous. The best-documented hazards are: musculoskeletal injuries; triggering of heart attack or sudden cardiac death; the so-called 'Female athlete triad' and the impairment of aspects of immune function.

MUSCULOSKELETAL INJURIES

Community studies in Europe suggest that every sixth unintentional injury is associated with leisure-time physical exercise, mainly sports. The majority are of low severity, but a minority require hospitalization. For example, at one university hospital in the Netherlands, sports injuries comprised about one-fifth of all injuries treated over a seven-year period, making these the second highest cause of accidental injuries (Dekker *et al.* 2000).

Injuries associated with physical activity fall into two categories: overuse and acute traumatic. Incidence rates for acute exercise-related (including sport-related) injuries are rather low in the general population. For example, about 5% of European adults who participated in a telephone survey reported such an injury in the previous month. Rates are higher, of course, among specific populations that are vigorously active; around 50% of people participating in team sports will sustain one or more injuries over a season and the annual rate of musculoskeletal injuries among military trainees is between 25% and 50%.

The majority of sports injuries are to the lower limb, especially to the knee and ankle (e.g. ligament sprains, meniscus tears) and two out of three occur during team sports. Soccer, in particular, gives rise to a high number of injuries, even when corrected for the number of people who play. Skiing is also associated with a high injury rate. Unfortunately, cervical spine injuries are occasionally incurred in sports such as rugby, diving, trampolining, gymnastics and horse-riding.

Running

Among recreational runners who are training steadily and participate in a long-distance run every now and then, the yearly incidence rate for injuries is between 37% and 56%, that is, 2.5 and 12.1 injuries per 1,000 hours of running (van Mechelen 1992). Most injuries are to the lower limb, predominantly the knee, and the majority appear to be due to the constant repetition of the same movement and impact, that is they are overuse injuries, such as stress fractures. Common sites for stress fractures, together with notes on definition, symptoms and diagnosis are show in Plate 11. Many overuse injuries lead to a reduction of training or to the cessation of training. Weekly distance run is the most important determinant of running injuries, for both men and women. Other predisposing factors include previous injury (injury recurrence is common), lack of running experience, running to compete and a rapid increase in training distance or intensity. Running on hard surfaces and running in poor shoes are implicated in about 5% of injuries. Age and sex do not appear to be important aetiological factors.

Moderate levels of physical activity

Information about injury rates among people who engage in 'ordinary' amounts of moderate-intensity activity is limited. However, researchers have documented the prevalence and nature of injuries among participants in the Aerobics Center Study, a prospective study of a physical activity intervention (Hootman *et al.* 2002). Subjects

Plate 11 Most common sites of stress fractures.

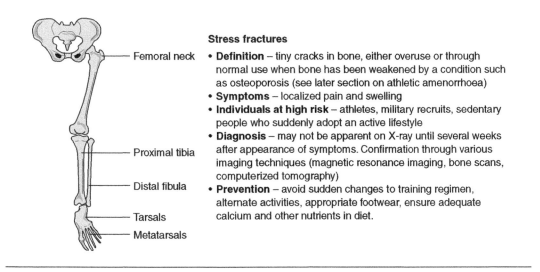

Femoral neck

Proximal tibia

Distal fibula

Tarsals

Metatarsals

Stress fractures
- **Definition** – tiny cracks in bone, either overuse or through normal use when bone has been weakened by a condition such as osteoporosis (see later section on athletic amenorrhoea)
- **Symptoms** – localized pain and swelling
- **Individuals at high risk** – athletes, military recruits, sedentary people who suddenly adopt an active lifestyle
- **Diagnosis** – may not be apparent on X-ray until several weeks after appearance of symptoms. Confirmation through various imaging techniques (magnetic resonance imaging, bone scans, computerized tomography)
- **Prevention** – avoid sudden changes to training regimen, alternate activities, appropriate footwear, ensure adequate calcium and other nutrients in diet.

Figure 12.1 Distribution and percentage of activity-related musculoskeletal injuries among participants in the US Aerobics Center Longitudinal Study.

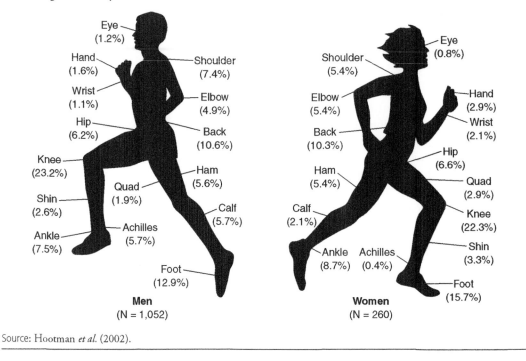

Eye (1.2%)
Hand (1.6%)
Wrist (1.1%)
Hip (6.2%)
Knee (23.2%)
Shin (2.6%)
Ankle (7.5%)
Shoulder (7.4%)
Elbow (4.9%)
Back (10.6%)
Ham (5.6%)
Quad (1.9%)
Calf (5.7%)
Achilles (5.7%)
Foot (12.9%)

Men
(N = 1,052)

Shoulder (5.4%)
Elbow (5.4%)
Back (10.3%)
Ham (5.4%)
Calf (2.1%)
Ankle (8.7%)
Achilles (0.4%)
Eye (0.8%)
Hand (2.9%)
Wrist (2.1%)
Hip (6.6%)
Quad (2.9%)
Knee (22.3%)
Shin (3.3%)
Foot (15.7%)

Women
(N = 260)

Source: Hootman *et al.* (2002).

(5,028 men, 1,285 women), who were aged 20–85, two-thirds of whom were physically active, provided information on physical activity habits and on injury experiences during one year. A quarter of participants reported at least one musculoskeletal injury and 83% of these were activity-related, two-thirds of them to the lower limb (Figure 12.1). Among both men and women, those participating in sports were the most likely to have an activity-related injury (27%), followed by runners (23–24%) and walkers (17–20%). However, 16% of subjects classified as sedentary also reported activity-related injuries, and so not all the injuries among the active groups can be attributed to physical activity purposefully taken for reasons of health benefit. In particular, those who walked for exercise experienced few 'excess' injuries, that is, above and beyond those reported in the sedentary group.

One of the few randomized intervention trials to report data on injuries associated with adopting a habit of moderate activity is the physical activity versus Metformin trial conducted by the Diabetes Prevention Program Group (details of this trial are discussed in Chapter 5). Their findings are broadly in line with those from the Aerobics Center study. Among men and women at risk of type 2 diabetes who increased their physical activity level ('moderate exercise such as brisk walking', around 6 MET-h per week, for an average of 2.8 years) the incidence rate of musculoskeletal injury was 24.1 per 100 person-years (Diabetes Prevention Program Research Group 2002). This was about the same as that experienced by the placebo group, which was 21.1 per 100 person-years.

Thus, moderate amounts and intensities of physical activity are not associated with a high risk of musculoskeletal injuries. Walking for exercise carries a particularly low risk of injury, even for the elderly. For example, among 21 men and women aged 70–79, who trained by walking briskly for three sessions per week, increasing to 45 minutes per session, only one injury was sustained over 13 weeks (Pollock *et al.* 1991).

SUDDEN CARDIAC DEATH, TRIGGERING OF HEART ATTACK

Vigorous physical activity, usually defined in the relevant literature as ≥ 6 METs, can acutely and transiently increase the risk of heart attack and sudden cardiac death in susceptible individuals. Who is 'susceptible' and why? Just how risky is vigorous exercise for the heart? What factors modify the risk? Research has provided some of the answers to these questions.

First, people who experience an exercise-related cardiac event invariably have underlying heart disease. In young adults this is typically some sort of hereditary or congenital cardiovascular abnormality, the most common being hypertrophic cardiomyopathy or coronary artery abnormalities. Among older people, the vast majority are individuals with atherosclerotic coronary artery disease. In this group, autopsy findings commonly show evidence of acute disruption of an atherosclerotic plaque, with thrombotic occlusion of a coronary artery. There may also be evidence, particularly in individuals known to have had symptomatic coronary heart disease (CHD), of ventricular fibrillation that may be explained by an abrupt loss of electrical instability when coronary blood flow is suddenly reduced.

Can the increased risk associated with vigorous exercise to be quantified? In one study in Seattle, limited to previously asymptomatic individuals, the incidence of cardiac arrest during exercise was 25 times higher than at other times (Siscovick *et al.* 1984). Findings from the US Physicians' Health Study bolster these conclusions (Albert *et al.* 2000). Among more than 12,000 men followed for 12 years, the risk of sudden cardiac death associated with an episode of vigorous exercise was 17 times higher than at all other times.

In studies of the potential 'triggers' to heart attack in Germany (Willich *et al.* 1993) and in the United States (Mittleman *et al.* 1993), researchers interviewed patients soon after they were admitted to hospital. Their activities during the hour before the onset of symptoms were recorded, as well as their usual level and type of physical activity. In the German study, the risk of a heart attack during or up to one hour after vigorous exertion was twice as high as during less strenuous activity or no activity. In the American study, the risk associated with vigorous exertion was around six times greater than at all other times. As Figure 12.2 shows, this relative risk varied greatly according to the men's usual frequency of vigorous exertion; it was 2.4 among those reporting regular vigorous exertion but 107 among individuals who were habitually sedentary, with clear evidence of a dose–response relationship. This effect modification by level of habitual exercise was even stronger in the German population studied.

Evidence for an increase in cardiovascular events during exercise among young individuals is necessarily much more limited. However, one Italian study among individuals aged 12–35 over a 21-year period found a 2.5-fold higher risk among athletes

Figure 12.2 Relative risk of myocardial infarction during a single session of heavy exertion, compared with all other times, according to the frequency of regular heavy exertion at ≥6 METs.

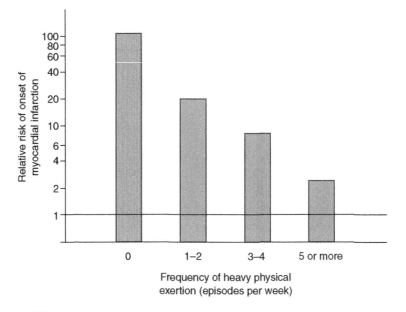

Source: Mittleman *et al.* (1993).
Note: The relative risk is shown on a logarithmic scale because the extremely high relative risk (107) in habitually sedentary people was so different from that (2.4, *P*<0.001) in people who reported heavy exertion five or more times per week. The horizontal line represents the baseline risk, that is, the risk during no exertion or during light exertion.

than among non-athletes (Corrado *et al.* 2003). This report included all deaths, however, not those solely during exertion, so the increased rate among athletes cannot be attributed to exercise alone.

At this point it is important to distinguish between the *relative* risk during exercise (discussed above) and the *absolute* risk. Although the *relative* risk is clearly increased during a session of exercise compared with other times, the *absolute* risk is extremely low in ostensibly healthy people. For example, the Physicians' Health Study reported just one death per 1.51 million episodes of exercise during a 12-year follow-up of nearly 21,500 men (Albert *et al.* 2000). Even in the marathon, the incidence of sudden death is low, about one in 50,000–74,000 competitors (Maron 2000). The incidence of sudden cardiac death in young athletes during competitive sports is even lower, about one in 200,000 student athletes per academic year.

On the other hand, the annual rate of exercise-related deaths among high-risk adults may be substantial. For example 0.2% of men with high cholesterol may be expected to have an exercise-related event annually. The incidence of exercise-related cardiovascular complications among people known to have established CHD is even higher. Based on reports of medically supervised cardiac rehabilitation programmes, one may expect one cardiac arrest per 116,906 patient hours, one myocardial infarction per 219,970 patient hours and one fatality per 752,365 patient hours (Thompson *et al.* 2007).

Paradoxically then, exercise is hazardous – as well as beneficial – to the heart. Does this diminish its role as part of a preventive strategy against CHD? The answer to this question – crucial for public health – is clearly 'no'. There is no evidence that the risks of physical activity outweigh the benefits for healthy subjects. Rather, the converse is true – benefits outweigh risks. The issue of benefit versus risk for CHD at a population level is discussed more fully in Chapter 13 in the context of public health.

FEMALE ATHLETE TRIAD

For most women, important health benefits accrue from leading a physically active lifestyle. On the other hand, very active girls and women participating in a range of physical activities may be at risk of developing a syndrome characterized by irregular or absent menses, low energy availability and low bone mineral density. The term 'Female Athlete Triad' was first adopted to describe these three interrelated medical problems in the early 1990s. Some scientists have challenged its existence (Stachenfeld and DiPietro 2006), but the prevailing view, endorsed by the 2005 International Olympic Committee Medical Commission Consensus Statement and the 2007 Position Stand of the ACSM, is that the Triad is a real phenomenon. Its characteristics can have clinical manifestations including eating disorders, hypothalamic amenorrhoea and osteoporosis that pose significant health risks. In this section, we will discuss the incidence, clinical consequences and aetiology of each component in turn. First, it is important to examine the prevalence of the syndrome and its predisposing factors.

The most robust findings on prevalence are from Norway, where all female elite athletes aged 13–39 ($n=938$) were invited to participate in a study, along with 900 controls in the same age group (Torstveit and Sundgot-Borgen 2005). Controls were randomly selected from the total female population of Norway in this age group. Eighty-eight per cent of athletes and 70% of controls completed a questionnaire and randomly selected sub-sets from each group completed all aspects of the study (186 athletes, 145 controls). Figure 12.3 shows the prevalence of the Triad and its components in elite athletes and non-athlete controls.

Figure 12.3 Prevalence of components of the Female Athlete Triad in elite Norwegian athletes and age-group-matched controls randomly selected from the Norwegian population. Data are given in numbers with percentages in brackets.

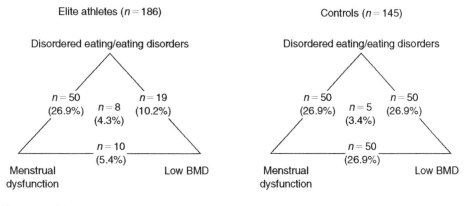

Source: Torstveit and Sundgot-Borgen (2005).

Eight athletes (4.3%) and five controls (3.4%) met all the criteria for the Triad, but many more from both groups exhibited two of its components. Based on the same study groups, more than six out of ten females were classified as being 'at risk' of developing the Triad, with those most at risk being non-athlete controls and athletes participating in sports where leanness and/or a specific weight were considered important. This last observation supports the view that pressure to meet unrealistic weight or body fat levels is one explanation for the development of the Triad or its components. It also demonstrates that the medical problems of the Triad co-exist among the general population of young women as well as among elite athletes.

Restriction of energy intake relative to energy expenditure leads to disordered eating and low energy availability – the defining feature of the Triad. Low energy availability impairs both reproductive function and bone turnover, with potentially important clinical consequences. Women restrict energy intake for many reasons. For athletes, the perception that decreasing body weight will improve performance creates pressure to be thin. However, pressure to be thin is also evident in the general population of young women where social success and attractiveness are often equated with thinness. These pressures are most strongly felt in individuals who seek to be high achievers and exhibit traits such as perfectionism.

Low energy availability

Energy availability is defined as dietary energy intake minus exercise energy expenditure, i.e. the amount of dietary energy available for other body functions after exercise training. When this is too low, physiological mechanisms reduce the amount of energy used for cellular maintenance, thermoregulation, growth and reproduction. While this compensation tends to restore energy balance and promote survival, it impairs health.

Some individuals reduce energy availability by increasing energy expenditure more than energy intake. Others reduce intake more than energy expenditure. Some practise abnormal eating behaviours that can progress to clearly defined clinical eating disorders such as anorexia nervosa or bulimia nervosa.

In anorexia nervosa food intake is severely restricted and the individual believes she is overweight even though she is below 85% of expected weight. Individuals with bulimia nervosa follow a cycle of binge eating followed by behaviours designed to rid the body of their 'unwanted calories'. These behaviours can include any or all of self-induced vomiting, use of laxatives, diuretics, fasting or excessive, compulsive exercise. Women suffering from bulimia nervosa or who have other, non-specific eating disorders can be within the normal range of weight for height. They are characterized, however, by a preoccupation with body image and weight as well as concern regarding eating. Dieting, that is restrictive eating for the purpose of losing weight, appears to be the primary precursor to the development of eating disorders.

The prevalence of disordered eating in athletes is high and, in general, studies have suggested that it is higher than in non-athletes. For example, a large controlled study of the entire population of Norwegian female elite athletes aged 15–39 ($n = 572$) found that 20% exhibited eating disorders, compared with 9% of controls (Sundgot-Borgen and Torstveit 2004). The prevalence of disorders was highest (42%) in athletes competing in sports described as 'aesthetic', including figure skating, gymnastics and dancing. In these sports, female athletes often feel under pressure to reduce weight in order to perform well. Disordered eating was also prevalent in sports where competitors are classified according to weight, for example judo and karate; many athletes in these sports want to have a low body fat mass and a high muscle mass and compete in a class below their 'ordinary' weight – hence the pressure for thinness. Particularly in sports or activities that emphasize leanness, there may be a distorted view as to what is an acceptable energy intake. Female dancers are a good example: dance students and professional ballerinas have been reported to consume less than 70% of the energy needed to meet body weight targets.

Disordered eating is not, however, a pre-requisite for low energy availability in very active women. An athlete may be eating normally for a non-athlete but not realize that her energy intake is insufficient to meet her enhanced energy needs because appetite is not necessarily a reliable indicator of energy requirements in athletes. Thus, disordered eating that restricts food intake can be unintentional. This may be a particular problem among girls as their food intake must also cover the energy costs of growth.

Menstrual disorders

Menarche has been reported to occur later in athletic girls – gymnasts and dancers for example – than in less active girls. However, this observation is probably accounted for by self-selection of late-maturing girls into these activities, rather than by a cause-and-effect relationship. By contrast, the high prevalence of menstrual dysfunction among women athletes is clearly associated with their eating and exercise behaviours.

The first systematic study found that between 6% and 43% of women runners participating in the 1977 US National Collegiate Cross-Country Championships had secondary amenorrhoea and that its prevalence was linearly related to training distance (Feicht *et al.* 1978) (Figure 12.4). Training intensity was highest among the

Figure 12.4 Incidence of secondary amenorrhoea in women runners in relation to distance run during training.

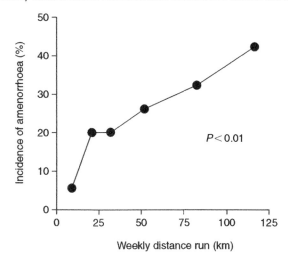

Source: Feicht *et al.* (1978).

amenorrhoeic athletes who were also better runners than those who were menstruating regularly.

Reports of the prevalence of menstrual disorders in athletes vary widely but, consistent with findings for eating disorders, it is highest in sports where leanness influences performance or where weight categories restrict competition. In rhythmic gymnasts, for example, as many as 61% have been reported to have oligomenorrhoea (irregular, long cycles), as have 21% of a group of English runners. These figures are substantially higher than those for the general population. Even in regularly menstruating athletes, asymptomatic subclinical disorders of reproductive function are common (these are evident only when researchers measure the concentrations of ovarian steroid hormones over at least one menstrual cycle). For example, in regularly menstruating recreational runners, the prevalence of luteal suppression and anovulation was 78%, much higher than in either the general population or in an age-matched group of sedentary women (~9%) (de Souza *et al.* 1998).

The prevalence of secondary amenorrhoea in adult athletes ranges from 3% to 66% (depending on the sport and the criteria used to define amenorrhoea), compared with only 2–5% of women of comparable age in the general population. Intense training for non-sporting activity is also associated with amenorrhoea; for example, around 40% of ballet dancers are amenorrhoeic. Predisposing factors include youth (women who take up a sport as adults are less likely to become amenorrhoeic), a low level of body fatness and a high training intensity or volume. Among US collegiate runners, the prevalence of amenorrhoea has been reported to range from 3% in those running less than 16 km week^{-1} with body mass >60 kg to around 60% in those running more than 113 km week^{-1} with body mass <50 kg.

Reproductive function is often impaired, however, even in women who have a normal pattern of menstrual bleeding. Researchers have undertaken careful comparisons of the characteristics of menstrual cycles of recreational runners with those of sedentary age- and weight-matched controls (de Souza *et al.* 1998). The exercising women ran an average of 32 km (20 miles) per week, had a body fat level of 20% and a VO_2max of 41.5 ml kg^{-1} min^{-1} – all characteristics consistent with a moderate habit of exercise rather than intense training and competition. Even though all the exercising women had repeatable menstrual cycle lengths in the normal range, their ovarian function was frequently abnormal: 55% of cycles monitored demonstrated either luteal phase deficiency (too short and/or inadequate because of low progesterone) (43%) or anovulation (12%). Cycles were more likely to be anovulatory as the severity of the disruption to endocrine function progressed.

The higher prevalence in athletes may be explained in part by self-selection, i.e. these women bring their menstrual disorders into sports. For example, women and girls with anorexia nervosa may self-select into sports where low body mass confers a competitive advantage. Other women acquire disorders through participation in sports. Endocrine studies have shed some light on the mechanisms responsible. In oligo/amenorrhoea, the mid-cycle surge in luteinizing hormone (LH) (on which ovarian function critically depends) is blunted and the characteristic pulsatility of the secretory pattern of this hormone is decreased. The increase in follicle-stimulating hormone in the luteal-to-follicular transition is also attenuated. These abnormalities reflect disturbances of the neuroendocrine functions of the hypothalamus and impair or prevent the normal processes of ovulation and implantation.

An early hypothesis that reproductive function is disrupted when body fat levels fall below a critical threshold has largely been disproved. Cross-sectional comparison of amenorrhoeic and normally menstruating athletes have failed to demonstrate a consistent association between menstrual status and body mass or composition. Meta analysis does demonstrate a 2.2% lower body fat content in amenorrhoeic athletes compared with their eumenorrhoeic peers, but this difference is unlikely to be important aetiologically.

The prevailing 'energy availability' hypothesis holds that exercise has no suppressive effect on the reproductive system beyond the impact of its energy cost. According to this hypothesis, the vital links between the hypothalamus and the pituitary are disrupted when some unknown signal, possibly leptin, indicates that dietary energy intake is inadequate to cover the energy costs of both reproduction and the considerable amount of energy expended in exercise.

If low energy availability is indeed the important causal factor in menstrual disorders, then these should be prevented or reversed by dietary intervention without any moderation of the exercise regimen. Using LH pulsatility as a marker of menstrual disorder, researchers have shown that the disruption of LH pulsatility in women with a habit of exercise is prevented by supplementing their diet to compensate fully for their exercise energy expenditure (Loucks *et al.* 1998). It is now clear that any combination of dietary restriction and exercise energy expenditure that reduces energy availability disrupts the pulsatile secretion of LH within days in proportion to the magnitude of the reduction in energy availability. These findings are consistent with an extensive literature showing that reproductive function is dependent on energy availability in animals.

So, what constitutes 'low' energy availability. For healthy, adequately nourished sedentary adult young women, energy balance occurs on average at energy availability of approx 190 kJ per kg of fat-free mass per day (45 kcal per kg of fat-free mass per day). LH pulsatility is disrupted when energy availability falls below approx 126 kJ per kg of fat-free mass per day (30 kcal per kg of fat-free mass per day), a threshold near resting metabolic rate and approximately 33% below energy balance. This threshold will be higher in growing adolescents.

'Athletic amenorrhoea' is reversed by modest weight gain (reflecting a return to adequate energy availability) and a reduced level of training, and so is not necessarily, in itself, a long-term hazard to reproductive health. Its most obvious short-term consequence is infertility; amenorrhoeic women are not developing egg cells that can be fertilized. Short luteal phases and low progesterone can also lead to infertility due to failures of implantation. Paradoxically, without contraception, irregularly menstruating athletes may be at increased risk for unwanted pregnancy because their day of ovulation is less predictable.

On the other hand, long episodes of amenorrhoea have important consequences for health beyond their impact on reproductive physiology. There are reports of reduced HDL-cholesterol and of impaired endothelium-dependent dilatation in athletes who experience this. Both changes may be expected to increase the risk for cardiovascular disease (CVD). The best-documented consequence of low oestrogen states is, however, skeletal demineralization.

Low bone mineral density

Amenorrhoea can predispose athletes to osteopenia and even premature osteoporosis, and put them at higher risk of stress fractures. These problems are a cause for special concern for adolescent athletes because impairment of bone formation during adolescence can prevent these individuals from achieving their genetic potential for peak bone mass.

Several reports in the early 1980s showed that women with exercise-associated amenorrhoea had lower spinal bone mineral density (BMD) than age-matched physically active or sedentary eumenorrhoeic women. Retrospective analysis of the menstrual histories of nearly 100 runners found that spinal BMD correlated with the duration of their amenorrhoea (Drinkwater *et al.* 1990) (Figure 12.5). Thus, the severity of bone loss increases with the degree of menstrual cycle disturbance. Moreover, as newer techniques became available, it has become clear that bone loss in amenorrhoeic athletes is not restricted to the spine, but may be observed at multiple skeletal sites, suggesting that this is a generalized effect and that even sites subjected to impact loading during exercise may be affected. The problem of low BMD is not restricted to women with exercise-associated oligo/amenorrhoea. Physically active women with regular menstrual cycles but who are anovulatory and/or have short luteal phases are also reported to experience bone loss.

Figure 12.5 Relationship between BMD and menstrual history for 97 active women aged between 18 and 38.

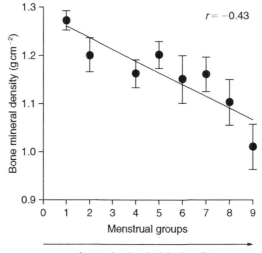

Source: Drinkwater *et al.* (1990).

Notes: Values are mean and standard error of the mean. Numbers of women in each group are 21, 7, 2 (not plotted but included in regression), 5, 22, 9, 10, 10 and 11 for groups 1–9 respectively. Subjects were categorized according to both patterns of menstrual function at time of observation and previous menstrual history. Group 1 – regular menstrual cycles at time of study and previously. Group 9 – amenorrhoeic at the time of study and previously. Other groups with histories intermediate between these two.

There are several studies reporting an increase in stress fractures among amenorrhoeic athletes. Among female recruits in basic training for the US Marine Corps, amenorrhoeic women had an almost three-fold increase in the risk of a lower extremity stress fracture (Rauh *et al.* 2006). The combination of amenorrhoea and demanding workouts increases the likelihood of stress fractures. In one study 100% of amenorrhoeic ballet dancers who practised for more than five hours per day had a stress fracture (Kadel *et al.* 1992). No large prospective trials are, however, available to evaluate the long-term consequences for skeletal health in women who have experienced long episodes of oligo/amenorrhoea. Eight-year follow-up data have been reported for a group of 29 athletes; despite several years of normal menses or use of oral contraceptives, formerly oligomenorrhoeic athletes still had values for vertebral BMD that were 15% lower than those of the athletes who had regular menses throughout (Keen and Drinkwater 1997). Amenorrhoeic athletes are clearly at risk for a decrease in bone mass and this may be irreversible. It is not known whether these women are at risk for premature osteoporotic fractures as they age.

Oestrogen deficiency is probably at least partly responsible for the low BMD found in amenorrhoeic women, in line with the observation that oestrogen deficiency is the principal cause of bone loss in women with ovarian failure. In oestrogen deficiencies, however, there is increased bone turnover with excessive bone *resorption* that is normalized by oestrogen replacement. By contrast, women distance runners with long-term amenorrhoea show reduced bone *formation*, compared with eumenorrhoeic runners or age-matched sedentary eumenorrhoeic women (Zanker and Swaine 1998). Moreover, low BMD in amenorrhoeic athletes is much less responsive to exogenous oestrogen therapy than in women with ovarian failure. These observations demonstrate that mechanisms other than low oestrogen are implicated. It may be that low energy availability accounts for imbalanced bone remodelling in active amenorrhoeic women, as it does for the amenorrhoea itself. Energy deficit has been shown to elicit the metabolic aberrations (increased cortisol, low thyroid hormones, IGF-1 deficiency) found in active amenorrhoeic women that can lead to inadequate bone formation. The impact of chronic low energy availability on BMD is thus a topic of active research interest.

What about male athletes?

The above discussion has focused on women. Do male athletes exhibit components of the Female Athlete Triad? Eating disorders have been reported in male athletes as well as in female athletes. The prevalence is lower, however, at around 4–8%. As with female athletes, the high-risk sports appear to be aesthetic sports, sports in which low body fat is advantageous and sports in which there is a need to make weight (Baum 2006). The scale of the problem is, however, much lower than among female athletes. One reason may be that, on average, female athletes consume 30% less energy per kilogram of body mass than their male counterparts in the same sports.

Reproductive hormone responses are probably depressed by regular exercise in men as well as in women but, in the absence of an overt sign such as absence of menses in women, are difficult to document. Male endurance runners have been reported to exhibit plasma testosterone concentrations that are around 15% lower than those of sedentary men, but clinical reproductive dysfunction is rare.

IMPAIRED IMMUNE FUNCTION

It was mentioned in connection with physical activity and the risk of cancer (Chapter 8) that the relationship between changes to the body's innate immune system and exercise intensity and/or volume appears to be J-shaped (Figure 12.6). Therefore, although moderate exercise probably benefits immune function, prolonged intense exercise may impair it.

The immune system distinguishes host cells from those of invading organisms in two ways: through the adaptive immune system, which detects a particular invading organism (specific recognition); and the innate system that detects such organisms in a non-specific manner. Evidence suggests that exercise appears to have effects on both adaptive and innate systems. There is no single marker of immune function, however, so many studies have used respiratory tract infection as a surrogate marker for altered immune function.

Epidemiological reports suggest that, during periods of heightened training or after marathon-type events, athletes are at increased risk of upper respiratory tract infections. For example, the incidence of such infections was studied in a group of 2,300 marathon runners who had applied to enter the Los Angeles marathon (Neiman *et al.* 1990). After the race, runners reported information about their training habits and about upper respiratory tract infections and symptoms before and for one week after the race. Nearly 13% of participants reported having an infectious episode during the week following the race, compared with only 2.2% of similarly experienced runners who had applied but did not participate (for reasons other than sickness). Participants were six times as likely to have an infection during the week after the race than the non-participating runners. Runners training more than 96 km per week were twice as likely as those running less than 32 km per week to have experienced an infection

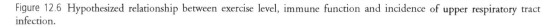

Figure 12.6 Hypothesized relationship between exercise level, immune function and incidence of upper respiratory tract infection.

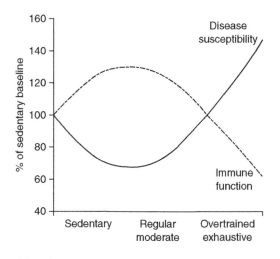

during the two months leading up to the marathon. These findings are supported by several smaller studies from South Africa on runners participating in 56 km and 90 km ultra-marathons.

The innate and adaptive immune systems help to defend the body against upper respiratory tract infections. After prolonged, intensive exercise there are complex changes to the populations of cells that constitute a first line of defence against infection: macrophages, neutrophils and natural killer cells. (Macrophages have phagocytic and cytotoxic capacities; neutrophils, also phagocytic, are important in the non-specific killing of bacteria; natural killer cells seek out and destroy virus-infected cells.) Macrophage antiviral function, neutrophil function and natural killer cell activity are all impaired for several hours after a session of high-intensity exercise, particularly if this is prolonged. One hypothesis is that the immune system's involvement in the inflammatory response following intensive exercise impairs its capability to protect against upper respiratory tract infection. The function of T lymphocytes (important cells of the adaptive immune system) is also altered following prolonged, intensive exercise. These cells are pivotal for anti-viral responses and are of particular relevance, given that athletes appear to suffer mainly from illnesses caused by respiratory viruses.

In the light of these findings, it has been suggested that a prolonged session of high-intensity endurance exercise leads to transient, but clinically important, changes in immune function. During this 'open window' of altered immunity (which may last 3–72 hours, depending on the parameter measured), viruses and bacteria may gain a foothold. A weakness of this argument is that investigators have yet to link most markers of immunosuppression after exercise with an increased incidence of infections. One study has reported a negative correlation between the concentration of an immune factor (immunoglobulin A) in the saliva and incidence of upper respiratory tract infection in elite swimmers during an intensive training period (Gleeson *et al.* 1999). As yet, however, there is no single marker of immune function to adopt as an outcome measure in studies, and the need to employ a large spectrum of parameters restricts research activity in this area.

PREVENTION

Some of the hazards of exercise are preventable. In some sports, protective equipment offers an obvious and effective strategy. Examples include helmets, mouth guards, shin pads and knee pads. The compulsory use of a face mask in ice hockey has virtually eliminated eye injuries. Safety is improved if cyclists display lights and wear reflective clothing. Helmets offer protection for the head for cyclists, although there are reports from Canada, Australia and the United States that the increasing use of these has not been associated with a reduction in fatalities. Runners can decrease their risk of injury through traffic accidents by wearing clothing that ensures that they can easily be seen, and selecting their routes carefully.

At least one community-based attempt to prevent injuries has been reported. Swedish researchers compared injury rates in a year-long injury prevention intervention population with those in a comparable control population (Timpka and Lindqvist 2001). The intervention comprised: an injury prevention course for physical education teachers; a programme for coaches and referees on discouraging foul play; compulsory use of shin pads in soccer; increased supervision of novices in all sports; and courses for coaches on proper physical preparation. In the intervention population the total morbidity rate for sports-related injuries decreased by 14%; the rate of moderately severe injuries halved and minor injuries increased, but there was no change in the rate of severe injuries. However, there was no tendency towards a decreased injury rate among the over 40s, probably because they do not participate as much in the traditional, mainly team, sports targeted by this particular intervention.

Prevention of running injuries may best be tackled through education on rehabilitation after injury, early recognition of symptoms of overuse and training principles (Bahr and Trosshaug 2005). Education on gradual entry into any sort of conditioning programme is particularly important for middle-aged and older people, especially if (often after long periods of a sedentary lifestyle) they intend to enter or re-enter the competitive arena.

Prevention of the Female Athlete Triad must focus on discouraging athletes from restrictive eating and on increasing understanding of nutritional principles among athletes, coaches and health-care professionals. Very active women – and female athletes in particular – need to take special care to maintain energy intake at a sufficient level to match their high levels of energy expenditure. Education, not only of athletes, but also of parents and coaches is the key for prevention and early intervention. For many athletes nutrition counselling and monitoring are sufficient, but the ACSM and the IOC both recommend that athletes are assessed for the Triad at any health screening opportunity or whenever they present with any of the associated clinical conditions. For a full discussion of issues concerning prevention, diagnosis, management and treatment, readers are referred to the 2005 IOC Medical Commission Consensus Statement and the 2007 Position Stand by the American College of Sports Medicine (details in Further Reading at the end of this chapter).

Finally, most of the hazards of exercise may be avoided by pursuing a habit of moderate exercise, rather than high-volume, intense training. As explained earlier, the transient risk of a cardiac event during exercise is much lower in people who are physically active on a regular basis than in those who rarely take exercise. Therefore, sedentary individuals who begin low-intensity activity and progress gradually to more and more intense activity will minimize their cardiovascular risk. Women who engage in moderate-intensity physical activity and allow the physiological mechanisms of hunger and satiety to govern their eating behaviour are not at high risk of menstrual dysfunction or its consequences. Similarly, recreational exercisers are unlikely to experience problems with immune function. It is clear from comprehensive literature published over a period of more than 50 years that substantial health benefits can be gained from regular physical activity. Recognition that some risks are associated with some types of activity – as described in this chapter – does not alter this conclusion.

SUMMARY

- A physically active lifestyle confers multiple health benefits, but participation in vigorous exercise or sports also carries risks. Moderate amounts and intensities of exercise are associated with few hazards.
- Exercise-related musculoskeletal injuries are common. The majority are to the lower limb and two out of three occur during team sports.
- Vigorous exertion can acutely and transiently increase the risk of sudden cardiac death and heart attack in susceptible people, i.e. those with existing cardiac disease. The transient increase in risk associated with a session of exercise is highest among people unaccustomed to vigorous exercise.
- The Female Athlete Triad is a syndrome evident in some women who are very active physically. It is characterized by three interrelated problems: irregular or absent menses, disordered eating and low bone mineral density.
- Menstrual dysfunction is common among women who engage in sports that emphasize leanness. Even when menstrual periods are regular, there may be abnormalities that will reduce fertility.
- Bone mineral density is lower in amenorrhoeic athletes than in those with normal menstrual periods. There is concern that this bone loss may be largely irreversible.
- Immune function may be compromised for some hours after prolonged vigorous exercise, and this may provide a 'window of opportunity' for infections to gain a foothold.
- Some hazards may be prevented through protective equipment. Those mainly associated with excessive exercise may be attenuated through avoidance of low energy availability (particularly for women) and/or by moderation of the training regimen.

STUDY TASKS

1. What are the most common musculoskeletal injuries among runners? Discuss the factors that predispose to these and suggest preventive strategies.
2. Explain the statement: 'Exercise is both hazardous and beneficial for the heart.' On average, what is the relative risk associated with a single session of vigorous exercise and how does this differ between sedentary people and those who are highly active?
3. Distinguish between eumenorrhoea, oligomenorrhoea and amenorrhoea. Give examples of sports where women are at high risk of menstrual dysfunction and suggest reasons.
4. Describe one cross-sectional study that suggests that spinal bone mineral density in women athletes is related to their menstrual history. What are the limitations to this study?
5. Describe the likely relationship between immune function and the intensity/volume of exercise. Identify the weakness in this explanation of the increased prevalence of upper respiratory tract infections in runners after marathon-type events and suggest what studies might be undertaken to address this.

■ FURTHER READING

American College of Sports Medicine (2007) 'Position stand: The Female Athlete Triad', *Medicine and Science in Sports and Exercise* 39: 1867–82.

Bennell, K.L., Malcolm, S.A., Wark, J.D. and Brukner, P.D. (1997) 'Skeletal effects of menstrual disturbances in athletes', *Scandinavian Journal of Medicine and Science in Sports* 7: 261–73.

International Olympic Committee Consensus Statement on the Female Athlete Triad (2005). Online., available at: http://multimedia.olympic.org/pdf/en_report_917.pdf (accessed 24 January 2007).

Loucks, A.B. (2006) 'The Female Athlete Triad: do female athletes need to take special care to avoid low energy availability? Prevailing view', *Medicine and Science in Sports and Exercise* 28: 1694–700.

Peterson, L. and Renstrom, P.A.F.H. (2001) *Sports Injuries: Their Prevention and Treatment*, 3rd edn, Champaign: Human Kinetics.

Redman, L.M. and Loucks, A.B. (2005) 'Menstrual disorders in athletes', *Sports Medicine* 35: 747–55.

Stachenfeld, N.S. and diPietro, L. (2006) 'The Female Athlete Triad: do female athletes need to take special care to avoid low energy availability? Challenging view', *Medicine and Science in Sports and Exercise* 28: 1694–700.

Thompson, P.D., Franklin, B.A. *et al.* (2007) 'Exercise and acute cardiovascular events: placing the risks into perspective: a scientific statement from the American Heart Association Council on nutrition, physical activity, and metabolism and the Council on clinical cardiology, in collaboration with the American College of Sports Medicine', *Circulation* 115: 2358–68.

13 Public health

Knowledge assumed
Common measures of disease
prevalence
Role of dose–response
relationships in establishing
causality in epidemiology

▊ INTRODUCTION

As mentioned in Chapter 1, after the Second World War research in public health began to focus on the influence of individual behaviours on chronic, non-communi-cable diseases. The work of Professor Jeremy Morris (who wrote the Foreword to this book) on the role of exercise in protection against heart attack, alongside that of Doll and Hill on smoking and lung cancer, was instrumental in defining this new vision of public health. Since the 1950s, when Professor Morris' first studies were published, there has been phenomenal growth of knowledge about the health benefits of physical activity and – in recent years – an increase in practical interventions that seek to increase levels of physical activity in the population, reflecting current public health priorities.

By 2003 non-communicable diseases explained some 60% of deaths and more than 50% of the global burden of disease, i.e. the sum of years of life lost because of premature mortality and years of life with disability. It is estimated that these diseases will contribute to 69% of deaths and 57% of the global burden of disease by 2030 (Mathers and Loncar 2006). Non-communicable diseases include cardiovascular disease (CVD), type 2 diabetes and many cancers; they share a relatively small number of preventable risk factors, especially lack of physical activity, obesity, tobacco use and an unhealthy diet. The potential benefits from changing these features of a population's behaviour are considerable: the World Health Organization (WHO) estimates that about 80% of premature heart disease and stroke, 80% of type 2 diabetes and 40% of all cancers are preventable.

Plate 12 The population burden of physical inactivity-related ill-health: measuring the public health impact of inactivity.

Population-attributable risk is the incidence of a disease in a population that is associated with (or attributed to) an exposure to a risk factor. It is a useful measure of the potential for prevention of disease, but caution is needed in extrapolating because PAR assumes a causal link between exposure and outcome.

The histogram shows population-attributable risk estimates for medical conditions related to physical activity in Australia in 2000 (vertical bars, EconTech 2007), in Australia in 1993–4 (solid circles, Stephenson *et al.* 2000 and in the United States in 1995 (open circles, Colditz 1999).

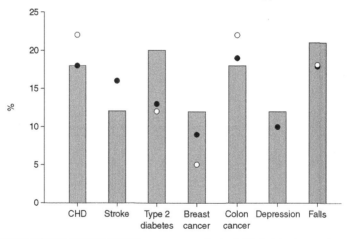

Disability adjusted life years (DALYs) are a measure of potential life lost due to premature mortality and the years of productive life lost due to disability.

Physical activity has been estimated as responsible for:
- 1% of DALYs lost globally and 3% in established market economies in 1990
- 3% of DALYs lost in the United Kingdom in 2002
- 6% of DALYs lost in Australia in 2003.

Sources: Murray and Lopez (1997), Allender *et al.* (2007) and Begg *et al.* (2008).

Table 13.1 Estimates of population-attributable risk for physical inactivity in Canada

DISEASE	PAR (%)
Coronary artery/heart disease	19.4
Stroke	24.3
Hypertension	13.8
Colon cancer	18.0
Breast cancer	14.2
Type 2 diabetes	21.1
Osteoporosis	24.0

Sources: Values from Katzmarzyk and Janssen (2004).

Note: Based on prevalence of physical inactivity of 53.5% and on estimates of relative risk from multiple studies of physical activity and each specific disease.

Population-attributable risk (PAR) values (explained in Chapter 2) estimate the effects of an individual risk factor on a given disease in a specified population. They inform public health strategies by helping policy makers to prioritize their efforts to change health-related behaviours. PAR values for major inactivity-related diseases in Australia and in the United States are presented in Plate 12 and for Canada in Table 13.1. Plate 12 also introduces a complex statistic, disability-adjusted life years (DALYs). DALYs take into account not only the duration of life, but also some notion of its quality. Collectively, these data illustrate the enormous public health impact of inactivity-related disease.

Of course, estimates of PARs are constrained by the definitions of inactivity adopted, by the methods used to measure prevalence and the extent of inactivity in the population(s) studied. They also assume that ceasing to be sedentary reduces the risk of the disease in question (there is epidemiological evidence for this in relation to CHD and type 2 diabetes (discussed in Chapters 4 and 5) but not for colon cancer). Despite these limitations, PARs clearly show that increases in the physical activity levels of a population may be expected markedly to reduce the incidence of several non-communicable diseases that have high prevalence world-wide.

What implications does this information have for public health strategies? Two approaches to primary prevention may be identified: the 'high-risk' approach and the population approach. The first requires selective screening for risk factors, followed by therapeutic interventions (in the present context, individual guidance on physical activity guidance and/or opportunities to participate in an exercise programme) with the group at greatest risk, i.e. the least active; the second approach aims to produce favourable shifts in the population distributions of risk factors (in the present context, encourage everyone to become a little more active). Of course, these approaches are not mutually exclusive. However, the priority for public health, as opposed to clinical medicine, is to reduce overall disease incidence and the most effective way to do this is probably to attempt to shift the whole distribution of risk. For physical inactivity, this requires a population-based strategy to increase activity across all sectors.

As the first generation in history to require little, often scarcely any, physical activity in our daily lives, we have therefore deliberately to introduce this ourselves, and commonly in an unhelpful environment. Manifestos by governments and the WHO underpin efforts to encourage people to become more active. A variety of health-promoting bodies such as, in England, Sustrans (promoting *sustainable transport*) and the National Heart Forum, work to change both personal behaviours and environmental factors that restrict activity. Complementary initiatives in medicine are evident: for example, in England the Department of Health initiated specialist training in Exercise and Sports Medicine, including an emphasis on disease prevention, in October 2005.

RECOMMENDATIONS FOR PHYSICAL ACTIVITY

Early in the twentieth century there was concern in the United Kingdom at the poor fitness of recruits to the armed services. As this impaired the country's capability to wage war, the government took action to improve the fitness of young people, introducing 'physical training' (PT as it was called) into schools. Nowadays, governments around the world instigate strategies to increase fitness and/or physical activity in their populations for a different reason – the benefits to personal and public health.

The development of recommendations on physical activity began in the middle of the twentieth century, when scientific interest in the biological effects of exercise and training gathered momentum. By the 1970s, this had generated a considerable literature about the type, intensity, frequency and duration of exercise needed to improve fitness – invariably interpreted as VO_2max. The first formal document was from the American College of Sports Medicine (ACSM) in their 'Position statement on the recommended quantity and quality of exercise for developing and maintaining fitness in healthy adults' (American College of Sports Medicine 1978). The recommendation was for 'continuous aerobic activity', 3–5 days per week at an intensity of 50–85% of VO_2max for 15–60 minutes per session. Both this position stand and the 1990 update (American College of Sports Medicine 1990) were soundly-based in that if most healthy adults followed their recommendations, they would improve personal fitness. Many people assumed, probably correctly, that this regimen would also lead to health benefits, but this was not the basis on which it was formulated.

The need to expand the 'exercise training-physical fitness' model to include a 'physical activity-health' model was addressed during the 1990s (Haskell 1994), leading to recommendations from several authorities, namely: the ACSM/US Centers for Disease Control and Prevention (Pate *et al.* 1995); the US National Institutes of Health Consensus Development Panel (1996); and the US Surgeon General's Report (US Department of Health and Human Services 1996). These recommendations had a strong influence on public health strategies and statements on physical activity in developed countries world-wide (e.g. US Healthy People 2010, UK Chief Medical Officer's Report in 2004 'At least five a week' and the 2005 National Physical Activity Guidelines for Adults, published by the Department of Health and Ageing in Australia). They differed in four important respects from earlier versions that were targeted at fitness improvements:

- by recognizing the benefit from 'moderate-intensity' activity;
- by asserting that multiple short spells of activity during a day are one way to fulfil the recommendations;
- by specifying a 'lifestyle' approach as an alternative to structured exercise;
- by emphasizing the need for 'frequent, preferably daily, activity'.

In 2007 updated recommendations for adults aged 18–65 were published jointly by the ACSM and the American Heart Association (Haskell *et al.* 2007). These largely confirmed the guidance included in the 1996 Surgeon General's Report, while placing greater emphasis on the possibility to combine moderate and vigorous activities and on the benefits from this. They also specified that aerobic activity is needed in addition to activities of daily living that are of light intensity, and that 'short' bouts of activity should last at least ten minutes.

The core recommendations from the 2007 statement are given in Box 13.1, alongside important differences in guidance for older adults, published in a companion paper by the same two authoritative bodies (Nelson *et al.* 2007).

There is concern that minimal compliance with the recommendations summarized in Box 13.1 may be insufficient to prevent the gradual transition in adulthood to overweight or obesity. For the prevention of unhealthy weight gain, Dietary Guidelines for Americans specify approximately 60 minutes of moderate-to-vigorous-intensity activity on most days of the week, while not exceeding energy intake requirements (US Department of Health and Human Services and US Department of Agriculture 2005). These guidelines, also adopted by the WHO, have their roots in earlier reports from the Institute of Medicine (2002) and the International Association for the Study of Obesity (Saris *et al.* 2003). To sustain weight loss in adults who were formerly overweight or obese, Dietary Guidelines for Americans recommend at least 60–90 minutes

---

BOX 13.1 US RECOMMENDATIONS FOR PHYSICAL ACTIVITY TO MAINTAIN AND IMPROVE THE HEALTH OF ADULTS 2007

- Adults aged 18–65 need moderate-intensity aerobic activity for a minimum of 30 minutes on five days each week or vigorous-intensity aerobic activity for a minimum of 20 minutes on three days each week.
- Combinations of moderate and vigorous activity can be performed because these are complementary in the production of health benefits.
- Moderate-intensity activities, generally equivalent to a brisk walk, can be accumulated toward the 30-minute minimum by performing bouts each lasting ten or more minutes.
- In addition, every adult should perform activities that maintain or increase muscular strength and muscular endurance on a minimum of two days each week.
- Further benefits (increased personal fitness, reduction of the risk for chronic diseases, avoidance of unhealthy weight gain) may be gained by exceeding the minimum recommendations.
- Differences in recommendations for older adults aged 65+ and for those aged 50–64 who are in receipt of regular medical care and treatment for a chronic condition or have functional limitations that limit movement are that:
  - Moderate intensity should be related to individual level of aerobic fitness.
  - Older adults should, in addition, undertake activities to maintain or increase flexibility and balance.
  - Activity plans should integrate preventive and therapeutic recommendations.

Sources: (Haskell *et al.* 2007) and (Nelson *et al.* 2007).

BOX 13.2 PHYSICAL ACTIVITY RECOMMENDATIONS FOR CHILDREN AND YOUNG PEOPLE

- Australia – at least 60 minutes of moderate-to-vigorous activity per day and not more than two hours per day using electronic media for entertainment.
- Canada – 90 minutes of moderate-to-vigorous activity per day, the equivalent of 16,500 steps.
- United States – at least 60 minutes of moderate activity most days of the week, preferably daily.
- United Kingdom – at least 60 minutes per day of at least moderate intensity and at least two session per week of activities that produce 'high physical stress'.

---

of daily moderate-intensity activity. In both instances, i.e. both for avoidance of weight gain and to sustain weight loss, the phrase 'while not exceeding caloric intake requirements' is added to the physical activity recommendation.

There is a consensus also that the recommendations for adults summarized in Box 13.1 are not sufficient for children and young people. Recommendations for those in the age range 5–18 are typically for 60 or more minutes of daily activity of at least moderate intensity. Examples from several different countries are given in Box 13.2.

Steps per day

Physical activity guidelines have been 'translated' into related indices based on pedometer readings of steps per day that approximate the associated energy expenditure. This approach, which reflects the notion that 'accumulating' activity is one valid way to achieve the recommended level of activity, has its origins in the Japanese walking clubs of more than 30 years ago. It is popular with the media because of the simplicity of the concept. For adults a target of 10,000 steps per day has been widely adopted as a reasonable estimate of an appropriate level of daily activity for apparently healthy adults. Studies are emerging that document the health benefits of attaining numbers of steps per day that approximate this target. The 10,000 target is, however, probably not sustainable for older adults or those whose capacities are constrained by chronic disease. On the other hand, this goal is probably too low for children; more suitable goals may

Table 13.2 Classification of pedometer-determined levels of physical activity in healthy adults

STEPS PER DAY	CLASSIFICATION
<5,000	Sedentary
5,000–7,499	Low active
7,500–9,999	Somewhat active
≥10,000	Active

Source: Based on Tudor-Locke and Bassett (2004)

Note: Individuals taking >12,500 steps/day are likely to be classified as 'highly active'.

be 15,000 steps per day and 12,000 steps per day for 5–12-year-olds. In Canada an even higher threshold of 16,500 steps per day is considered desirable for children and young people. Besides simplicity, the 'steps per day' approach facilitates objective assessment. It may be utilized to motivate individuals and as a tool for surveillance of changes of physical activity in population levels. Suggested cut-off points for classifying levels of activity according to recorded steps per day are shown in Table 13.2.

RATIONALE FOR RECOMMENDATIONS

The rationale for aspects of public health recommendations that differ from the older 'exercise–training–physical fitness' paradigm is explained briefly in the next section – and more comprehensively by Haskell *et al.* (2007).

Intensity – moderate to vigorous[1]

Intensity of exercise can be described both in *absolute* terms or *relative* to the capacity of the individual. In absolute terms, intensity is the rate of energy expenditure demanded by an activity, invariably estimated from the associated oxygen uptake; in relative terms, intensity is this oxygen uptake expressed as a percentage of the individual's maximum. This distinction is important because it is the relative intensity of activity that determines not only many of the favourable adaptations, but also some of the risks associated with physical activity. For practical reasons, large population studies have to measure and describe intensity in absolute terms. On the other hand, experimental studies invariably express intensity relative to each individual's capacity, making it difficult sometimes to reconcile evidence from these different sources.

In many epidemiological studies the type of physical activity associated with favourable health outcomes, for example, lower risk of all-cause or CVD mortality, incidence of type 2 diabetes and some cancers, has been of light-to-moderate intensity (Chapters 3, 4, 5 and 8 provide further discussion and main references). Recent studies with careful classification of self-reported physical activity have confirmed these findings. The amount and/or speed of walking – moderate-intensity exercise for most middle-aged people – has been specifically linked to the risk of each of these endpoints. Moreover, lower rates of CHD are consistently reported for people in the moderate category for physical activity or fitness than for those in the least active or least fit categories (Chapter 4).

Exercise training studies have found that moderate-intensity activity is sufficient to improve fitness in previously sedentary people (see section on walking) and benefit some health-related outcomes. For example, moderate exercise is at least as effective in reducing blood pressure as more vigorous exercise (Chapter 4); and low or moderate activity clearly improves some metabolic risk factors for CVD (Chapter 7).

Two other considerations underpin the decision to recommend moderate- – as well as vigorous- – intensity physical activity for previously sedentary individuals. First, the hazards of physical activity appear to be associated more with its intensity than with its frequency or duration (discussed in Chapter 12). Moreover, unaccustomed vigorous activity is particularly hazardous for sedentary people – the group specifically targeted by public health recommendations. Second, experience world-wide with earlier recommendations and campaigns have shown how difficult it is to alter the proportion of people engaging in vigorous exercise.

However, the few studies that have compared the benefits of different intensities of exercise while controlling for energy expenditure have rather consistently found greater benefits – at least in terms of protection against heart disease – from vigorous, rather than moderate, exercise (Swain and Franklin 2006). Thus, a continuum of cardioprotective benefit may exist from low to high exercise intensities, a finding that is also suggested by the relationships observed between the level of fitness and the incidence of heart disease. Evidence on this for other health outcomes is scant.

Accumulation

This principle assumes that multiple short periods of activity spread throughout the day will benefit health to the same extent as fewer, longer periods of equivalent energy expenditure.

Support for this view comes from the fact that much of the activity reported in epidemiological studies and found to be associated with favourable health outcomes was probably not undertaken in sessions of long duration. Examples include walking, stair climbing, gardening and household chores. There are few data to confirm the (probably fairly safe) assumption that most such activities are performed intermittently, but one report from the Harvard Alumni study provides some evidence. Between 1988 and 1993 participants reported the frequency and average duration of each episode of activity; researchers found that longer sessions did not have a different effect on risk than shorter sessions, as long as the total energy expended was similar (Lee and Paffenbarger 2000).

Experimental studies that have compared responses to contrasting patterns of activity of the same total duration are another source of data on the efficacy of accumulating activity. For example, in one classic study, previously inactive middle-aged men did 30 minutes of jogging per day, five days per week for eight weeks (DeBusk et al. 1990). One group did this in a single, 30-minute session per day, while a second group did three ten-minute sessions per day (no control group). Both patterns of activity led to an increase in VO$_2$max and weight loss was similar in both groups. Another study, this one randomly controlled, allocated middle-aged women to train by brisk walking in either one 30-minute session or three ten-minute sessions per day (Murphy and Hardman 1998). Fitness improvements were similar in each walking group (relative to controls who remained sedentary) and three ten-minute sessions were at least as effective in decreasing body fatness as one long bout (Table 13.3). A subsequent study found that three ten-minute sessions per day of brisk walking resulted in similar increases in high-density lipoprotein (HDL)-cholesterol and similar decreases in total cholesterol and triglycerides as one 30-minute session (Murphy et al. 2002).

If the principle that it is total energy expenditure that mainly determines benefits to health-related outcomes is correct, then it should be possible to 'trade' intensity for duration. We can be fairly confident that this is true for weight control because reviews and meta-analyses have consistently found that it is the total energy expended in physical activity or exercise that determines its influence on body weight or fatness

Table 13.3 Changes with different patterns of brisk walking in previously sedentary, middle-aged women

	CONTROLS $n=10$	THREE TEN-MINUTE SESSIONS, $n=12$	ONE 30-MINUTE SESSION, $n=12$
Body mass, kg	+0.6 (0.7)	−1.7 (1.7)*	−0.9 (2.0)
Sum of four skinfold thicknesses, mm	+2.6 (2.8)	−3.3 (3.5)*	−2.8 (3.8)*
Waist circumference, cm	+0.6 (1.0)	−3.0 (2.4)*	−1.8 (2.4)
Systolic blood pressure, mm Hg	−2.0 (6.9)	−7.4 (7.3)	−4.6 (5.9)
$\dot{V}O_2$max, ml kg^{-1} min^{-1}	−0.5 (0.1)	+2.3 (0.1)*	+2.4 (0.1)*

Source: Murphy and Hardman (1998).

Note: Values are mean (standard deviation). *Change from baseline significantly different from change in controls, $P<0.05$. Training was either one 30-minute session per day or three ten-minute sessions per day, five days per week for ten weeks. Comparisons are with controls who remained sedentary.

(Chapter 6). A few studies have specifically compared the effects on a health outcome of exercise sessions that differ in intensity, but expend the same energy. In one, described in more detail in Chapter 7, researchers found that the postprandial triglyceride response was decreased by the same amount after either 90 minutes of exercise at 60% $\dot{V}O_2$max or after 180 minutes at 30% $\dot{V}O_2$max (Figure 7.8). Similarly, in a study of women with type 2 diabetes, insulin sensitivity was enhanced to the same degree after a longer session of exercise at 50% $\dot{V}O_2$max or a shorter session at 75% $\dot{V}O_2$max of equivalent energy expenditure (Braun *et al.* 1995). Thus, at least for these two outcomes, there is some evidence that intensity *can* be traded for duration.

However, given the prominence afforded in public health recommendations to the efficacy of accumulating physical activity throughout the day, research on this topic is still inadequate: the total number of subjects in studies comparing short with longer bouts of activity is small; information on the effects of sessions of activity shorter than 8–10 minutes is lacking, so the most recent recommendations (referred to above) stipulate that ten minutes should be the minimum duration of a 'short' bout; few studies have compared the effects of longer bouts of moderate activity with those of shorter bouts of more vigorous activity; and a rather small number of health-related outcomes have been studied.

Lifestyle activity

There is overlap here with topics discussed earlier as many so-called 'lifestyle' activities are of moderate intensity and undertaken intermittently. These are self-selected occupational or household activities or activities involved in 'getting about' (e.g. stair climbing) engaged in as part of a daily routine and are invariably of moderate intensity. Observational and prospective epidemiological studies have linked such activities to health benefits, although there are few intervention trials.

In one two-year randomized (but not controlled) trial, called Project Active, researchers compared the effects of increased lifestyle activities with those of a traditional structured exercise programme (Dunn *et al.* 1999): changes in fitness, body fatness and several risk factors for CVD were measured in 235 healthy, slightly over-weight men and women aged 35–60. Estimated energy expenditure increased by a similar amount in both groups. Although the structured exercise group showed a greater improvement in fitness after six months, they failed to maintain this advantage and, by 24 months, there was no significant difference between groups in the increase in $\dot{V}O_2$max (mean values: lifestyle $0.77\,ml\,kg^{-1}\,min^{-1}$; structured $1.34\,ml\,kg^{-1}\,min^{-1}$). Both groups experienced similar (small) decreases in body fatness and blood pressure. This study and a few others (several of overweight or obese individuals) provide support for the proposition that increases in lifestyle activities lead to favourable changes in health-related outcomes. An important limitation to this literature, however, is the lack of randomized trials that include a control group.

Frequent, almost daily, activity

Physical activity does not need to result in a training effect to elicit a health benefit – although benefits may be enhanced when it does. Some health-related changes are due largely to acute biological responses that persist for some time following each session. For example, blood pressure is decreased for up to 12 hours after an exercise session, and plasma triglyceride concentrations are reduced for even longer after a session of aerobic exercise. Of course, for such changes to decrease disease risk, people need to be physically active on an almost daily basis. This is well illustrated by 'de-training' studies. At least two beneficial metabolic characteristics (low postprandial triglycerides, good insulin sensitivity) have been shown to deteriorate rapidly when the habit of exercise is interrupted (Figure 13.1).

Figure 13.1 (a) Changes in fasting and postprandial plasma concentrations of triglyceride in ten endurance-trained athletes during a 6.5-day interruption to training (mean and standard error); and (b) changes in insulin sensitivity in nine moderately trained men and women during a seven-day interruption to training (mean and standard deviation).

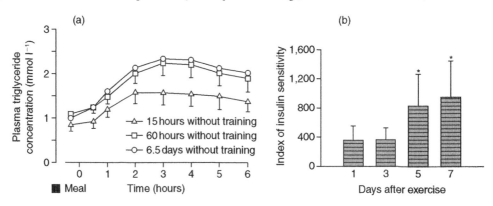

Sources: Hardman *et al.* (1998) and King *et al.* (1995).
Notes: (a) A high-fat mixed meal was completed at time 0 h. The area under the plasma triglyceride x time curve was 45% lower at 15 h than at 60 h ($P<0.05$); (b) insulin sensitivity measured as the product of insulin and glucose areas under concentration versus time curves (low values indicate good sensitivity). *Significantly different from one and three days after interruption to training.

Two small studies are especially relevant because they have looked at the acute effects of several short sessions of brisk walking (a lifestyle activity of moderate intensity) accumulated throughout the day. In the first, plasma triglycerides were measured in ten middle-aged overweight people over three separate days during which they ate three ordinary meals (Murphy *et al.* 2000). During one trial, subjects sat down all day (control); during another they walked for 30 minutes before breakfast; and during the other they walked for ten minutes before each of the three meals. Both patterns of brisk walking decreased triglycerides by a similar amount (Figure 13.2). In the second study, changes in ambulatory blood pressure after four ten-minute walks were compared with changes after one 40-minute walk in 21 healthy but pre-hypertensive people (Park *et al.* 2006). Both systolic and diastolic pressures were reduced for longer after multiple short bouts of walking (11 hours) than after the single longer bout (seven hours). Thus, it is not only long, continuous episodes of activity which result in acute biological changes – accumulating activity throughout the day is effective too.

Acute responses to bouts of exercise are likely to be augmented when a person's fitness improves because the absolute intensity of exercise that can be sustained during a session is increased. This will hold for any benefit determined by the magnitude of the energy expended during an exercise session. Thus there is an interaction between the acute and chronic (training) effects in this regard.

Figure 13.2 Effect of 30 minutes of brisk walking on plasma triglyceride concentrations throughout the day.

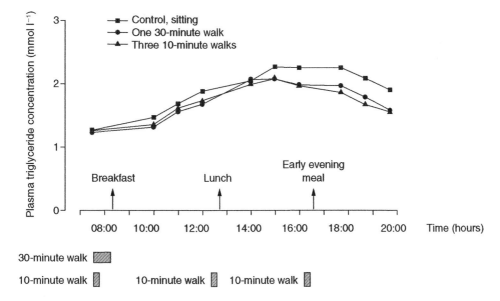

Source: Adapted from Murphy *et al.* (2000).
Notes: Ten subjects aged 34–66 each undertook three trials: control (sitting down all day); one 30-minute walk before breakfast; and three ten-minute walks, one before each meal. Plasma triglycerides were significantly lower than control with each pattern of walking.

Muscular strength and endurance

Activities that increase muscular strength and endurance in non-elderly people promote musculoskeletal health benefits. In particular, mechanical loading by resistance exercise stimulates an increase in bone formation in young adults and slows bone loss in middle-age. These effects will be expected to confer a lower risk for osteopenia, osteoporosis and bone fracture. Moreover, activities that increase muscular strength promote the development and maintenance of metabolically active lean muscle mass, helping to maintain insulin sensitivity. Muscle-strengthening activities can help older individuals to continue to live independently and, alongside balance exercises, decrease the risk for falls (Chapters 9 and 11).

Overall evaluation of the basis for newer aspects of physical activity recommendations

Despite the evidence described in the previous section, dose–response relationships with physical activity are still poorly described for many health outcomes. The need for more research is still clear despite increased interest in this topic over recent years. However, the evidence that physical activity benefits health is irrefutable and concerns about the inadequacy of information on dose–response should be viewed in the context of this certainty.

The process of refining evidence-based recommendations is on-going as dose–response relationships are better described. For example, the US Department of Health and Human Services published the first federal Physical Activity Guidelines for Americans in late 2008. Future recommendations may be expected to increasingly reflect evidence specific to particular diseases. For example, changes to bone mineral density relate to the level of strain to which bone is exposed during activity rather than to the energy expended. Public health recommendations can never reflect all these complexities, however, and so individuals (or those who counsel them) will always have to interpret recommendations in relation to personal needs, priorities and physical capabilities.

Finally, as the Canadian HERITAGE Family Study has shown, individual responses to a given amount and/or type of activity are heterogeneous (this study is investigating the heritable component of the heterogenicity in the responses to exercise). People will get different 'rewards' for their investment in activity. Changes in fitness, HDL-cholesterol and blood pressure have all been found to vary greatly among more than 700 participants, despite a carefully standardized 20-week training programme. This variation tended to cluster in families and so must reflect a degree of genetic predisposition and/or gene–environment interactions. For further discussion of this topic the reader is referred to Rankinen and Bouchard (2007).

The relative importance of physical activity versus physical fitness for health benefits has been widely debated. As the level and intensity of activity is one determinant of fitness and the indices used to measure these parameters have different attributes, this is not always helpful. However, the emphasis on moderate-intensity exercise in current recommendations has been widely interpreted to mean that physical activity is the only goal and that fitness does not matter. This is wrong: it does matter. Fitness enables an individual to expend more energy and to sustain a higher rate of energy expenditure without becoming fatigued. This, in turn, helps weight regulation, enhances the acute biological responses to each session of activity and opens up a wide choice of leisure-time pursuits. A given task (e.g. shovelling snow, playing football with children) demands a lower proportion of $\dot{V}O_2$max for a fit person, so he/she can do it with something in reserve.

CHANGING PHYSICAL ACTIVITY BEHAVIOURS

Researchers world-wide are addressing the question 'What works to improve physical activity levels in a population?' but the answer is far from clear. A wide range of different interventions is documented. More information is needed concerning the uptake, sustainability and cost-effectiveness of physical activity associated with particular interventions, and how widely these could be disseminated. Moreover, a 'one-size fits all' approach is not likely to succeed – interventions need to be adapted to different cultures.

Physical activity and exercise take place in different settings, namely: in or around the home, at work, in commuting/transportation and of course in active leisure. Interventions can target any or all of these, in the population at large or in subgroups such as children, the elderly or patient groups. They vary enormously, from educational materials and self-help materials to changes to organizations and the physical environment.

Structured programmes

Structured exercise programmes usually involve exercise at a rather high intensity, say 60–70% $\dot{V}O_2$max, and require frequent attendance at an exercise facility such as a gymnasium over a number of weeks or months. Sessions are generally supervised, and this may help previously sedentary people to avoid injury or other adverse events. It may also help them to appreciate the need to start gently, progress gradually and to incorporate different modes of activity – stretching, aerobic activity and muscle strengthening. Adherence to structured interventions has been reported to be good, with at least 80% of participants completing the programme. Moreover, these programmes appear to motivate people to be more active outside the structured activity; for example, they may do more walking, even on the days they attend an exercise class. Structured exercise programmes clearly lead to increased physical activity and improved fitness in those who participate. On the other hand, their effectiveness at a population level is limited because only a small proportion of the sedentary population enrol, i.e. those who have already reached a decision to become more active.

Interventions with unstructured activity

Interventions based on integrating more physical activity into daily life reflect recommendations for at least moderate-intensity activity on an almost daily basis. They aim to heighten awareness of the many and varied opportunities for activity that suit individual preferences. Research literature shows that such interventions can be as effective as structured programmes in increasing fitness, energy expenditure and in modifying heart disease risk factors. They are most successful when home-based participants receive training (including behavioural skills) and follow-up. It is likely that adherence is not as good as that reported for structured programmes, but this may simply reflect the difference in the type of people who enrol.

Interventions that specifically promote walking have been extensively studied because of the popularity and accessibility of this activity and its suitability for the most sedentary. Nearly 50 trials (randomized and non-randomized) including advice to individuals, group-based and community-level approaches, as well as a number based on walking as a means of transport, have been reviewed (Ogilvie *et al.* 2007). There is clear evidence that people can be encouraged to walk more by interventions tailored to their needs, targeted at the most sedentary or at those most motivated to change and delivered either at the level of the individual, household or group. The most successful increased walking amongst target groups by some 30–60 minutes per week.

The availability of inexpensive pedometers means that individuals can monitor their levels of walking and use feedback to reinforce this behaviour change. Thirty minutes of moderate-intensity activity per day are likely to be achieved with 8,000 steps daily (Table 13.2).

Children and young people

Interventions targeted at children and adolescents appear an attractive way to increase activity levels before sedentary behaviours become entrenched. However, simply increasing school physical education classes does not increase activity sufficiently to meet recommended thresholds. At least in adolescents, effective interventions generally have many components and are undertaken in multiple settings (school, home and community), facilitating physical activity by providing opportunities and a supportive environment (van Sluijs *et al.* 2007). Promoting active commuting to and from school is one intervention with great potential to increase activity generally. In the United Kingdom for example, about 20% of all car journeys during the weekday morning rush hour are short and undertaken by parents taking children to school. Thus, creating environments that support safe local walking and cycling is a pre-requisite if more children (and parents) are to make these frequent, short journeys without the use of a car.

Role of physicians in promoting physical activity and exercise

Physical activity has long been considered by doctors to be important in the management of patients suffering from a variety of conditions – for example, cardiovascular and respiratory diseases and osteoarthritis of the knee. However, despite clear evidence that exercise helps people to make the most of functional capacities that are limited by their disease – and in some instances decreases the risk of further manifestations – compliance with such programmes is generally poor (Kujala 2004). A detailed discussion of this topic is beyond the scope of this book and the interested reader is referred to Durstine and Moore (2002) and Pedersen and Saltin (2006).

The potential for primary care physicians to counsel sedentary, but apparently healthy, people to increase physical activity is increasingly recognized. A number of randomly controlled trials (advice from a physician versus no advice) have found counselling is effective, at least over 6–12 months. Physicians can give advice themselves, offer educational materials delivered by an ever-increasing range of media and/or refer patients to exercise specialists. The efficacy of these (probably complementary) approaches is a topic of continuing research interest, although there is still little information about longer-term effects on patients' physical activity levels. Trials in the United Kingdom have shown that a variety of interventions, including exercise referral schemes, motivational interviewing and introducing sedentary patients to more active 'peer mentors' can all be effective, particularly among people initially classed as sedentary or minimally active.

The initiative 'Exercise is Medicine' was launched in 2007 by the American College of Sports Medicine and the American Medical Association in an attempt to make physical activity a standard component of disease prevention. A specific goal is to encourage all physicians 'to assess, to advocate for, and to review every patient's physical activity program during every comprehensive visit'. A web site provides physicians, health and fitness professionals, policy makers, the media and the public with every kind of educational and practical resource to support the initiative (Exercise is Medicine 2007). Physicians are encouraged to sign up to the policy and the public are encouraged to put pressure on their physicians to do so. The range of supporting organizations is vast and bodes well for the success of this initiative.

EXAMPLES OF GOOD PRACTICE IN PUBLIC HEALTH

Lifestyle activity is strongly influenced by the built environment. For instance, the more attractive and 'walkable' streets and parks are, the higher the levels of walking (Owen *et al.* 2007). Policies and legislation can therefore help to sustain increases in physical activity for personal transport at a population level. Several examples are described briefly below.

The Danish government has introduced legislation requiring that every child has a safe route to school. If there is no such route, free bus transport must be provided, giving authorities a financial incentive to invest in safe routes. As a consequence, some 50% of Danish children walk or cycle to school (compared with 2% in Great Britain) and this has been achieved alongside a reduction in the accident rate.

Increasingly, regulations governing urban design and land use specify that plans should facilitate walking, cycling and public transport to minimize dominance by the car. These sorts of changes may influence activity levels, even in people who have no conscious intention to become more active. For example, in the Netherlands motorized traffic entering 6,500 residential zones or 'Woonerf' is restricted to a speed of 'walking pace'. These areas typically combine shared walking/cycling/driving surfaces and use trees, planters and children's play areas to create a street space so unlike a traditional street that vehicle speeds are markedly reduced by the instinctive, behavioural change in drivers. Moreover, under the unique Dutch legal system, motorists must yield to cyclists unless there are special road markings and are held automatically to be responsible in collisions with cyclists, regardless of the circumstances of an accident.

With the aim of making Paris a quieter place, with less pollution and where people 'take up more of the space', the city has vigorously encouraged bicycling through a variety of schemes. It now boasts some 370 km of bike paths, and bicycle use increased by 48% between 2001 and 2007. Accident rates remained stable despite this big increase. It seems that, with more cyclists on the road, they are more visible to other road users who have become more used to their presence. The initiative 'Paris Breathes' permits, on Sundays and Bank Holidays, pedestrians, cyclists and people on roller blades to benefit from the closure of many roads to cars. 'Paris Rando Vélo' organizes free guided trips by bicycle around the city. The boldest scheme – 'Vélib' (from vélo, a bicycle and libre, free) – was launched on 15 July 2007. By the end of 2007, Paris had 20,600 low-cost rental bicycles at 1,451 stations, with a station every 300 m or so! Users pick up a bicycle from any station, returning it to any other. The first 30 minutes of use is free, with a charge of €1 for each subsequent 30-minute period. Regular users can pay a subscription for a week or a year, but can expect to ride them almost for free because the duration of 96% of journeys is less than 30 minutes.

Actions by businesses and organizations can also promote active living. For example, in one intervention, installing locker rooms led to an increase in the number of employees walking or cycling to work. Simple changes within buildings, such as clear signing of staircases, can increase daily activity.

WALKING: 'THE NEAREST TO PERFECT EXERCISE' (Morris and Hardman 1997)

Walking is cheap, safe, popular and sociable[2] and can take place in all sorts of environments, urban and rural. It is the obvious starting point for previously sedentary people.

At a 'normal/ordinary' pace, say (4.8 km h^{-1} or 3 mile h^{-1}) on level ground, walking increases the metabolic rate more than three-fold, demanding about 3.5 METs. At a 'brisk' pace of around 5.6 km h^{-1} (3.5 mile h^{-1}), this rises to 3.8 METs. Such brisk walking constitutes light activity for the average young person, but moderate or even vigorous activity for those with lower functional capacities, such as the elderly (Figure 13.3). Notice that Figure 13.3 expresses the intensity of exercise relative to $\dot{V}O_2$max reserve, i.e. capacity above the resting metabolic rate of 1 MET (see Chapter 2), as well as to $\dot{V}O_2$max. For people with very low $\dot{V}O_2$max values, such as patients with cardiac or respiratory problems, this distinction is important as there is little capability to increase oxygen uptake above the resting level. For such individuals brisk – or even normal-paced – walking constitutes vigorous exercise.

When asked to walk 'briskly', inactive middle-aged men and women typically select a pace that elicits nearly 60% $\dot{V}O_2$max and thus sufficient to improve their fitness. It is therefore not surprising that regular brisk or fast walking has been found to improve fitness in controlled trials in both men and women of this age group. Based on meta-analysis of intervention studies with a mean length of 35 weeks, the average increase is typically 9%, for subjects with initial $\dot{V}O_2$max values around 30 ml kg^{-1} min^{-1} (Murphy et al. 2007). Such increases, although modest, are consistent with meaningful reductions to the risk of CVD morbidity and mortality (see Chapter 4).

Walking (amount and/or usual pace) has been specifically studied in observational and prospective studies and shown to be independently associated with a lower risk of

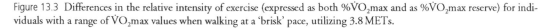

Figure 13.3 Differences in the relative intensity of exercise (expressed as both %$\dot{V}O_2$max and as %$\dot{V}O_2$max reserve) for individuals with a range of $\dot{V}O_2$max values when walking at a 'brisk' pace, utilizing 3.8 METs.

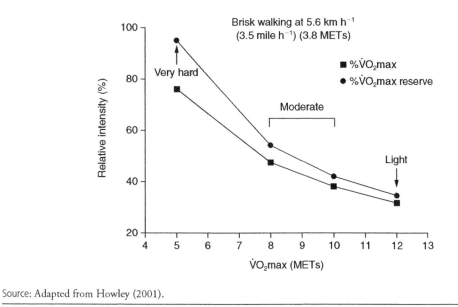

Source: Adapted from Howley (2001).

all-cause mortality, CHD/CVD, ischemic stroke, type 2 diabetes, cognitive decline and weight gain (on average, the risk of CHD is 30–40% lower for individuals who walk briskly at least half an hour per day compared with sedentary individuals). Some analyses of walking behaviour are comprehensive, particularly among cohorts of women. For example, the Women's Health Initiative Observational Study (Manson *et al.* 2002) found that both amount and pace of walking were strongly related to the risk of a cardiovascular event (Figure 13.4).

The increasing age of the population, one of three important modern trends identified in Chapter 1, makes research on the risk factors for diminished cognitive function essential. Cohort studies of people in their 70s have reported that regular walking is associated with better cognitive function and less cognitive decline in women (Weuve *et al.* 2004) and with a lower risk of developing dementia in men (Abbott *et al.* 2004). Associations between walking and opportunities for walking are relevant to another modern trend, the epidemic of obesity. People are more likely to be overweight or obese if they live in less 'walkable' areas (Giles-Corti *et al.* 2003). In a travel survey of 10,878 participants in Atlanta, each additional kilometre walked per day was associated with a 4.8% reduction in the likelihood of obesity (Frank *et al.* 2004). This observational evidence fits with findings from intervention studies that regular walking for exercise decreases body weight and/or adiposity (or avoids increases seen in controls).

In a number of surveys, regular walking has been associated with a lower risk of hip fracture in women. Potential explanations include an osteogenic effect and/or improvements in strength and balance that reduce the risk of falling (see Chapters 9 and 11). While walking does not elicit an *optimal* osteogenic response, if brisk or fast it can stimulate activity in the lower limb skeleton through alterations to the direction and

Figure 13.4 Effect of volume (a) and pace (b) of walking on the relative risk of CVD among postmenopausal women in the US Women's Health Initiative Observational Study.

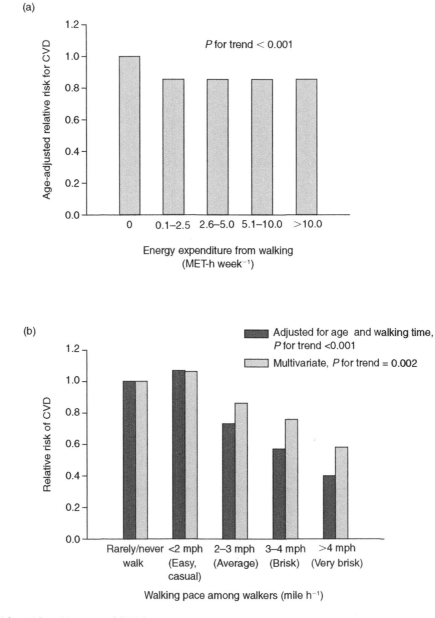

Source: Adapted from Manson *et al.* (2002).
Note: 10 MET-h is equivalent to walking for 3 h 20 min at an 'ordinary' pace of 4.8 km h^{-1} (3 mile h^{-1}).

BOX 13.3 WALKING AND PUBLIC HEALTH – IMPLICATIONS FOR PREVENTION

- Adding three hours of walking per week to all participants in the US Health Professionals Follow-up Study suggests that this would lead to a 17% decrease in colon cancer (Colditz *et al.* 1997).
- In the Honolulu Heart Study of Japanese men aged 61–81, for every five men who walked at least 2 miles a day, one fewer died over 12 years, compared with those who walked less than 1 mile per day (Hakim *et al.* 1998). A walking group that includes 60 men in this age group may therefore be expected to save one life each year.
- In a prospective study of nearly 3,000 diabetics in the United States, walking half an hour per day was associated with a 50% lower risk of cardiovascular and total mortality. Researchers estimated that '1 death per year may be preventable for every 61 people who could be persuaded to walk at least 2 h per week.' (Gregg *et al.* 2003).

---

rate of loading that increase ground and hip reaction forces. Controlled trials have found either no effect of brisk or fast walking on BMD at the lumbar spine or just a small benefit in postmenopausal women. However, even a small difference in BMD can reduce the propensity to fracture. Moreover, older women enjoy walking and compliance can be excellent. For example, one large trial ($n = 78$) reported 91% adherence among women aged 60–70 during the first year of the intervention and 94% during the follow-up year (Brooke-Wavell *et al.* 2001).

Even as planned exercise with the goal to improve fitness, walking is very injury-free. For example, as mentioned in Chapter 12, among participants in the Aerobics Center Study, the prevalence of injuries in walkers was similar to that in sedentary people (Hootman *et al.* 2002). Moreover, increased duration of walking for exercise did not increase the risk of injury. These findings are important because fear of sustaining an injury and stopping activity because of an injury have both been associated with failure to start or maintain a physically active lifestyle. Furthermore, because walking constitutes light- or moderate-intensity activity for so many people, it carries little risk for sudden cardiovascular events.

Promoting walking for health offers an opportunity to shift the population distribution of levels of physical activity. The potential benefits for public health that may be expected through increased levels of walking are illustrated in Box 13.3.

PHYSICALLY ACTIVE COMMUTING

One reason walking and cycling for personal transportation can be health-enhancing is because these activities are regular and performed on a near-daily basis. Commuting to work by walking and cycling has been studied, particularly in Finland. Meta-analytic review of eight prospective cohort and case-control studies of physically active commuting concluded that this was associated with an 11% reduction in cardiovascular risk (Hamer and Chida 2007). Other health-related outcomes reported to be associated with a lower risk in people with a habit of active commuting include certain cancers (Hou *et al.* 2004; Matthews *et al.* 2005) and all-cause mortality (Matthews *et al.* 2007).

The potential to increase walking and cycling for short journeys (as opposed to active leisure) is considerable. In Britain in 2003, 58% of people surveyed stated that they currently use a car to make journeys within walking or cycling distance (Department of Transport 2003).

BENEFITS VERSUS RISKS

As discussed in Chapter 12, physical activity can be hazardous as well as beneficial. The risk–benefit ratio of exercise is therefore an important concern for public health, as well as for the individual (for whom it will be modified by pre-existing medical conditions) because interventions need to provide guidance on how to maximize benefits and minimize risks.

Cardiovascular events

Some risk–benefit analysis is available for cardiac events (Thompson *et al.* 2007). As discussed in Chapter 12, vigorous exercise is associated with a transient increase in the risk of a cardiovascular event during or soon after exertion. Nevertheless, no evidence suggests that the risks of physical activity outweigh the benefits for healthy people. Indeed, the converse is true; epidemiological, scientific and clinical evidence shows that habitual activity decreases the risk of cardiovascular events over time.

The reader will recall that the increase in risk associated with exertion varies greatly according to the level of habitual activity and a disproportionate number of cardiac events occur in sedentary people performing unaccustomed, vigorous activity. For example, in a study, the relative risk of cardiac arrest was greater during exercise than at rest for all levels of habitual activity (Siscovick *et al.* 1984). However, the overall risk of the physically active men, that is, during and not during vigorous exercise, was only 40% of that of the sedentary men.[3] The transient increase in the risk of a cardiac event associated with a single session of exercise was clearly outweighed by the long-term benefit.

Thus, one of the most important defences against exercise-related cardiac events is to acquire and maintain physical fitness through regular physical activity, and the single most important public health strategy must be to encourage a high level of physical activity in the population. To minimize cardiovascular risk, this must emphasize the need for sedentary people to begin with low/moderate-intensity activity, progressing only gradually to longer-duration, high-intensity activity if they seek greater benefits.

As well as recommending prudent exercise programmes, other strategies to reduce cardiovascular events include: preparing fitness personnel and facilities to identify and deal with cardiovascular emergencies; increasing health care professionals' knowledge of pathological conditions that may increase risk; and educating physically active adults to recognize symptoms that may be indicative of cardiac disease.

Another potential strategy is to screen individuals before they participate in sports or programmes of exercise. This would reduce exercise-related cardiac events by restricting vigorous exercise among high-risk individuals. For adults with known CVD, screening through exercise testing is clearly advisable, but the value of exercise testing in asymptomatic adults is uncertain. Consensus statements from the American College of Sports Medicine and the American College of Cardiology/American Heart Association propose that only individuals who appear to be at greater risk (because they have two or more risk factors or because they are diabetic) should be considered for exercise testing before beginning a vigorous exercise programme (defined as ≥60% VO_2max reserve). On the other hand, the US Preventive Services Task Force states that insufficient evidence exists to determine the benefits and harm from exercise testing before exercise programmes.

For young athletes, practices vary (the issue here is that, in contrast to adults in whom vigorous exercise appears to reduce the overall risk of CHD, exercise in young subjects with hidden CVD may increase both exercise- and non-exercise-related sudden death). The European Society of Cardiology recommends that routine ECGs be obtained for all athletes as part of a comprehensive pre-participation evaluation. This is based largely on an Italian observational study among athletes 12–35 years old that found that the introduction of screening was associated with a nearly 90% decrease in the annual incidence of sudden death. The American Heart Association, while recommending cardiovascular pre-participation screening for high school and college athletes and at 2–4-year intervals subsequently, does not advocate routine testing by ECG. In the United Kingdom, there is provision for elite athletes with relevant family history or who have experienced symptoms to be screened at the Olympic Medical Institute, but there are no recommendations from authoritative bodies for widespread screening. Reasons for not instigating widespread screening for young athletes include the low incidence of cardiac events in this group, cost–benefit issues and concerns about the problem of 'false positives'.

Injuries

Unfortunately, little useful risk–benefit analysis is available for musculoskeletal and other injuries. This is a cause for concern because their prevalence will increase if the population becomes more active and more provision for treatment will be required. Injury avoidance may be particularly important for old people, for whom the consequences of a fall may be catastrophic.

Pharmacological interventions carry risks too

Finally, physical activity is not the only intervention aiming to benefit health that carries risks. Drugs have side effects too, ranging from the discomforting to the life-threatening. Their packaging therefore carries instructions on how to optimize effectiveness and minimize risks – rather like physical activity recommendations. In some circumstances, physical activity may be as (or more) effective than a drug in decreasing disease risk and it may incur fewer side effects. For example, the Diabetes Prevention Program Group trial compared physical activity and Metformin as means to prevent the development of type 2 diabetes in people with impaired glucose tolerance (Diabetes Prevention Program Research Group 2002). Subjects allocated to the drug therapy group were more likely not only to develop type 2 diabetes but also to experience a high incidence of gastrointestinal disturbances (a side effect of the drug) than those in the lifestyle intervention group.

A 'BEST BUY IN PUBLIC HEALTH'? (Morris 1994)

Physical inactivity confers an enormous economic burden, world-wide. The associated direct medical costs (hospital care, drugs, physician care, etc.) have been estimated as £1.06 billion in the United Kingdom in 2002 and US$75 billion in the United States in 2000, some 3–6% of total health care costs. Indirect costs, i.e. the value of economic input lost because of illness, injury-related work disability or premature death, inflate these figures still further. Thus, substantial economic benefit may be expected if the prevalence of physical inactivity can be decreased. Some examples are presented in Box 13.4.

BOX 13.4 ECONOMIC BENEFITS FROM INCREASING LEVELS OF PHYSICAL ACTIVITY

- Data from the United States show that workplace physical activity programmes can reduce short-term sick-leave (by 6–32%), health care costs (by 20–55%) and increase productivity (by 2–52%).
- In Australia (based on only three diseases, i.e. CHD, type 2 diabetes and colon cancer), gross savings of US$3.6 million per annum in health care costs could be achieved for every 1% gain in the proportion of the population who are sufficiently active.
- Reducing the sedentary proportion of the population in Northern Ireland from 20% to 15% would, by saving at least 121 lives per year, lead to economic benefit of £131 million and savings to the health services of £0.62 million annually.
- Based on a reduced incidence of CHD, stroke and colon cancer, a 5% increase in physically active individuals in Scotland (achieved over a five-year period) would avert 157 deaths, with an estimated saving to the NHS of approximately £3.5 million over this period. It would also lead to a 7% reduction in days lost from sickness, generating a substantial increase in productivity, output and employment.

These data on health economics are compelling but, as a justification for the promotion of physical activity, they are neither necessary nor sufficient. Low fitness and physical inactivity are a waste of human potential, at the population level as well as at a personal level. For these reasons alone, physical activity should be widely and enthusiastically promoted.

SUMMARY

- Non-communicable diseases are a major and increasing public health burden, in developing countries as well as those with established market economies. Increasing physical activity levels would have an important impact on the incidence of these diseases.
- Adults need moderate-intensity aerobic activity for a minimum of 30 minutes on five days each week, or vigorous-intensity aerobic activity for a minimum of 20 minutes on three days each week. Children need more activity, of the order of 60 minutes most days of the week.
- Exercise programmes (structured and unstructured) are effective, but changes to the built environment to facilitate walking and cycling may have more impact at a population level.
- Physical activity has some adverse side effects, but these are mainly avoided if the intensity of activity is moderate. Overall, for the majority of individuals, benefits outweigh risks.
- Brisk or fast walking will improve fitness in most middle-aged and older men and in almost all adult women. Walking for exercise is very injury-free.
- The promotion of physical activity may lead to economic benefits.

STUDY TASKS

1 Provide a reasoned argument for promoting activity of a moderate, rather than vigorous, intensity in the general population.
2 Explain why walking can be light or vigorous activity for different individuals, giving illustrative examples.
3 It is asserted that one way to meet physical activity recommendations is to accumulate short bouts throughout the day. Do you think the available evidence is sufficient in quantity and quality to justify this assertion? Give full reasons for your point of view.
4 Explain why there is so much research interest in the dose–response relationships between physical activity and health outcomes.
5 Identify and discuss the relative strengths of potential strategies to improve public health through increasing physical activity.

NOTES

1 Moderate – absolute intensity 3–6 METs, relative intensity 40–60% $\dot{V}O_2$max: vigorous ≥6 METs, relative intensity >60% $\dot{V}O_2$max.
2 Dogs are good companions as well as people – in one Australian study 23% of all walking was dog walking! Moreover, dog owners are much more likely than non-owners to be sufficiently active.
3 The media appreciate the relative risk (e.g. five-fold, 56-fold) but, in reporting sudden exercise-related deaths, do not explain to their readership that the absolute risk of a cardiac event during exercise is very low (Chapter 12).

FURTHER READING

Biddle, S.J.H. and Mutrie, N. (2008) *Psychology of Physical Activity: Determinants, Well-being and Interventions,* 2nd edn, London: Routledge.

Blair, S.N., LaMonte, M.J. and Nichaman, M.Z. (2004) 'The evolution of physical activity recommendations: how much is enough?', *American Journal of Clinical Nutrition* 79: S913–20.

Exercise is Medicine (2007) A programme launched by the American College of Sports Medicine and the American Heart Association. Online, available at: www.exerciseismedicine.org.

Frank, L.D., Saelens, B.E., Powell, K.E. and Chapman, J.E. (2007) 'Stepping towards causation: do built environments or neighborhood and travel preferences explain physical activity, driving, and obesity?', *Social Science and Medicine* 65: 1898–914.

Haskell, W.L. (2006) 'Dose–response issues in physical activity, fitness, and health', in C. Bouchard, S.N. Blair and W.L. Haskell (eds) *Physical Activity and Health,* Champaign: Human Kinetics, pp. 303–17.

Haskell, W.L., Lee, I.-M., Pate, R.R., Powell, K.E., Blair, S.N., Franklin, B.A., Macera, C.A., Heath, G.W., Thompson, P.D., and Bauman, A. (2007) 'Physical activity and public health: updated recommendation for adults from the American College of Sports Medicine and the American Heart Association', *Medicine and Science in Sports and Exercise* 39: 1423–34.

Health Canada and the US Centers for Disease Control and Prevention (2001) 'Collection of papers from a symposium organized by "Dose–response issues concerning physical activity and health: an evidence-based symposium"', *Medicine and Science in Sports and Exercise* 33 (6) Supplement.

Nelson, M.E., Haskell, W.L, and Kennedy, M. (2008) 'The birth of physical activity guidelines for Americans', *Journal of Physical Activity and Health* 5: 485–7.

Ogilivie, D., Foster, C.E., Rothnie, H., Cavill, N., Hamilton, V., Fitzimons, C.F., Mutrie, N. on behalf of the Scottish Physical Activity Research Collaboration (2007) 'Interventions to promote walking: systematic review', *British Medical Journal* 334: 1204–14.

Swain, D.P. and Franklin, B.A. (2006) 'Comparison of cardioprotective benefits of vigorous versus moderate intensity aerobic exercise', *American Journal of Cardiology* 97: 141–7.

United States Department of Health and Human Services (2008) 'Physical activity guidelines fors Americans'. Online, available at http://www.health.gov/paguidelines

Glossary

Abdominal fat   Fat on the trunk of the body between the waist and the diaphragm.

Accelerometer   A device that senses motion in one or more planes. It yields a count of movements in arbitrary units.

Accuracy   The extent to which measured values reflect the true values.

Acute biological response   Physiological or metabolic changes arising from a single session of exercise.

Adventitia   External coat of an artery or vein.

All-cause mortality   Death from any cause.

Amenorrhoea   Absence of menses. Primary amenorrhoea – normal menses never established; secondary amenorrhoea – cessation of menses after they were established.

Aneurysm   Rupture of an artery wall weakened by atherosclerosis, leading to internal bleeding.

Angina   Severe but temporary attack of cardiac pain.

Angiography   Radiography of arteries (e.g. coronary, carotid) after injecting a radio-opaque substance, such as iodine, into an artery.

Anorexia nervosa   A common psychological illness. There is minimal food intake, leading to loss of weight and sometimes death from starvation.

Apoptosis   Active ('programmed') cell death.

Arteriovenous difference for oxygen   The difference between the oxygen content of arterial and mixed venous blood. This indicates how much oxygen has been extracted from arterial blood and utilized (predominantly) by muscle. Often written as $(a-\bar{v})$ O_2 diff.

Asthma   Episodic obstruction resulting from airway inflammation; characterized by cough, wheeze and breathlessness.

Atheroma   Infiltration of lipid into the arterial wall, leading to tissue degeneration.

Atherosclerosis   A progressive disease that leads to hardening and thickening of the walls of arteries and to narrowing of these vessels.

β-hydroxyacyl-CoA dehydrogenase   The rate-limiting enzyme in the mitochondrial β-oxidation pathway.

Bias   Error that produces results that differ in a systematic manner from the true values.

Body mass index   Body mass (in kilograms) divided by height (in metres) squared, i.e. body mass (kg)/height (m)^2. Used as a measure of obesity.

Bronchitis A lung disease characterized by excessive mucus production in the bronchial tree, causing coughing to get rid of sputum. Small airways become inflamed and narrowed and mucus may occlude small bronchi.

Bulimia nervosa Self-induced vomiting after meals.

Cancer A set of diseases characterized by unregulated cell growth, leading to invasion of surrounding tissues and spread to other parts of the body.

Carcinogen Agent capable of causing cancer.

Carcinogenesis Processes involved in the production of a cancer.

Cardiomyopathy Disorder of the heart muscle of unknown aetiology.

Case-control study A study comparing the occurrence of a possible cause/risk factor between cases (people with a disease or other outcome variable) and suitable controls (unaffected by the disease or outcome variable).

Case-report or case-series A study describing the characteristics of a patient or number of patients with a specific disease or attribute.

Cerebrovascular disease Stroke.

Cholesterol A steroid molecule necessary for the synthesis of steroid hormones and bile salts and an integral component of cell membranes.

Cholesterol esters Cholesterol in combination with long chain fatty acids, i.e. esterified.

Chylomicron A lipoprotein, its main function is the transport of dietary fat (triglyceride) to adipose tissue and muscle.

Citrate synthase An enzyme involved in oxidative metabolism within the mitochondria. One of the enzymes in Kreb's cycle.

Coronary collaterals Additional blood vessels that may grow in the heart, enhancing coronary blood flow.

Chronic heart failure The inability of the heart to pump blood at a sufficient rate to meet the metabolic demands of the body.

Chronic obstructive pulmonary disease Progressive, sometimes partially reversible, airflow obstruction that does not vary over a long period. Predominantly caused by cigarette smoking that results in emphysema, chronic bronchitis and small airways disease.

Cohort study A study in which a group of people (a cohort), free of disease, are followed up to see how the development of new cases of the disease (or other outcome) differs between subgroups of the cohort classified according to their exposure to a potential cause/risk factor.

Confounding A factor associated both with an exposure (for example, physical activity) and the outcome being studied which, if unequally distributed between the exposure subgroups, may confuse the findings. This distorts the estimated exposure effect.

Correlational study A study describing relationships between potential risk factors and a disease (or other outcome). Populations or groups are the units of analysis, rather than individuals.

Cortical bone Dense, strong ivory-like bone.

Cytotoxic Toxic to cells.

Diabetes insipidus A disease caused by a low secretion of vasopressin. (antidiuretic hormone, ADH) from the pituitary gland and hence a low rate of reabsorption of water in the kidneys.

Diabetes mellitus　A disease characterized by either an inability of the pancreas to secrete insulin (type 1 diabetes) or an inability of the cells to respond to insulin (type 2 diabetes).

Diabetic foot　An informal term for the damages caused by microvascular disease of the extremities. Tissue damage leads to pain and, in severe cases, can lead to the need for amputation.

Disability　Restriction or lack of ability to perform an activity in a manner or within the range considered normal for a human being.

Dyslipidaemia　Abnormal concentrations in the blood of plasma lipoprotein lipids.

Dyspnoea　Uncomfortable sensation of breathlessness, difficulty in breathing or laboured breathing.

Dose–response　The relationship between level of exposure to a factor such as physical activity and the response to this in terms of health (or disease) outcome.

Effect modification　The magnitude or direction of the association under study differs according to the level of another factor.

Effect size　A statistic used to determine whether or not a difference between two means (different groups or same group in different conditions) is sufficiently large to be considered meaningful.

Emphysema　A lung disease characterized by enlargement of air spaces distal to the terminal bronchiole, with destruction of their walls. Parts of the capillary bed are destroyed.

Endosteum　The inner surface of bone that faces the bone marrow.

Endothelial function　Ability of the endothelium to invoke vasodilation or vasoconstriction by interacting with vascular smooth muscle.

Epidemiology　The study of the distribution and determinants of health-related states or events in specified populations, and the application of this study to control of health problems.

Euglycaemic clamp technique　Also known as the 'hyperinsulinaemic euglycaemic clamp' or the 'glucose clamp'. A technique used to determine insulin sensitivity by measuring how much glucose the body can dispose of (via oxidation and storage) in response to a fixed insulin concentration.

Eumenorrhoea　Normal menses, 10–13 cycles per year.

Excess post-exercise oxygen consumption　The elevation in oxygen consumption above resting levels which occurs following an acute bout of exercise.

Experimental study　A study in which researchers attempt to change a variable in one or more groups. Also called an intervention study.

Exposure　A measure of an individual's experience or 'dose' of a specified risk factor. (Exposure has two dimensions, level and duration; for physical activity it depends not only on the level of activity but also on number of years during which an individual has engaged in physical activity.)

Fat-free mass　Total body mass minus fat mass.

Fibrillation　Rapid uncoordinated contraction or twitching of cardiac muscle.

Fibrin　A protein polymer that traps erythrocytes and other cells in the blood to form a clot.

Fibrinogen　A plasma protein, the precursor of fibrin.

Fibrinolysis　The breakdown of fibrin in blood clots.

Flow-induced arterial vasodilation Vasodilation in response to the increased shear stress on the endothelium when blood flow is increased.

Free radical A highly chemically reactive molecule or molecular fragment that can damage cellular components such as DNA and lipid-rich membranes.

Generalizability The extent to which results are applicable to different populations.

Gluconeogenesis The synthesis of glucose from non-carbohydrate sources including pyruvate, lactate, glycerol and amino acids.

Glucose tolerance The ability of the body to respond to the ingestion of glucose. Usually determined using the blood glucose concentration measured at the 2-hour point in an oral glucose tolerance test.

GLUT4 An insulin-sensitive receptor located on membranes of cells in muscle and adipose tissue, which aids in the transport of glucose across the membrane into the cell.

Glycosuria The presence of excessive amounts of glucose in the urine.

Gonadotrophins Hormones that control the endocrine functions of the gonads (ovaries in women, testes in men).

Haemorrhagic Due to a haemorrhage (bleed).

Health status Disease-specific quality of life (a concept), usually measured with questionnaires.

High-density lipoproteins Species of lipoproteins that, amongst other functions, promote the removal of excess cholesterol from cells in a process termed 'reverse cholesterol transport'.

Hypercholesterolaemia Abnormally high concentration of cholesterol in the blood.

Hyperglycaemia Abnormally high concentration of glucose in the blood.

Hyperinsulinaemia Abnormally high concentration of insulin in the blood.

Hypertriglycerideaemia Abnormally high concentration of triglycerides in the blood.

Homocysteine A sulphur-containing amino acid, high plasma concentrations of which may be associated with an increased risk of cardiovascular disease.

Hypertension Abnormally high arterial blood pressure.

Hypertrophic An increase in the size of tissues or structures.

Hypertrophic cardiomyopathy A familial cardiac disease characterized morphologically by an enlarged and non-dilated left ventricle.

Hypotension Abnormally low arterial blood pressure.

Incidence The number of new events/cases that develop in a defined population during a specified time interval.

Infarction Death of a section of tissue because the blood supply has been cut off, as in myocardial infarction (heart attack).

Insulin resistance A loss of sensitivity to the effects of insulin.

Insulin sensitivity A measure of how effectively the cells remove glucose from the blood in response to insulin.

Insulin-dependent diabetes mellitus Alternative name for type 1 diabetes.

Intima Internal coat of a blood vessel.

Ischemic Impaired blood flow.

Isokinetic Movement at a constant speed or angular velocity.

Ketoacidosis A life-threatening situation in which an excess of ketone bodies leads to an increase in the acidity (reduction in pH) of the blood.

Ketogenesis   The formation of ketone bodies.

Lipaemia   Increased lipids, particularly triglycerides, in the blood.

Lipolytic   Chemical breakdown of fat by enzymes.

Lipoproteins   Macromolecular complexes composed of lipid and protein, responsible for transporting triglycerides and cholesterol in the blood.

Low-density lipoprotein   The main carrier of cholesterol in the blood, responsible for delivering cholesterol to the cells.

Lymphoma   Tumour of lymphatic tissue.

Macrophages   Cells that scavenge foreign bodies and cell debris.

Maximal oxygen uptake   The highest rate of oxygen uptake. This is reached when there is little or no further increase in oxygen uptake despite an increase in exercise intensity during a maximal exercise test. Expressed either in absolute terms (units $l\,min^{-1}$) or relative to body mass ($ml\,kg^{-1}\,min^{-1}$). Sometimes predicted from heart rate and oxygen uptake during sub-maximal exercise. Used as a marker for aerobic/endurance fitness.

Media   Middle coat of a blood vessel.

MET   A multiple of the resting metabolic rate. One MET is defined as the energy requirement at rest, designated as an oxygen uptake of $3.5\,ml\,kg^{-1}\,min^{-1}$.

Meta-analysis   The statistical analysis of a collection of analytic results for the purpose of integrating the findings.

Metastasis   Process by which cancers escape to other parts of the body.

Metformin   A drug used in the treatment of type 2 diabetes.

Mutation   A heritable change in DNA.

Nitric oxide   A gas released by endothelial cells which acts as a vasodilator.

Non-esterified fatty acids   Fatty acids not combined with glycerol in triglyceride.

Non-insulin dependent diabetes mellitus   Alternative term for type 2 diabetes. An imprecise term since insulin is required by some individuals with type 2 diabetes.

Non-enzymatic glycation   A process whereby glucose molecules are bound to proteins to form glycoproteins.

Odds ratio   The ratio of the odds (likelihood) of exposure to the variable of interest in one group to the odds of exposure to this variable in another group.

Oligomenorrhoea   Infrequent menstruation, cycle prolonged beyond 35 days.

Oncogenes   A gene whose protein product contributes to carcinogenesis.

Osteoblasts   Cells that produce bone matrix to build new bone.

Osteoclasts   Cells responsible for bone resorption, removing old bone.

Osteocytes   Mature bone cells which may be involved in activation of bone turnover and regulation of extracellular calcium.

Osteomalacia   Demineralization of the mature skeleton, with softening of the bone and bone pain.

Osteopenia   Low bone mineral density without evidence of non-traumatic fractures.

Osteoporosis   A condition characterized by generalized skeletal fragility, leading to fractures with minimal trauma.

Phagocyte   A cell capable of engulfing bacteria or other particles.

Phospholipids   Compounds of fatty acids, phosphoric acid and a nitrogenous base: important constituents of all cell membranes.

Plaques   Complicated atheromatous lesions that are raised and obstruct blood flow.

Population-attributable risk   The incidence of a disease or characteristic in a population that is associated with an exposure to a risk factor. Describes the relative importance of an exposure for that population.

Postprandial   After a meal.

Precision   The extent to which the same measurements, when repeated, yield the same values. Also called repeatability.

Prevalence   The number of cases in a defined population at a specified point in time.

Primary care   First-level contact with the health care system (in the United Kingdom, with general practitioners).

Primary prevention   Prevention of the development of disease in healthy people.

Procoagulant   Leading to formation of a blood clot.

Relative risk   The ratio of occurrence of a disease (or other outcome) among exposed people to that among the unexposed.

Repeated measures   An experimental design where measurements are repeated on the same individuals in different conditions.

Resorption   The breaking down of bone into soluble constituents.

Resting metabolic rate   The energy expenditure at rest following an overnight fast and eight hours of sleep.

Reverse cholesterol transport   The process whereby high-density lipoproteins collect cholesterol from cells and return it to the liver where it can be excreted as bile salts in the bile.

Rhabdomyolisis   Sporadic appearance in blood of abnormal levels of myoglobin, indicative of muscle damage.

Rheumatic heart disease   Damage to the myocardium due to rheumatic fever.

Rickets   A disorder of calcium and phosphate metabolism, associated with deficiency of vitamin D, and beginning most often in infancy and early childhood. It leads to softening and bending of the long weight-bearing bones.

Risk difference   The (absolute) difference in rates of occurrence between exposed and unexposed groups.

Sarcoma   Cancer of connective tissues.

Secondary prevention   Decrease in the risk of mortality and further morbidity in patients with existing disease.

Sensitivity (of clinical tests)   The proportion of true positives that are correctly identified by the test.

Shear stress   The force exerted on the endothelium by blood flow.

Specificity (of clinical tests)   The proportion of true negatives that are correctly identified by the test.

Stenoses   Narrowing, for example, of coronary vessels due to atherosclerosis.

Statistical power   The ability of a study to detect a specified (often 'clinically important') difference, i.e. the probability of rejecting the null hypothesis when this is in fact false and should be rejected. It depends on sample size, and on the level of significance chosen.

Stoichiometry   Calculation of quantitative relationships between the reactants and products in a chemical reaction. The mathematics of chemistry.

Strain   Deformation of a material, measured as the change in dimension produced by force, divided by the original dimension. One 'strain' is thus equivalent to a 1 per cent change.

Subcutaneous abdominal fat   Abdominal fat stored under the skin.

Succinate dehydrogenase   An enzyme involved in oxidative metabolism within the mitochondria. One of the enzymes in Kreb's cycle.

Syndrome   A group of symptoms which, occurring together, produce a pattern typical of a particular disease.

Thermic effect   Increase in energy expenditure. For example, the thermic effect of food is the increase in energy expenditure due to digestion, absorption, and storage of food; the thermic effect of activity is the increase in energy expenditure due to physical activity.

Thrombin   The enzyme responsible for converting fibrinogen into fibrin.

Thrombosis   Formation of a blood clot.

Thromboembolytic   Due to the formation of a thrombus (blood clot) that has blocked a blood vessel. Sometimes called an ischaemic stroke.

Thrombus   A blood clot.

Trabecular bone   An open type of bone (always enclosed in a hard outer crust of cortical bone) made up of a three-dimensional lattice-work of trabeculae. It has more remodelling sites and a more active metabolism than cortical bone.

Trabeculae   Curved plates and tubes organized to withstand the particular forces to which each part of a bone is normally subjected. They confer bone's essential property of 'strength with lightness'.

Training effect   An adaptive response to training, not merely a short-term biological response to a single session of exercise.

Triglyceride   A lipid molecule composed of glycerol and three fatty acids that is the storage form of fat in the body. From a biochemical perspective, it is correctly called triacyglycerol, but the term triglyceride is still widely used, particularly in the clinical literature.

Tumour   A swelling or growth, i.e. a mass of tissue which fulfils no useful purpose and which grows at the expense of the body. It can be benign or cancerous.

Type I (alpha) error   Rejecting the null hypothesis when this is true, i.e. finding an effect when there is none (a 'false positive').

Type II (beta) error   Accepting the null hypothesis when this is false, i.e. failing to find an effect when one is there (a 'false negative').

Validity   The extent to which a study measures what it purports to measure.

Visceral fat   Fat stored within the abdominal cavity.

Waist–hip ratio   The ratio of waist circumference to hip circumference, used as a surrogate marker for abdominal obesity.

Waist circumference   The preferred surrogate marker for abdominal obesity.

Bibliography

Abbott, R.D., White, L.R., Ross, G.W., Masaki, K.H., Curb, J.D. and Petrovitch, H. (2004) 'Walking and dementia in physically capable elderly men', *Journal of the American Medical Association* 292: 1447–53.

Adams, K.F., Schatzkin, A., Harris, T.B., Kipnis, V., Mouw, T., Ballard-Barbash, R., Hollenbeck, A. and Leitzmann, M.F. (2006) 'Overweight, obesity, and mortality in a large prospective cohort of persons 50 to 71 years old', *New England Journal of Medicine* 355: 763–78. (See also the commentary by Beyers, T. (2006) 'Overweight and mortality among baby boomers – now we're getting personal', *New England Journal of Medicine* 355: 758–60.)

Adams, T.D., Gress, R.E., Smith, S.C., Halverson, R.C., Simper, S.C., Rosamond, W.D., LaMonte, M.J., Stroup, A.M. and Hunt, S.C. (2007) 'Long-term mortality after gastric bypass surgery', *New England Journal of Medicine* 357: 753–61. (See also the editorial by Bray, G.A. (2007) 'The missing link – lose weight, live longer', *New England Journal of Medicine* 357: 818–20.)

Ades, P.A., Ballor, D.L., Ashikaga, T., Utton, J.L. and Nair, K.S. (1996) 'Weight training improves walking endurance in healthy elderly persons', *Annals of Internal Medicine* 124: 568–72.

Ainsworth, B.E., Haskell, W.L., Whitt, M.C., Irwin, M.L., Swartz, A.M., Strath, S.J., O'Brien, W.L., Bassett, D.R., Schmitz, K.H., Emplaincourt, P.O., Jacobs, D.R. and Leon, A.S. (2000) 'Compendium of physical activities: an update of activity codes and MET intensities', *Medicine and Science in Sports and Exercise* 32 (Supplement): S498–504.

Albert, C.M., Mittleman, M.A., Chae, C.U., Lee, I.-M., Hennekens, C.H. and Manson, J.E. (2000) 'Triggering of sudden death from cardiac causes by vigorous exertion', *New England Journal of Medicine* 343: 1355–61.

Alberti, K.G., Zimmet, P. and Shaw, J. (2006) 'Metabolic syndrome – a new world-wide definition. A Consensus Statement from the International Diabetes Federation', *Diabetic Medicine* 23: 469–80.

Albright, A., Franz, M., Hornsby, G., Kriska, A., Marrero, D., Ullrich, I. and Verity, L.S. (2000) 'American College of Sports Medicine Position Stand: exercise and type 2 diabetes', *Medicine and Science in Sports and Exercise* 32: 1345–60.

Alexander, L.M., Inchley, J., Todd, J., Currie, D., Cooper, A.R. and Currie, C. (2005) 'The broader impact of walking to school among adolescents: seven day accelerometry based study', *British Medical Journal* 331: 1061–2.

Allender, S., Foster, C., Scarborough, P. and Rayner, M. (2007) 'The burden of physical activity-related ill health in the UK', *Journal of Epidemiology and Community Health* 61: 344–8.

Alley, D.E. and Chang, V.W. (2007) 'The changing relationship of obesity and disability, 1988–2004', *Journal of the American Medical Association* 298: 2020–7. (See also the editorial by Gregg, E.W. and Guralnik, J.M. (2007) 'Is disability obesity's price of longevity?', *Journal of the American Medical Association* 298: 2066–7.

Allison, D.B., Fontaine, K.R., Manson, J.E., Stevens, J. and VanItallie, T.B. (1999) 'Annual deaths attributable to obesity in the United States', *Journal of the American Medical Association* 282: 1530–8.

American College of Sports Medicine (1978) 'The recommended quantity and quality of exercise for developing and maintaining fitness in healthy adults', *Medicine and Science in Sports* 10: vii–ix.

American College of Sports Medicine (1990) 'Position Stand: the recommended quantity and quality of exercise for developing and maintaining cardiorespiratory and muscular fitness in healthy adults', *Medicine and Science in Sports and Exercise* 22: 265–74.

American College of Sports Medicine (1998) 'Position Stand: the recommended quantity and quality of exercise for developing and maintaining cardiorespiratory and muscular fitness, and flexibility in healthy adults', *Medicine and Science in Sports and Exercise* 30: 975–91.

American Heart Association (2008) 'Heart disease and stroke statistics 2008 update: a report from the American Heart Association Statistics Committee and Stroke Statistics Subcommittee', *Circulation* 117: E25–146.

Andersen, L.B., Harro, M., Sardinha, L.B., Froberg, K., Ekelund, U., Brage, S. and Anderssen, S.A. (2006) 'Physical activity and clustered cardiovascular risk in children: a cross-sectional study (The European Youth Heart Study)', *Lancet* 368: 299–304. (See also the comment by Weiss, R. and Raz, I. (2006) 'Focus on fitness not just fatness', *Lancet* 368: 261–2.)

Andersen, R.E., Crespo, C.J., Bartlett, S.J., Cheskin, L.J. and Pratt, M. (1998) 'Relationship of physical activity and television watching with body weight and level of fatness among children: results from the Third National Health and Nutrition Examination Survey', *Journal of the American Medical Association* 279: 938–42.

Andersen, R.E., Wadden, T.A., Bartlett, S.J., Zemel, B., Verde, T.J. and Franckowiak, S.C. (1999) 'Effects of lifestyle activity vs structured aerobic exercise in obese women: a randomized trial', *Journal of the American Medical Association* 281: 335–40.

Åstrand, P.-O., Bergh, U. and Kilbom, Å. (1997) 'A 33-yr follow-up of peak oxygen uptake and related variables of former physical education students', *Journal of Applied Physiology* 82: 1844–52.

Atlantis, E., Barnes, E.H. and Fiatorone Singh, M.A. (2006) 'Efficacy of exercise for treating overweight in children and adolescents: a systematic review', *International Journal of Obesity* 30: 1027–40.

Australian Bureau of Statistics (2006) 'Physical activity in Australia: a snapshot, 2004–05'. Online, available at: www.abs.gov.au/ausstats/abs@.nsf/mf/4835.0.55.001 (accessed 12 March 2008).

Avenell, A., Sattar, N. and Lean, M. (2006) 'ABC of obesity: management: part 1 – behaviour change, diet, and activity', *British Medical Journal* 333: 740–3.

Aylin, P., Williams, S. and Bottle, A. (2005) 'Obesity and type 2 diabetes in children, 1996–7 to 2003–4', *British Medical Journal* 331: 1167.

Badman, M.K. and Flier, J.S. (2005) 'The gut and energy balance: visceral allies in the obesity wars', *Science* 307: 1909–14.

Bahr, R. and Trosshaug, T. (2005) 'Understanding injury mechanisms: a key component of preventing injuries in sport', *British Journal of Sports Medicine* 39: 324–9.

Baird, J., Fisher, D., Lucas, P., Kleijnen, J., Roberts, H. and Law, C. (2005) 'Being big or growing fast: systematic review of size and growth in infancy and later obesity', *British Medical Journal* 331: 929.

Baker, J.L., Olsen, L.W. and Sørensen, T.I.A. (2007) 'Childhood body mass index and the risk of coronary heart disease in adulthood', *New England Journal of Medicine* 357: 2329–37. (See also the perspective by Ludwig, D.S. (2007) 'Childhood obesity: the shape of things to come', *New England Journal of Medicine* 357: 2325–7.)

Balady, G.J. (2002) 'Survival of the fittest: more evidence', *New England Journal of Medicine* 346: 852–4 (editorial).

Balkau, B., Deanfield, J.E., Després, J.P., Bassand, J.P., Fox, K.A.A., Smith, S.C., Barter, P., Tan, C.E., Van Gaal, L., Wittchen, H.U., Massien, C. and Haffner, S.M. (2007) 'International day for the evaluation of abdominal obesity (IDEA): a study of waist circumference, cardiovascular disease, and diabetes mellitus in 168,000 primary care patients in 63 countries', *Circulation* 116: 1942–51.

Barengo, N.C., Nissinen, A., Tuomilehto, J. and Pekkarinen, H. (2002) 'Twenty-five-year trends in physical activity of 30- to 59-year-old populations in eastern Finland', *Medicine and Science in Sports and Exercise* 34: 1302–7.

Basham, P. and Luik, J. (2008) 'Is the obesity epidemic exaggerated? Yes', *British Medical Journal* 336: 244.

Bass, S.L. (2000) 'The prepubertal years: a uniquely opportune stage of growth when the skeleton is most responsive to exercise?', *Sports Medicine* 30: 73–8.

Bass, S.L., Naughton, G., Saxon, L., Iuliano-Burns, S., Daly, R., Briganti, E.M., Hume, C. and Nowson, C. (2007) 'Exercise and calcium combined results in a greater osteogenic effect than either factor alone: a blinded randomized placebo-controlled trial in boys', *Journal of Bone and Mineral Research* 22: 458–64.

Bassuk, S.S. and Manson, J.E. (2005) 'Epidemiological evidence for the role of physical activity in reducing the risk of type 2 diabetes and cardiovascular disease', *Journal of Applied Physiology* 99: 1193–204.

Batterham, R.L., Cohen, M.A., Ellis, S.M., Le Roux, C.W., Withers, D.J., Frost, G.S., Ghatei, M.A. and Bloom, S.R. (2003) 'Inhibition of food intake in obese subjects by peptide YY_{3-36}', *New England Journal of Medicine* 349: 941–8.

Batty, G.D. and Lee, I.M. (2002) 'Physical activity for preventing strokes: better designed studies suggest that it is effective', *British Medical Journal* 325: 350–1 (editorial).

Baum, A. (2006) 'Eating disorders in male athletes', *Sports Medicine* 36: 1–6.

Beaglehole, R., Bonita, R. and Kjellström, T. (1993) *Basic Epidemiology*, Geneva: World Health Organization.

Begg, S.J., Vos, T., Barker, B., Stanley, L. and Lopez, A.D. (2008) 'Burden of disease and injury in Australia in the new millennium: measuring health loss from diseases, injuries and risk factors', *Medical Journal of Australia*, 188: 36–40.

Berlin, J.A. and Colditz, G.H. (1990) 'A meta-analysis of physical activity in the prevention of coronary heart disease', *American Journal of Epidemiology* 132: 612–28.

Bernstein, L., Henderson, B.E., Hanisch, R., Sullivan-Halley, J. and Ross, R.K. (1994) 'Physical exercise and reduced risk of breast cancer in young women', *Journal of the National Cancer Institute* 86: 1403–8.

Bhargava, S.K., Sachdev, H.S., Fall, C.H.D., Osmond, C., Lakshmy, R., Barker, D.J.P., Biswas, S.K.D., Ramji, S., Prabhakaran, D. and Reddy, K.S. (2004) 'Relation of serial changes in childhood body-mass index to impaired glucose tolerance in young adulthood', *New England Journal of Medicine* 350: 865–75.

Bibbins-Domingo, K., Coxson, P., Pletcher, M.J., Lightwood, J. and Goldman, L. (2007) 'Adolescent overweight and future adult coronary heart disease', *New England Journal of Medicine* 357: 2371–9. (See also the perspective by Ludwig, D.S. (2007) 'Childhood obesity: the shape of things to come', *New England Journal of Medicine* 357: 2325–7.)

Birdwood, G. (1996) *Understanding Osteoporosis and its Treatment: A Guide for Physicians and their Patients*, New York: Parthenon.

Black, C., Collins, A. and Snell, M. (2001) 'Encouraging walking: the use of journey-to-school trips in compact urban areas', *Urban Studies* 38: 1121–41.

Blair, S.N. and Church, T.S. (2004) 'The fitness, obesity, and health equation: is physical activity the common denominator?', *Journal of the American Medical Association* 292: 1232–4 (editorial).

Blair, S.N. and Haskell, W.L. (2006) 'Objectively measured physical activity and mortality in older adults', *Journal of the American Medical Association* 296: 216–18 (editorial).

Blair, S.N. and LaMonte, M.J. (2006) 'Commentary: current perspectives on obesity and health: black and white, or shades of grey?', *International Journal of Epidemiology* 35: 69–72.

Blair, S.N., Cheng, Y. and Holder, J.S. (2001) 'Is physical activity or physical fitness more important in defining health benefits?', *Medicine and Science in Sports and Exercise* 33 (Supplement): S379–99.

Blair, S.N., Goodyear, N.N., Gibbons, L.W. and Cooper, K.H. (1984) 'Physical fitness and incidence of hypertension in healthy normotensive men and women', *Journal of the American Medical Association* 252: 487–90.

Blair, S.N., Kampert, J.B., Kohl, H.W., Barlow, C.E., Macera, C.A., Paffenbarger, R.S. and Gibbons, L.W. (1996) 'Influences of cardiorespiratory fitness and other precursors on cardiovascular disease and all-cause mortality in men and women', *Journal of the American Medical Association* 276: 205–10.

Blair, S.N., Kohl, H.W., Barlow, C.E., Paffenbarger, R.S., Gibbons, L.W. and Macera, C.A. (1995) 'Changes in physical fitness and all-cause mortality: a prospective study of healthy and unhealthy men', *Journal of the American Medical Association* 273: 1093–8.

Blair, S.N., Kohl, H.W., Paffenbarger, R.S., Clark, D.G., Cooper, K.H. and Gibbons, L.W. (1989) 'Physical fitness and all-cause mortality: a prospective study of healthy men and women', *Journal of the American Medical Association* 262: 2395–401.

Bliss, M. (2007) *The Discovery of Insulin*, Chicago: University of Chicago Press.

Boreham, C., Twisk, J., Neville, C., Savage, M., Murray, L. and Gallagher, A. (2002) 'Associations between physical fitness and activity patterns during adolescence and cardiovascular risk factors in young adulthood: the Northern Ireland Young Hearts Project', *International Journal of Sports Medicine* 23 (Supplement): S22–6.

Bouchard, C., Tremblay, A., Després, J.P., Nadeau, A., Lupien, P.J., Thériault, G., Dussault, J., Moorjania, S., Pinault, S. and Fournier, G. (1990) 'The response to long-term overfeeding in identical twins', *New England Journal of Medicine* 322: 1477–82.

Bouchard, C., Tremblay, A., Després, J.P., Thériault, G., Nadeau, A., Lupien, P.J., Moorjani, S., Prudhomme, D. and Fournier, G. (1994) 'The response to exercise with constant energy intake in identical twins', *Obesity Research* 2: 400–10.

Boulé, N.G., Haddad, E., Kenny, G.P., Wells, G.A. and Sigal, R.J. (2001) 'Effects of exercise on glycemic control and body mass in type 2 diabetes mellitus: a meta-analysis of controlled clinical trials', *Journal of the American Medical Association* 286: 1218–27.

Boulé, N.G., Kenny, G.P., Haddad, E., Wells, G.A. and Sigal, R.J. (2003) 'Meta-analysis of the effect of structured exercise training on cardiorespiratory fitness in type 2 diabetes mellitus', *Diabetologia* 46: 1071–81.

Braun, B., Zimmermann, M.B. and Kretchmer, N. (1995) 'Effects of exercise intensity on insulin sensitivity in women with non-insulin-dependent diabetes mellitus', *Journal of Applied Physiology* 78: 300–6.

Bray, G.A. (1969) 'Effect of caloric restriction on energy expenditure in obese patients', *Lancet*, 23 August 1969: 397–8.

British Heart Foundation Statistics Database (2007) 'Coronary heart disease statistics 2007'. Online, available at: www.heartstats.org (accessed 18 March 2008).

British Heart Foundation Statistics Database (2008) 'European cardiovascular disease statistics 2008'. Online, available at: www.heartstats.org (accessed 18 March 2008).

Broocks, A., Pirke, K.M., Schweiger, U., Tuschl, R.J., Laessle, R.G., Strowitzki, E., Hörl, T., Haas, W. and Jeschke, D. (1990) 'Cyclic ovarian function in recreational athletes', *Journal of Applied Physiology* 68: 2083–6.

Brooke-Wavell, K., Jones, P.R.M., Hardman, A.E., Tsuritani, I. and Yamada, Y. (2001) 'Commencing, continuing and stopping brisk walking: effects on bone mineral density, quantitative ultrasound of bone and markers of bone metabolism in postmenopausal women', *Osteoporosis International* 12: 581–7.

Buchwald, H., Avidor, Y., Braunwald, E., Jensen, M.D., Pories, W., Fahrbach, K. and Schoelles, K. (2004) 'Bariatric surgery: a systematic review and meta-analysis', *Journal of the American Medical Association* 292: 1724–37.

Cameron, A.J., Shaw, J.E. and Zimmet, P.Z. (2004) 'The metabolic syndrome: prevalence in worldwide populations', *Endocrinology and Metabolism Clinics of North America* 33: 351–75.

Campos, P., Saguy, A., Ernsberger, P., Oliver, E. and Gaesser, G. (2006) 'The epidemiology of overweight and obesity: public health crisis or moral panic?', *International Journal of Epidemiology* 35: 55–60.

Canadian Fitness and Lifestyle Research Institute (2005) 'Physical activity and sport monitor'. Online, available at: www.cflri.ca/eng/statistics/surveys/documents/pam2005_sec1.pdf. (accessed 24 March 2008).

Carnethon, M.R., Gidding, S.S., Nehgme, R., Sidney, S., Jacobs, D.R. and Liu, K. (2003) 'Cardiorespiratory fitness in young adulthood and the development of cardiovascular disease risk factors', *Journal of the American Medical Association* 290: 3092–100.

Carnethon, M.R., Gulati, M. and Greenland, P. (2005) 'Prevalence and cardiovascular disease correlates of low cardiorespiratory fitness in adolescents and adults', *Journal of the American Medical Association* 294: 2981–8.

Carola, R., Harley, J.P. and Noback, C.R. (1992) *Human Anatomy*, New York: McGraw-Hill.

Castaneda, C., Layne, J.E., Munoz-Orians, L., Gordon, P.L., Walsmith, J., Foldvari, M., Roubenoff, R., Tucker, K.L. and Nelson, M.E. (2002) 'A randomized controlled trial of resistance exercise training to improve glycemic control in older adults with type 2 diabetes', *Diabetes Care* 25: 2335–41.

Cauza, E., Hanusch-Enserer, U., Strasser, B., Ludvik, B., Metz-Schimmerl, S., Pacini, G., Wagner, O., Georg, P., Prager, R., Kostner, K., Dunky, A. and Haber, P. (2005) 'The relative benefits of endurance and strength training on the metabolic factors and muscle function of people with type 2 diabetes mellitus', *Archives of Physical Medicine and Rehabilitation* 86: 1527–33.

Chacko, K.M., Bauer, T.A., Dale, R.A, Dixon, J.A., Schrier, R.W. and Estacio, R.O. (2008) 'Heart rate recovery predicts mortality and cardiovascular events in patients with type 2 diabetes', *Medicine and Science in Sports and Exercise* 40: 288–95.

Chakravarty, E.F., Hubert, H.B., Lingala, V.B. and Fries, J.F. (2008) 'Reduced disability and mortality among aging runners: a 21-year longitudinal study', *Archives of Internal Medicine* 168: 1638–46. (See also the editorial by Mackey, R.H. (2008) 'Weighing benefits for older runners', *Archives of Internal Medicine* 168: 1948–9.)

Chang, J.T., Morton, S.C., Rubenstein, L.Z., Mojica, W.A., Maglione, M., Suttorp, M.J., Roth, E.A. and Shekelle, P.G. (2004) 'Interventions for the prevention of falls in older adults: systematic review and meta-analysis of randomised clinical trials', *British Medical Journal* 328: 653–4.

Chanoine, J.P., Hampl, S., Jensen, C., Boldrin, M. and Hauptman, J. (2005) 'Effect of orlistat on weight and body composition in obese adolescents: a randomized controlled trial', *Journal of the American Medical Association* 294: 1491. (See also the editorial by Joffe, A. (2005) 'Pharmacotherapy for adolescent obesity: a weighty issue', *Journal of the American Medical Association* 293: 2932–4.)

Cherkas, L.F., Hankin, J.L., Kato, B.S., Richards, B., Gardner, J.P., Surdulescu, G.L., Kimura, M., Lu, X., Spector, T.D. and Aviv, A. (2008) 'The association between physical activity in leisure time and leukocyte telomere length', *Archives of Internal Medicine* 168: 154–8. (See also the editorial by Guralnik, J.M. (2008) 'Successful aging', *Archives of Internal Medicine* 168: 131–2.)

Chin A Paw, M.J.M., van Uffelen, J.G.Z., Riphagen, I. and van Mechelen, W. (2008) 'The functional effects of physical exercise training in frail older people: a systematic review', *Sports Medicine* 38: 781–93.

Chinn, S., and Rona, R.J. (2001) 'Prevalence and trends in overweight and obesity in three cross sectional studies of British children, 1974–94', *British Medical Journal* 322: 24–6.

Christou, D.D., Gentile, C.L., De Souza, C.A., Seals, D.R. and Gates, P.E. (2005) 'Fatness is a better predictor of cardiovascular disease risk factor profile than aerobic fitness in healthy men', *Circulation* 111: 1904–14.

Church, T.S., Cheng, Y.J., Earnest, C.P., Barlow, C.E., Gibbons, L.W., Priest, E.L. and Blair, S.N. (2004) 'Exercise capacity and body composition as predictors of mortality among men with diabetes', *Diabetes Care* 27: 83–8.

Church, T.S., Earnest, C.P., Skinner, J.S. and Blair, S.N. (2007) 'Effects of different doses of physical activity on cardiorespiratory fitness among sedentary, overweight or obese postmenopausal women with elevated blood pressure: a randomized controlled trial', *Journal of the American Medical Association* 297: 2081–91.

Clark, E.M., Ness, A.R. and Tobias, J.H. (2008) 'Vigorous physical activity increases fracture risk in children irrespective of bone mass: a prospective study of the independent risk factors for fractures in healthy children', *Journal of Bone and Mineral Research* 23: 1012–22.

Coggan, A.R., Spina, R.J., King, D.S., Rogers, M.A., Brown, M., Nemeth, P.M. and Holloszy, J.O. (1992) 'Skeletal muscle adaptations to endurance training in 60- to 70-yr-old men and women', *Journal of Applied Physiology* 72: 1780–6.

Coggan, A.R., Spina, R.J., Rogers, M.A., King, D.S., Brown, M., Nemeth, P.M. and Holloszy, J.O. (1990) 'Histochemical and enzymatic characteristics of skeletal muscle in masters athletes', *Journal of Applied Physiology* 68: 1896–901.

Colditz, G.A. (1999) 'Economic costs of obesity and inactivity', *Medicine and Science in Sports and Exercise* 31 (Supplement): S663–7.

Colditz, G.A., Cannuscio, C.C. and Frazier, A.L. (1997) 'Physical activity and reduced risk of colon cancer: implications for prevention', *Cancer Causes and Control* 8: 649–67.

Colditz, G.A., Willett, W.C., Stampfer, M.J., Manson, J.E., Hennekens, C.H., Arky, R.A. and Speizer, F.E. (1990) 'Weight as a risk factor for clinical diabetes in women', *American Journal of Epidemiology* 132: 501–13.

Cole, C.R., Blackstone, E.H., Pashkow, F.J., Snader, C.E. and Lauer, M.S. (1999) 'Heart-rate recovery immediately after exercise as a predictor of mortality', *New England Journal of Medicine* 341: 1351–7.

Cole, T.J. (2006) 'Childhood obesity: assessment and prevalence', in N. Cameron, N.G. Norgan and G.T.H. Ellison (eds) *Childhood Obesity: Contemporary Issues*, Boca Raton: CRC Press, pp. 3–12.

Cole, T.J., Bellizzi, M.C., Flegal, K.M. and Dietz, W.H. (2000) 'Establishing a standard definition for childhood overweight and obesity worldwide: international survey', *British Medical Journal* 320: 1240–3.

Cole, T.J., Flegal, K.M., Nicholls, D. and Jackson, A.A. (2007) 'Body mass index cut offs to define thinness in children and adolescents: international survey', *British Medical Journal* 335: 194–7. (See also the editorial by Cameron, N. (2007) 'Body mass index cut offs to define thinness in children and adolescents: a new chart will be most useful in countries in social, economic and nutritional transition where both undernutrition and overnutrition are prevalent', *British Medical Journal* 335: 166–7.)

Commonwealth Department of Health (2000) *The Costs of Illness Attributable to Physical Inactivity*, Canberra: Commonwealth Department of Health.

Cordain, L., Latin, R.W. and Behnke, J.J. (1986) 'The effects of an aerobic running program on bowel transit time', *Journal of Sports Medicine* 26: 101–4.

Cornelissen, V.A. and Fagard, R.H. (2005) 'Effects of endurance training on blood pressure, blood pressure-regulating mechanisms, and cardiovascular risk factors', *Hypertension* 46: 667–75.

Corrado, D., Basso, C., Rizzoli, G., Schiavon, M. and Thiene, G. (2003) 'Does sports activity enhance the risk of sudden death in adolescents and young adults?', *Journal of the American College of Cardiology* 42: 1959–63.

Couillard, C., Bergeron, N., Prud'homme, D., Bergeron J., Tremblay, A., Bouchard, C., Mauriège, P. and Després, J.-P. (1998) 'Postprandial triglyceride response in visceral obesity in men', *Diabetes* 47: 953–60.

Courteix, D., Jaffré, C., Lespessailles, E. and Benhamou, L. (2005) 'Cumulative effects of calcium supplementation and physical activity on bone accretion in premenarchal children: a double-blind randomised placebo-controlled trial', *International Journal of Sports Medicine* 26: 332–8.

Craig, C.L., Marshall, A.L., Sjöström, M., Bauman, A.E., Booth, M.L., Ainsworth, B.E., Pratt, M., Ekelund, U., Yngve, A., Sallis, J.F. and Oja, P. (2003) 'International physical activity questionnaire: 12-country reliability and validity', *Medicine and Science in Sports and Exercise* 35: 1381–95.

Cummings, D.E., Weigle, D.S., Frayo, R.S., Breen, P.A., Ma, M.K., Dellinger, E.P. and Purnell, J. (2002) 'Plasma ghrelin levels after diet-induced weight loss or gastric bypass surgery', *New England Journal of Medicine* 346: 1623–30.

Cummings, S.R., Nevitt, M.C., Browner, W.S., Stone, K., Fox, K.M., Ensrud, K.E., Cauley, J., Black, D. and Vogt, T.M. (1995) 'Risk factors for hip fracture in white women', *New England Journal of Medicine* 332: 767–73.

Curioni, C.C. and Lourenço, P.M. (2005) 'Long-term weight loss after diet and exercise: a systematic review', *International Journal of Obesity* 29: 1168–74.

Currens, J.H. and White, P.D. (1961) 'Half a century of running: clinical, physiologic and autopsy findings in the case of Clarence DeMar ("Mr. Marathon")', *New England Journal of Medicine* 16: 988–93.

Cust, A.E., Armstrong, B.K., Friedenreich, C.M., Slimani, N. and Bauman, A. (2007) 'Physical activity and endometrial cancer risk: a review of the current evidence, biologic mechanisms and the quality of physical activity measurements', *Cancer Causes and Control* 18: 243–58.

Daley, M.J. and Spinks, W.L. (2000) 'Exercise, mobility and aging', *Sports Medicine* 29: 1–12.

Danaei, G., Vander Hoorn, S., Lopez, A.D., Murray, C.J.L. and Ezzati, M. (Comparative Risk Assessment collaborating group, cancers) (2005) 'Causes of cancer in the world: comparative risk assessment on nine behavioural and environmental factors', *Lancet* 366: 1784–93.

Daniels, S.R., Arnett, D.K., Eckel, R.H., Gidding, S.S., Hayman, L.L., Kumanyika, S., Robinson, T.N., Scott, B.J., St. Jeor, S. and Williams, C.L. (2005) 'Overweight in children and adolescents: pathophysiology, consequences, prevention and treatment', *Circulation* 111: 1999–2012.

Davey Smith, G., Bracha, Y., Svendsen, K.H., Neaton, J.D., Haffner, S.M. and Kuller, L.H., for the Multiple Risk Factor Intervention Trial Research Group (2005) 'Incidence of type 2 diabetes in the randomized multiple risk factor intervention trial', *Annals of Internal Medicine* 142: 313–22.

Day, L., Fildes, B., Gordon, I., Fitzharris, M., Flamer, H. and Lord, S. (2002) 'Randomised factorial trial of falls prevention among older people living in their own homes', *British Medical Journal* 325: 128–33.

DeBusk, R.F., Stenestrand, U., Sheehan, M. and Haskell, W.L. (1990) 'Training effects of long versus short bouts of exercise in healthy subjects', *American Journal of Cardiology* 65: 1010–13.

Dekker, R., Kingma, J., Groothoff, J.W., Eisma, W.H. and Ten Duis, H.J. (2000) 'Measurement of severity of sports injuries: an epidemiological study', *Clinical Rehabilitation* 14: 651–6.

Dela, F., von Linstow, M.E., Mikines, K.J. and Galbo, H. (2004) 'Physical training may enhance β-cell function in type 2 diabetes', *American Journal of Physiology Endocrinology and Metabolism* 287: E1024–31.

Dencker, M., Thorsson, O., Karlsson, M.K., Lindén, C., Svensson, J., Wollmer, P. and Andersen, L.B. (2006) 'Daily physical activity and its relation to aerobic fitness in children aged 8–11 years', *European Journal of Applied Physiology* 96: 587–92.

Department of Transport (2003) 'Attitudes to walking and cycling'. Online, available at: www.dft.gov. uk/pgr/statistics/datatablespublications/trsnstatsatt/earlierreports/attitudestowalkingandcycling (accessed 5 May 2007).

de Souza, M.J., Miller, B.E., Loucks, A.B., Luciano, A.A., Pescatello, L.S., Campbell, C.G. and Lasley, B.L. (1998) 'High frequency of luteal phase deficiency and anovulation in recreational women runners: blunted elevation in follicle-stimulating hormone observed during luteal-follicular transition', *Journal of Clinical Endocrinology and Metabolism* 83: 4220–32.

Diabetes Prevention Program Research Group (2002) 'Reduction in the incidence of type 2 diabetes with lifestyle intervention or metformin', *New England Journal of Medicine* 346: 393–403.

Doak, C.M., Visscher, T.L.S., Renders, C.M. and Seidell, J.C. (2006) 'The prevention of overweight and obesity in children and adolescents: a review of intervention programmes', *Obesity Reviews* 7: 111–36.

Dolan, S.H., Williams, D.P., Ainsworth, B.E. and Shaw, J.M. (2006) 'Development and reproducibility of the bone loading history questionnaire', *Medicine and Science in Sports and Exercise* 38: 1121–31.

Donnelly, J.E., Blair, S.N., Jakicic, J.M., Manore, M.M., Rankin, J.W. and Smith, B.K. (2009) 'Appropriate physical activity intervention strategies for weight loss and prevention of weight regain in adults', *Medicine and Science in Sports and Exercise* 41: 459–71.

Donnelly, J.E., Hill, J.O., Jacobsen, D.J., Potteiger, J., Sullivan, D.K., Johnson, S.L., Heelan, K., Hise, M., Fennessey, P.V., Sonko, B., Sharp, T., Jakicic, J.M., Blair, S.N., Tran, Z.V., Mayo, M., Gibson, C. and Washburn, R.A. (2003) 'Effects of a 16-month randomized controlled exercise trial on body weight and composition in young, overweight men and women', *Archives of Internal Medicine* 163: 1343–50.

Dorn, J., Naughton, J., Imamura, D. and Trevisan, M. (1999) 'Results of a multicenter randomized clinical trial of exercise and long-term survival in myocardial infarction patients: the National Exercise and Heart Disease Project (NEHDP)', *Circulation* 100: 1764–9.

Drake, A.J., Smith, A., Betts, P.R., Crowne, E.C. and Shield, J.P.H. (2002) 'Type 2 diabetes in obese white children', *Archives of Disease in Childhood* 86: 207–8.

Drinkwater, B.L., Bruemner, B. and Chesnut, C.H. (1990) 'Menstrual history as a determinant of current bone density in young athletes', *Journal of the American Medical Association* 263: 545–8.

Druce, M.R., Wren, A.M., Park, A.J., Milton, J.E., Patterson, M., Frost, G., Ghatei, M.A., Small, C. and Bloom, S.R. (2005) 'Ghrelin increases food intake in obese as well as lean subjects', *International Journal of Obesity* 29: 1130–6.

Duncan, G.E., Li, S.M. and Zhou, X.-H. (2005) 'Cardiovascular fitness among U.S. adults: NHANES 1999–2000 and 2001–2002', *Medicine and Science in Sports and Exercise* 37: 1324–8.

Dunn, A.L., Marcus, B.H., Kampert, J.B., Garcia, M.E., Kohl, H.W. and Blair, S.N. (1999) 'Comparison of lifestyle and structured interventions to increase physical activity and cardiorespiratory fitness', *Journal of the American Medical Association* 281: 327–34.

Dunstan, D.W., Salmon, J., Owen, N., Armstrong, T., Zimmet, P.Z., Welborn, T.A., Cameron,

A.J., Dwyer, T., Jolley, D. and Shaw, J.E. (2005) 'Associations of TV viewing and physical activity with the metabolic syndrome in Australian adults', *Diabetologia* 48: 2254–61.

Durstine, J.L. and Lyerly, G.W. (2007) 'No physical activity or exercise is not an option', *Journal of Applied Physiology* 103: 417–18 (editorial).

Durstine, J.L. and Moore, G.E. (2002) *ACSM's Exercise Management for Persons with Chronic Diseases and Disabilities*, Champaign: Human Kinetics.

Eckel, R.H., Daniels, S.R., Jacobs, A.K. and Robertson, R.M. (2005) 'America's children: a critical time for prevention', *Circulation* 111: 1866–8.

EconTech (2007) 'Economic modelling of the net costs associated with non-participation in sport and physical activity'. Online, available at: www.econtech.com.au/information/Social/Medibank_Sports_Final_300707.pdf (accessed 24 October 2008).

Eisenmann, J.C., Katzmarzyk, P.T., Perusse, L., Tremblay, A., Després, J.P. and Bouchard, C. (2005a) 'Aerobic fitness, body mass index, and CVD risk factors among adolescents: the Québec family study', *International Journal of Obesity* 29: 1077–83.

Eisenmann, J.C., Wickel, E.E., Welk, G.J. and Blair, S.N. (2005b) 'Relationship between adolescent fitness and fatness and cardiovascular disease risk factors in adulthood: the Aerobics Centre Longitudinal Study (ACLS)', *American Heart Journal* 149: 46–53.

Ekelund, U., Åman, J., Yngve, A., Rennman, C., Westerterp, K. and Sjöström, M. (2002) 'Physical activity but not energy expenditure is reduced in obese adolescents: a case-control study', *American Journal of Clinical Nutrition* 76: 935–41.

Ekelund, U., Neovius, M., Linné, Y., Brage, S., Wareham, N.J. and Rössner, S. (2005) 'Associations between physical activity and fat mass in adolescents: the Stockholm Weight Development Study', *American Journal of Clinical Nutrition* 81: 355–60. (See also the editorial by Styne, D.M. (2005) 'Obesity in childhood: what's activity got to do with it?', *American Journal of Clinical Nutrition* 81: 337–8.)

Enos, W.F., Beyer, J. and Holmes, R.H. (1955) 'Pathogenesis of coronary disease in American soldiers killed in Korea', *Journal of the American Medical Association* 158: 912–14.

Enos, W.F., Holmes, R.H. and Beyer, J. (1953) 'Coronary disease among United States soldiers killed in action in Korea', *Journal of the American Medical Association* 152: 1090–3.

Erikssen, G. (2001) 'Physical fitness and changes in mortality: the survival of the fittest', *Sports Medicine* 31: 571–6.

Erikssen, G., Liestøl, K., Bjørnhold, J., Thaulow, E., Sandvik, L. and Erikssen, J. (1998) 'Changes in physical fitness and changes in mortality', *Lancet* 352: 759–62.

Eriksson, K.F. and Lindgärde, F. (1991) 'Prevalence of type 2 (non-insulin dependent) diabetes mellitus by diet and physical exercise: the 6-year Malmö feasibility study', *Diabetologia* 34: 891–8.

Eriksson, K.F. and Lindgärde, F. (1998) 'No excess 12-year mortality in men with impaired glucose tolerance who participated in the Malmö Preventive Trial with diet and exercise', *Diabetologia* 41: 1010–16.

Esparza, J., Fox, C., Harper, I.T., Bennett, P.H., Schulz, L.O., Valencia, M.E. and Ravussin, E. (2000) 'Daily energy expenditure in Mexican and USA Pima Indians: low physical activity as a possible cause of obesity', *International Journal of Obesity* 24: 55–9.

Ettinger, W.H., Burns, R., Messier, S.P., Applegate, W., Rejeski, W.J., Morgan, T., Sumaker, S., Berry, M.J., O'Toole, M., Monu, J. and Craven, T. (1997) 'A randomized trial comparing aerobic exercise and resistance exercise with a health education programme in older adults with knee osteoarthritis: the Fitness Arthritis and Seniors Trial (FAST)', *Journal of the American Medical Association* 277: 25–31.

European Commission (2006) 'Health and food: special Eurobarometer 246/Wave 64.3 – TNS opinion and social'. Online, available at: http://ec.europa.eu/health/ph_publication/eb_food_ en.pdf. (accessed 13 March 2008).

Exercise is Medicine (2007) A programme launched by the American College of Sports Medicine and the American Heart Association. Online, available at: www.exerciseismedicine.org.

Expert Committee on the Diagnosis and Classification of Diabetes Mellitus (1999) 'Report of the Expert Committee on the Diagnosis and Classification of Diabetes Mellitus', *Diabetes Care* 22 (Supplement 1): S5–19.

ExTraMATCH Collaborative (2004) 'Exercise training meta-analysis of trials in patients with chronic heart failure (ExTraMATCH)', *British Medical Journal* 328: 189–92.

Farooqi, I.S., Jebb, S.A., Langmack, G., Lawrence, E., Cheetham, C.H., Prentice, A.M., Hughes, I.A., McCamish, M.A. and O'Rahilly, S. (1999) 'Effects of recombinant leptin therapy in a child with congenital leptin deficiency', *New England Journal of Medicine* 341: 879–84.

Feicht, C.B., Johnson, T.S., Martin, B.J., Sparkes, K.E. and Wagner, W.W. (1978) 'Secondary amenorrhoea in athletes', *Lancet* 2: 1145–6.

Fernhall, B. and Agiovlasitis, S. (2008) 'Arterial function in youth: window into cardiovascular risk', *Journal of Applied Physiology* 105: 325–33.

Feskanich, D., Willett, W.C. and Colditz, G.A. (2002) 'Walking and leisure-time activity and risk of hip fracture in postmenopausal women', *Journal of the American Medical Association* 288: 2300–6.

Fiatarone, M.A., O'Neill, E.F., Ryan, N.D., Clements, K.M., Solares, G.R., Nelson, M.E., Roberts, S.B., Kehayias, J.J., Lipsitz, L.A. and Evans, W.J. (1994) 'Exercise training and nutritional supplementation for physical frailty in very elderly people', *New England Journal of Medicine* 330: 1769–75.

Fitzgerald, M.D., Tanaka, H., Tran, Z.V. and Seals, D.R. (1997) 'Age-related declines in maximal aerobic capacity in regularly exercising vs. sedentary women: a meta-analysis', *Journal of Applied Physiology* 83: 160–5.

Fleg, J.L. and Lakatta, E.G. (1988) 'Role of muscle loss in the age-associated reduction in $\dot{V}O_2$max', *Journal of Applied Physiology* 65: 1147–51.

Flegal, K.M. (2006) 'Commentary: the epidemic of obesity – what's in a name?', *International Journal of Epidemiology* 35: 72–4.

Flegal, K.M., Graubard, B.I., Williamson, D.F. and Gail, M.H. (2005) 'Excess deaths associated with underweight, overweight, and obesity', *Journal of the American Medical Association* 293: 1861–7. (See also the editorial by Mark, D.H. (2005) 'Deaths attributable to obesity', *Journal of the American Medical Association* 293: 1918–19.)

Flegal, K.M., Graubard, B.I., Williamson, D.F. and Gail, M.H. (2007) 'Cause-specific excess deaths associated with underweight, overweight, and obesity', *Journal of the American Medical Association* 298: 2028–37.

Flodmark, C.E., Marcus, C. and Britton, M. (2006) 'Interventions to prevent obesity in children and adolescents: a systematic literature review', *International Journal of Obesity* 30: 579–89.

Folsom, A.R., Kushi, L.H. and Hong, C.-P. (2000) 'Physical activity and incident diabetes mellitus in postmenopausal women', *American Journal of Public Health* 90: 134–8.

Fontaine, K.R., Redden, D.T., Wang, C., Westfall, A.O. and Allison, D.B. (2003) 'Years of life lost due to obesity', *Journal of the American Medical Association* 289: 187–93. (See also the editorial by Manson, J.E. and Bassuk, S.S. (2003) 'Obesity in the United States: a fresh look at its high toll', *Journal of the American Medical Association* 289: 229–30.)

Ford, E.S. and Li, C. (2006) 'Physical activity or fitness and the metabolic syndrome', *Expert Review Cardiovascular Therapies* 4: 897–915.

Ford, E.S., Kohl III, H.W., Mokdad, A.H. and Ajani, U.A. (2005) 'Sedentary behavior, physical activity, and the metabolic syndrome among U.S. adults', *Obesity Research* 13: 608–14.

Forwood, M.R. (2008) 'Physical activity and bone development during childhood: insights from animal models', *Journal of Applied Physiology* 105: 334–41.

Frändin, K., Grimby, G., Mellström, D. and Svanborg, A. (1991) 'Walking habits and health-related factors in a 70-year-old population', *Gerontology* 37: 281–8.

Frank, L.D., Andresen, M.A. and Schmid, T.L. (2004) 'Obesity relationships with community design, physical activity, and time spent in cars', *American Journal of Preventive Medicine* 27: 87–96.

Frayn, K.N. (2003) *Metabolic Regulation: A Human Perspective*, 2nd edn, Oxford: Blackwell Science Ltd.

Friedenreich, C.M. (2001) 'Physical activity and cancer prevention: from observational to intervention research', *Cancer Epidemiology, Biomarkers and Prevention* 10: 287–301.

Friedenreich, C.M., Bryant, H.E. and Courneya, K.S. (2001) 'Case-control study of lifetime physical activity and breast cancer risk', *American Journal of Epidemiology* 154: 336–47.

Frontera, W.R., Hughes, V.A., Fielding, R.A., Fiatarone, M.A., Evans, W.J. and Roubenoff, R. (2000) 'Aging skeletal muscle: a 12-yr longitudinal study', *Journal of Applied Physiology* 88: 1321–6.

Frontera, W.R., Hughes, V.A., Lutz, K.J. and Evans, W.J. (1991) 'A cross-sectional study of muscle strength and mass in 45- to 78-year old men and women', *Journal of Applied Physiology* 71: 644–50.

Frontera, W.R., Meredith, C.N., O'Reilly, K.P., Knuttgen, H.G. and Evans, W.J. (1988) 'Strength conditioning in older men: skeletal muscle hypertrophy and improved function', *Journal of Applied Physiology* 64: 1038–44.

Funatogawa, I., Funatogawa, T. and Yano, E. (2008) 'Do overweight children necessarily make overweight adults? Repeated cross-sectional annual nationwide survey of Japanese girls and women over nearly six decades', *British Medical Journal* 337: 500–2.

Gæde, P., Lund-Andersen, H., Parving, H.-H. and Pedersen, O. (2008) 'Effect of multifactorial intervention on mortality in type 2 diabetes', *New England Journal of Medicine* 358: 580–91.

Gæde, P., Vedel, P., Larsen, N., Jensen, G.V.H., Parving, H.-H. and Pedersen, O. (2003) 'Multifactorial intervention and cardiovascular disease in patients with type 2 diabetes', *New England Journal of Medicine* 348: 383–93. (See also the editorial by Solomon, C.G. (2003) 'Reducing cardiovascular risk in type 2 diabetes', *New England Journal of Medicine* 348: 457–9).

Garn, S.M. and Clark, D.C. (1976) 'Trends in fatness and the origins of obesity', *Pediatrics* 57: 443–56.

Gielen, S., Schuler, G. and Hambrecht, R. (2001) 'Exercise training in coronary artery disease and coronary vasomotion', *Circulation* 103: E1–6.

Giles-Corti, B., Macintyre, S., Clarkson, J.P., Pikora, T. and Donovan, R.J. (2003) 'Environmental and lifestyle factors associated with overweight and obesity in Perth, Australia', *American Journal of Health Promotion* 18: 93–102.

Gill, J.M.R. and Malkova, D. (2006) 'Physical activity, fitness and cardiovascular disease risk in adults: interactions with insulin resistance and obesity', *Clinical Science* 110: 409–25.

Gill, J.M.R, Al-Mamari, A., Ferrell, W.R., Cleland, S.J., Packard, C.J., Sattar, N., Petrie, J.R. and Caslake, M.J. (2004) 'Effects of prior moderate exercise on postprandial metabolism and vascular function in lean and centrally obese men', *Journal of the American College of Cardiology* 44: 2375–82.

Gillies, C.L., Abrams, K.R., Lambert, P.C., Cooper, N.J., Sutton, A.J., Hsu, R.T. and Khunti, K. (2007) 'Pharmacological and lifestyle interventions to prevent or delay type 2 diabetes in people with impaired-glucose tolerance: systematic review and meta-analysis', *British Medical Journal* 334: 299.

Giovannucci, E., Ascherio, A., Rimm, E.B., Colditz, G.A., Stampfer, M.J. and Willett, W.C. (1995) 'Physical activity, obesity, and risk for colon cancer and adenoma in men', *Annals of Internal Medicine* 122: 327–34.

Gleeson, M., McDonald, W.W., Pyne, D.B., Cripps, A.W., Francis, J.L., Fricker, P.A. and Clancy, R.L. (1999) 'Salivary gland IgA levels and infection risk in swimmers', *Medicine and Science in Sports and Exercise* 31: 67–73.

Glew, R.H., Williams, M., Conn, C.A., Cadena, S.M., Crossey, M., Okolo, S.N. and VanderJagt, D.J. (2001) 'Cardiovascular disease risk factors and diet of Fulani pastoralists of northern Nigeria', *American Journal of Clinical Nutrition* 74: 730–6.

Gordon-Larsen, P. and Popkin, B.M. (2006) 'Global perspectives on adolescent obesity', in N. Cameron, N.G. Norgan and G.T.H Ellison (eds) *Childhood Obesity: Contemporary Issues*, Boca Raton: CRC Press, pp. 13–23.

Great Britain Athletics UK All-Time lists. Online, available at: www.gbrathletics.com/uk (accessed 1 November 2008).

Gregg, E.W., Cauley, J.A., Stone, K., Thompson, T.J., Bauer, D.C., Cummings, S.R. and Ensrud, K.E. (2003a) 'Relationship of changes in physical activity and mortality among older women', *Journal of the American Medical Association* 289: 2379–86.

Gregg, E.W., Cheng, Y.J., Cadwell, B.L., Imperatore, G., Williams, D.E., Flegal, K.M., Venkat Narayan, K.M. and Williamson, D.F. (2005) 'Secular trends in cardiovascular disease risk factors according to body mass index in US adults', *Journal of the American Medical Association* 293: 1868–74. (See also the editorial by Mark, D.H. (2005) 'Deaths attributable to obesity', *Journal of the American Medical Association* 293: 1918–19.)

Gregg, E.W., Gerzoff, R.B., Caspersen, C.J., Williamson, D.F. and Narayan, K.M.V. (2003b) 'Relationship of walking to mortality among US adults with diabetes', *Archives of Internal Medicine* 163: 1440–7. (See also the editorial by Hu, F.B. and Manson, J.E. (2003b) 'Walking: the best medicine for diabetes?', *Archives of Internal Medicine* 163: 1397–8.)

Gulati, M., Black, H.R., Shaw, L.J., Arnsdorf, M.F., Merz, N.B., Lauer, M.S., Marwick, T.H., Pandey, D.K., Wicklund, R.H. and Thisted, R.A. (2005) 'The prognostic value of a nomogram for exercise capacity in women', *New England Journal of Medicine* 353: 468–75.

Gunter, K., Baxter-Jones, A.D.G., Mirwald, R.L., Almstedt, H., Fuchs, R.K., Durski, S. and Snow, C. (2008) 'Impact exercise increases BMC during growth: an 8-year longitudinal study', *Journal of Bone and Mineral Research* 23: 986–93.

Guralnik, J.M., Ferrucci, L., Simonsick, E.M., Salive, M.E. and Wallace, R.B. (1995) 'Lower-extremity function in persons over the age of 70 years as a predictor of subsequent disability', *New England Journal of Medicine* 332: 556–61.

Haapanen, N., Miilunpalo, S., Pasanen, M., Oja, P. and Vuori, I. (1997) 'Association between leisure time physical activity and 10-year body mass change among working-aged men and women', *International Journal of Obesity* 21: 288–96.

Haapasalo, H., Kannus, P., Sievänen, H., Pasanen, M., Uusi-Rasi, K., Heinonen, A., Oja, P. and Vuori, I. (1998) 'Effect of long-term unilateral activity on bone mineral density of female junior tennis players', *Journal of Bone and Mineral Research* 13: 310–19.

Hadjiolova, I., Mintcheva, L., Dunev, S., Daleva, M., Handjiev, S. and Balabanski, L. (1982) 'Physical working capacity in obese women after an exercise programme for body weight reduction', *International Journal of Obesity* 6: 405–10.

Hagberg, J.M., Graves, J.E., Limacher, M., Woods, D.R., Leggett, S.H., Cononie, C., Gruber, J.J. and Pollock, M.L. (1989) 'Cardiovascular responses of 70- to 79-yr-old men and women to exercise training', *Journal of Applied Physiology* 66: 2589–94.

Haines, L., Barrett, T.G., Wan, K.C., Shield, J.P.H. and Lynn, R. (2007) 'Rising incidence of type 2 diabetes in children in the UK', *Diabetes Care* 30: 1097–101.

Hajjar, D.P. and Nicholson, A.C. (1995) 'Atherosclerosis: an understanding of the cellular and molecular basis of the disease promises new approaches for its treatment in the near future', *American Scientist* 83: 460–7.

Hakanen, M., Lagström, H., Kaitosaari, T., Niinikoski, H., Nüntö-Salonen, K., Jokinen, E., Sillan-mäki, L., Viikari, J., Rönnemaa, T. and Simell, O. (2006) 'Development of overweight in an atherosclerosis prevention trial starting in early childhood: the STRIP study', *International Journal of Obesity* 30: 618–26.

Hakim, A.A., Petrovitch, H., Burchfiel, C.M., Ross, G.W., Rodriguez, B.L., White, L.R., Yano, K., Curb, J.D. and Abbott, R.D. (1998) 'Effects of walking on mortality among non-smoking retired men', *New England Journal of Medicine* 338: 94–9.

Hallal, P.C., Wells, J.C.K., Reichert, F.F., Anselmi, L. and Victoria, C.G. (2006) 'Early determinants of physical activity in adolescence: prospective birth cohort study', *British Medical Journal* 332: 1002–7.

Hambrecht, R., Walther, C., Möbius-Winkler, S., Gielen, S., Linke, A., Conradi, K., Erbs, S., Kluge, R., Kendziorra, K., Sabri, O., Sick, P. and Schuler, G. (2004) 'Percutaneous coronary angioplasty compared with exercise training in patients with stable coronary artery disease: a randomized trial', *Circulation* 109: 1371–8.

Hambrecht, R., Wolf, A., Gielen, S., Linke, A., Hofer, J., Erbs, S., Schoene, N. and Schuler, G. (2000) 'Effect of exercise on coronary endothelial function in patients with coronary artery disease', *New England Journal of Medicine* 342: 454–60.

Hamer, M. and Chida, Y. (2007) 'Active commuting and cardiovascular risk: a meta-analytic review', *Preventive Medicine* 20: 20.

Hamer, M. and Chida, Y. (2008) 'Walking and primary prevention: a meta-analysis of prospective cohort studies', *British Journal of Sports Medicine* 42: 238–43.

Han, T.S., Sattar, N. and Lean, M. (2006) 'ABC of obesity; assessment of obesity and its clinical implications', *British Medical Journal* 333: 695–8.

Hancox, R.J., Milne, B.J. and Poulton, R. (2004) 'Association between child and adolescent television viewing and adult health: a longitudinal birth cohort study', *Lancet* 364: 257–62. (See also the comment by Ludwig, D.S. and Gortmaker, S.L. (2004) 'Programming obesity in childhood', *Lancet* 364: 226–7.)

Hardman, A.E., Lawrence, J.E.M. and Herd, S.L. (1998) 'Postprandial lipemia in endurance-trained people during a short interruption to training', *Journal of Applied Physiology* 84: 1895–901.

Haskell, W.L. (1994) 'Health consequences of physical activity: understanding and challenges regarding dose–response', *Medicine and Science in Sports and Exercise* 26: 649–60.

Haskell, W.L., Lee, I.M., Pate, R.R., Powell, K.E., Blair, S.N., Franklin, B.A., Macera, C.A., Heath, G.W., Thompson, P.D. and Bauman, A. (2007) 'Physical activity and public health: updated recommendation for adults from the American College of Sports Medicine and the American Heart Association', *Medicine and Science in Sports and Exercise* 39: 1423–34.

Haskell, W.L., Sims, C., Myll, J., Bortz, W.M., Goar, F.G. and Alderman, E.L. (1993) 'Coronary artery size and dilating capacity in ultradistance runners', *Circulation* 87: 1076–82.

Haslam, D.W. and James, W.P.T. (2005) 'Obesity', *Lancet* 366: 1197–209.

Haslam, D.W., Sattar, N. and Lean, M. (2006) 'ABC of obesity: obesity – time to wake up', *British Medical Journal* 333: 640–2.

Hasselstrøm, H., Hansen, S.E., Froberg, K. and Andersen, L.B. (2002) 'Physical fitness and physical activity during adolescence as predictors of cardiovascular disease risk in young adulthood: Danish

Youth and Sports Study: an eight-year follow-up study', *International Journal of Sports Medicine* 23: S27–31.

Hawkins, S.A. and Wiswell, R.A. (2003) 'Rate and mechanism of maximal oxygen consumption decline with aging', *Sports Medicine* 33: 877–88.

Hayden, J.A., van Tulder, M.W., Malmivaara, A. and Koes, B.W. (2005) 'Exercise therapy for treatment of non-specific low back pain', *Cochrane Database Systematic Review* 3: CD000335.

Health Canada (2007) 'Older but not wiser: Canada's future at risk: Canada's Report Card on physical activity and youth 2007'. Online, available at: www.jeunesenforme.ca/Ophea/Active-HealthyKids_v2/programs_2007reportcard.cfm (accessed 28 February 2008).

Heath, G.W., Hagberg, J.M., Ehsani, A.A. and Holloszy, J.O. (1981) 'A physiological comparison of young and older endurance athletes', *Journal of Applied Physiology* 51: 634–40.

Heilbronn, L.K., de Jonge, L., Frisard, M.I., DeLany, J.P., Larson-Meyer, D.E., Rood, J., Nguyen, T., Martin, C.K., Volaufova, J., Most, M.M., Greenway, F.I., Smith, S.R., Deutsch, W.A., Williamson, D.A. and Ravussin, E. for the Pennington CALERIE Team (2006) 'Effect of 6-month calorie restriction on biomarkers of longevity, metabolic adaptation, and oxidative stress in overweight individuals: a randomized trial', *Journal of the American Medical Association* 295: 1539–48. (See also the editorial by Fontana, L. (2006) 'Excessive adiposity, calorie restriction, and aging', *Journal of the American Medical Association* 295: 1577–8.)

Heinonen, A., Kannus, P., Sievänen, H., Oja, P., Pasanen, M., Rinne, M., Uusi-Rasi, K. and Vuori, I. (1996) 'Randomised controlled trial of the effect of high-impact exercise on selected risk factors for osteoporotic fractures', *Lancet* 348: 1343–7.

Heinonen, A., Oja, P., Sievänen, H., Pasanen, M. and Vuori, I. (1998) 'Effect of two training regimens on bone mineral density in healthy perimenopausal women: a randomized controlled trial', *Journal of Bone and Mineral Research* 13: 483–90.

Helmrich, S.P., Ragland, D.R., Leung, R.W. and Paffenbarger, R.S. (1991) 'Physical activity and reduced occurrence of non-insulin-dependent diabetes mellitus', *New England Journal of Medicine* 325: 147–52.

Hennekens, C.H. and Buring, J.E. (1987) *Epidemiology in Medicine*, Philadelphia: Lippincott, Williams and Wilkins.

Hill, J.O. and Wyatt, H.R. (1999) 'Relapse in obesity treatment: biology or behaviour?', *American Journal of Clinical Nutrition* 69: 1064–5 (editorial).

Hill, J.O. and Wyatt, H.R. (2005) 'Role of physical activity in preventing and treating obesity', *Journal of Applied Physiology* 99: 765–70.

Hill, J.O., Hauptman, J., Anderson, J.W., Fujioka, K., O'Neil, P.M., Smith, D.K., Zavoral, J.H. and Aronne, L.J. (1999) 'Orlistat, a lipase inhibitor, for weight maintenance after conventional dieting: a 1-y study', *American Journal of Clinical Nutrition* 69: 1108–16.

Hill, J.O., Seagle, H.M., Johnson, S.L., Smith, S., Reed, G.W., Tran, Z.V., Cooper, D., Stone, M. and Peters, J.C. (1998) 'Effects of 14 d covert substitution of olestra for conventional fat on spontaneous food intake', *American Journal of Clinical Nutrition* 67: 1178–85.

Hill, J.O., Wyatt, H.R., Reed, G.W. and Peters, J.C. (2003) 'Obesity and the environment: where do we go from here?', *Science* 299: 853–5.

Hind, K. and Burrows, M. (2007) 'Weight-bearing exercise and bone mineral accrual in children and adolescents: a review of controlled trials', *Bone* 40: 14–27.

Holloszy, J.O. (2005) 'Exercise-induced increase in muscle insulin sensitivity', *Journal of Applied Physiology* 99: 338–43.

Holmes, M.D., Chen, W.Y., Feskanich, D., Kroenke, C.H. and Colditz, G.A. (2005) 'Physical activity and survival after breast cancer diagnosis', *Journal of the American Medical Association* 293: 2479–86.

Holten, M.K., Zacho, M., Gaster, M., Juel, C., Wojtaszewski, J.F.P. and Dela, F. (2004) 'Strength training increases insulin-mediated glucose uptake, GLUT4 content, and insulin signalling in skeletal muscle in patients with type 2 diabetes', *Diabetes* 53: 294–305.

Hootman, J.M., Macera, C.A., Ainsworth, B.E., Addy, C.L., Martin, M. and Blair, S.N. (2002) 'Epidemiology of musculoskeletal injuries among sedentary and physically active adults', *Medicine and Science in Sports and Exercise* 34: 838–44.

Hou, L., Ji, B.T., Blair, A., Dai, Q., Gao, Y.T. and Chow, W.H. (2004) 'Commuting physical activity and risk of colon cancer in Shanghai, China', *American Journal of Epidemiology* 160: 860–7.

Houmard, J.A., Tanner, C.J., Slentz, C.A., Duscha, B.D., McCartney, J.S. and Kraus, W.E. (2004) 'Effect of the volume and intensity of exercise training on insulin sensitivity', *Journal of Applied Physiology* 96: 101–6.

Howley, E.T. (2001) 'Type of activity: resistance, aerobic, anaerobic and leisure-time versus occupational physical activity', *Medicine and Science in Sports and Exercise* 33: S364–9.

Hu, F.B., Manson, J.E., Stampfer, M.J., Colditz, G., Liu, S., Solomon, C.G. and Willett, W.C. (2001a) 'Diet, lifestyle, and the risk of type 2 diabetes mellitus in women', *The New England Journal of Medicine* 345: 790–7.

Hu, F.B., Sigal, R.J., Rich-Edwards, J.W., Colditz, G.A., Solomon, C.G., Willett, W.C., Speizer, F.E. and Manson, J.E. (1999) 'Walking compared with vigorous physical activity and risk of type 2 diabetes in women: a prospective study', *Journal of the American Medical Association* 282: 1433–9.

Hu, F.B., Stampfer, M.J., Colditz, G.A., Ascherio, A., Rexrode, K.M., Willett, W.C. and Manson, J.A. (2000) 'Physical activity and risk of stroke in women', *Journal of the American Medical Association* 283: 2961–7.

Hu, F.B., Stampfer, M.J., Solomon, C., Liu, S., Colditz, G.A., Speizer, F.E., Willett, W.C. and Manson, J.E. (2001b) 'Physical activity and risk for cardiovascular events in diabetic women', *Annals of Internal Medicine* 134: 96–105.

Hu, F.B., Willet, W.C., Li, T., Stampfer, M.J., Colditz, G.A. and Manson, J.E. (2004) 'Adiposity as compared with physical activity in predicting mortality among women', *New England Journal of Medicine* 351: 2694–703.

Hu, G., Eriksson, J., Barengo, N.C., Lakka, T.A., Valle, T.T., Nissinen, A., Jousilahti, P. and Tuomilehto, J. (2004a) 'Occupational, commuting, and leisure-time physical activity in relation to total and cardiovascular mortality among Finnish subjects with type 2 diabetes', *Circulation* 110: 666–73.

Hu, G., Lindström, J., Valle, T.T., Eriksson, J.G., Jousilahti, P., Silventoinen, K., Qiao, Q. and Tuomilehto, J. (2004b) 'Physical activity, body mass index, and risk of type 2 diabetes in patients with normal or impaired glucose regulation', *Archives of Internal Medicine* 164: 892–6.

Hu, G., Qiao, Q., Silventoinen, K., Eriksson, J.G., Jousilahti, P., Lindström, J., Valle, T.T., Nissinen, A. and Tuomilehto, J. (2003) 'Occupational, commuting, and leisure-time physical activity in relation to risk for type 2 diabetes in middle-aged Finish men and women', *Diabetologia* 46: 322–9.

Imhof, A. and Koenig, W. (2001) 'Exercise and thrombosis', *Cardiology Clinics* 19: 389–400.

Imperatore, G., Fulton, J., Cheng, Y.J., Gregg, E.W. and Williams, D.E. (2006) 'Physical activity, cardiovascular fitness, and insulin sensitivity among U.S. adolescents: the National Health and Nutrition Examination Survey, 1999–2002', *Diabetes Care* 29: 1567–72.

Information Centre (2008) 'Statistics on obesity, physical activity and diet: England, January 2008'. Online, available at: www.ic.nhs.uk/webfiles/publications/opan08/OPAD%20Jan%202008%20 final%20v6%20with%20links%20and%20buttons.pdf (accessed 17 February 2008).

Ingram, D.K. (2000) 'Age-related decline in physical activity: generalization to nonhumans', *Medicine and Science in Sports and Exercise* 32: 1623–9.

Institute of Medicine (2002) *Dietary Reference Intake, Energy, Carbohydrate, Fiber, Fat, Fatty Acids, Cholesterol, Protein and Amino Acids*, Washington: National Academy Press.

International Agency for Research on Cancer (2002) *Weight Control and Physical Activity*, IARC Handbooks on Cancer Prevention Vol. 6, Lyon: International Agency for Research on Cancer Press.

International Diabetes Federation (2007) *The Diabetes Atlas*, 3rd edn, Brussels: International Diabetes Federation.

Irwin, M.L., Yasui, Y., Ulrich, C.M., Bowen, D., Rudolph, R.E., Schwartz, R.S., Yukawa, M., Aiello, E., Potter, J.D. and McTiernan, A. (2003) 'Effect of exercise on total and intra-abdominal body fat in postmenopausal women: a randomized controlled trial', *Journal of the American Medical Association* 289: 323–30.

Jakicic, J.M. and Otto, A.D. (2005) 'Physical activity considerations for the treatment and prevention of obesity', *American Journal of Clinical Nutrition* 82 (Supplement): S226–9.

Jakicic, J.M., Marcus, B.H., Gallagher, K.I., Napolitano, M. and Lang, W. (2003) 'Effect of exercise duration and intensity on weight loss in overweight, sedentary women: a randomized trial', *Journal of the American Medical Association* 290: 1323–30. (See also the editorial by Lee, I.M. (2003) 'Physical activity in women: how much is good enough?', *Journal of the American Medical Association* 290: 1377–9.)

Jakicic, J.M., Winters, C., Lang, W. and Wing, R.R. (1999) 'Effects of intermittent exercise and use of home exercise equipment on adherence, weight loss, and fitness in overweight women: a randomized trial', *Journal of the American Medical Association* 282: 1554–60.

James, W.P.T. (1995) 'A public health approach to the problem of obesity', *International Journal of Obesity and Related Metabolic Disorders* 19: S37–45.

James, W.P.T. (2008) 'The epidemiology of obesity: the size of the problem', *Journal of Internal Medicine* 263: 336–52.

JBS 2 (2005) *Joint British Societies' Guidelines on Prevention of Cardiovascular Disease in Clinical Practice* (prepared by British Cardiac Society, British Hypertension Society, Diabetes UK, HEART UK, Primary Care Cardiovascular Society and the Stroke Association) 91 (Supplement V): V1–52.

Jee, S.H., Sull, J.W., Park, J., Lee, S.Y., Ohrr, H., Guallar, E. and Samet, J.M. (2006) 'Body-mass index and mortality in Korean men and women', *New England Journal of Medicine* 355: 779–87. (See also the commentary by Beyers, T. (2006) 'Overweight and mortality among baby boomers: now we're getting personal', *New England Journal of Medicine* 355: 758–60.)

Jeffery, R.W. and Sherwood, N.E. (2008) 'Is the obesity epidemic exaggerated? No', *British Medical Journal* 336: 245.

Jeffrey, R.W., Wing, R.R., Sherwood, N.E. and Tate, D.F. (2003) 'Physical activity and weight loss: does prescribing higher physical activity goals improve outcome?', *American Journal of Clinical Nutrition* 78: 684–9. (See also the editorial by Schoeller, D.A. (2003) 'But how much physical activity?', *American Journal of Clinical Nutrition* 78: 669–70.)

Jensen, M.K., Chiuve, S.E., Rimm, E.B., Dethlefsen, C., Tjønneland, A., Joensen, A.M. and Overvad, K. (2008) 'Obesity, behavioural lifestyle factors, and risk of acute coronary events', *Circulation* 117: 3062–9. (See also the editorial by Poirier, P. (2008) 'Healthy lifestyle: even if you are doing everything right, extra weight carries an excess risk of acute coronary events', *Circulation* 117: 3057–9.)

Jeon, C.Y., Lokken, R.P., Hu, F.B. and van Dam, R.M. (2007) 'Physical activity of moderate intensity and risk of type 2 diabetes', *Diabetes Care* 30: 744–52.

Jessen, N. and Goodyear, L.J. (2005) 'Contraction signalling to glucose transport in skeletal muscle', *Journal of Applied Physiology*, 99: 330–7.

Jette, A.M. and Branch, L.G. (1981) 'The Framingham disability study: II-Physical disability among the aging', *American Journal of Public Health* 71: 1211–16.

Joint National Committee on Detection, Evaluation and Treatment of High Blood Pressure (1997) 'The 6th report of the Joint National Committee on Detection, Evaluation and Treatment of High Blood Pressure (JNC VI)', *Archives of Internal Medicine* 157: 2413–46.

Jones, W.H.S. (1967) *Hippocrates* (trans. W.H.S. Jones), Cambridge: Harvard University Press.

Jurca, R., Lamonte, M.J., Barlow, C.E., Kampert, J.B., Church, T.S. and Blair, S.N. (2005) 'Association of muscular strength with incidence of metabolic syndrome in men', *Medicine and Science in Sports and Exercise* 37: 1849–55.

Jurca, R., Lamonte, M.J., Church, T.S., Earnest, C.P., Fitzgerald, S.J., Barlow, C.E., Jordan, A.N., Kampert, J.B. and Blair, S.N. (2004) 'Associations of muscle strength and fitness with metabolic syndrome in men', *Medicine and Science in Sports and Exercise* 36: 1301–7.

Kadel, N.J., Teitz, C.C. and Kronmal, R.A. (1992) 'Stress fractures in ballet dancers', *American Journal of Sports Medicine* 20: 445–9.

Kahn, H.S., Tatham, L.M., Rodriguez, C., Calle, E.E., Thun, M.J. and Heath, C.W. (1997) 'Stable behaviors associated with adults' 10-year change in body mass index and likelihood of gain at the waist', *American Journal of Public Health* 87: 747–54.

Kahn, S.E., Hull, R.L. and Utzschneider, K.M. (2006) 'Mechanisms linking obesity to insulin resistance and type 2 diabetes', *Nature* 444: 840–6.

Kannus, P., Haapasalo, H., Sankelo, M., Sievanen, H., Pasanen, M., Heinonen, A., Oja, P. and Vuori, I. (1995) 'Effect of starting age of physical activity on bone mass in the dominant arm of tennis and squash players', *Annals of Internal Medicine* 123: 27–31.

Karlsson, M.K., Linden, C., Karlsson, C., Johnell, O., Obrant, K. and Seeman, E. (2000) 'Exercise during growth and bone mineral density and fractures in old age', *Lancet* 355: 469–70.

Katch, F.I. and McArdle, W.D. (1993) *Introduction to Nutrition, Exercise and Health*, 4th edn, Philadelphia and London: Lea and Febiger.

Katzmarzyk, P.T. and Craig, C.L. (2002) 'Musculoskeletal fitness and risk of mortality', *Medicine and Science in Sports and Exercise* 34: 740–4.

Katzmarzyk, P.T. and Janssen, I. (2004) 'The economic costs associated with physical inactivity and obesity in Canada: an update', *Canadian Journal of Applied Physiology* 29: 90–115.

Katzmarzyk, P.T., Church, T.S. and Blair, S.N. (2004) 'Cardiorespiratory fitness attenuates the effects of the metabolic syndrome on all-cause and cardiovascular disease mortality in men', *Archives of Internal Medicine* 164: 1092–7.

Katzmarzyk, P.T., Leon, A.S., Wilmore, J.H., Skinner, J.S., Rao, D.C., Rankinen, T. and Bouchard, C. (2003) 'Targeting the metabolic syndrome with exercise: evidence from the HERITAGE Family Study', *Medicine and Science in Sports and Exercise* 35: 1703–9.

Keen, A.D. and Drinkwater, B.L. (1997) 'Irreversible bone loss in former amenorrheic athletes', *Osteoporosis International* 7: 311–15.

Keith, S.W., Redden, D.T., Katzmarzyk, P.T., Boggiano, M.M., Hanlon, E.C., Benca, R.M., Ruden, D., Pietrobelli, A., Barger, J.L., Fontaine, K.R., Wang, C., Aronne, L.J., Wright, S.M., Baskin, M., Dhurandhar, N.V., Lijoi, M.C., Grilo, C.M., DeLuca, M., Westfall, A.O. and Allison, D.B. (2006) 'Putative contributors to the secular increase in obesity: exploring the roads less traveled', *International Journal of Obesity* 30: 1585–94.

Kelley, D.A. (1998) 'Exercise and regional bone mineral density in postmenopausal women', *American Journal of Physical Medicine and Rehabilitation* 77: 76–87.

Kelley, G.A. and Kelley, K.S. (2006) 'Exercise and bone mineral density at the femoral neck in post-menopausal women: a meta-analysis of controlled clinical trials with individual patient data', *American Journal of Obstetrics and Gynecology* 194: 760–7.

Kelley, G.A., Kelley, K.S. and Tran, Z.V. (2005) 'Aerobic exercise, lipids and lipoproteins in over-weight and obese adults: a meta-analysis of randomized controlled trials', *International Journal of Obesity* 29: 881–93.

Kettaneh, A., Oppert, J.M., Heude, B., Deschamps, V., Borys, J.M., Lommez, A., Ducimetière, P. and Charles, M.A. (2005) 'Changes in physical activity explain paradoxical relationship between baseline physical activity and adiposity changes in adolescent girls: the FLVS II study', *International Journal of Obesity* 29: 586–93.

Keys, A. (1980) *Seven Countries: A Multivariate Analysis of Death and Coronary Heart Disease*, Boston: Harvard University Press.

Khan, K.M., McKay, H.A., Kannus, P., Bailey, D., Wark, J. and Bennell, K. (2001) *Physical Activity and Bone Health*, Champaign: Human Kinetics.

Khaw, K.T., Wareham, N., Binhman, S., Welch, A., Luben, R. and Day, N. (2008) 'Combined impact of health behaviours and mortality in men and women: the EPIC-Norfolk prospective population study', *Public Library of Science Medicine* 5: E12.

Kimm, S.Y.S., Glynn, N.W., Kriska, A.M., Barton, B.A., Kronsberg, S.S., Daniels, S.R., Crawford, P.B., Sabry, Z.I. and Liu, K. (2002) 'Decline in physical activity in black girls and white girls during adolescence', *New England Journal of Medicine* 347: 709–15.

Kimm, S.Y.S., Glynn, N.W., Obarzanek, E., Kriska, A.M., Daniels, S.R., Barton, B.A. and Liu, K. (2005) 'Relation between changes in physical activity and body-mass index during adolescence: a multicentre longitudinal study', *Lancet* 366: 301–7. (See also the editorial by Reilly, J.J. (2005) 'Physical activity and obesity in childhood and adolescence', *Lancet* 366: 268–9.)

King, D.S., Baldus, R.J., Sharp, R.L., Kesl, L.D., Feltmeyer, T.L. and Riddle, M.S. (1995) 'Time course for exercise-induced alterations in insulin action and glucose tolerance in middle-aged people', *Journal of Applied Physiology* 78: 17–22.

Klarlund Pedersen, B.K. and Hoffman-Goetz, L. (2000) 'Exercise and the immune system: regulation, integration, and adaptation', *Physiological Reviews* 80: 1055–81.

Klem, M.L., Wing, R.R., McGuire, M.T., Seagle, H.M. and Hill, J.O. (1997) 'A descriptive study of individuals successful at long-term maintenance of substantial weight loss', *American Journal of Clinical Nutrition* 66: 239–46.

Knoops, K.T.B., de Groot, L.C.P.G.M., Kromhout, D., Perrin, A.E., Moreiras-Varela, O., Menotti, A. and van Staveren, W.A. (2004) 'Mediterranean diet, lifestyle factors, and 10-year mortality in elderly European men and women: the Hale Project', *Journal of the American Medical Association* 292: 1433–9. (See also the editorial by Rimm, E.B. and Stampfer, M.J. (2004) 'Diet, exercise, and longevity: the next steps?', *Journal of the American Medical Association* 292: 1490–2.)

Knowler, W.C., Barrett-Connor, E., Fowler, S.E., Hamman, R.F., Lachin, J.M., Walker, E.A. and Nathan, D.M. for the Diabetes Prevention Program Research Group (2002) 'Reduction in the incidence of type 2 diabetes with lifestyle intervention or Metformin', *The New England Journal of Medicine* 346: 393–403.

Koh-Banerjee, P., Chu, N.F., Spiegelman, D., Rosner, B., Colditz, G., Willett, W. and Rimm, E. (2003) 'Prospective study of the association of changes in dietary intake, physical activity, alcohol consumption, and smoking with 9-y weight gain in waist circumference among 16,587 US men', *American Journal of Clinical Nutrition* 78: 719–27.

Kohl, H.W., Gordon, N.F., Villegas, J.A. and Blair, S.N. (1992) 'Cardiorespiratory fitness, glycemic status, and mortality risk in men', *Diabetes Care* 15: 184–92.

Kohrt, W.M., Bloomfield, S.A., Little, K.D., Nelson, M.E. and Yingling, V.R. (2004) 'American College of Sports Medicine Position Stand: physical activity and bone health', *Medicine and Science in Sports and Exercise* 36: 1985–96.

Kohrt, W.M., Ehsani, A.A. and Birge, S.J. (1997) 'Effects of exercise involving predominantly either joint-reaction or ground-reaction forces on bone mineral density in older women', *Journal of Bone and Mineral Research* 12: 1253–61.

Kolonel, L.N. and Wilkens, L.R. (2006) 'Migrant studies' in D. Schottenfeld and J.F. Fraumeni (eds) *Cancer Epidemiology, Biomarkers and Prevention*, 3rd edn, New York: Oxford University Press, pp. 189–201.

Kontulainen, S., Heinonen, A., Kannus, P., Pasanen, M., Sievänen, H. and Vuori, I. (2004) 'Former exercisers of an 18-month intervention display residual aBMD benefits compared with control women 3.5 years post-intervention: a follow-up of a randomized controlled high-impact trial', *Osteoporosis International* 15: 248–51.

Kontulainen, S., Kannus, P., Haapasalo, H., Heinonen, A., Sievänen, H., Oja, P. and Vuori, I. (1999) 'Changes in bone mineral content with decreased training in competitive young adult tennis players and controls: a prospective 4-yr follow-up', *Medicine and Science in Sports and Exercise* 31: 646–52.

Kontulainen, S., Sievänen, H., Kannus, P., Pasanen, M. and Vuori, I. (2003) 'Effect of long-term impact-loading on mass, size, and estimated strength of humerus and radius of female racquet-sports players: a peripheral quantitative computed tomography study between young and old starters and controls', *Journal of Bone and Mineral Research* 18: 352–9.

Koopman, R., Manders, R.J.F., Zorenc, A.H.G., Hul, G.B.J., Kuipers, H., Keizer, H.A. and van Loon, L.J.C. (2005) 'A single session of resistance exercise enhances insulin sensitivity for at least 24 h in healthy men', European *Journal of Applied Physiology* 94: 180–7.

Korner, J. and Aronne, L.J. (2003) 'The emerging science of body weight regulation and its impact on obesity treatment', *Journal of Clinical Investigation* 111: 565–70.

Kragelund, C. and Omland, T. (2005) 'A farewell to the body-mass index?' *Lancet* 366: 1589–91 (editorial).

Kramsch, D.M., Aspen, A.J., Abramowitz, B.M., Kreimendahl, T. and Hood, W.B. (1981) 'Reduction of coronary atherosclerosis by moderate conditioning exercise in monkeys on an atherogenic diet', *New England Journal of Medicine* 305: 1483–9.

Kraus, W.E. and Douglas, P.S. (2005) 'Where does fitness fit in?', *New England Journal of Medicine* 353: 517–19 (editorial).

Kraus, W.E., Houmard, J.A., Duscha, B.D., Knetzger, K.J., Wharton, M.B., McCartney, J.S., Bales, C.W., Henes, S., Samsa, G.P., Otvos, J.D., Kulkarni, K.R. and Slentz, C.A. (2002) 'Effects of the amount and intensity of exercise on plasma lipoproteins', *New England Journal of Medicine* 347: 1483–92.

Kujala, U.M. (2004) 'Evidence for exercise therapy in the treatment of chronic disease based on three randomized controlled trials – summary of published systematic reviews', *Scandinavian Journal of Medicine and Science in Sports* 14: 339–45.

Kurl, S., Laukkanen, J.A., Rauramaa, R., Lakka, T.A., Sivenius, J. and Salonen, J.T. (2003) 'Cardiorespiratory fitness and the risk of stroke in men', *Archives of Internal Medicine* 163: 1682–8.

Laaksonen, D.E., Lakka, H.M., Salonen, J.T., Niskanen, L.K., Rauramaa, R. and Lakka, T.A. (2002) 'Low levels of leisure-time physical activity and cardiorespiratory fitness predict development of the metabolic syndrome', *Diabetes Care* 25: 1612–18.

LaCroix, A.Z., Leveille, S.G., Hecht, J.A., Grothaus, L.C. and Wagner, E.H. (1996) 'Does walking decrease the risk of cardiovascular disease hospitalizations and death in older adults', *Journal of the American Geriatric Society* 44: 113–20.

Lahti-Koski, M., Pietinen, P., Heliövaara, M. and Vartiainen, E. (2002) 'Associations of body mass index and obesity with physical activity, food choices, alcohol intake, and smoking in the 1982–97 FINRISK Studies', *American Journal of Clinical Nutrition* 75: 809–17.

Lakka, T.A., Laaksonen, D.E., Lakka, H.-M., Männikkö, N., Niskanen, L.K., Rauramaa, R. and Salonen, J.T. (2003) 'Sedentary lifestyle, poor cardiorespiratory fitness, and the metabolic syndrome', *Medicine and Science in Sports and Exercise* 35: 1279–86.

Lakka, T.A., Laukkanen, J.A., Rauramaa, R., Salonen, R., Lakka, H.-M., Kaplan, G.A. and Salonen, J.T. (2001) 'Cardiorespiratory fitness and the progression of carotid atherosclerosis in middle-aged men', *Annals of Internal Medicine* 134: 12–20.

LaMonte, M.J., Barlow, C.E., Jurca, R., Kampert, J.B., Church, T.S. and Blair, S.N. (2005a) 'Cardiorespiratory fitness is inversely associated with the incidence of metabolic syndrome: a prospective study of men and women', *Circulation* 112: 505–12.

LaMonte, M.J., Blair, S.N. and Church, T.S. (2005b) 'Physical activity and diabetes prevention', *Journal of Applied Physiology* 99: 1205–13.

Langlois, J.A., Keyl, P.M., Guralnik, J.M., Foley, D.J., Marottoli, R.A. and Wallace, R.B. (1997) 'Characteristics of older pedestrians who have difficulty crossing the street', *American Journal of Public Health* 87: 393–7.

LaPorte, R.E., Brenes, G., Dearwater, S., Murphy, M.A., Cauley, J.A., Dietrick, R. and Robertson, R. (1983) 'HDL Cholesterol across a spectrum of physical activity from quadriplegia to marathon running', *Lancet* 1: 1212–13.

Laukkanen, J.A., Lakka, T.A., Rauramaa, R., Kuhanen, R., Venäläinen, J.M., Salonen, R. and Salonen, J.T. (2001) 'Cardiovascular fitness as a predictor of mortality in men', *Archives of Internal Medicine* 161: 825–31.

Lautenschlager, N.T., Cox, K.L., Flicker, L., Foster, J.K., van Bockxmeer, F.M., Xiao, J., Greenop, K.R. and Almeida, O.P. (2008) 'Effect of physical activity on cognitive function in older adults at risk for Alzheimer disease: a randomized trial', *Journal of the American Medical Association* 300: 1027–37. (See also the editorial by Larson, E.B. (2008) 'Physical activity for older adults at risk for Alzheimer disease', *Journal of the American Medical Association* 300: 1077–9.)

Lavrencic, A., Salobir, G. and Keber, I. (2000) 'Physical training improves flow-mediated dilation in patients with the polymetabolic syndrome', *Arteriosclerosis, Thrombosis and Vascular Biology* 20: 551–5.

Lazar, M.A. (2005) 'How obesity causes diabetes: not a tale', *Science* 307: 373–5.

Lean, M. and Finer, N. (2006) 'ABC of obesity: management: Part II – Drugs', *British Medical Journal* 333: 794–7.

Lee, C.D. and Blair, S.N. (2002) 'Cardiorespiratory fitness and stroke mortality in men', *Medicine and Science in Sports and Exercise* 34: 592–5.

Lee, C.D., Blair, S.N. and Jackson, A.S. (1999) 'Cardiorespiratory fitness, body composition, and all-cause and cardiovascular disease mortality in men', *American Journal of Clinical Nutrition* 69: 373–80.

Lee, I.-M. and Oguma, Y. (2006) 'Physical activity', in D.A. Schottenfeld and J.F.J. Fraumeni (eds) *Cancer Epidemiology and Prevention,* San Francisco: Oxford University Press.

Lee, I.-M. and Paffenbarger, R.S. (1996) 'Do physical activity and physical fitness avert premature mortality?', *Exercise and Sport Sciences Reviews* 24: 135–71.

Lee, I.-M. and Paffenbarger, R.S. (1998) 'Physical activity and stroke incidence: the Harvard Alumni Health Study', *Stroke* 29: 2049–54.

Lee, I.-M. and Paffenbarger, R.S. (2000) 'Associations of light, moderate, and vigorous intensity physical activity with longevity', *American Journal of Epidemiology* 151: 293–9.

Lee, I.-M. and Skerrett, P.J. (2001) 'Physical activity and all-cause mortality: what is the dose–response relation?', *Medicine and Science in Sports and Exercise* 33: S459–71.

Lee, I.-M., Hsieh, C.C. and Paffenbarger, R.S. (1995) 'Exercise intensity and longevity in men: the Harvard Alumni Health Study', *Journal of the American Medical Association* 273: 1179–84.

Lee, I.-M., Paffenbarger, R.S. and Hsieh, C.C. (1991) 'Physical activity and the risk of developing colorectal cancer among college alumni', *Journal of the National Cancer Institute* 83: 1324–9.

Lee, I.-M., Paffenbarger, R.S. and Hsieh, C.C. (1992) 'Physical activity and risk of prostatic cancer among college alumni', *American Journal of Epidemiology* 135: 169–79.

Lee, I.-M., Rexrode, K.M., Cook, N.R., Hennekens, C.H. and Buring, J.E. (2001a) 'Physical activity and breast cancer risk: the Women's Health Study (United States)', *Cancer Causes and Control* 12: 137–45.

Lee, I.-M., Sesso, H.D., Oguma, Y. and Paffenbarger, R.S. (2003) 'Relative intensity of physical activity and risk of coronary heart disease', *Circulation* 107: 1110–16.

Lee, I.-M., Sesso, H.D. and Paffenbarger, R.S. (2000) 'Physical activity and coronary heart disease risk in men: does the duration of exercise episodes predict risk?', *Circulation* 102: 981–6.

Lee, I.-M., Sesso, H.D. and Paffenbarger, R.S. (2001b) 'A prospective cohort study of physical activity and body size in relation to prostate cancer risk (United States)', *Cancer Causes and Control* 12: 187–93.

Lee, J.M., Herman, W.H., Okumura, M.J., Gurney, J.G. and Davis, M.M. (2006) 'Prevalence and determinants of insulin resistance among U.S. adolescents', *Diabetes Care* 29: 2427–32.

Lee, L., Kumar, S. and Chin Leong, L. (1994) 'The impact of five month basic military training on the body weight and body fat of 197 moderately to severely obese Singaporean males aged 17 to 19 years', *International Journal of Obesity* 18: 105–9.

Lee, W.R.W. (2000) 'The changing demography of diabetes mellitus in Singapore', *Diabetes Research and Clinical Practice* 50 (Supplement): S35–9.

Lefevre, J., Philippaerts, R., Delvaux, K., Thomis, M., Claessens, A.L., Lysens, R., Renson, R., Vanden Eynde, B., Vanreusel, B. and Beunen, G. (2002) 'Relation between cardiovascular risk factors at adult age, and physical activity during youth and adulthood: the Leuven Longitudinal Study on Lifestyle, Fitness and Health', *International Journal of Sports Medicine* 23: S32–8.

Lehmann, R., Vokac, A., Niedermann, K., Agosti, K. and Spinas, G.A. (1995) 'Loss of abdominal fat and improvement of the cardiovascular risk profile by regular moderate exercise training in patients with NIDDM', *Diabetologia* 38: 1313–19.

Leibel, R.L., Rosenbaum, M. and Hirsch, J. (1995) 'Changes in energy expenditure resulting from altered body weight', *New England Journal of Medicine* 332: 621–8.

Levine, J.A., Lanningham-Foster, L.M., McCrady, S.K., Krizan, A.C., Olson, L.R., Kane, P.H., Jensen, M.D. and Clark, M.M. (2005) 'Interindividual variation in posture allocation: possible role in human obesity', *Science* 307: 584–6.

Levine, J.A., McCrady, S.K., Lanningham-Foster, L.M., Kane, P.H., Foster, R.C. and Manohar, C.U. (2008) 'The role of free-living daily walking in human weight gain and obesity', *Diabetes* 57: 548–54.

Levine, J.A., Vander Weg, M.W., Hill, J.O. and Klesges, R.C. (2006) 'Non-exercise activity thermogenesis: the crouching tiger hidden dragon of societal weight gain', *Arteriosclerosis, Thrombosis, and Vascular Biology* 26: 729–36.

Licinio, J., Caglayan, S., Ozata, M., Yildiz, B.O., de Miranda, P.B., O'Kirwan, F., Whitby, R., Liang, L., Cohen, P., Bhasin, S., Krauss, R.M., Veldhuis, J.D., Wagner, A.J., DePaoli, A., McCann, S.M. and Wong, M.L. (2004) 'Phenotypic effects of leptin replacement on morbid obesity, diabetes mellitus, hypogonadism, and behaviour in leptin-deficient adults', *Proceedings of the National Academy of Sciences* 101: 4531–6.

Lindsay, J., Laurin, D., Verreault, R., Hébert, R., Helliwell, B., Hill, G.B. and McDowell, I. (2002) 'Risk factors for Alzheimer's disease: a prospective analysis from the Canadian study of health and aging', *American Journal of Epidemiology* 156: 445–53.

Lindström, J., Ilanne-Parikka, P., Peltonen, M., Aunola, S., Eriksson, J.G., Hemiö, K., Hämäläinen, H., Härkönen, P., Keinänen-Kiukaanniemi, S., Laakso, M., Louheranta, A., Mannelin, M., Paturi, M., Sundvall, J., Valle, T.T., Uusitupa, M. and Tuomilehto, J. on behalf of the Finnish Diabetes Prevention Study Group (2006) 'Sustained reduction in the incidence of type 2 diabetes by lifestyle intervention: follow-up of the Finnish Diabetes Prevention Study', *Lancet* 368: 1673–9.

Lipman, R.L., Raskin, P., Love, T., Triebwasser, J., Lecocq, F.R. and Schnure, J.J. (1972) 'Glucose intolerance during decreased physical activity in man', *Diabetes* 21: 101–7.

Littman, A.J., Kristal, A.R. and White, E. (2005) 'Effects of physical activity intensity, frequency, and activity type on 10-y weight change in middle-aged men and women', *International Journal of Obesity* 29: 524–33.

Lobstein, T.J., James, W.P.T. and Cole, T.J. (2003) 'Increasing levels of excess weight among children in England', *International Journal of Obesity* 27: 1136–8.

Loucks, A.B. (1996) 'The reproductive system' in O. Bar-Or, D. Lamb and P. Clarkson (eds) *Perspectives in Exercise Science and Sports Medicine, Vol. 9: Exercise and the Female: A Life Span Approach*, Carmel: Cooper Publishing, pp. 41–71.

Loucks, A.B., Verdun, M. and Heath, E.M. (1998) 'Low energy availability, not stress of exercise, alters LH pulsatility in exercising women', *Journal of Applied Physiology* 84: 37–46.

Lowell, B.B. and Shulman, G.I. (2005) 'Mitochondrial dysfunction and type 2 diabetes', *Science* 307: 384–7.

McArdle, W.D., Katch, F.I. and Katch, V.L. (2006) *Exercise Physiology: Energy, Nutrition, and Human Performance*, Philadelphia: Lippincott Williams and Wilkins.

McAuley, K.A., Williams, S.M., Mann, J.I., Goulding, A., Chisholm, A., Wilson, N., Story, G., McLay, R.T., Harper, M.J. and Jones, I.E. (2002) 'Intensive lifestyle changes are necessary to improve insulin sensitivity', *Diabetes Care* 25: 445–52.

McCarthy, H.D., Cole, T.J., Fry, T., Jebb, S.A. and Prentice, A.M. (2006) 'Body fat reference curves for children', *International Journal of Obesity* 30, 598–602.

McCarthy, H.D., Ellis, S.M. and Cole, T.J. (2003) 'Central overweight and obesity in British youth aged 11–16 years: cross sectional surveys of waist circumference', *British Medical Journal* 326: 624–6.

Macdonald, H.M., Kontulainen, S.A., Khan, K.M. and McKay, H.A. (2007) 'Is a school-based physical activity intervention effective for increasing tibial bone strength in boys and girls?', *Journal of Bone and Mineral Research* 22: 434–46.

MacDonald, J.R. (2002) 'Potential causes, mechanisms, and implications of post exercise hypotension', *Journal of Human Hypertension* 16: 225–36.

McGill, H.C., McMahan, C.A., Herderick, E.E., Malcom, G.T., Tracy, R.E. and Strong, J.P., for the Pathobiological Determinants of Atherosclerosis in Youth (PDAY) Research Group (2000) 'Origin of atherosclerosis in childhood and adolescence', *American Journal of Clinical Nutrition* 72 (Supplement): S1307–15.

McGill, H.C. Jr., Geer, J.C. and Strong, J.P. (1963) 'Natural history of human atherosclerotic lesions', in M. Sandler and G.H. Bourne (eds) *Atherosclerosis and its Origin*, New York: Academic Press, pp. 39–65.

McGuire, D.K., Levine, B.D., Williamson, J.W., Snell, P.G., Blomqvist, G., Saltin, B. and Mitchell, J.H. (2001a) 'A 30-year follow-up of the Dallas bed rest and training study: I: effect of age on the cardiovascular response to exercise', *Circulation* 104: 1350–7.

McGuire, D.K., Levine, B.D., Williamson, J.W., Snell, P.G., Blomqvist, G., Saltin, B. and Mitchell, J.H. (2001b) 'A 30-year follow-up of the Dallas bed rest and training study: II: effect of age on cardiovascular adaptation to exercise training', *Circulation* 104: 1358–66.

McKay, H.A. and Smith, E. (2008) 'Winning the battle against childhood physical inactivity: the key to bone strength?', *Journal of Bone and Mineral Research* 23: 980–5.

McKay, H.A., MacLean, L., Petit, M., MacKelvie-O'Brien, K., Janssen, P., Beck, T. and Kahn, K.M. (2005) ' "Bounce at the Bell": a novel program of short bouts of exercise improves proximal femur bone mass in early pubertal children', *British Journal of Sports Medicine* 39: 521–6.

McMillan, D.C., Sattar, N., Lean, M. and McArdle, C.S. (2006) 'ABC of obesity: obesity and cancer', *British Medical Journal* 333: 1109–11.

McNamara, J.J., Molot, M.A., Stremple, J.F., Cutting, R.T. (1970) 'Coronary artery disease in combat casualties in Vietnam', *Journal of the American Medical Association* 216: 1185–7.

MacRae, P.G., Asplund, L.A., Schnelle, J.F., Ouslander, J.G., Abrahamse, A. and Morris, C. (1996) 'A walking program for nursing home residents: effects on walk endurance, physical activity, mobility, and quality of life', *Journal of the American Geriatric Society* 44: 175–80.

McTiernan, A., Tworoger, S.S., Ulrich, C.M., Yasui, Y., Irwin, M.L., Rajan, K.B., Sorensen, B., Rudolph, R.E., Bowen, D., Stanczyk, F.Z., Potter, J.D. and Schwartz, R.S. (2004) 'Effect of exercise on serum estrogens in postmenopausal women: a 12-month randomized clinical trial', *Cancer Research* 64: 2923–8.

Magnus, K., Matroos, A. and Strackee, J. (1979) 'Walking, cycling, or gardening, with or without seasonal interruption, in relation to acute coronary events', *American Journal of Epidemiology* 110: 724–33.

Majeed, A. and Aylin, P. (2005) 'The ageing population of the United Kingdom and cardiovascular disease', *British Medical Journal* 331: 1362.

Malbut, K.E., Dinan, S. and Young, A. (2002) 'Aerobic training in the "oldest old": the effect of 24 weeks of training', *Age and Ageing* 31: 255–60.

Mallam, K.M., Metcalf, B.S., Kirkby, J., Voss, L.D. and Wilkin, T.J. (2003) 'Contribution of time-tabled physical education to total physical activity in primary school children: cross sectional study', *British Medical Journal* 327: 592–3.

Manini, T.M., Everhart, J.E., Patel, K.V., Schoeller, D.A., Colbert, L.H., Visser, M., Tylavsky, F., Bauer, D.C., Goodpaster, B.H. and Harris, T.B. (2006) 'Daily activity energy expenditure and mortality among older adults', *Journal of the American Medical Association* 296: 171–9. (See also the editorial by Blair, S.N. and Haskell, W.L. (2006) 'Objectively measured physical activity and mortality in older adults', *Journal of the American Medical Association* 296: 216–18.)

Manson, J.E., Greenland, P., LaCroix, A.Z., Stefanik, M.L., Mouton, C.P., Oberman, A., Perri, M.G., Sheps, D.S., Pettinger, M.B. and Sisovick, D.S. (2002) 'Walking compared with vigorous exercise for the prevention of cardiovascular events in women', *New England Journal of Medicine* 347: 716–25.

Manson, J.E., Hu, F.B., Rich-Edwards, J.W., Colditz, G.A., Stampfer, M.J., Willett, W.C., Speizer, F.E. and Hennekens, C.H. (1999) 'A prospective study of walking as compared with vigorous exercise in the prevention of coronary heart disease in women', *New England Journal of Medicine* 341: 650–8.

Manson, J.E., Nathan, D.M., Krolewski, A.S., Stampfer, M.J., Willett, W.C. and Hennekens, C.H. (1992) 'A prospective study of exercise and incidence of diabetes among US male physicians', *Journal of the American Medical Association* 268: 63–7.

Maron, B.J. (2000) 'Sudden death in sports and the marathon' in D. Tunstall-Pedoe (ed.) *Marathon Medicine*, London: Royal Society of Medicine Press, pp. 208–25.

Marshall, S.J., Gorely, T. and Biddle, S.J. (2006) 'A descriptive epidemiology of screen-based media use in youth: a review and critique', *Journal of Adolescence* 29: 333–49.

Martínez, M.E., Giovannucci, E., Spiegelman, D., Hunter, D.J., Willett, W.C. and Colditz, G.A. (1997) 'Leisure-time physical activity, body size, and colon cancer in women', *Journal of the National Cancer Institute* 89: 948–55.

Martínez, M.E., Heddens, D., Earnest, D.L., Bogert, C.L., Roe, D., Einspahr, J., Marshall, J.R. and Alberts, D.S. (1999) 'Physical activity, body mass index, and prostaglandin E_2 levels in rectal mucosa', *Journal of the National Cancer Institute* 91: 950–3.

Martínez-González, M.Á., Alfredo Martínez, J., Hu, F.B., Gibney, M.J. and Kearney, J. (1999) 'Physical inactivity, sedentary lifestyle and obesity in the European Union', *International Journal of Obesity* 23: 1192–201.

Mathers, C.D. and Loncar, D. (2006) 'Projections of global mortality and burden of disease from 2002 to 2030', *PLoS Medicine* 3: E442.

Matthews, C.E., Jurj, A.L., Shu, X.O., Li, H.L., Yang, G., Li, Q., Gao, Y.T. and Zheng, W. (2007) 'Influence of exercise, walking, cycling, and overall nonexercise physical activity on mortality in Chinese women', *American Journal of Epidemiology* 165: 1343–50.

Matthews, C.E., Xu, W.H., Zheng, W., Gao, Y.T., Ruan, Z.X., Cheng, J.R., Xiang, Y.B. and Shu, X.O. (2005) 'Physical activity and risk of endometrial cancer: a report from the Shanghai endometrial cancer study', *Cancer Epidemiology, Biomarkers and Prevention* 14: 779–85.

Mattocks, C., Ness, A., Deere, K., Tilling, K., Leary, S., Blair, S.N. and Riddoch, C. (2008) 'Early life determinants of physical activity in 11 to 12 year olds: cohort study', *British Medical Journal* 336: 26–9.

Matton, L., Thomis, M., Wijndaele, K., Duvigneaud, N., Beunen, G., Claessens, A.L., Vanreusel, B., Philippaerts, R. and Lefevre, J. (2006) 'Tracking of physical fitness and physical activity from youth to adulthood in females', *Medicine and Science in Sports and Exercise* 38: 1114–20.

Mayer-Davis, E.J., D'Agostino, R., Karter, A.J., Haffner, S.M., Rewers, M.J., Saad, M. and Bergman, R.N. (1998) 'Intensity and amount of physical activity in relation to insulin sensitivity: the Insulin Resistance Atherosclerosis Study', *Journal of the American Medical Association* 279: 669–74.

Mazzeo, R.S., Cavanagh, P., Evans, W.J., Fiatarone, M., Hagberg, J., McAuley, E. and Startzell, J. (1998) 'American College of Sports Medicine Position Stand: exercise and physical activity for older adults', *Medicine and Science in Sports and Exercise* 30: 992–1008.

Meisinger, C., Döring, A., Thorand, B., Heier, M. and Löwel, H. (2006) 'Body fat distribution and risk of type 2 diabetes in the general population: are there differences between men and women? The MONICA/KORA Augsburg Cohort Study', *American Journal of Clinical Nutrition* 84: 483–9.

Merrill, J.R., Holly, R.G., Anderson, R.L., Rifai, N., King, M.E. and DeMeersman, R. (1989) 'Hyperlipidemic response of young trained and untrained men after a high fat meal', *Arteriosclerosis* 9: 217–23.

Messerli, F.H., Williams, B. and Ritz, E. (2007) 'Essential hypertension', *Lancet* 370: 591–603.

Metcalf, B., Voss, L., Jeffery, A., Perkins, J. and Wilkin, T. (2004) 'Physical activity cost of the school run: impact on schoolchildren of being driven to school (EarlyBird 22)', *British Medical Journal* 329: 832–3.

Middleton, L.E., Mitnitski, A., Fallah, N., Kirkland, S.A. and Rockwood, K. (2008) 'Changes in cognition and mortality in relation to exercise in later life: a population based study', *PLoS ONE* 3: E3124.

Mittleman, M.A., Maclure, M., Tofler, G.H., Sherwood, J.B., Goldberg, R.J. and Muller, J.E. (1993) 'Triggering of acute myocardial infarction by heavy physical exertion: protection against triggering by regular exertion', *New England Journal Medicine* 329: 1677–83.

Mokdad, A.H., Ford, E.S., Bowman, B.A., Dietz, W.H., Vinicor, F., Bales, V.S. and Marks, J.S. (2003) 'Prevalence of obesity, diabetes, and obesity-related health risk factors, 2001', *Journal of the American Medical Association* 289: 76–9.

Mootha, V.K., Lindgren, C.M., Eriksson, K.-F., Subramanian, A., Sihag, S., Lehar, J., Puigserver, P., Carlsson, E., Ridderstråle, M., Laurila, E., Houstis, N., Daly, M.J., Patterson, N., Mesirov, J.P., Golub, T.R., Tamayo, P., Spiegelman, B., Lander, E.S., Hirschhorn, J.N., Altshuler, D. and Groop, L.C. (2003) 'PGC-1α-responsive genes involved in oxidative phosphorylation are coordinately downregulated in human diabetes', *Nature Genetics* 34: 267–73.

Mora, S., Lee, I.-M., Buring, J.E. and Ridker, P.M. (2006) 'Association of physical activity and body mass index with novel and traditional cardiovascular biomarkers in women', *Journal of the American Medical Association* 295: 1412–19.

Mora, S., Redberg, R.F., Cui, Y., Whiteman, M.K., Flaws, J.A., Sharrett, A.R. and Blumenthal, R.S. (2003) 'Ability of exercise testing to predict cardiovascular and all-cause death in asymptomatic women: a 20-year follow-up of the Lipid Research Clinics Prevalence Study', *Journal of the American Medical Association* 290: 1600–7.

Morbidity and Mortality Weekly Report (2004) 'Trends in intake of energy and macronutrients: United States, 1971–2000', 6 February.

Morbidity and Mortality Weekly Report (2005) 'Barriers to children walking to or from school: United States, 2004', *Journal of the American Medical Association* 294: 2160–2.

Morio, B., Montaurier, C., Pickering, G., Ritz, P., Fellmann, N., Coudert, J., Beaufrère, B. and Vermorel, M. (1998) 'Effects of 14 weeks of progressive endurance training on energy expenditure in elderly people', *British Journal of Nutrition* 80: 511–19.

Morris, J.N. (1994) 'Exercise in the prevention of coronary heart disease: today's best buy in public health', *Medicine Science Sports Exercise* 26: 807–14.

Morris, J.N. and Hardman, A.E. (1997) 'Walking to health', *Sports Medicine* 23: 306–32.

Morris, J.N., Clayton, D.G., Everitt, M.G., Semmence, A.M. and Burgess, E.H. (1990) 'Exercise in leisure time: coronary attack and death rates', *British Heart Journal* 63: 325–34.

Morris, J.N., Everitt, M.G., Pollard, R., Chave, S.P.W. and Semmence, A.M. (1980) 'Vigorous exercise in leisure-time: protection against coronary heart disease', *Lancet* 2: 1207–10.

Morris, J.N., Heady, J.A., Raffle, P.A.B., Parks, J.W. and Roberts, C.G. (1953) 'Coronary heart disease and physical activity of work', *Lancet* 2: 1053–7, 1111–20.

Murphy, K.G. and Bloom, S.R. (2006) 'Gut hormones and the regulation of energy homeostasis', *Nature* 444: 854–9.

Murphy, M.H. and Hardman, A.E. (1998) 'Training effects of short and long bouts of brisk walking in sedentary women', *Medicine and Science in Sports and Exercise* 30: 152–7.

Murphy, M.H., Nevill, A.M. and Hardman, A.E. (2000) 'Different patterns of brisk walking are equally effective in decreasing postprandial lipaemia', *International Journal of Obesity* 24: 1303–39.

Murphy, M.H., Nevill, A.M., Murtagh, E.M. and Holder, R.L. (2007) 'The effect of walking on fitness, fatness and resting blood pressure: a meta-analysis of randomised, controlled trials', *Preventive Medicine* 44: 377–85.

Murphy, M.H., Nevill, A.M., Neville, C., Biddle, S.J.H. and Hardman, A.E. (2002) 'Accumulating brisk walking for fitness, cardiovascular risk, and psychological health', *Medicine and Science in Sports and Exercise* 34: 1468–74.

Murray, C.J.L. and Lopez, A.D. (1997) 'Global mortality, disability, and the contribution of risk factors: Global Burden of Disease Study', *Lancet* 349: 1436–42.

Must, A. and Anderson, S.E. (2006) 'Body mass index in children and adolescents: considerations for population-based application', *International Journal of Obesity* 30: 590–4.

Must, A., Jacques, P.F., Dallal, G.E., Bajema, C.J. and Dietz, W.H. (1992) 'Long-term morbidity and mortality of overweight adolescents: a follow-up of the Harvard Growth Study of 1922 to 1935', *New England Journal of Medicine* 327: 1350–5.

Must, A., Spadano, J., Coakley, E.H., Field, A.E., Colditz, G. and Dietz, W.H. (1999) 'The disease burden associated with overweight and obesity', *Journal of the American Medical Association* 282: 1523–9.

Myers, J., Kaykha, A., George, S., Abella, J., Zaheer, N., Lear, S., Yamazaki, T. and Froelicher, V. (2004) 'Fitness versus physical activity patterns in predicting mortality in men', *American Journal of Medicine* 117: 912–18.

Myers, J., Prakash, M., Froelicher, V., Do, D., Partington, S. and Atwood, J.E. (2002) 'Exercise capacity and mortality among men referred for exercise testing', *New England Journal of Medicine* 346: 793–801.

Nader, P.R., Bradley, R.H., Houts, R.M., McRichie, S.L. and O'Brien, M. (2008) 'Moderate-to-vigorous physical activity from ages 9 to 15 years', *Journal of the American Medical Association* 300: 295–305.

Nair, K.S. (2005) 'Aging muscle', *American Journal of Clinical Nutrition* 81: 953–63.

Narayan, K.M.V., Boyle, J.P., Thompson, T.J., Sorensen, S.W. and Williamson, D.F. (2003) 'Lifetime risk of diabetes mellitus in the United States', *Journal of the American Medical Association* 290: 1884–90.

National Institutes of Health (2001) 'Executive summary of the third report of the National Cholesterol Education Program (NECP) expert panel on the detection, evaluation, and treatment of high blood cholesterol in adults (Adult Treatment Panel III)', *Journal of the American Medical Association* 285: 2486–97.

National Institutes of Health Consensus Development Panel (1996) 'Physical activity and cardiovascular health', *Journal of the American Medical Association* 276: 241–6.

National Institutes of Health and the National Heart, Lung, and Blood Institute (1998) 'Clinical guidelines on the identification, evaluation, and treatment of overweight and obesity in adults: the Evidence Report', *Obesity Research* 6: S51–209.

Neiman, D.C., Nehlsen-Cannarella, S.L., Markoff, P.A., Balk-Lamberton, A.J., Yang, H., Chritton, D.B.W., Lee, J.W. and Arabatzis, K. (1990) 'The effects of moderate exercise training on natural killer cells and acute upper respiratory tract infections', *International Journal Sports Medicine* 11: 467–73.

Nelson, K.M., Reiber, G. and Boyko, E.J. (2002) 'Diet and exercise among adults with type 2 diabetes: findings from the Third National Health and Nutrition Examination Survey (NHANES III)', *Diabetes Care* 25: 1722–8.

Nelson, L., Jennings, G.L., Esler, M.D. and Korner, P.I. (1986) 'Effect of changing levels of physical activity on blood-pressure and haemodynamics in essential hypertension', *Lancet* 2: 473–6.

Nelson, M.E., Fiatorone, M.A., Morganti, C.M., Trice, I., Greenberg, R.A. and Evans, W.J. (1994) 'Effects of high-intensity strength training on multiple risk factors for osteoporotic fractures: a randomized controlled trial', *Journal of the American Medical Association* 272: 1909–14.

Nelson, M.E., Haskell, W.L, and Kennedy, M. (2008) 'The birth of physical activity guidelines for Americans', *Journal of Physical Activity and Health* 5: 485–7.

Nelson, M.E., Rejeski, J.W., Blair, S.N., Duncan, P.W., Judge, J.O., King, A.C., Macera, C.A. and Castaneda-Sceppa, C. (2007) 'Physical activity and public health in older adults: recommendation from the American College of Sports Medicine and the American Heart Association', *Medicine and Science in Sports and Exercise* 39: 1435–45.

Nevitt, M.C., Cummings, S.R., Stone, K.L., Palermo, L., Black, D.M., Bauer, H.K., Genant, M.C., Hochberg, M.C., Ensrud, K.E., Hillier, T.A. and Cauley, J.A. (2005) 'Risk factors for a first-incident radiographic vertebral fracture in women ≥65 years of age: the study of osteoporotic fractures', *Journal of Bone and Mineral Research* 20: 131–40.

Newman, A.B., Simonsick, E.M., Naydeck, B.L., Boudreau, R.M., Kritchevsky, S.B., Nevitt, M.C., Pahor, M., Satterfield, S., Brach, J.S., Studenski, S.A. and Harris, T.B. (2006) 'Association of long-distance corridor walk performance with mortality, cardiovascular disease, mobility limitation, and disability', *Journal of the American Medical Association* 295: 2018–26.

Nikander, R., Sievänen, H., Uusi-Rasi, K., Heinonen, A. and Kannus, P. (2006) 'Loading modalities and bone structures at nonweight-bearing upper extremity and weight-bearing lower extremity: a pQCT study of adult female athletes', *Bone* 39: 886–94.

Ogden, C.L., Carroll, M.D., Curtin, L.R., McDowell, M.A., Tabak, C.J. and Flegal, K.M. (2006) 'Prevalence of overweight and obesity in the United States, 1999–2004', *Journal of the American Medical Association* 295: 1549–55.

Ogden, C.L., Carroll, M.D. and Flegal, K.M. (2008) 'High body mass index for age among US children and adolescents, 2003–6', *Journal of the American Medical Association* 299: 2401–5. (See also the editorial by Ebbeling, C.B. and Ludwig, D.S. (2008) 'Tracking pediatric obesity: an index of uncertainty', *Journal of the American Medical Association* 299: 2442–3.

Ogilvie, D., Foster, C.E., Rothnie, H., Cavill, N., Hamilton, V., Fitzsimons, C.F. and Mutrie, N. (2007) 'Interventions to promote walking: systematic review', *British Medical Journal* 334: 1204–14.

Ohlson, L.-O., Larsson, B., Svärdsudd, K., Welin, L., Eriksson, H., Wilhelmsen, L., Björntrop, P. and Tibblin, G. (1985) 'The influence of body fat distribution on the incidence of diabetes mellitus: 13.5 years of follow-up of the participants in the study of men born in 1913', *Diabetes* 34: 1055–8.

Okada, K., Hayashi, T., Tsumura, K., Suematsu, C., Endo, G. and Fujii, S. (2000) 'Leisure-time physical activity at weekends and the risk of type 2 diabetes mellitus in Japanese men: the Osaka Health Survey', *Diabetic Medicine* 17: 53–8.

Olshansky, S.J., Passaro, D.J., Hershow, R.C., Layden, J., Carnes, B.A., Brody, J., Hayflick, L., Butler, R.N., Allison, D.B. and Ludwig, D.S. (2005) 'A potential decline in life expectancy in the United States in the 21st century', *New England Journal of Medicine* 352: 1138–45.

O'Rahilly, S., Barroso, I. and Wareham, N.J. (2005) 'Genetic factors in type 2 diabetes: the end of the beginning?', *Science* 307: 370–3.

Ornish, D., Scherwitz, L.W., Billings, J.H., Gould, L., Merritt, T.A., Sparler, S., Armstrong, W.T., Ports, T.A., Kirkeide, R.L., Hogeboom, C. and Brand, R.J. (1998) 'Intensive lifestyle changes for reversal of coronary heart disease', *Journal of the American Medical Association* 280: 2001–7.

Orsini, N., Bellocco, R., Bottai, M., Pagano, M. and Wolk, A. (2006) 'Age and temporal trends of total physical activity among Swedish women', *Medicine and Science in Sports and Exercise* 38: 240–5.

Ortega, F.B., Tresaco, B., Ruiz, J.R., Moreno, L.A., Martin-Matillas, M., Mesa, J.L., Warnberg, J., Bueno, M., Tercedor, P., Gutiérrez, Á., Castillo, M.J. and the AVENA Study group (2007) 'Cardiorespiratory fitness and sedentary activities are associated with adiposity in adolescents', *Obesity* 15: 1589–99.

Owen, N., Cerin, E., Leslie, E., du Toit, M.S., Coffee, N., Frank, L.D., Bauman, A.E., Hugo, G., Saelens, B.E. and Sallis, J.F. (2007) 'Neighborhood walkability and the walking behavior of Australian adults', *American Journal of Preventive Medicine* 33: 387–95.

Paffenbarger, R.S. and Hale, W.E. (1975) 'Work activity and coronary heart mortality', *New England Journal of Medicine* 292: 545–50.

Paffenbarger, R.S., Hyde, R.T., Wing, A.L. and Hsieh, C.C. (1986) 'Physical activity, all-cause mortality, and longevity of college alumni', *New England Journal of Medicine* 314: 605–13.

Paffenbarger, R.S., Hyde, R.T., Wing, A.L., Lee, I.-M., Jung, D.L. and Kampert, J.B. (1993) 'The association of changes in physical-activity level and other lifestyle characteristics with mortality among men', *New England Journal of Medicine* 328: 538–45.

Paffenbarger, R.S., Wing, A.L. and Hyde, R.T. (1978) 'Physical activity as an index of heart attack risk in college alumni', *American Journal of Epidemiology* 108: 161–75.

Paffenbarger, R.S., Wing, A.L., Hyde, R.T. and Jung, D.L. (1983) 'Physical activity and incidence of hypertension in college alumni', *American Journal of Epidemiology* 117: 245–57.

Pan, X.R., Li, G.W., Hu, Y.H., Wang, J.X., Yang, W.Y., An, Z.X., Hu, Z.X., Lin, J., Xiao, J.Z., Cao, H.B., Liu, P.A., Jiang, X.G., Jiang, Y.Y., Wang, J.P., Zheng, H., Zhang, H., Bennett, P.H. and Howard, B.V. (1997) 'Effects of diet and exercise in preventing NIDDM in people with impaired glucose tolerance', *Diabetes Care* 20: 537–44.

Park, S., Rink, L.D. and Wallace, J.P. (2006) 'Accumulation of physical activity leads to a greater blood pressure reduction than a single continuous session, in prehypertension', *Journal of Hypertension* 24: 1761–70.

Parsons, T.J., Manor, O. and Power, C. (2006) 'Physical activity and change in body mass index from adolescence to mid-adulthood in the 1958 British cohort', *International Journal of Epidemiology* 35: 197–204.

Pate, R.R., Pratt, M., Blair, S.N., Haskell, W.L., Macera, C.A., Bouchard, C., Buchner, D., Ettinger, W., Heath, G.W., King, A.C., Kriska, A., Leon, A.S., Marcus, B.H., Morris, J., Paffenbarger, R.S., Patrick, K., Pollock, M.L., Rippe, J.M., Sallis, J. and Wilmore, J.H. (1995) 'Physical activity and public health: a recommendation from the Centers for Disease Control and Prevention and the American College of Sports Medicine', *Journal of the American Medical Association* 273: 402–7.

Pate, R.R., Wang, C.-Y., Dowda, M., Farrell, S.W. and O'Neill, J.R. (2006) 'Cardiorespiratory fitness levels among US youth 12 to 19 years of age: findings from the 1999–2002 National Health and Nutrition Examination Survey', *Archives of Pediatric and Adolescent Medicine* 160: 1005–12.

Pedersen, B.K. and Saltin, B. (2006) 'Evidence for prescribing exercise as therapy in chronic disease', *Scandinavian Journal of Medicine and Science in Sports* 16: 3–63.

Perseghin, G., Price, T.B., Petersen, K.F., Roden, M., Cline, G.W., Gerow, K., Rothman, D.L. and Shulman, G.I. (1996) 'Increased glucose transport-phosphorylation and muscle glycogen synthesis after exercise training in insulin-resistant subjects', *New England Journal of Medicine* 335: 1357–62.

Pescatello, L.S., Franklin, B.A., Fagard, R., Farquhar, W.B., Kelley, G.A. and Ray, C.A. (2004) 'Exercise and hypertension: American College of Sports Medicine Position Stand', *Medicine and Science in Sports and Exercise* 36: 533–53.

Petersen, A.M.W. and Pedersen, B.K. (2005) 'The anti-inflammatory effect of exercise', *Journal of Applied Physiology* 98: 1154–62.

Petrie, J., Barnwell, B. and Grimshaw, J. (1995) *Clinical Guidelines: Criteria for Appraisal for National Use*, Edinburgh: Royal College of Physicians.

Pinhas-Hamiel, O. and Zeitler, P. (2005) 'The global spread of type 2 diabetes mellitus in children and adolescents', *The Journal of Pediatrics* 146: 693–700.

Plasqui, G., Joosen, A.M., Kester, A.D., Goris, A.H. and Westerterp, K.R. (2005) 'Measuring free-living energy expenditure and physical activity with triaxial accelerometry', *Obesity Research* 13: 1363–9.

Pollock, M.L., Carroll, J.F., Graves, J.E., Leggett, S.H., Braith, R.W., Linacher, M. and Hagberg, J. (1991) 'Injuries and adherence to walk/jog and resistance training programs in the elderly', *Medicine and Science in Sports and Exercise* 23: 1194–200.

Pollock, M.L., Mengelkoch, L.J., Graves, J.E., Lowenthal, D.T., Limacher, M.C., Foster, C. and Wilmore, J.H. (1997) 'Twenty-year follow-up of aerobic power and body composition of older track athletes', *Journal of Applied Physiology* 82: 1508–16.

Porta, M. (2008) *Dictionary of Epidemiology* (5th edn), Oxford: Oxford University Press for the International Epidemiological Association.

Pouliot, M.-C., Després, J.-P., Nadeau, A., Moorjani, S., Prud'homme, D., Lupien, P.J., Tremblay, A. and Bouchard, C. (1992) 'Visceral obesity in men: associations with glucose tolerance, plasma insulin, and lipoprotein levels', *Diabetes* 41: 826–34.

Powell, K.E., Thompson, P.D., Caspersen, C.J. and Kendrick, J.S. (1987) 'Physical activity and incidence of coronary heart disease', *Annual Review of Public Health* 8: 253–87.

Powers, S.K., Demirel, H.A., Vincent, H.K., Coombes, J.S., Naito, H., Hamilton, K.L., Shanely, R.A. and Jessup, J. (1998) 'Exercise training improves myocardial tolerance to in vivo ischemia-reperfusion in the rat', *American Journal of Physiology* 44: R1468–77.

Powers, S.K., Murlasits, Z., Wu, M. and Kavazis, A.N. (2007) 'Ischemia-reperfusion-induced cardiac injury: a brief review', *Medicine and Science in Sports and Exercise* 39: 1529–36.

Praet, S.F.E. and van Loon, L.J.C. (2007) 'Optimizing the therapeutic benefits of exercise in Type 2 diabetes', *Journal of Applied Physiology* 103: 1113–20.

Prentice, A.M. (2006) 'The emerging epidemic of obesity in developing countries', *International Journal of Epidemiology* 35: 93–9.

Prentice, A.M. and Jebb, S.A. (1995) 'Obesity in Britain: gluttony or sloth?' *British Medical Journal* 311: 437–9.

Ramachandran, A., Snehalatha, C., Mary, S., Mukesh, B., Bhaskar, A.D. and Vijay, V., for the Indian Diabetes Prevention Programme (2006) 'The Indian Diabetes Prevention Programme shows that lifestyle modification and metformin prevent type 2 diabetes in Asian Indian subjects with impaired glucose tolerance (IDPP-1)', *Diabetalogia* 49: 289–97.

Rankinen, T. and Bouchard, C. (2007) 'Genetic differences in the relationships among physical activity, fitness, and health', in C. Bouchard, S.N. Blair and W.L. Haskell (eds) *Physical Activity and Health*, Champaign: Human Kinetics, pp. 337–358.

Rauh, M.J., Macera, C.A., Trone, D.W., Shaffer, R.A. and Brodine, S.K. (2006) 'Epidemiology of stress fracture and lower-extremity overuse injury in female recruits', *Medicine and Science in Sports and Exercise* 38: 1571–7.

Ravussin, E., Lillioja, S., Knowler, W.C., Christin, L., Freymond, D., Abbott, W.G.H., Boyce, V., Howard, B.V. and Bogardus, C. (1988) 'Reduced rate of energy expenditure as a risk factor for body weight gain', *New England Journal of Medicine* 318: 467–72.

Ravussin, E., Valencia, M.E., Esparza, J., Bennet, P.H. and Schulz, L.O. (1994) 'Effects of a traditional lifestyle on obesity in Pima Indians', *Diabetes Care* 17: 1067–74.

Reaven, G.M. (1988) 'Role of insulin resistance in human disease', *Diabetes* 37: 1595–607.

Reeves, G.K., Pirie, K., Beral, V., Green, J., Spencer, E. and Bull, D. (2007) 'Cancer incidence and mortality in relation to body mass index in the Million Women Study: cohort study', *British Medical Journal* 7630: 1134–8. (See also the editorial by Calle, E.E. (2007) 'Obesity and cancer: substantial evidence supports the link between increasing adiposity and a higher risk of many cancers', *British Medical Journal* 335: 1107–8.)

Regan, F. and Betts, P. (2006) 'A brief review of the health consequences of childhood obesity', in N. Cameron, N.G. Norgan and G.T.H. Ellison (eds) *Childhood Obesity: Contemporary Issues*, Boca Raton: CRC Press, pp. 25–38.

Reilly, J.J. (2006a) 'Diagnostic accuracy of the BMI for age in paediatrics', *International Journal of Obesity* 30: 595–7.

Reilly, J.J. (2006b) 'Obesity prevention in childhood and adolescence: a review of systematic reviews', in N. Cameron, N.G. Norgan and G.T.H. Ellison (eds) *Childhood Obesity: Contemporary Issues*, Boca Raton: CRC Press, pp. 205–22.

Reilly, J.J. and Wilson, D. (2006) 'ABC of obesity: childhood obesity', *British Medical Journal* 333: 1207–10.

Reilly, J.J., Armstrong, J., Dorosty, A.R., Emmett, P.M., Ness, A., Rogers, I., Steer, C. and Sherriff, A., for the Avon Longitudinal Study of Parents and Children Study Team (2005) 'Early life risk factors for obesity in childhood: cohort study', *British Medical Journal* 330: 1357–9.

Reilly, J.J., Jackson, D.M., Montgomery, C., Kelly, L.A., Slater, C., Grant, S. and Paton, J.Y. (2004) 'Total energy expenditure and physical activity in young Scottish children: mixed longitudinal study', *Lancet* 363: 211–12. (See also the commentary by Hill, J. (2004) 'Physical activity and obesity', *Lancet* 363: 182).

Reilly, J.J., Kelly, L., Montgomery, C., Williamson, A., Fisher, A., McColl, J.H., Lo Conte, R., Paton, J.Y. and Grant, S. (2006) 'Physical activity to prevent obesity in young children: cluster randomised controlled trial', *British Medical Journal* 333: 1041.

Reinehr, T., de Sousa, G., Toschke, A.M. and Andler, W. (2006) 'Long-term follow-up of cardiovascular disease risk factors in children after an obesity intervention', *American Journal of Clinical Nutrition* 84: 490–6.

Rennie, K.L., Livingstone, M.B.E., Wells, J.C.K., McGloin, A., Coward, W.A., Prentice, A.M. and Jebb, S.A. (2005) 'Association of physical activity with body-composition indexes in children aged 6–8 y at varied risk of obesity', *American Journal of Clinical Nutrition* 82: 13–20.

Rhodes, C.J. (2005) 'Type 2 diabetes: a matter of β-cell life and death?', *Science* 307: 380–3.

Riddoch, C.J., Mattocks, C., Deere, K., Saunders, J., Kirkby, J., Tilling, K., Leary, S.D., Blair, S.N. and Ness, A.R. (2006) 'Objective measurement of levels and patterns of physical activity', *Archives of Disease is Childhood* 92: 963–9.

Rifkin, E. and Bouwer, E. (2007) *The Illusion of Certainty: Health Benefits and Risks*, New York: Springer.

Rizzo, N.S., Ruiz, J.R., Oja, L., Veidebaum, T. and Sjöström, M. (2008) 'Associations between physical activity, body fat, and insulin resistance (homeostasis model assessment) in adolescents: the European Youth Heart Study', *American Journal of Clinical Nutrition* 87: 586–92.

Roberts, S.B., Savage, J., Coward, W.A., Chew, B. and Lucas, A. (1988) 'Energy expenditure and intake in infants born to lean and overweight mothers', *New England Journal of Medicine* 318: 461–6.

Robinson, T.N. (1999) 'Reducing children's television viewing to prevent obesity', *Journal of the American Medical Association* 282: 1561–7.

Rockhill, B., Willett, W.C., Hunter, D.J., Manson, J.E., Hankinson, S.E. and Colditz, G.A. (1999) 'A prospective study of recreational physical activity and breast cancer risk', *Archives of Internal Medicine* 159: 2290–6.

Rogers, M.A., King, D.S., Hagberg, J.M., Ehsani, A.A. and Holloszy, J.O. (1990) 'Effect of 10 days of physical inactivity on glucose tolerance in master athletes', *Journal of Applied Physiology* 68: 1833–7.

Romero-Corral, A., Montori, V.M., Somers, V.K., Korinek, J., Thomas, R.J., Allison, T.G., Mookadam, F. and Lopez-Jimenez, F. (2006) 'Association of bodyweight with total mortality and with cardiovascular events in coronary artery disease: a systematic review of cohort studies', *Lancet* 368: 666–78. (See also the editorial by Franzosi M.G. (2006) 'Should we continue to use BMI as a cardiovascular risk factor?' *Lancet* 368: 624–5).

Rondon, M.U.P.B., Alves, M.J.N.N., Braga, A.M.F.W., Teixeira, O.T.U.N., Barretto, A.C.P., Krieger, E.M. and Negrão, C.E. (2002) 'Postexercise blood pressure reduction in elderly hypertensive patients', *Journal of the American College of Cardiology* 39: 676–82.

Rosen, E.D. and Spiegelman, B.M. (2006) 'Adipocytes as regulators of energy balance and glucose homeostasis', *Nature* 444: 847–53.

Ross, R. (1997) 'Effects of diet and exercise induced weight loss on visceral adipose tissue in men and women', *Sports Medicine* 24: 55–64.

Ross, R. and Janssen, I. (2007) 'Physical activity, fitness, and obesity', in C. Bouchard, S.N. Blair and W.L. Haskell (eds) *Physical Activity and Health*, Champaign: Human Kinetics, pp. 173–89.

Ross, R., Freeman, J.A. and Janssen, I. (2000) 'Exercise alone is an effective strategy for reducing obesity and related comorbidities', *Exercise and Sports Sciences Reviews* 28: 165–70.

Rovio, S., Kåreholt, I., Helkala, E.-L., Viitanen, M., Winblad, B., Tuomilehto, J., Soininen, H., Nissinen, A. and Kivipelto, M. (2005) 'Leisure-time physical activity at midlife and the risk of dementia and Alzheimer's disease', *Lancet Neurology* 4: 705–11.

Rowland, T.W. (2007) 'Physical activity, fitness and children', in C. Bouchard, S.N. Blair and W.L. Haskell (eds) *Physical Activity and Health*, Champaign: Human Kinetics, pp. 259–70.

Rucker, D., Padwal, R., Li, S.K., Curioni, C. and Lau, D.C.W. (2007) 'Long term pharmacotherapy for obesity and overweight: updated meta-analysis', *British Medical Journal* 335: 1194–9.

Ruiz, J.R., Ortega, F.B., Warnberg, J. and Sjöström, M. (2007) 'Associations of low-grade inflammation with physical activity, fitness and fatness in prepubertal children: the European Youth Heart Study', *International Journal of Obesity* 31: 1545–51.

Ruiz, J.R., Rizzo, N.S., Hurtig-Wennlof, A., Ortega, F.B., Warnberg, J. and Sjöström, M. (2006) 'Relations of total physical activity and intensity to fitness and fatness in children: the European Youth Heart Study', *American Journal of Clinical Nutrition* 84: 299–303.

Russ, D.W. and Kent-Braun, J.A. (2004) 'Is skeletal muscle oxidative capacity decreased in old age?', *Sports Medicine* 34: 221–9.

Sacco, R.L., Gan, R., Boden-Albala, B., Lin, I.F., Kargman, D.E., Hauser, A., Shea, S. and Paik, M.C. (1998) 'Leisure-time physical activity and ischemic stroke risk: the Northern Manhattan Stroke Study', *Stroke* 29: 380–7.

Saris, W.H.M., Blair, S.N., van Baak, M.A., Eaton, S.B., Davies, P.S., Di Pietro, L., Fogelholm, M., Rissanen, A., Schoeller, D., Swinburn, B., Tremblay, A., Westerterp, K.R. and Wyatt, H. (2003) 'How much physical activity is enough to prevent unhealthy weight gain? Outcome of the IASO 1st Stock Conference and consensus statement', *Obesity Research* 4: 101–14.

Savoye, M., Shaw, M., Dziura, J., Tamborlane, W.V., Rose, P., Guandalini, C., Goldberg-Gell, R., Burget, T.S., Cali, A.M.G., Weiss, R. and Caprio, S. (2007) 'Effects of a weight management program on body composition and metabolic parameters in overweight children: a randomized controlled trial', *Journal of the American Medical Association* 297: 2697–704.

Sawada, S.S., Lee, I.M., Muto, T., Matuszaki, K. and Blair, S.N. (2003) 'Cardiorespiratory fitness and the incidence of type 2 diabetes: prospective study of Japanese men', *Diabetes Care* 26: 2918–22.

Schwartz, M.W. and Porte, D. (2005) 'Diabetes, obesity, and the brain', *Science* 307: 375–9.

Seip, R.L., Angelopoulos, T.J. and Semenkovich, C.F. (1995) 'Exercise induces human lipoprotein lipase gene expression in skeletal muscle but not adipose tissue', *American Journal of Physiology* 268: E229–36.

Shephard, R.J. (1986) *Fitness of a Nation: Lessons from the Canada Fitness Survey*, Basel: Karger.

Sigal, R.J., Kenny, G.P., Boulé, N.G., Wells, G.A., Prud'homme, D., Fortier, M., Reid, R.D., Tulloch, H., Coyle, D., Phillips, P., Jennings, A. and Jaffey, J. (2007) 'Effects of aerobic training, resistance training, or both on glycemic control in type 2 diabetes', *Annals of Internal Medicine* 147: 357–69. (See also the editorial by Kraus, W.E. and Levine, B.D. (2007) 'Exercise training for diabetes: the "strength" of the evidence', *Annals of Internal Medicine* 147: 423–4).

Sileno, A.P., Brandt, G.C., Spann, B.M. and Quay, S.C. (2006) 'Lower mean weight after 14 days intravenous administration peptide YY_{3-36} (PYY_{3-36}) in rabbits', *International Journal of Obesity* 30: 68–72.

Simsolo, R.B., Ong, J.M. and Kern, P.A. (1993) 'The regulation of adipose tissue and muscle lipo-protein lipase in runners by detraining', *Journal of Clinical Investigation* 92: 2124–30.

Singh, S.J., Morgan, M.D., Scott, S., Walters, D. and Hardman, A.E. (1992) 'Development of a shuttle walking test of disability in patients with chronic airways obstruction', *Thorax* 47: 1019–24.

Sinha, R., Fisch, G., Teague, B., Tamborlane, W.V., Banyas, B., Allen, K., Savoye, M., Rieger, V., Taksali, S., Barbetta, G., Sherwin, R.S. and Caprio, S. (2002) 'Prevalence of impaired glucose tolerance among children and adolescents with marked obesity', *New England Journal of Medicine* 346: 802–10. (See also the editorial by Rocchini, A.P. (2002) 'Childhood obesity and a diabetes epidemic', *New England Journal of Medicine* 346: 854–5.)

Siscovick, D.S., Weiss, N.S., Fletcher, R.H. and Lasky, T. (1984) 'The incidence of primary cardiac arrest during vigorous exercise', *New England Journal of Medicine* 311: 874–7.

Sjöström, L., Narbro, K., Sjöström, C.D., Karason, K., Larsson, B., Wedel, H., Lystig, T., Sullivan, M., Bouchard, C., Carlsson, B., Bengtsson, C., Dahlgren, S., Gummesson, A., Jacobson, P., Karlsson, J., Lindroos, A.K., Lönroth, H., Näslund, I., Olbers, T., Stenlöf, K., Torgerson, J., Ågren, G. and Carlsson, L.M.S., for the Swedish Obese Subjects Study (2007) 'Effects of bariat-ric surgery on mortality in Swedish obese subjects', *New England Journal of Medicine* 357: 741–52. (See also the editorial by Bray, G.A. (2007) 'The missing link: lose weight, live longer', *New England Journal of Medicine* 357: 818–20.)

Skelton, D.A. and Dinan-Young, S.M. (2008) 'Ageing and older people', in J. Buckley (ed.) *Exercise Physiology in Special Populations*, Edinburgh: Churchill Livingstone Elsevier, pp. 161–223.

Slattery, M.L., Edwards, S.L., Ma, K.N., Friedman, G.D. and Potter, J.D. (1997) 'Physical activity and colon cancer: a public health perspective', *Annals of Epidemiology* 7: 137–45.

Slentz, C.A., Houmard, J.A., Johnson, J.L., Bateman, L.A., Tanner, C.J., McCartney, J.S., Duscha, B.D. and Kraus, W.E. (2007) 'Inactivity, exercise training and detraining, and plasma lipopro-teins: STRRIDE: a randomized, controlled study of exercise intensity and amount', *Journal of Applied Physiology* 103: 432–42.

Smith, J.K. (2001) 'Exercise and atherogenesis', *Exercise and Sport Sciences Reviews* 29: 49–53.

Snowling, N.J. and Hopkins, W.G. (2006) 'Effects of different modes of exercise training on glucose control and risk factors for complications in type 2 diabetes patients: a meta-analysis', *Diabetes Care* 29: 2518–27.

Snyder, K.A., Donnelly, J.E., Jabobsen, D.J., Hertner, G. and Jakicic, J.M. (1997) 'The effects of long-term, moderate intensity, intermittent exercise on aerobic capacity, body composition, blood lipids, insulin and glucose in overweight females', *International Journal of Obesity* 21: 1180–9.

Sørensen, T.I.A., Rissanen, A., Korkeila, M. and Kaprio, J. (2005) 'Intention to lose weight, weight changes, and 18-y mortality in overweight individuals without co-morbidities', *Public Library of Science Medicine* 2: E171.

Speiser, P.W., Rudolf, M.C.J., Anhalt, H., Camacho-Hubner, C., Chiarelli, F., Eliakim, A., Free-mark, M., Gruters, A., Hershkovitz, E., Iughetti, L., Krude, H., Latzer, Y., Lustig, R.H., Pesco-vitz, O.H., Pinhas-Hamiel, O., Rogol, A.D., Shalitin, S., Sultan, C., Stein, D., Vardi, P., Werther, G.A., Zadik, Z., Zuckerman-Levin, N. and Hochberg, Z., on behalf of the Obesity Consensus Working Group (2005) 'Consensus statement: childhood obesity', *Journal of Clinical Endocrinology and Metabolism* 60: 1871–7.

Spina, R.J., Ogawa, T., Kohrt, W.M., Martin, W.H., Holloszy, J.O. and Ehsani, A.A. (1993) 'Dif-ferences in cardiovascular adaptations to endurance exercise training between older men and women', *Journal of Applied Physiology* 75: 849–55.

Spirduso, W.W. and Cronin, D.L. (2001) 'Exercise dose–response effects on quality of life and inde-pendent living in older adults', *Medicine and Science in Sports and Exercise* 33: S598–608.

Sports Council and Health Education Authority (1992) *National Fitness Survey: Main Findings*, London: Sports Council and Health Education Authority.

Stachenfeld, N.S. and DiPietro, L. (2006) 'The female athlete triad: do female athletes need to take special care to avoid low energy availability? The challenging view', *Medicine and Science in Sports and Exercise* 28: 1694–700.

Stamatakis, E., Primatesta, P., Chinn, S., Rona, R. and Falascheti, E. (2005) 'Overweight and obesity trends from 1974 to 2003 in English children: what is the role of socioeconomic factors?', *Archives of Disease in Childhood* 90: 999–1004.

Stampfer, M.J., Hu, F.B., Manson, J.E., Rimm, E.B. and Willett, W.C. (2000) 'Primary prevention of coronary heart disease in women through diet and lifestyle', *New England Journal of Medicine* 343: 16–22.

Statistics New Zealand (2008) 'National population projections 2006 (base) to 2061', Online, available at: www.stats.govt.nz/schools-corner/find-info-by-subject/population/our-ageing-pop-activity.htm. (accessed 21 January 2008).

Steele, R.M., Brage, S., Corder, K., Wareham, N.J. and Ekelund, U. (2008) 'Physical activity, cardiorespiratory fitness, and metabolic syndrome in youth', *Journal of Applied Physiology* 105: 342–51.

Steinberger, J., Jacobs, D.R., Raatz, S., Moran, A., Hong, C.-P., and Sinaiko, A.R. (2005) 'Comparison of body fatness measurements by BMI and skinfolds vs dual energy X-ray absorptiometry and their relation to cardiovascular risk factors in adolescents', *International Journal of Obesity* 29: 1346–52. Corrigendum in *International Journal of Obesity* (2006) 30: 1170.

Stephenson, P., Bauman, A., Armstrong, T., Smith, B. and Bellew, B. (2000) *The Cost of Illness Attributable to Physical Inactivity in Australia: A Preliminary Study*, Canberra: The Commonwealth Department of Health and Aged Care and the Australian Sports Commission.

Sternfeld, B., Jacobs, M.K., Quesenberry, C.P., Gold, E.B. and Sowers, M. (2003) 'Physical activity and menstrual cycle characteristics in two prospective cohorts', *American Journal of Epidemiology*, 156: 402–9.

Stewart, K.J., Hiatt, W.R., Regensteiner, J.G. and Hirsch, A.T. (2002) 'Exercise training for claudication', *New England Journal of Medicine* 347: 1941–51.

Stewart, W.K. and Fleming, L.W. (1973) 'Features of a successful therapeutic fast of 382 days' duration', *Postgraduate Medical Journal* 49: 203–9.

Stratton, G., Canoy, D., Boddy, L.M., Taylor, S.R., Hackett, A.F. and Buchan, I.E. (2007) 'Cardiorespiratory fitness and body mass index of 9–11-year-old English children: a serial cross-sectional study from 1998 to 2004', *International Journal of Obesity* 31: 1172–8.

Stunkard, A.J., Foch, T.T. and Hrubec, Z. (1986a) 'A twin study of human obesity', *Journal of the American Medical Association* 256: 51–4.

Stunkard, A.J., Sorensen, T.I.A., Hanis, C., Teasdale, T.W., Chakraborty, R., Schull, W.J. and Schulsinger, F. (1986b) 'An adoption study of human obesity', *New England Journal of Medicine* 314: 193–8.

Sui, X., Hooker, S.P., Lee, I.M., Church, T.S., Colabianchi, N., Lee, C.-D. and Blair, S.N. (2008) 'A prospective study of cardiorespiratory fitness and risk of type 2 diabetes in women', *Diabetes Care* 31: 550–5.

Sui, X., LaMonte, M.J., Laditka, J.N., Hardin, J.W., Chase, N., Hooker, S.P. and Blair, S.N. (2007) 'Cardiorespiratory fitness and adiposity as mortality predictors in older adults', *Journal of the American Medical Association* 298: 2507–16.

Sulemana, H., Smolensky, M.H. and Lai, D. (2006) 'Relationship between physical activity and body mass index in adolescents', *Medicine and Science in Sports and Exercise* 38: 1182–6.

Sundgot-Borgen, J. and Torstveit, M.S. (2004) 'Prevalence of eating disorders in elite athletes is higher than in the general population', *Clinical Journal of Sports Medicine* 14: 25–32.

Swain, D.P. and Franklin, B.A. (2006) 'Comparison of cardioprotective benefits of vigorous versus moderate intensity aerobic exercise', *American Journal of Cardiology* 97: 141–7.

Tall, A.R. (2002) 'Exercise to reduce cardiovascular risk: how much is enough?', *New England Journal of Medicine* 347: 1522–4 (editorial).

Tanaka, H. and Seals, D.R. (1997) 'Age and gender interactions in physiological functional capacity: insight from swimming performance', *Journal of Applied Physiology* 82: 846–51.

Tanasescu, M., Leitzmann, M.F., Rimm, E.B. and Hu, F.B. (2003) 'Physical activity in relation to cardiovascular disease and total mortality among men with type 2 diabetes', *Circulation* 107: 2435–9.

Tanasescu, M., Leitzmann, M.F., Rimm, E.B., Willett, W.C., Stampfer, M.J. and Hu, F.B. (2002) 'Exercise type and intensity in relation to coronary heart disease in men', *Journal of the American Medical Association* 288: 1994–2000.

Taubes, G. (1995) 'Epidemiology faces its limits', *Science* 269: 164–9.

Taylor, H.L., Klepetar, E., Keys, A., Parlin, W., Blackburn, H. and Puchner, T. (1962) 'Death rates among physically active and sedentary employees of the railroad industry', *American Journal of Public Health* 52: 1697–707.

Taylor, R.S., Brown, A., Ebrahim, S., Jolliffe, J., Noorani, H., Rees, K., Skidmore, B., Stone, J.A., Thompson, D.R. and Oldridge, N. (2004) 'Exercise-based rehabilitation for patients with coronary heart disease: systematic review and meta-analysis of randomized controlled trials', *American Journal of Medicine* 116: 682–92.

Teri, L., Gibbons, L.E., McCurry, S.M., Logsdon, R.G., Buchner, D.M., Barlow, W.E., Kukull, W.A., LaCroix, A.Z., McCormick, W. and Larson, E.B. (2003) 'Exercise plus behavioural management in patients with Alzheimer disease: a randomized controlled trial', *Journal of the American Medical Association* 290: 2015–22.

Thomas, J.R., Nelson, J.K. and Silverman, S.J. (2005) *Research Methods in Physical Activity*, Champaign: Human Kinetics.

Thompson, P.D. (2002) 'Additional steps for cardiovascular health', *New England Journal of Medicine* 347: 755–6 (editorial).

Thompson, P.D., Franklin, B.A., Balady, G.J., Blair, S.N., Corrado, D., Estes III, N.A., Fulton, J.E., Gordon, N.F., Haskell, W.L., Link, M.S., Maron, B.J., Mittleman, M.A., Pelliccia, A., Wenger, N.K., Willich, S.N., Costa, F., Taylor-Piliae, R.E., Norton, L.C., Mahbouda, M.H., Fair, J.M., Iribarren, C., Hlatky, M.A., Go, A.S. and Fortmann, S.P. (2007) 'Exercise and acute cardiovascular events placing the risks into perspective: a scientific statement from the American Heart Association Council on Nutrition, Physical Activity, and Metabolism and the Council on Clinical Cardiology', *Circulation* 115: 2358–68.

Thune, I., Brenn, T., Lund, E. and Gaard, M. (1997) 'Physical activity and the risk of breast cancer', *New England Journal of Medicine* 336: 1269–75.

Timpka, T. and Lindqvist, K. (2001) 'Evidence based prevention of acute injuries during physical exercise in a WHO safe community', *British Journal of Sports Medicine* 35: 20–7.

Torstveit, M.S. and Sundgot-Borgen, J. (2005) 'The female athlete triad: are elite athletes at increased risk?', *Medicine and Science in Sports and Exercise* 37: 184–93.

Trappe, S.W., Costill, D.L., Fink, W.J. and Pearson, D.R. (1995) 'Skeletal muscle characteristics among distance runners: a 20-yr follow-up study', *Journal of Applied Physiology* 78: 823–9.

Trappe, S.W., Costill, D.L., Vukovich, M.D., Jones, J. and Melham, T. (1996) 'Aging among elite distance runners: a 22-yr longitudinal study', *Journal of Applied Physiology* 80: 285–90.

Tremblay, M.S., Barnes, J.D., Copeland, J.L. and Esliger, D.W. (2005) 'Conquering childhood inactivity: is the answer in the past?', *Medicine and Science in Sports and Exercise* 37: 1187–94.

Truswell, A.S., Kennelly, B.M., Hansen, J.D.L. and Lee, R.B. (1972) 'Blood pressure of Kung Bushmen in northern Botswana', *American Heart Journal* 84: 5–12.

Tsetsonis, N.V. and Hardman, A.E. (1996) 'Reduction in postprandial lipemia after walking: influence of exercise intensity', *Medicine and Science in Sports and Exercise* 28: 1235–42.

Tudor-Locke, C. and Bassett, D.R. (2004) 'How many steps/day are enough? Preliminary pedometer indices for public health', *Sports Medicine* 34: 1–8.

Tuomilehto, J., Lindström, J., Eriksson, J.G., Valle, T.T., Hämäläinen, H., Ilanne-Parikka, P., Keinänen-Kiukaanniemi, S., Laakso, M., Louheranta, A., Rastas, M., Salminen, V. and Uusitupa, M., for the Finnish Diabetes Prevention Study Group (2001) 'Prevention of type 2 diabetes mellitus by changes in lifestyle among subjects with impaired glucose tolerance', *The New England Journal of Medicine* 344: 1343–50. (See also the editorial by Tataranni, P.A. and Bogardus, C. (2001) 'Changing habits to delay diabetes', *New England Journal of Medicine* 344: 1390–2).

Twisk, J.W.R., Kemper, H.C.G. and van Mechelen, W. (2002) 'The relationship between physical fitness and physical activity during adolescence and cardiovascular disease risk factors at adult age: the Amsterdam Growth and Health Longitudinal Study', *International Journal of Sports Medicine* 23: S8–14.

UK Department of Health (2004) *At Least Five a Week: Evidence on the Impact of Physical Activity and Its Relationship to Health*, London: UK Department of Health. Online, available at: www.dh.gov.uk/en/Publicationsandstatistics/Publications/PublicationsPolicyAndGuidance/DH_4080994 (accessed 27 August 2008).

United Nations Department of Economic and Social Affairs, Population Division (2007) 'World population prospects: the 2006 revision: population ageing'. Online, available at: www.un.org/esa/population/publications/wpp.2006/wpp.2006_ageing.pdf. (accessed 11 March 2008).

US Department of Health and Human Services (1996) *Physical Activity and Health: A Report of the Surgeon General*, Atlanta: Centers for Disease Control and Prevention.

US Department of Health and Human Services and US Department of Agriculture (2005) *Dietary Guidelines for Americans, 2005*, 6th edn, Washington: US Government Printing Office.

US National Institutes of Health Consensus Development Panel (1995) 'Physical activity and cardiovascular health', Online, available at: http://consensus.nih.gov/1995/1995ActivityCardiovascularHealth101html.htm, (accessed 18 March 2009).

van der Ploeg, H.P., Merom, D., Corpuz, G. and Bauman, A.E. (2008) 'Trends in Australian children traveling to school 1971–2003: burning petrol or carbohydrates?', *Preventive Medicine* 46: 60–2.

van Mechelen, W. (1992) 'Running injuries: a review of the epidemiological literature', *Sports Medicine* 14: 320–35.

van Sluijs, E.M.F., McMinn, A.M. and Griffin, S.J. (2007) 'Effectiveness of interventions to promote physical activity in children and adolescents: systematic review of controlled trials', *British Medical Journal* 335: 703. (See also the editorial by Giles-Corti, B. and Salmon, J. (2007) 'Encouraging children and adolescents to be more active: well evaluated complex interventions are still needed', *British Medical Journal* 335: 677–8.)

Vicente-Rodríguez, G. (2006) 'How does exercise affect bone development during growth?', *Sports Medicine* 36: 561–9.

Vignon, E., Valat, J.P., Rossignol, M., Avouac, B., Rozenberg, S., Thoumie, P., Avouac, J., Nordin, M. and Hilliquin, P. (2006) 'Osteoarthritis of the knee and hip and physical activity; a systematic international review and synthesis (OASIS)', *Joint Bone Spine* 73: 442–55.

Villareal, D.T., Miller, B.V., Banks, M., Fontana, L., Sinacore, D.R. and Klein, S. (2006) 'Effect of lifestyle intervention on metabolic coronary heart disease risk factors in obese older adults', *American Journal of Clinical Nutrition* 84: 1317–23. (See also the editorial by van Baak, M.A. and Visscher, T.L.S. (2006) 'Public health success in recent decades may be in danger if lifestyles of the elderly are neglected', *American Journal of Clinical Nutrition* 84: 1257–8.)

Viner, R.M., Segal, T.Y., Lichtarowicz-Krynska, E. and Hindmarsh, P. (2005) 'Prevalence of the insulin resistance syndrome in obesity', *Archives of Disease in Childhood* 90: 10–14. (See also the perspective by Dunger, D.B. (2005) 'Obesity and the insulin resistance syndrome', *Archives of Disease in Childhood* 90: 1).

Visser, M., Pluijm, S.M.F., Stel, V.S., Bosscher, R.J. and Deeg, D.J.H. (2002) 'Physical activity as a determinant of change in mobility performance: the Longitudinal Aging Study Amsterdam', *Journal of the American Geriatric Society* 50: 1774–81.

Vita, J.A. and Keaney, J.F. (2000) 'Exercise: toning up the endothelium?', *New England Journal of Medicine* 342: 503–5 (editorial).

Vuori, I., Lankenau, B. and Pratt, M. (2004) 'Physical activity policy and program development: the experience in Finland', *Public Health Reports* 119: 331–45.

Wadden, T.A., Berkowitz, R.I., Womble, L.G., Sarwer, D.B., Phelan, S., Cato, R.K., Hesson, L.A., Osei, S.Y., Kaplan, R. and Stunkard, A.J. (2005) 'Randomized trial of lifestyle modification and pharmacotherapy for obesity', *New England Journal of Medicine* 353: 2111–20.

Wallace, J.P. (2003) 'Exercise in hypertension: a clinical review', *Sports Medicine* 33: 585–98.

Wang, Y., Rimm, E.B., Stampfer, M.J., Willett, W.C. and Hu, F.B. (2005) 'Comparison of abdominal adiposity and overall obesity in predicting risk of type 2 diabetes among men', *American Journal of Clinical Nutrition* 81: 555–63.

Wannamethee, S.G., Shaper, A.G. and Alberti, G.M.M. (2000) 'Physical activity, metabolic factors, and the incidence of coronary heart disease and type 2 diabetes', *Archives of Internal Medicine* 160: 2108–16.

Wannamethee, S.G., Shaper, A.G. and Walker, M. (1998) 'Changes in physical activity, mortality, and incidence of coronary heart disease in older men', *Lancet* 351: 1603–8.

Wardle, J., Carnell, S., Haworth, C.M.A. and Plomin, R. (2008) 'Evidence for a strong genetic influence on childhood adiposity despite the force of the obesogenic environment', *American Journal of Clinical Nutrition* 87: 398–404. (See also the editorial by Musani, S.K., Erickson, S. and Allison, D.B. (2008) 'Obesity: still highly heritable after all these years', *American Journal of Clinical Nutrition* 87: 275–6.)

Wareham, N.J., van Sluijs, E.M.F. and Ekelund, U. (2005) 'Physical activity and obesity prevention: a review of the current evidence', *Proceedings of the Nutrition Society* 64: 229–47.

Watts, K., Jones, T.W., Davis, E.A. and Green, D. (2005) 'Exercise training in obese children and adolescents: current concepts', *Sports Medicine* 35: 375–92.

Weeks, B.K., Young, C.M. and Beck, B.R. (2008) 'Eight months of regular in-school jumping improves indices of bone strength in adolescent boys and girls: the POWER PE Study', *Journal of Bone and Mineral Research* 23: 1002–11.

Wei, M., Gibbons, L.W., Kampert, J.B., Nichaman, M.Z. and Blair, S.N. (2000) 'Low cardiorespiratory fitness and physical inactivity as predictors of mortality in men with type 2 diabetes', *Annals of Internal Medicine* 132: 605–11.

Wei, M., Gibbons, L.W., Mitchell, T.L., Kampert, J.B., Lee, C.D. and Blair, S.N. (1999a) 'The association between cardiorespiratory fitness and impaired fasting glucose and type 2 diabetes mellitus in men', *Annals of Internal Medicine* 130: 89–96.

Wei, M., Kampert, J.B., Barlow, C.E., Nichaman, M.Z., Gibbons, L.W., Paffenbarger, R.S. and Blair, S.N. (1999b) 'Relationship between low cardiorespiratory fitness and mortality in normal weight, overweight and obese men', *Journal of the American Medical Association* 282: 1547–53.

Weinsier, R.L., Hunter, G.R., Desmond, R.A., Byrne, N.M., Zuckerman, P.A. and Darnell, B.E. (2002) 'Free-living activity energy expenditure in women successful and unsuccessful at maintaining normal body weight', *American Journal of Clinical Nutrition* 75: 499–504. (See also the editorial by Wyatt, H.R. and Hill, J.O. (2002) 'Let's get serious about promoting physical activity', *American Journal of Clinical Nutrition* 75: 449–50.

Weinstein, A.R., Sesso, H.D., Lee, I.M., Cook, N.R., Manson, J.E., Buring, J.E. and Gaziano, J.M. (2004) 'Relationship of physical activity vs body mass index with type 2 diabetes in women', *Journal of the American Medical Association* 292: 1188–94.

Westerterp, K.R. and Speakman, J.R. (2008) 'Physical activity energy expenditure has not declined since the 1980s and matches energy expenditures of mammals', *International Journal of Obesity* 32: 1256–63.

Weuve, J., Kang, J.H., Manson, J.E., Breteler, M.M., Ware, J.H. and Grodstein, F. (2004) 'Physical activity, including walking, and cognitive function in older women', *Journal of the American Medical Association* 292: 1454–61.

Wheater, P.R., Burkitt, H.G., Stevens, A. and Lowe, J.S. (1985) *Basic Histopathology: A Colour Atlas and Text*, Edinburgh: Churchill Livingstone.

Whelton, S.P., Chin, A., Xin, X. and He, J. (2002) 'Effect of aerobic exercise on blood pressure: a meta analysis of randomized, controlled trials', *Annals of Internal Medicine* 136: 493–503.

Whitaker, R.C., Wright, J.A., Pepe, M.S., Seidel, K.D. and Dietz, W.H. (1997) 'Predicting obesity in young adulthood from childhood and parental obesity', *New England Journal of Medicine* 337: 869–73.

Wild, S.H. and Byrne, C.D. (2006) 'ABC of obesity: risk factors for diabetes and coronary heart disease', *British Medical Journal* 333: 1009–11.

Wilfley, D.E., Stein, R.I., Saelens, B.E., Mockus, D.S., Matt, G.E., Hayden-Wade, H.A., Welch, R.R., Schechtman, K.B., Thompson, P.A. and Epstein, L.H. (2007) 'Efficacy of maintenance treatment approaches for childhood overweight: a randomized controlled trial', *Journal of the American Medical Association* 298: 1661–73. (See also the editorial by Rhodes, E.T. and Ludwig, D.S. (2007) 'Childhood obesity as a chronic disease: keeping the weight off', *Journal of the American Medical Association* 298: 1695–6.

Wilkin, T.J., Mallam, K.M., Metcalf, B.S., Jeffery, A.N. and Voss, L.D. (2006) 'Variation in physical activity lies with the child, not his environment: evidence for an "activitystat" in young children (EarlyBird 16)', *International Journal of Obesity* 30: 1050–5.

Will, J.C., Williamson, D.F., Ford, E.S., Calle, E.E. and Thun, M.J. (2002) 'Intentional weight loss and 13-year diabetes incidence in overweight adults', *American Journal of Public Health* 92: 1245–8.

Willcox, B.J., He, Q., Chen, R., Yano, K., Masaki, K.H., Grove, J.S., Donlon, T.A., Willcox, D.C. and Curb, J.D. (2006) 'Midlife risk factors and healthy survival in men', *Journal of the American Medical Association* 296: 2343–50.

Williams, P.D. (1996) 'High-density lipoprotein cholesterol and other risk factors for coronary heart disease in female runners', *New England Journal of Medicine* 334: 1298–303.

Williams, P.T. and Pate, R.R. (2005) 'Cross-sectional relationships of exercise and age to adiposity in 60,617 male runners', *Medicine and Science in Sports and Exercise* 37: 1329–37.

Williams, P.T. and Wood, P.D. (2006) 'The effects of changing exercise levels on weight and age-related weight gain', *International Journal of Obesity* 30: 543–51.

Williamson, D.F., Madans, J., Anda, R.F., Kleinman, J.C., Kahn, H.S. and Byers, T. (1993) 'Recreational physical activity and ten-year weight change in a US national cohort', *International Journal of Obesity* 17: 279–86.

Willich, S.N., Lewis, M., Löwel, H., Arntz, H.-R., Schubert, F. and Schröder, R. (1993) 'Physical exertion as a trigger of acute myocardial infarction', *New England Journal Medicine* 329: 1684–90.

Wilmore, J.H. and Costill, D.L. (2004) *Physiology of Exercise and Sport*, 3rd edn, Champaign: Human Kinetics.

Wilson, P.W., D'Agostino, R.B., Levy, D., Belanger, A.M., Silbershatz, H. and Kannel, W.B. (1998) 'Prediction of coronary heart disease using risk factor categories', *Circulation* 97: 1837–47.

Wilson, P.W., Kannel, W.B., Silbershatz, H. and D'Agostino, R.B. (1999) 'Clustering of metabolic risk factors and coronary heart disease', *Archives of Internal Medicine* 159: 1104–9.

Wing, R.R. and Phelan, S. (2005) 'Long-term weight loss maintenance', *American Journal of Clinical Nutrition* 82 (Supplement): S222–5.

Wisløff, U., Najjar, S.M., Ellingsen, Ø., Haram, P.M., Swoap, S., Al-Share, Q., Fernström, M., Rezaei, K., Lee, S.J., Koch, L.G. and Britton, S.L. (2005) 'Cardiovascular risk factors emerge after artificial selection for low aerobic capacity', *Science* 307: 418–20.

Wolff, I., van Croonenborg, J.J., Kemper, H.C.G., Kostense, P.J. and Twisk, J.W.R. (1999) 'The effect of exercise training programs on bone mass: a meta-analysis of published controlled trials in pre- and postmenopausal women', *Osteoporosis International* 9: 1–12.

Wood, P.D., Stefanick, M.L., Dreon, D.M., Frey-Hewitt, B., Garay, S.C., Williams, P.T., Superko, H.R., Fortmann, S.P., Albers, J.J., Vranizan, K.M., Ellsworth, N.M., Terry, R.B. and Haskell, W.L. (1988) 'Changes in plasma lipids and lipoproteins in overweight men during weight loss through dieting as compared with exercise', *New England Journal of Medicine* 319: 1173–9.

Woods, P.D., Davis, J.M., Smith, J.A. and Nieman, D.C. (1999) 'Exercise and cellular innate immune function', *Medicine and Science in Sports and Exercise* 31: 57–66.

World Cancer Research Fund (2007) 'Physical activity' in *Food, Nutrition, Physical Activity, and the Prevention of Cancer: A Global Perspective*, Washington: American Institute for Cancer Research, pp. 198–209. Online, available at: www.dietandcancerreport.org/downloads/chapters/chapter_05.pdf (accessed 16 January 2008).

World Health Organization (1946) Preamble to the Constitution of the World Health Organization as adopted by the International Health Conference, New York, 19–22 June 1946; signed on 22 July 1946 by the representatives of 61 States (*Official Records of the World Health Organization* 2: 100) and entered into force on 7 April 1948.

World Health Organization (expert consultation) (2004) 'Appropriate body-mass index for Asian populations and its implications for policy and intervention strategies', *Lancet* 363: 157–63.

World Health Organization (2008a) 'Physical activity and young people'. Online, available at: www.who.int/dietphysicalactivity/factsheet_young_people/en/index.html (accessed 13 March 2008).

World Health Organization (2008b) 'Physical inactivity: a global health problem'. Online, available at: www.who.int/dietphysicalactivity/factsheet_inactivity/en/index.html (accessed 9 March 2008).

Wren, A.M., Seal, L.J., Cohen, M.A., Brynes, A.E., Frost, G.S., Murphy, K.G., Dhillo, W.S., Ghatei, M.A. and Bloom, S.R. (2001) 'Ghrelin enhances appetite and increases food intake in humans', *Journal of Clinical Endocrinology and Metabolism* 86: 5992–5.

Wright, C.M., Parker, L., Lamont, D. and Craft, A.W. (2001) 'Implications of childhood obesity for adult health: findings from thousand families cohort study', *British Medical Journal* 323: 1280–4.

Writing Group for the SEARCH for Diabetes in Youth Study Group (2007) 'Incidence of diabetes in youth in the United States', *Journal of the American Medical Association* 297: 2716–24. (See also the editorial by Lipton, R.B. (2007) 'Incidence of diabetes in children and youth: tracking a moving target', *Journal of the American Medical Association* 297: 2760–2.)

Wynne, K., Park, A.J., Small, C.J., Meeran, K., Ghatei, M.A., Frost, G.S. and Bloom, S.R. (2006) 'Oxyntomodulin increases energy expenditure in addition to decreasing energy intake in overweight and obese humans: a randomised controlled trial', *International Journal of Obesity* 30: 1729–36.

Wynne, K., Park, A.J., Small, C.J., Patterson, M., Ellis, S.M., Murphy, K.G., Wren, A.M., Frost, G.S., Meeran, K., Ghatei, M.A. and Bloom, S.R. (2005) 'Subcutaneous oxyntomodulin reduces body weight in overweight and obese subjects: a double-blind randomized controlled trial', *Diabetes* 54: 2390–5.

Young, A. and Dinan, S. (2005) 'Activity in later life', *British Medical Journal* 330: 189–91.

Yu, C.C.W., Sung, R.Y.T., So, R.C.H., Lui, K.C., Lau, W., Lam, P.K.W. and Lau, E.M.C. (2005) 'Effects of strength training on body composition and bone mineral content in children who are obese', *Journal of Strength and Conditioning Research* 19: 667–72.

Yusuf, S., Hawken, S., Ounpuu, S., Bautista, L., Franzosi, M.G., Commerford, P., Lang, C.C., Rumboldt, Z., Onen, C.L., Lisheng, L., Tanomsup, S., Wangai, P., Razak, F., Sharma, A.M. and Anand, S.S. (2005) 'Obesity and the risk of myocardial infarction in 27,000 participants from 52 countries: a case-control study', *Lancet* 366: 1640–9. (See also the editorial by Kragelund, C. and Omland, T. (2005) 'A farewell to the body-mass index?' *Lancet* 366: 1589–91).

Zanker, C.L. and Swaine, I.L. (1998) 'Bone turnover in amenorrhoeic and eumenorrhoeic distance runners', *Scandinavian Journal of Medicine and Science in Sports* 8: 20–6.

Zhang, C., Rexrode, K.M., van Dam, R.M., Li, T.Y. and Hu, F.B. (2008) 'Abdominal obesity and risk of all-cause, cardiovascular, and cancer mortality: sixteen years of follow-up in US women', *Circulation* 117: 1658–67. (See also the editorial by Cameron, A.J. and Zimmet, P.Z. (2008) 'Expanding evidence for the multiple dangers of epidemic abdominal obesity', *Circulation* 117: 1624–6.)

Zmuda, J.M., Yurgalevitch, S.M., Flynn, M.M., Bausserman, L.L., Saratelli, A., Spannaus-Martin, D.J., Herbert, P.N. and Thompson, P.D. (1998) 'Exercise training has little effect on HDL levels and metabolism in men with initially low HDL cholesterol', *Atherosclerosis* 137: 215–21.

Index

Children, Obesity and Exercise

Prevention, treatment and management of childhood and adolescent obesity

Andrew P. Hills, Queensland University of Technology, Australia
Neil A. King, Queensland University of Technology, Australia
Nuala M. Byrne, Queensland University of Technology, Australia

Throughout the developed world there is an increasing prevalence of childhood obesity. Because of this increase, and awareness of the risks to long term health that childhood obesity presents, the phenomena is now described by many as a global epidemic.

2007 HB: 978-0-415-40883-7 **£80.00** / PB: 978-0-415-40884-4: **£24.99**

Children, Obesity and Exercise provides sport, exercise and medicine students and professionals with an accessible and practical guide to understanding and managing childhood and adolescent obesity. It covers:

- overweight, obesity and body composition;
- physical activity, growth and development;
- psycho-social aspects of childhood obesity;
- physical activity behaviours;
- eating behaviours;
- measuring children's behaviour;
- interventions for prevention and management of childhood obesity.

Children, Obesity and Exercise addresses the need for authoritative advice and innovative approaches to the prevention and management of this chronic problem.

Contents:

1. Introduction: The Nature of the Problem 2. Tracking of Obesity from Childhood to Adulthood: Implications for Health 3. Clinical Correlates of Overweight and Obesity 4. Body Composition Assessment in Children and Adolescents: Implications for Obesity 5. The Importance of Physical Activity in the Growth and Development of Children 6. The Role of Perceived Competence in the Motivation of Obese Children to be Physically Active 7. Psycho-Social Factors and Childhood Obesity 8. Physical Activity, Appetite Control and Energy Balance: Implications for Obesity 9. Eating Behaviour in Children and the Measurement of Food Intake 10. Physical Activity Behaviour in Children and the Measurement of Physical Activity 11. Environmental Factors and Physical Activity in Children: Implications for Active Transport Programs 12. Interventions for the Prevention, Treatment and Management of Childhood Obesity (including Family, School and Community)

Visit www.routledge.com/9780415408844 for more details.

Routledge
Taylor & Francis Group

For more details, or to request a copy for review, please contact:

Gemma-Kate Hartley, Senior Marketing Co-ordinator
Gemma-kate.hartley@tandf.co.uk   020 7017 5911

The Obesity Epidemic
Science, Morality and Ideology

Michael Gard, Leeds Metropolitan University, UK and
Jan Wright, University of Wollongong, Australia

Increasing obesity levels are currently big news but do we think carefully enough about what this trend actually means? Everybody – including doctors, parents, teachers, sports clubs, businesses and governments – has a role to play in the 'war on obesity'. But is talk of an obesity 'crisis' justified? Is it the product of measured scientific reasoning or age-old 'habits of mind'? Why is it happening now? And are there potential risks associated with talking about obesity as an 'epidemic'?

The Obesity Epidemic proposes that obesity science and the popular media present a complex mix of ambiguous knowledge, familiar (yet unstated) moral agendas and ideological assumptions.

THE OBESITY EPIDEMIC
SCIENCE, MORALITY and IDEOLOGY

MICHAEL GARD and JAN WRIGHT

2005 HB: 978-0-415-31895-2 £95.00 / PB: 978-0-415-31896-9: £27.50

'*The Obesity Epidemic* is a superb contribution to the sociology of knowledge, and an essential text for anyone who wants to understand the current moral panic over fat.' - Paul Campos, University of Colorado, author of *The Obesity Myth*

'The strength in this book lies in its ability to provide its readers with a critical view of obesity science by challenging them to go beyond traditional thinking ... reminding them of the harmful and stigmatizing consequences of adopting a 'war on obesity' mentality ... This book is an essential read for anyone who is interested in health, obesity, health promotion, and public health.' - *Krista Rondeau, Dieticians of Canada*

Contents:

1. Science and Fatness
2. The War on Obesity
3. The Ghost of a Machine
4. 'Modernity's Scourge': A brief history of obesity science
5. Fat or Fiction: Weighing in the 'obesity epidemic'
6. The search for a cause
7. Obesity Science for the People
8. Feminism and the 'obesity epidemic'
9. Interrogating expert knowledge: risk and the ethics of body weight
10. Beyond Body Weight

Visit www.routledge.com/9780415318969 for more details.

Routledge
Taylor & Francis Group

For more details, or to request a copy for review, please contact:

Gemma-Kate Hartley, Senior Marketing Co-ordinator
Gemma-kate.hartley@tandf.co.uk   020 7017 5911

2ND Edition

Psychology of Physical Activity

Determinants, Well-Being and Interventions

Nanette Mutrie, Strathclyde University, UK

Stuart J.H. Biddle, Loughborough University, UK

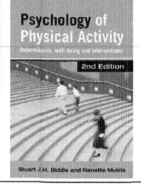

This text covers the field of exercise psychology in detail. Issues covered include motivation, attitudes, wellbeing, depression and mental illness, clinical populations, interventions and research consensus.

2007 HB: 978-0-415-36664-9 **£90.00** / PB: 978-0-415-36665-6: **£29.99**

'This second edition of Biddle and Mutrie's book reflects their broad grasp of contemporary public health concerns. Their sophisticated and practically-grounded perspectives allow them to a guide the reader through an inherently complex field, highlighting what is most relevant and important. ' - *Dr Neville Owen, Director, Cancer Prevention Research Centre, The University of Queensland, Australia*

'This new edition is a welcome and important contribution to a rapidly-expanding field of knowledge, in which Biddle and Mutrie's guiding ideas and synthesis of diverse research is much needed.' - *Dr Neville Owen, Director, Cancer Prevention Research Centre, The University of Queensland, Australia*

Contents:

Visit www.routledge.com/9780415366656 for more details.

Routledge
Taylor & Francis Group

For more details, or to request a copy for review, please contact:

Gemma-Kate Hartley, Senior Marketing Co-ordinator
Gemma-kate.hartley@tandf.co.uk   020 7017 5911